The Limits and Legitimacy of Referendums

The Limits and Legitimacy of Referendums

Edited by

RICHARD ALBERT AND RICHARD STACEY

OXFORD
UNIVERSITY PRESS

OXFORD
UNIVERSITY PRESS

Great Clarendon Street, Oxford, OX2 6DP,
United Kingdom

Oxford University Press is a department of the University of Oxford.
It furthers the University's objective of excellence in research, scholarship,
and education by publishing worldwide. Oxford is a registered trade mark of
Oxford University Press in the UK and in certain other countries

First Edition published in 2022

Impression: 1

Published in the United States of America by Oxford University Press
198 Madison Avenue, New York, NY 10016, United States of America

British Library Cataloguing in Publication Data

Data available

Library of Congress Control Number: 2022930080

ISBN 978–0–19–886764–7

DOI: 10.1093/oso/9780198867647.001.0001

Printed and bound in Great Britain by
Clays Ltd, Elcograf S.p.A.

Acknowledgements

The seeds for this book were planted in the John Willis Room at the University of Toronto in September 2017. We spent two days discussing all aspects of referendums: why they are held, what explains their success or failure, when they became synonymous (rightly or wrongly) with democracy, how to reconcile their use with the core commitments of constitutionalism, and so much more. Our group included the contributors to this volume and a fabulous roster of discussants who pressed the authors on their ideas and suggested ways to deepen and improve their already strong papers. Those papers have since been revised quite substantially, and now appear as scholarly chapters in this book.

We thank each of the discussants for the integral part they played in bringing this book to life: Jacques Bertrand, Jamie Cameron, Yasmin Dawood, David Dyzenhaus, Courtney Jung, Ran Hirschl, and David Schneiderman.

We thank also the many persons who devoted their time and talent to organizing the conference and to producing this book, including in particular Trish Do, Katelin Everson, Seána Glennon, Nadia Gulezko, and Bobby Nguyen. We also benefited from the support of our partners across the University of Toronto, including the Faculty of Arts and Sciences, the Faculty of Law, the Centre for Ethics, and the Munk School of Global Affairs.

And we give a standing ovation to each of the contributors. They have produced magnificent chapters, often through difficult circumstances, not the least of which was the public health emergency that began in 2020 and persists still today in 2022. The entire team at Oxford University Press—led by Brianne Bellio, Jordan Burke, and Jamie Berezin—was patient and understanding through it all. We are grateful to the Press for supporting this project. We hope the editorial team is as proud of this book as we are.

We wish to acknowledge, finally, that we came together to exchange ideas on the traditional land of the Huron-Wendat, the Seneca, and the Mississaugas of the Credit River. For thousands of years this meeting place has been home to many

Indigenous people from across Turtle Island, and we are grateful to have had the opportunity to work on this land.

Richard Albert
Austin, Texas
Richard Stacey
Toronto, Ontario
28 January 2022

Contents

List of Contributors

Richard Albert, William Stamps Farish Professor in Law, Professor of Government, and Director of Constitutional Studies, The University of Texas at Austin

Antoni Abat i Ninet, Visiting Professor, The Hebrew University of Jerusalem, Research affiliate at the CEU Democracy Institute, and Research Faculty at the Edwin Jaeckle Center for Democracy, Law SUNY at Buffalo

Carlos Bernal, Professor, School of Law, University of Dayton

Zachary Elkins, Department of Government, The University of Texas at Austin

Anna Fruhstorfer, Postdoctoral Researcher, Faculty of Economic and Social Sciences, University of Potsdam

Alexander Hudson, International IDEA, Stockholm

Aileen Kavanagh, Trinity College Dublin

David Kenny, Trinity College Dublin

Janna Promislow, Associate Professor, Faculty of Law, University of Victoria

Richard Stacey, Associate Professor, Faculty of Law, University of Toronto

Stephen Tierney, Professor of Constitutional Theory, School of Law, University of Edinburgh

Leah Trueblood, Fellow in Public Law, Worcester College, University of Oxford

Introduction

Democracy, Liberalism and Constitutional Referendums: When Does Popular Sovereignty Legitimate Constitutional Change?

Richard Stacey and Richard Albert

I. Introduction—from liberalism to democracy

'Liberal democracy' is a term people often use to describe political systems with a commitment to principles like the rule of law, constitutionalism and equality. What distinguishes these systems from less liberal or less democratic systems is a set of basic rules, often collected in a constitution, that obliges the government to treat all those subject to its authority as equals both in the formation of government and in the application of law. It is notable that in describing these political systems, the adjective ('liberal') almost always precedes the noun ('democracy'). The lexical ordering of the phrase suggests that what is valuable about these democracies is their liberalism.

The essence of democracy, however, is that the people who constitute a political community choose the arrangements according to which they will live together.[1] The post-colonial constitution imposed on an Indigenous people by a departing coloniser, or the constitution hurriedly decreed by a military junta after a coup, tends to lack these democratic foundations, regardless of whether it contains liberal features like a bill of rights. For a constitution to claim to represent the will of a people, the people must be involved in its design, at least to some extent. The referendum has emerged as a primary mechanism for involving a community of peoples in constitutional creation.[2]

[1] Frank Michelman argues that any commitment to democracy must mean that a country's citizens must be able to decide 'for themselves all of the politically decidable matters about which they have good moral and material reason to care. That apparently must include the contents of a country's constitution, the laws that organise the institutions of government and set limits to governmental powers in that country' (*Brennan and Democracy* (Princeton: Princeton University Press, 1999), 6).

[2] Stephen Tierney, 'Whose Political Constitution?' Citizens and Referendums' (2013) 14 *German Law Journal* 2185.

Richard Stacey and Richard Albert, *Introduction* In: *The Limits and Legitimacy of Referendums*. Edited by: Richard Albert and Richard Stacey, Oxford University Press.
DOI: 10.1093/oso/9780198867647.003.0001

We might also wonder, then, whether a constitution's democratic foundations necessarily lead to liberal content.[3] While it follows from a commitment to democratic constitutional design that everyone must have an opportunity to participate in determining the shape of their political arrangements, it does not seem to follow that they will or must choose a liberal political system when they exercise that opportunity. Indeed, there is an extensive literature from the first two decades of the 21st century which uses phrases like 'illiberal democracy', 'abusive constitutionalism', or 'authoritarian constitutionalism' to describe non-liberal (or less liberal) regimes.[4]

It may be more realistic, then, especially as these illiberal political systems show no immediate signs of retreating, to consider whether 'democratic' should instead be the adjective that describes whatever regime-identifying noun comes afterwards. In this lexical ordering, liberalism is just one option among a range of other forms of political system from which a people may freely choose. 'Democratic liberalism' is just as available and legitimate as 'democratic socialism' or 'democratic authoritarianism'.[5]

Why do we begin by shifting focus from political systems' liberal credentials to their democratic foundations? The short answer is that it is our response to the rise in constitutional referendums over the last several decades. The reliance on referendums in shaping and reshaping political systems' fundamental arrangements suggests that the members and leaders of political communities

[3] One of us has suggested elsewhere that there is a connection between a commitment to popular sovereignty and liberal norms (Richard Stacey, 'Popular Sovereignty and Revolutionary Constitution-Making' in D Dyzenhaus and M Thorburn (eds), *Philosophical Foundations of Constitutional Law* (Oxford: OUP, 2016), 161; and Richard Stacey, 'Constituent Power and Carl Schmitt's Theory of Constitution in Kenya's Constitution-Making Process' (2011) 9 *International Journal of Constitutional Law* 587). Joel Cólon-Ríos has argued similarly that a commitment to principles of democracy puts (liberal) limits on exercises of constituent power and in turn popular constitution-making (*Weak Constitutionalism: Democratic Legitimacy and the Question of Constituent Power* (London and New York: Routledge, 2012). For criticism of these positions, see George Duke, 'Inherent Constraints on Constituent Power' (2020) 40 *Oxford Journal of Legal Studies* 795.

[4] See, for example, Mark A Graber, Sanford Levinson and Mark Tushnet (eds), *Constitutional Democracy in Crisis* (New York: Oxford University Press, 2018), Fareed Zakaria, *The Future of Freedom: Illiberal Democracy at Home and Abroad* (New York: WW Norton and Company, 2003); David Landau, 'Abusive Constitutionalism' (2013) 47 *UC Davis Law Review* 189; Mark Tushnet, 'Authoritarian Constitutionalism' (2015) 100 *Cornell Law Review* 391; Boris Vormann and Michael D Weinman (eds), *The Emergence of Illiberalism: Understanding a Global Phenomenon* (New York: Routledge, 2020).

[5] John Locke made this point in the *Second Treatise of Government*, ch X § 132: 'The Majority having . . . the whole power of the Community, naturally in them, may imploy all that power in making Laws for the Community from time to time; and then the *Form* of Government is a perfect *Democracy:* Or else may put the power of making Laws into the hands of a few select Men, and the Heirs or Successors; and then it is an *Oligarchy:* Or else into the hands of one Man, and then it is a *Monarchy:* If to him and his Heirs, it is a *Hereditary Monarchy:* If to him only for Life, but upon his Death the Power of only nominating a successor to return to them; an *Elective Monarchy.*' For a modern account of democratic liberalism, see Richard Holden & Rosalind Dixon, From Free to Fair Markets: Liberalism after Covid (Oxford University Press, 2022).

care at least as much about being able to make political arrangements as they do about what those arrangements are. Those who care about either liberalism or democracy will do well to understand the relationship between them.[6] Referendums on constitutional and other fundamental issues bring the two into sharp relief.

II. Referendum's moment

At its most basic, a referendum is a mechanism for involving the public in choosing among available options in law and public policy, for instance to ratify a constitutional reform,[7] to secede or stay,[8] and to settle political disagreements.[9] There are other mechanisms, of course, such as regular elections to a representative legislature. Yet electoral systems rarely produce legislatures that faithfully and comprehensively reflect a society's diverse make-up—even if they have been designed to do so.

A referendum, however, is a form of direct democracy. Without the complex calculations of an electoral system or the bargaining of parliamentary politics, a referendum allows a people to express their political will in, arguably, the purest way possible. If we care about democracy, and it turns out that referendum does in fact present a pure and straightforward mechanism of exercising democracy, then the political arrangements that the people happen to make at referendum is perhaps less important than the fact that the people made them.

This proposition is alarming to many, however. Shortly after Britons voted in 2016 to leave the European Union, Harvard economist Kenneth Rogoff decried the use of referendums in modern constitutional democracy. 'This isn't democracy,' he said. 'It is Russian roulette for republics.'[10] And the Brexit referendum is just one of many popular decisions in the 2010s that produced unexpectedly non-liberal results.

[6] See, for example, James Allen, 'Democracy, Liberalism, and Brexit' (2018) 39 *Cardozo Law Review* 879, considering the consequences of resolving the tension between liberalism and democracy too frequently in favour of liberalism.

[7] See, for example, Fernando Mendez et al, *Referendums and the European Union* (Cambridge: Cambridge University Press, 2014).

[8] See, for example, Matt Qvortrup, 'Referendums on Independence and Secession' in Gëzim Visoka et al, (eds), *Routledge Handbook of State Recognition* (London: Routledge, 2019).

[9] See, for example, Ron Levy et al, *Deliberative Peace Referendums* (Oxford: Oxford University Press, 2021).

[10] Kenneth Rogoff, 'Britain's Democratic Failure' (June 24, 2016) *Project Syndicate*, at: <https://www.project-syndicate.org/commentary/brexit-democratic-failure-for-uk-by-kenneth-rogoff-2016-06?barrier=true> (accessed 22 January 2022).

In 2016 alone, Colombians rejected the historic peace pact between the government and the Revolutionary Armed Forces of Colombia (FARC), Italian voters rejected constitutional reforms reducing the size of the legislature and (in theory) increasing its responsiveness to voter input, and Thai voters approved a new constitution that entrenches military control while offering little in the way of democratic reform. In 2014, Crimea voted to secede from Ukraine and join Russia as a federal subject. Grenadians opted twice, in 2016 and 2018, to keep the Judicial Committee of the Privy Council as the court of final appeal for Grenada rather than accede to the appellate jurisdiction of the Caribbean Court of Justice.

On the other hand, referendums also offer opportunities for citizen-led progressive change. In June 2016, two-thirds of Swiss voters approved a more welcoming procedure for asylum seekers. In Ireland, voters chose to constitutionally recognise same-sex marriage (in May 2015) and to remove the constitutional prohibition of abortion (in May 2018). Referendums can also stymie leaders' attempts to consolidate power: in 2016, Hungary's populist president Viktor Orbán failed to win referendal approval for his government's rejection of EU-imposed migrant quotas because voter turnout was so low (although a majority of voters who did turn out approved the measure).[11] And in Italy in 2020, voters finally approved constitutional amendments reducing the number of elected representatives, easing the gridlock between the two chambers of the legislature.

A. In this volume

One motivation for this collection of chapters is to explore how a referendum distils the tension between liberalism and democracy, and to consider whether, and how, a referendum can bring these commitments together. Our starting point is the reality that the people may choose (democratically) to endorse or make changes to their political arrangements that trend away from liberal orthodoxy. These chapters capture how referendums can be abused on one hand to achieve short-term political or even personal gains, and how they can be deliberative, innovative, democracy-enhancing exercises on the other.

[11] Matt Qvortrup, *The Referendum and Other Essays on Constitutional Politics* (Oxford: Hart, 2019), 6, and Eoin Daly, 'A Republican Defence of the Constitutional Referendum' (2015) 35 *Legal Studies* 30. It is worth noting that both liberal and populist or conservative governments have 'lost' referendums. Elkins and Hudson (in this volume) describe the conditions under which governments are likely to achieve the results they want when they put constitutional questions to referendum.

This oscillation between democracy-enhancing use and anti-democratic misuse leads us to the quandary of referendums: how can it be that a mechanism of democracy can be used to establish a political system or alter it in ways that appear to care little for the basic principles that have come to be associated with democracy? By what standards can we assess the democratic legitimacy of a referendum if we are no longer to rely on the norms of traditional liberal democracy? In short, when is a referendum legitimate?

We approach this guiding question from three broad perspectives, which in turn provide the larger structure for the volume. First, why have referendums on issues of fundamental political importance become so frequent? Are there connections, at a theoretical level, between notions of constitutionalism, democracy, liberalism and referendum that explain this frequency, or are there reasons to be sceptical of claims of any such connections? In Part I of the volume we ask, 'Why referendum?', through Richard Albert's inquiry into the reasons for and consequences of holding a referendum when doing so is not required, Richard Stacey's argument that a referendum is not necessary in order for a people to act as sovereign, and Zachary Elkins and Alexander Hudson's historical account of successful and unsuccessful constitutional referendums.

Second, who are—or who *should* be—the people that make decisions about a political community's future? The question is particularly relevant in societies divided along ethnic, religious, linguistic or other lines, and in federal countries. The all-or-nothing nature of an up-or-down referendum can be homogenising, obscuring the diversity and difference that characterises political communities in a globalising world. If there is value in pluralism, how can the reliance on referendum preserve the multi-throated nature of modern societies? On the other hand, a referendum may have the capacity to bridge divisions in society, forging a sense of national identity and unity where perhaps that was lacking before. In Part II of the volume, entitled 'Who are the people?', we include Stephen Tierney's chapter on referendums in federal systems, Antoni Abat's examination of Catalonia's sovereignty referendum in 2017, and Anna Frushtorfer's inquiry into the use of referendums in less democratic post-Soviet regimes.

Third, is it possible to say after closely examining a handful of specific referendums that the referendum is an effective and reliable mechanism of popular sovereignty or democratic choice? This raises questions about what it means to be sovereign or for people to exercise sovereignty within an existing political community, and whether we can conclude with any degree of certainty that the outcome of a referendum faithfully reflects the actual will of the people. Part III of the volume, 'Are the people sovereign?', features Leah Trueblood's chapter on the Brexit referendum, Carlos Bernal's discussion of referendum during the Colombian peace process, Janna Promislow's examination of community-based decision-making within First Nations communities in Canada, and Aileen Kavanagh and David Kenny's inquiry into the transportability of Ireland's exemplary referendum experience.

These chapters bring together perspectives on referendums, constitutionalism, liberalism and democracy in ways that we hope offer tentative answers to some of these questions, and to the overarching question about the legitimacy of referendums. At the very least, we hope that the volume will go some way to helping scholars, public lawyers, politicians and citizens think more deeply about the questions.

In this Introduction we consider, first, why the incidence of referendum has increased, and what this means for democracy; second, how referendums have been or can be used and abused; and third, how referendums relate to constitutions and the tensions that arise between commitments to constitutionalism and direct democracy.

III. The rise of referendum

We begin by emphasising the primary reason for this volume, namely, the increasing reliance on referendums to settle disagreements of constitutional or otherwise significant importance. The brief roundup above of recent referendums is just a snapshot of a broader trend. Although the French Revolution was followed by a referendum on constitutional change way back in 1793, there were relatively few referendums in the 1800s compared to the 1900s. And even in the 1900s, it is really only since 1980 that the use of referendums has taken off.[12] As Stephen Tierney notes in the opening lines of his 2012 book:

> The use of referendums around the world has proliferated remarkably in the past 30 years. It has been estimated that of the 58 functioning electoral democracies with a population of more than three million, 39 had conducted at least one national referendum between 1975 and 2000.[13]

[12] Matt Qvortrup, 'Two Hundred years of Referendums' in Qvortrup (ed), *Referendums around the World* (Cham: Springer International Publishing AG, 2017) 263, 263.

[13] Stephen Tierney, *Constitutional Referendums: The Theory and Practice of Republican Deliberation* (Oxford: OUP, 2012), 1, referring to Lawrence LeDuc, *The Politics of Direct Democracy: Referendums in Global Perspective* (Peterborough: Broadview Press, 2003) 29. See also Tor Bjorklund, 'The Demand for Referendum: When does it Arise and When does it Succeed?' (1982) 5 *Scandinavian Political Studies* 237.

Tierney refers here to a rise in referendums in 'functioning electoral democracies'. Although there has been a similar increase in the use of referendums in non-democratic political systems over the same period, the increased incidence of referendums is generally correlated with more democracy worldwide.[14] What Samuel Huntington called the 'third wave' of democratisation is more-or-less contemporaneous with the proliferation of referendums.[15] Also, referendums have occurred more frequently in democracies than in authoritarian or non-democratic regimes.[16]

This correlation between democracy and referendum challenges the post-Brexit notion that referendums constitute an unmitigated threat to 'true' democracy, or even to the liberal values that are associated with democracy. It makes intuitive sense that once democratic methods for choosing governments have become ingrained in a political community, members of that community might begin to demand democratic methods for answering more fundamental questions of constitutional design as well.[17]

But the more frequent use of referendums in democracies does raise another question: is there a deficiency in representative democratic systems that has led to this turn to direct democracy in the late 20th and early 21st century? There are at least a few possible answers here.

[14] Qvortrup, 'Two Hundred years of Referendums' (above n 12), 263–64.

[15] Samuel P Huntington, *The Third Wave: Democratization in the Late Twentieth Century* (Norman: University of Oklahoma Press, 1991).

[16] Between 1900 and 2017 there were 262 plebiscites in authoritarian or 'not free' countries (as defined on the Polity IV scale), while there were 331 referendums in democratic countries over the same period (not including the 400 in Switzerland alone): Qvortrup, 'Two Hundred years of Referendums' (above n 12), 263–64; Qvortrup, 'The Rise of Referendums: Demystifying Direct Democracy' (2017) 28 *Journal of Democracy* 141, 142.

[17] Canada's experience of constitutional change is instructive here. The statutes that led to the enactment of the *Constitution Act, 1982* were not approved at referendum but rather negotiated and enacted by elected representatives (Peter Russell calls this a Burkean approach to constitutional change: *Constitutional Odyssey: Can Canadians become a Sovereign People* (Toronto: University of Toronto Press, 2004)). The compromise these elected representatives struck in 1982 led to two further rounds of negotiations about constitutional change, at Meech Lake in 1987 and Charlottetown in 1992. The Meech Lake Accord fell apart the longer the process went on without significant popular involvement, and to remedy that flaw the Charlottetown Accord was always intended to be put to referendum (a majority of voters rejected the Charlottetown Accord). For a more detailed overview, see Mary Dawson, 'From the Backroom to the Front Line: Making Constitutional History: Encounters with the Constitution: Patriation, Meech Lake, and Charlottetown' (2012) 57 *McGill Law Journal* 955.

A. Voter dealignment and the crisis of representative democracy

The first is what political scientists have identified as the 'dealignment' of political parties and their historical voting blocs.[18] An increase in electoral volatility begins in about the 1970s, with voters more willing to shift allegiance—or 'de-align'—from political parties on individual issues. For fear of alienating voters in general elections, governments took 'hot button' individual issues off the electoral agenda by putting them to referendum instead.[19] David Cameron's decision to put Britain's future in the EU to a referendum can largely be explained as an attempt to prevent eurosceptic Tory voters turning to the UK Independence Party (UKIP).

The phenomenon of dealignment on particular issues, however, is a symptom of a more fundamental worry: that representative politics fails altogether at representing the people. Considering how representative and direct democracy can coexist in mature democracies, David Altman puts the paradox as follows:

> If democracy works reasonably well (i.e., is relatively institutionalized), why should it embrace institutions that might bring uncertainties, inconsistencies, and doubts; cost money; and be potentially manipulable? My answer is rather simple: Because institutionalized party systems may go one step further and become overinstitutionalized, they have serious dilemmas of channeling social demands, they lack the required flexibility for doing so, and ultimately they will be subject to massive demands for movement toward citizens' preferences.[20]

The referendum has come to function as a safety valve in situations where the inefficiencies of party politics leave constituents' desires unfulfilled.[21] The old

[18] Richard Rose and Ian McAllister, *Voters begin to choose: From closed class to open elections in Britain* (London: Sage, 1986); Asa von Schoultz, 'Party systems and voter alignments' in Kai Arzheimer, Jocelyn Evans and Michael S Lewis-Beck (eds), *The Sage handbook of Electoral Behaviour* (London: Sage, 2017); Ruth Dassonville, 'Electoral volatility and parties' ideological responsiveness' (2018) 57 *European Journal of Political Research* 808.

[19] Qvortrup, 'Two Hundred Years' (above n 12), 264–65.

[20] David Altman, *Direct Democracy Worldwide* (New York: Cambridge University Press, 2011), 197.

[21] Qvortrup, *The Referendum and Other Essays* (above n 11), 30–31, Francis Cheneval and Alice el-Wakil, 'The Institutional Design of Referendums: Bottom-Up and Binding' (2018) 24 *Swiss Political Science Review* 294 (arguing that referendums can supplement representative systems when referendums are launched by citizens (bottom-up) and when governments are bound by the outcome), Benjamin Barber, *Strong Democracy: Participatory Politics for a New Age* (Berkeley: University of California Press, 1984), and Dimitrios Kivotidis, 'The *Pharmakon* of Democracy: General Will and the People in the Context of the Greek Referendum' (2018) 27 *Social and Legal Studies* 755.

and familiar political parties (labour, religious, social-democratic, conservative) may no longer represent electoral interests in multicultural societies where the issues that matter cut across these traditional social or class divisions.

A second answer follows from this. If the referendum is a way to supplement or salvage representative democracy in practice, it is also a mechanism for averting a legitimacy crisis in representative democracy more broadly. When members of a political community begin to feel that they do not have a say in the resolution of disputes that matter to them, the political structures that are meant to represent them may begin to leach legitimacy.[22]

AV Dicey argued as the 19th century waned, for example, that Parliament cannot legitimately pass laws making fundamental changes to Britain's unwritten constitution without consulting the people. Although Parliament is legally sovereign, he maintained, the people are politically sovereign.[23] The UK did not have a formal process for referendum in Dicey's time, but he suggested that the relationship between the Houses of Parliament infused electoral politics with the spirit of referendum. For Dicey, the House of Lords' rejection of a Commons' bill on a constitutional issue (a matter of 'first rate importance'), transformed the following parliamentary election into a referendum on that issue.[24] The House of Lords' legislative veto acted as a safeguard of popular sovereignty, and in turn as a bulwark of Parliament's democratic legitimacy.

The gears of direct democracy and representative democracy do not always mesh, however. If the referendum can be a safety valve that preserves the institutions of democracy, it can also function as a democratic bypass valve altogether. The dealignment of political parties and their traditional electoral bases may in time widen into a chasm between the political elite and voters

[22] Qvortrup, *The Referendum and Other Essays* (above n 11), 8–9.

[23] For an argument that the United Kingdom's constitutional system should not be seen as including separate political and legal sovereigns, but rather that it has a collaborative constitution combining political and legal accountability into a multi-dimensional constitutional order, see Aileen Kavanagh, 'Recasting the Political Constitution: From Rivals to Relationships' (2019) 30 *King's Law Journal* 43. See also Martin Loughlin, *The Idea of Public Law* (Oxford and New York: Oxford University Press, 2003), 83–86.

[24] AV Dicey, 'The Parliament Act, 1911, and the Destruction of all Constitutional Safeguards' in WR Anson et al, (eds), *The Rights of Citizenship: A Survey of Safeguards for the People* (London: Warne, 1912); Dicey, 'Democracy in Switzerland' (1890) 171 *Edinburgh Review* 113, 141; Dicey, 'Ought the Referendum to be Introduced into England?' (1890) 57 (Jan/June) *Contemporary Review* 489–511; Dicey 'The United States and the Swiss Confederation' (8 October 1885) 41 *Nation* 297–98. There has been a recent resurgence of interest in Dicey's work on referendum. In addition to Leah Trueblood's essay in this volume, see, for example, Rivka Weill, 'Dicey was not Diceyan' (2003) 62 *Cambridge Law Journal* 474, Mark Walters, *AV Dicey and the Common Law Constitutional Tradition: A Legal Turn of Mind* (Cambridge: Cambridge University Press, 2020). For somewhat older work on Dicey, see Vernon Bogdanor, *The People and the Party System: The Referendum and Electoral Reform in British Politics* (Cambridge and New York: Cambridge University Press, 1981), and Richard A Cosgrove, *The Rule of Law: Albert Venn Dicey, Victorian Jurist* (Chapel Hill: University of North Carolina Press, 1980).

disillusioned with politics.[25] Poland's slide to 'plebiscitarian authoritarianism' and the electoral success of the Law Justice (PiS) party since 2015 is explained in part by voters' disenchantment with a political establishment seen as arrogant and out of touch with the people's real needs.[26] A maverick leader who promises to operate outside the stultified and ossified channels of politics-as-usual is appealing in these circumstances. A referendum unconstrained by legislative rules or liberal constitutional norms is an obvious side door to political results.

Turkey's experience is illustrative. In 2017, the ruling Justice and Development Party (AKP) proposed constitutional amendments that abolish the office of the prime minister, centralise power in the president while reducing the role of the legislature in government, weaken legislative and judicial oversight of the president and, effectively, enable President Recep Tayyip Erdoğan to stay in office until 2029.[27] The proposals failed to win the required support of two-thirds of the legislature, but they nevertheless became law with just over 51 per cent of voter support at referendum. In Turkey, referendum is the engine that has moved the system away from liberal democracy and towards competitive authoritarianism.[28]

This is not to suggest that parliamentary bypass always leads away from democracy. Uruguay remains a relatively stable democracy even though its constitution allows constitutional amendment by a majority vote in a referendum, even if only a minority of the legislature agrees.[29] France, too, remains a functioning constitutional democracy even though the referendum Charles de Gaulle relied on in 1962 to transform the Fifth Republic into a semi-presidential system amounted to an unconstitutional parliamentary bypass (see further in section V below, and Richard Albert's contribution to this volume).

Just as Erdoğan did in 2017, De Gaulle sidestepped a recalcitrant legislature to shift the balance of political power from the representative legislature to the president.[30] While Erdoğan marches on with constitutional reform in Turkey,

[25] Stephen Holmes, 'How Democracies Perish' in Cass R Sunstein (ed), *Can It Happen Here? Authoritarianism in America* (New York: Dey St, 2018), 387, 412.

[26] Wojciech Sadurski, *Poland's Constitutional Breakdown* (Oxford: Oxford University Press, 2019), 168–73.

[27] One of us has described these transformative changes as more than mere constitutional amendments. See Richard Albert, *Constitutional Amendments: Making, Breaking, and Changing Constitutions* (Oxford: Oxford University Press, 2019) at 7, 91.

[28] Ioannis N Grigoriadis, *Democratic Transition and the Rise of Populist Majoritarianism: Constitutional Reform in Greece and Turkey* (Cham: Palgrave Macmillan, 2018) 65–67, and David Landau, 'Populist Constitutions' (2018) 85 *University of Chicago Law Review* 521, 540–41.

[29] Constitution of the Oriental Republic of Uruguay, 1966, article 331(b).

[30] Saskia Hollander, *The Politics of Referendum Use in European Democracies* (Cham, Springer International, 2019), 128–30.

announcing in early 2021 that his government will draft a new constitution, De Gaulle's further proposals for a stronger presidency were ultimately rejected at referendum in 1969.

In a twist on this bypass model, the Colombian government has relied on representative democratic channels to pursue its agenda regardless of popular opposition. After a majority of voters rejected the peace deal the government negotiated with FARC rebels, the government simply ignored the plebiscite result and enacted the peace deal into law through the legislative process. Carlos Bernal argues in his contribution to this volume that this was unconstitutional: a constitution that takes it legitimacy from the will of the people does not allow the government to bypass the results of a direct vote in which the people express their will.

B. Finding the people

If the basic model of representative democracy has struggled with a legitimacy crisis and dealignment in general, the problem is exacerbated in federations and systems with existing social divisions. The referendum has emerged as a useful tool in precisely those situations where a group of people within a broader political community does not see themselves represented in federal democratic structures.

Sub-state entities have relied on referendums in their attempts to secede, for instance Catalonia from Spain, in large part because people in these regions have not felt represented at the national level. Even though Catalonia has not forged a new nation separate from Spain, the referendum has been a tool at the very least to allow the sub-state people to distinguish their identity from the rest of the jurisdiction.

Of course, the complication in such cases, and in federal systems more broadly, is that it matters greatly who votes in a referendum.[31] In the Supreme Court of Canada's response to the 1995 secession referendum, it stressed that Quebec's nationalist ambitions would have to be balanced with the views of the rest of Canada. Even if a referendum returned a clear majority in favour of secession, the only political consequence would be an obligation on the other partners in Confederation to negotiate in good faith with Quebec.[32]

[31] See, for example, Bleddyn Davies, 'Brexit and Sovereignty—the EU Referendum: Who Were The British People?' (2016) 27 *King's Law Journal* 323.

[32] Reference re Secession of Quebec [1998] 2 SCR 217, para 88.

The chapter in this volume by Antoni Abat discusses the Catalonia case, while Stephen Tierney's chapter fills a significant gap in the theoretical understanding of referendums in federal systems. Tierney begins against the background of the existing tension between open democratic decision-making and constitutional entrenchment, then goes on to ask how a constitutional commitment to territorial and societal pluralism, especially in cases of marked demotic difference, affects our understanding of the role and practice of referendum.

Janna Promislow approaches a similar question from a somewhat different angle: the decision-making processes of First Nations in Canada. She describes how First Nations rely on internal democratic processes in order to decide how to go about engaging with the Canadian Crown. Decisions about whether to negotiate or ratify a treaty, to engage with private corporations seeking to develop Indigenous land, to launch a rights claim or litigate Indigenous rights, are frequently the subject of referendums within First Nations.

While these democratic decision-making processes afford Indigenous community members some measure of autonomy and political self-determination within Canada, they are nevertheless constrained by the far-reaching implications of Canada's settler legal structure. At the same time, many of the factors that complicate referendums in general, and sub-national referendums in federal systems in particular, are at play in these Indigenous settings too.

It is likely that referendums will continue to be favoured tool for the expression of distinct political and social identities within existing systems. In Scotland, for example, independence from the United Kingdom was the subject of an unsuccessful referendum in 2014.[33] The result of the Brexit referendum, where over 60 per cent of Scottish voters favoured remaining in the EU, has spurred renewed interest in a second independence referendum in Scotland. The pro-independence Scottish National Party failed to capture a majority in the Scottish parliamentary elections on 6 May 2021, but support from the pro-independence Green Party may help build momentum for a second independence referendum.[34]

[33] See Ross Bond, 'National Identities and the 2014 Independence Referendum in Scotland' (2015) 20 *Sociological Research Online* 1, and Tom Mullen, 'The Scottish Independence Referendum, 2014' (2014) 41 *Journal of Law and Society* 627, for analyses of how the 2014 referendum affected national identity in Scotland. Around 45 per cent of voters favoured an independent Scotland in the 2014 referendum.

[34] Stephen Castle, 'Scenes of Scotland, as it weighs its future within Britain', *New York Times*, 6 May 2021, <https://www.nytimes.com/2021/05/06/world/scotland-election-brexit-independence.html> (accessed 6 May 2021).

C. Necessary referendums

A third reason for the correlation between democratisation and referendum has to do with constitutions themselves, although in two quite different ways. On one hand, a constitution's amendment procedures may require approval at referendum. As more constitutions begin to include mandatory amendment referendums, the incidence of constitutional referendums will increase. We consider these mandatory constitutional referendums in more detail in section V of this Introduction.

On the other hand, the circumstances in which new constitutions are made are sometimes ripe for referendum. When authoritarian or other non-democratic regimes are brought down by revolution or civil resistance, when a new nation is carved out of an existing one, or when an autonomous sub-national region is established within a state, the leaders proposing new constitutional arrangements usually have little or no basis on which to claim to represent the people of the new state or region.[35]

Writing in this volume, Richard Stacey calls these moments of 'constitutional interregnum', in which a society suddenly finds itself with no popular foundation for the exercise of authority. Under these circumstances, a new constitution's democratic legitimacy must come from a source other than the now-defunct representative institutions or constitution. A referendum has the capacity to provide this democratic legitimacy to the new institutions or constitution.

On the other hand, as Stacey notes further, a referendum can also provide cover to a constitution that is decidedly less democratic than the one it replaces.[36] As Egypt's example of constitutional reform in the 2010s shows, a regime that is intolerant of political dissent, even one that has just overthrown a non-democratic or illiberal regime, can engineer referendal approval for a new constitution despite opposition to it.[37] In section IV of this Introduction, we consider what it means for a referendum to be held in unfree circumstances.

[35] Stephen Tierney identifies these as three of four situations in which 'direct constitutional democracy' is regularly used. The fourth is a state's accession to a supranational confederation, like the EU (Tierney, *Constitutional Referendums* (above n 13), 1.

[36] See, for example, Richard Bellamy, *Political Constitutionalism: A Republican Defence of the Constitutionality of Democracy* (Cambridge: Cambridge University Press, 2007), 132.

[37] Human Rights Watch detailed how opponents of Egypt's then-draft constitution had been harassed and arrested in the weeks leading up to the referendum: 'The [2014] referendum comes in the midst of widening repression against political dissent in which arbitrary arrests solely for the exercise of peaceful expression and assembly have increased. While streets are awash with billboards and signs calling for a "yes" vote, "no" posters have been virtually absent from the public square.' (Human Rights Watch, 'Egypt: Activists arrested for "No" campaign: Repression intensified ahead of referendum', 13 January 2014, <https://www.hrw.org/news/2014/01/13/egypt-activists-arrested-no-campaign> (accessed 12 April 2021). The Christian Science Monitor called the 2014 referendum, 'by any standard ... the least

The connection between democracy and referendums is not straightforward. Referendums can supplement democracy and enhance the participation of citizens in government, but they have also been used to clad non-democratic or democracy-eroding changes in a veneer of democratic legitimacy. In the remaining sections of this introductory chapter, we consider several facets of referendum's duality.

IV. The use and abuse of referendums

It is tempting to describe any referendum that produces non-liberal results as a misuse of referendum. In March 2021 Swiss voters approved a ban on religious face coverings, for example. There is no doubt that this referendum was an exercise in democracy, even though a majority of people supported a measure that liberal constitutions might prohibit as an unjustifiable limitation on rights to religious freedom were it enacted by ordinary legislation.[38] Indeed, liberal principles and the preferences of a majority are often in tension.[39] But to criticise this result for its illiberalism is quite different from arguing that it is undemocratic. As we observed at the outset of this Introduction, liberalism is not what makes a political system democratic.

But what about a referendum that produces anti-democratic results? The reason referendums are valuable is because they offer citizens a direct say in the resolution of disputes that matter to them. In some cases, a referendum may provide a solution to disputes that representative democratic institutions

free and fair of the five national referendums and elections held since Egypt's military-backed dictator Hosni Mubarak was pushed from power by mass protests in February 2011' (Dan Murphy, 'Egypt's constitutional referendum: It's not about democracy any more', 15 January 2014, *Christian Science Monitor*, <https://www.csmonitor.com/World/Security-Watch/Backchannels/2014/0115/Egypt-s-constitutional-referendum-It-s-not-about-democracy-any-more>(accessed 12 April 2021).

[38] In April 2021, the Quebec Superior Court found that Quebec's statutory ban on religious dress in public employment infringed Charter rights to religious freedom, but that Quebec's reliance on the Charter's 'notwithstanding' clause (section 33 of the Charter) made it constitutional: *Hak v Attorney General of Canada* 2021 QCCS 1466 (CanLII), 20 April 2021.

[39] This tension is a theme in work that might be considered classics of constitutional and political theory today: see, for example, Michelman, *Brennan and Democracy* (above n 1), Robert Dahl, *Democracy and its Critics* (New Haven: Yale UP, 1989), Michael Walzer, 'Philosophy and Democracy' (1981) 9 *Political Theory* 379, Randall G Holcombe, *From Liberty to Democracy: The Transformation of American Government* (Ann Arbor: University of Michigan Press, 2002). It is also a theme in more recent work on the populist illiberalism of the 2010s: see, for example, Michael D Weinman and Boris Vormann, 'From a Politics of No Alternative to a Politics of Fear: Illiberalism and its Variants' in Vormann and Weinman (eds), *The Emergence of Illiberalism*, 3 (above n 4), and Simone Chambers, 'Democracy and Constitutional Reform: Deliberative versus Populist Constitutionalism' (2019) 45 *Philosophy and Social Criticism* 1116.

cannot resolve. Because referendum works on democratic principles, a referendum that reduces opportunities for democratic participation in the future seems inconsistent with referendum's democratic foundations. Could this be described as a misuse of referendum?

In considering this idea, we think it is important to be sensitive to the existing political conditions in which a referendum is held. When a government calls a referendum while actively suppressing opposition, flooding the public square with pro-government propaganda and controlling access to the media, or simply limiting suffrage to certain groups of people, we might be sceptical about whether the process could be described as democratic at all. With this in mind, we distinguish between two broad categories of referendums (unfree and free) and suggest a nuanced distinction within the latter category (between illiberal and undemocratic results).

A. Unfree referendums

We think of unfree referendums as those where a government works the levers of state power to influence voting and manipulate results. Many of these unfree referendums ratify constitutional changes that strengthen the government's grip on power by reducing constitutional limits on the exercise of power, undermining political opposition, and suppressing dissent in civil society. Anna Fruhstorfer's chapter in this volume describes how autocratic leaders in the former Soviet region relied on constitutional referendums to institutionalise party hegemony and narrow avenues for political opposition. More importantly, ostensible referendal support for these changes allows the government to describe them as exercises in sovereign or democratic constitutional design, and to clothe what is otherwise little more than a power-grab in the legitimacy of popular sovereignty.[40]

Simone Chambers calls this 'populist constitutionalism', and identifies Erdoğan in Turkey, Orbán in Hungary, Duda in Poland and Chávez and Maduro in Venezuela as masters of the craft.[41] In Hungary, constitutional reforms 'in the name of the people' have reduced opportunities for the people to express political opinions: they amount to 'a concerted effort to stifle dissent, debate and criticism in the public sphere'.[42] In Poland, Duda and PiS have relied

[40] Nancy Bermeo, 'On Democratic Backsliding' (2016) 27 *Journal of Democracy* 5.
[41] Chambers, 'Democracy and Constitutional Reform' (above n 39), 1118–20.
[42] Ibid, 1121. See also Zolán Tibor Pállinger, 'Direct Democracy in an Increasingly Illiberal Setting: The Case of the Hungarian National Referendum' (2019) 25 *Contemporary Politics* 62.

on the rhetoric of the people's sovereignty to erode constraints on political authority, even without holding a referendum. As Wojciech Sadurski notes:

> The 'will of the sovereign', expressed allegedly through an electoral choice ('winner takes all'), was declared a fundamental legitimation for a general transformation of the state ... and as a reason to downplay checks and controls upon the executive and legislative branches. PiS's campaigns against first the [Constitutional Tribunal] and later the regular courts have rested upon the idea that any restraints upon the political majority are by their nature anti-democratic.[43]

For Chambers, these cases highlight the paradox of populist constitutionalism, and of unfree referendums in particular: namely, that formally democratic mechanisms such as referendum or competitive elections produce anti-democratic results. The very exercise of democracy results in the weakening of a political system's democracy. Chambers puts the problem as follows:

> One of the identifying features of populist constitutionalism is the tension between the means and justification of constitutional reform, on the one hand, and the institutional ends sought through constitutional reform, on the other hand. The means and justification are all about the people, participation, democracy and citizen power. The ends are all about the consolidation and concentration of power and ultimately the limitation and suppression of the people, participation, democracy and citizen power.[44]

Egypt tells a similar story. The 2014 Constitution was drafted by an interim military government (the Supreme Council of the Armed Forces) after General Abdel Fattah el-Sisi led a coup against Mohammed Morsi's government in July 2013. It includes a number of provisions that cement the military's political influence, limit expression, association and political opposition, and increase presidential power while reducing legislative and judicial oversight.[45] In April 2019, further amendments were approved at referendum. These amendments lengthen the president's term of office and allow el-Sisi a third term as president (he can now hold office until 2030), as well as extending the president's

[43] Sadurski, *Poland's Constitutional Breakdown* (above n 26), 3.
[44] Ibid.
[45] Zaid Al-Ali, 'Egypt's Third Constitution in Three Years: A Critical Analysis' in Bernard Rougier and Stéphane Lacroix (eds), *Egypt's Revolutions: Politics, Religion and Social Movements* (London: Palgrave Macmillan, 2016) 123.

control over the legislature and judiciary and cementing the military's role in cabinet. Despite these anti-democratic features, 98 per cent of voters supported the 2014 Constitution at referendum, and nearly 89 per cent approved the 2019 amendments.

The paradox of democracy-weakening democratic processes disappears, however, as soon as we recognise that the processes are not democratic at all. Referendums that are unfree from the outset, in other words, should not be considered democratic. As Matt Qvortrup notes, there is little to learn about democratic referendums from plebiscites in dictatorships: 'the votes in dictatorships are, almost by definition rigged'.[46] During Turkey's 2017 constitutional referendum expanding presidential power, for example, the government ensured that there was little public debate or discussion before the vote and silenced opponents of the proposed measures.[47] The vote itself was opened to manipulation by a Supreme Court ruling—on the very day of the vote—allowing the counting of ballots from which an official stamped seal was missing.[48] Similar concerns arose about the freeness of Egypt's 2014 referendum.[49]

The danger here is that a referendum, even an unfree one, provides a sheen of democracy to reforms that are undemocratic. Perhaps a popular vote that does not meet basic requirements of democratic participation and voter freedom should not even be called a referendum. Maybe—we take no position in this definitional debate. We conclude, more relevantly for our purposes, that it amounts to a misuse or an abuse of the referendum to pursue democracy-weakening reforms through an unfree popular vote.

[46] Qvortrup, *The Referendum and Other Essays* (above n 11), 83.

[47] Mehmet Emin Caliskan, 'With media muzzled, Turkish 'no' voters seek alternative channels', *Reuters*, 11 April 2017, <https://www.reuters.com/article/us-turkey-referendum-no-campaign/with-media-muzzled-turkish-no-voters-seek-alternative-channels-idUSKBN17D235> (accessed 14 April 2021); Tuğçe Erçetin and Emre Erdoğan, 'Mirror, Mirror on the wall, please tell me ... ': the Populist Rhetoric of the "New" Media of "New Turkey" During the April 16, 2017 referendum' (2021) 22 *Turkish Studies* 290; Ryan Lavigne, 'The End of Opposition: the AKP's Ten-Year War on Press Freedom in Turkey' (2019) 17 *UCLA Journal of Islamic and Near Eastern Law* 1.

[48] Jennifer Amur, 'Why Turkish opposition parties are contesting the referendum results', *Washington Post*, 17 April 2017, <https://www.washingtonpost.com/news/worldviews/wp/2017/04/16/heres-why-turkish-opposition-parties-are-contesting-the-referendum-results/> (accessed 14 April 2021).

[49] David D Kirkpatrick, 'Overwhelming vote for Egypt's constitution raises concern', *New York Times*, 18 January 2014, <https://www.nytimes.com/2014/01/19/world/middleeast/vote-validates-egypts-constitution-and-military-takeover.html> (accessed 17 April 2021): 'The near unanimity of the vote was plausible because the government thoroughly suppressed any opposition to the new charter. A campaign of arrests and mass shootings has crippled the Brotherhood, the main opposition group, which was formally outlawed three weeks ago, and it had called for a boycott of the plebiscite. Almost no critics of the charter were able to express their views in the news media or on the streets. And several activists were arrested just for hanging signs urging a "no" vote.' See also *The Economist*, 'Deepening rifts; Egypt's referendum', 25 January 2014.

B. Free referendums (and their results)

We contrast unfree referendums, where the vote and the results are manipulated by the government to its advantage, with free referendums that meet basic conditions of fair and democratic competition.[50] Free referendums might nevertheless return results we might think of as illiberal: Switzerland's 2021 referendum on face coverings is intolerant of religious diversity, while Britain's choice to leave the EU is a repudiation of a liberal orthodoxy that embraces universal human rights, free trade and globalisation.

We do not think of these as misuses of referendums, however. Neither the Swiss nor the Brexit referendum can be faulted from the perspective of democracy, no matter how anyone feels about the wisdom or desirability of the results. To belabour the point: what we value about referendums is their democracy, not their liberalism. The appeal of, and ultimately the justification for a referendum, is the opportunity it provides for the members of a political community to express their policy preferences directly (or at least, more directly than through elected representatives), freely and fairly. Any referendum that gives a political community that opportunity should therefore be considered legitimate.

Even under conditions of freedom, though, a referendum may nevertheless fail to produce the kind of widespread civic participation, meaningful and deep deliberation, and good-faith argument that leads proponents of referendum to describe them as pure and unadulterated expressions of a people's true desires. As Aileen Kavanagh and David Kenny argue in their chapter in this volume, Ireland's positive experience with referendum is in part attributable to a deep-seated 'culture of referendum' that does not necessarily exist elsewhere.[51] It may be difficult to replicate Ireland's referendums in places other than Ireland, even if those places are otherwise well-functioning, free democracies.[52]

It is conceivable, then, that a free referendum held in sub-optimal conditions in a country other than Ireland could produce the kinds of

[50] Robert Dahl famously offered a set of criteria that a political system must have in order to satisfy the democratic requirement that citizens are able to participate equally and freely in their own governance: effective participation, voting equality, reasonable opportunities for all members of the community to learn about policy proposals and alternatives (enlightened understanding), popular control of the agenda, and the extension of full rights of citizenship to all adult permanent residents (inclusion). See *On Democracy* 2 ed (Ian Shapiro, ed, London: Yale University Press, 2015), 37–40.

[51] See also Gavin Barrett, 'The use of Referendums in Oreland: An analysis' (2017) 23 *Journal of Legislative Studies* 71.

[52] Simone Chambers suggests similarly that without a sufficiently deliberative debate preceding a referendum, the referendum may degenerate into a tool of populist or majoritarian politics: 'Making Referendums Safe for Democracy: A Call for More and Better Deliberation' (2018) 24 *Swiss Political Science Review* 305.

democracy-weakening results we see emerging from unfree referendums. There is no structural or ontological reason that democracy-weakening changes could not win the support of a majority in a free referendum. One example is Lichtenstein's 1968 referendum on women's suffrage. Although it was a free referendum—women were allowed to vote in this referendum—a majority of voters still rejected expanding suffrage to women. And by the same token, a 1984 referendum limited to male voters—arguably an unfree one for that reason—did ultimately extend suffrage to female adults.

In our view, free referendums with anti-democratic results must be considered a legitimate use of referendum. There is nothing inherent in the machinery of democracy that prevents a government from asking its citizens if they would prefer a less democratic system. A commitment to democracy must mean that we uphold and respect changes that the members of a political community (or at least, a majority of them) make to the constitutional and political arrangements under which they live—even if those changes reduce opportunities for democratic participation later on.

Despite taking this position in principle, we nevertheless have a couple of reasons to think that most democracy-weakening referendums will make only minor changes in practice, whose effects will be dampened by the system as a whole. To begin with, constitutional change exists on a spectrum. Some constitutional changes to an otherwise democratic system pose more of a threat to democracy than others. Minor chips at the edifice of democracy are a quite different thing from huge bites that undermine the foundations of democracy. And there is a notable status-quo bias among referendum voters: they are more likely to reject far-reaching and complicated constitutional reforms than relatively minor and simple ones.[53] With this in mind, we think it unlikely that major democracy-weakening reforms will see much success in otherwise free and democratic constitutional referendums.

Zachary Elkins and Alexander Hudson's chapter in this volume confirms this preference for easy-to-understand constitutional change. They find that referendums on entirely new, replacement constitutions are more likely to succeed than referendums on individual amendments. They call this the 'bundling' effect: voters turn out to be more receptive to a package of reforms that comes together in a curated constitutional bundle than they are to smaller,

[53] Zohal Hessami and Sven Resnjanskij, 'Complex Ballot Propositions, Individual Voting Behavior, And Status Quo Bias' (2019) 58 *European Journal of Political Economy* 82, 85; William Samuelson and Richard Zeckhauser, 'Status Quo Bias in Decision Making' (1988) 1 *Journal of Risk and Uncertainty* 7.

stand-alone tweaks to a constitutional system that may affect the rest of the constitution in complicated and unanticipated ways.

If simplicity is key to the success of a referendum on constitutional change, and constitutional replacements are simpler for voters to understand than piecemeal changes that must be fitted into the existing system, then the lesson here is 'go big or go home', constitutionally speaking. It is nevertheless unlikely that a referendum to replace a constitution in its entirety will succeed—or even occur—in a well-functioning democracy. Indeed, Elkins and Hudson note that 'yes' votes in replacement referendums are far more frequent in less-democratic regimes than in democratic regimes.

Second, and related to this last point, even when a government makes small democracy-undermining changes to one part of the system—an expansion of presidential power, say—other institutional safeguards like a strong judiciary or a free press are usually capable of limiting the anti-democratic effects of that change. Wojcech Sadurski describes how Poland's descent into populist authoritarianism was achieved by making a swath of quite small changes all at once, without giving the system a chance to correct itself. It is also worth noting that none of these changes were made by referendum: rather, PiS and President Duda made the changes in the legislature, relying on their electoral majority to claim the support of the sovereign people for these reforms.[54]

All this is to suggest that even though a free referendum approving an anti-democratic change remains a legitimate use of direct democracy, we expect only rarely to see referendums making changes that shake a democratic system to its foundations.

V. Constitutional, non-constitutional and unconstitutional referendums

This volume focuses on constitutional referendums, but there are a number of different ways this phrase can be understood. In this section we outline three such understandings, and the distinctions to which each understanding gives rise. First, referendums can be about constitutional changes or non-constitutional but nevertheless fundamental changes; second, referendums can be required by a constitution, or not (mandatory and non-mandatory or discretionary referendums); and third, a constitution may allow discretionary referendums on some matters, while prohibiting referendums on other matters or

[54] *Poland's Constitutional Breakdown* (above n 26), 5.

limiting the manner in which they may be called. This creates the possibility of an unconstitutional referendum.

A. Small-c and capital-C constitutional change

We draw a distinction between referendums that change the text of a written constitution, and referendums that make important or fundamental changes to a community's social and political arrangements without changing the text of a written constitution. This amounts to a distinction between what we might think of as 'capital-C' constitutional change on one hand, and changes to the 'small-c' constitution on the other hand.[55]

This terminology captures the idea that the capital-C Constitution—the tangible document that codifies a community's foundational rules, principles and political architecture—does not necessarily codify all the principles or structures on which rests the exercise of political authority in a particular community. Most political communities have a body of unwritten principles, norms, conventions and practices that govern the exercise of political authority just as much as the rules written down in the capital-C constitution. Similarly, many of a community's important rules and principles are written down in places other than in the capital-C constitution, such as ordinary statutes, organic statutes, or international conventions and treaties. The rules and principles that constitute the small-c constitution can provide just as important a constitutional foundation for a political community as the capital-C constitution.

Despite the difference between the formal legal effects of capital-C and small-c constitutional change, referendums in either case can have equally significant political and social effects. In either case, a successful vote can make profound changes to the way authority is organised and exercised, and how people in the community and its leaders interact with one another. The referendums by which former Soviet states approved new constitutions and embraced the free market and a more-or-less liberal democratic orthodoxy are examples of capital-C constitutional referendums that brought deep social, political and economic change to a large region. Britain's vote to leave the EU did not result in capital-C constitutional change, but there is no doubt that Britain's departure from the continental bloc will bring profound changes to social, political and economic life in the UK.

[55] See, for example, Anthony King, *The British Constitution* (Oxford: Oxford University Press, 2007).

The United Kingdom is in the rare position, of course, of being without a single, tangible document called 'The Constitution'. All changes to the constitution of the United Kingdom will be small-c constitutional changes. But not all profound changes bring constitutional amendments even in places where there are venerated capital-C constitutions.[56] Compare the referendums in Ireland and Australia on whether to legalise same-sex marriage. In Ireland, voters' approval of same-sex marriage in 2015 gave effect to the 34th Amendment of the Constitution of Ireland. In Australia, Parliament merely had to pass an ordinary statute to give effect to voters' desire to legalise same-sex marriage in 2017.[57] In a social sense, the change is the same in both countries even though in a formal legal sense, constitutional amendment and ordinary legislation are quite different things.

While profound changes can result from both capital-C constitutional referendums and small-c constitutional referendums, not all capital-C constitutional referendums make deeply significant political and social changes. Switzerland, for example, held a referendum in 1866 on amendments to the text of the capital-C Constitution about whether to adopt a standardised system for weights and measures (it failed).

Our point is less that a referendum may be the vehicle by which a new constitution is ratified or an existing one amended, and more that a referendum can bring fundamental changes whether or not it affects the text of a written constitution. What makes a referendum noteworthy is not that it leads to capital-C constitutional amendment—although this is often important—but that it affords the members of a political community an opportunity to involve themselves in decisions about social, political, or economic issues that matter to them. It is merely an accident of history whether or not a nation inscribes these important issues into the text of its written constitution.

Our use of the phrase 'constitutional referendum', then, is meant to capture the connection between referendum and a broad understanding of constitutional change, without regard to whether the formality of the change is in the

[56] King points out that parts of the British constitution are in fact written down, even if there is no single document that amounts to The Constitution: 'What Britain lacks is not a written constitution but a *codified* Constitution, a Constitution with a capital 'C', one that has been formally adopted in accordance with some legal process generally acknowledged as appropriate to the purpose. … On the one hand, large chunks of Britain's small-c constitution *are* written down. On the other hand, large and important chunks of other countries' capital-C Constitutions are *not* written down' (*The British Constitution* (above n 55), 5).

[57] A voluntary postal survey was held in Australia in 2017, posing the question 'Should the law be changed to allow same-sex couples to marry?' Over 60 per cent of respondents voted yes, with a turnout of nearly 80 per cent (although participation in elections and formal referendums is mandatory in Australia, this postal survey was voluntary). Australia's Parliament enacted The Marriage Amendment (Definition and Religious Freedoms) Act, 2017 in December 2017.

capital-C or small-c sense. We are more concerned with the proposition that referendum allows a people to express a desire for fundamental change, than we are with whether constitutional amendment or ordinary legislation gives effect to the referendum.

B. Mandatory and non-mandatory constitutional referendums

It is important, however, to distinguish referendums about small-c or capital-C constitutional issues from referendums that the capital-C constitution requires. There are many written constitutions that include a requirement for a referendum in their amendment procedures. These capital-C constitutions cannot be amended, in other words, without a referendum approving the proposed changes. Other capital-C constitutions provide for the discretionary or non-mandatory use of a referendum for constitutional amendment. Others include no constitutional avenue for amendment by referendum.[58]

We begin here with mandatory constitutional referendums. The rationale for requiring a referendum for constitutional change is closely tied to the sovereign and democratic flavour that constitutions carry, and to notions of constituent power. The argument is that if a constitution is the product of the people's constituent power, then changes to the constitution must also follow from an exercise of constituent power. If a constitution reflects (or claims to reflect) an agreement among the members of a political community about the basic rules by which they will live, then changes to those rules require the consent of those same people.

That a constitution carries the imprimatur of constituent power is so self-evident to some that a requirement for a constitutional referendum can be read into the fabric of constitutionalism even if the capital-C constitution says nothing about referendum. In a 2004 judgment, *Njoya v Attorney General*, the Kenyan High Court set aside a process of constitutional reform because it did not culminate in a referendum:

[58] Dag Anckar, 'Constitutional Referendums in the Countries of the World' (2014) 7 *Journal of Politics and Law* 12, inquiring why 98 countries provide for amendment by mandatory or discretionary referendum and 95 others do not. The author suggests that amendment referendums are more likely in plurality electoral systems, rather than in proportional systems. Bleddyn Davies notes that in the United Kingdom, constitutional change occurs both by ordinary legislation and by referendum, and argues that each plays a part, but not a decisive role, in legitimising the system as a whole ('Popular Participation and Legitimacy in Constitutional Change: Finding the Sovereign' (2015) 36 *Liverpool Law Review* 277). See also, generally, Richard Albert, Xenophon Contiades and Alkmene Fotiadou (eds), *The Foundations and Traditions of Constitutional Amendment* (Oxford: Hart, 2017).

> The most important attribute of a sovereign people is their possession of the constituent power. And lest somebody wonder why, the supremacy of the Constitution … is not explicable only on the basis that the Constitution is the supreme law, the grundnorm on Kelsenian dictum; nay, the Constitution is not supreme because it says so: its supremacy is a tribute to its having been made by a higher power, a power higher than the Constitution itself or any of its creatures. The Constitution is supreme because it is made by they in whom the constituent power is reposed, the people themselves.… In short, I am of the persuasion that the constituent power of the people has a juridical status within the Constitution of Kenya and is not an extra-constitutional notion without import in constitutional adjudication.[59]

We should note that in this case the Kenyan court was seized with the question of how to replace a constitution in its entirety. Amending Kenya's 1963 Constitution did not require a referendum, but in the court's view there is a qualitative difference between amendment and replacement.[60] When a statute merely amends a constitution in terms of the amendment procedures it sets out itself, the amending statute can still claim to be consistent with the sovereign will of the constitution's authors.

Nevertheless, the rationale that constitutional changes including amendments require referendal approval has been persuasive. Perhaps influenced by the court's comments in *Njoya*, Kenya's 2010 Constitution does require a referendum for constitutional amendments relating to certain fundamental matters.[61] Other constitutions require a referendum to approve amendments

[59] *Njoya & Others v Attorney General & Others*, [2004] LLR 4788 (HCK), High Court of Kenya at Nairobi, 25 March 2004, at 15.

[60] The distinction between constitutional amendment and constitutional replacement is a recurring theme in Carl Schmitt's attack on liberalism. See *Constitutional Theory* (Durham: Duke University Press, 2008) (Jeffrey Seitzer transl) at 79–81, 144–146, 150–155.

[61] Article 255 of Kenya's 2010 Constitution provides:

A proposed amendment to this Constitution shall be enacted in accordance with Article 256 or 257, and approved in accordance with clause (2) by a referendum, if the amendment relates to any of the following matters-

a) the supremacy of this Constitution;
b) the territory of Kenya;
c) the sovereignty of the people;
d) the national values and principles of governance mentioned in Article 10(2)(a) to (d);
e) the Bill of Rights;
f) the term of office of the President;
g) the independence of the Judiciary and the commissions and independent offices to which Chapter Fifteen applies;
h) the functions of Parliament;
i) the objects, principles and structure of devolved government; or
j) the provisions of this Chapter.

under certain procedural circumstances (Constitution of France, 1958, article 89; Constitution of the Republic of Slovenia, 1991, article 170), and others require a referendum for all constitutional amendments (Constitution of the Republic of Ireland, 1937, article 46(2); Constitution of the Arab Republic of Egypt, 2014, article 226).

Most of these mandatory or obligatory referendums on constitutional amendment are confirmatory, with the people expressing their views only at the end of the amendment process. In effect, voters hold a veto over constitutional amendment. Article 46(2) of the Irish Constitution follows this approach:

> Every proposal for an amendment of this Constitution shall be initiated in Dáil Éireann as a Bill, and shall upon having been passed or deemed to have been passed by both Houses of the Oireachtas, be submitted by Referendum to the decision of the people in accordance with the law for the time being in force relating to the Referendum.

A non-mandatory referendum, on the other hand, lies at the discretion of the government. In some cases the constitution is explicit in giving the government the option to hold a referendum, on both capital-C constitutional amendments or small-c constitutional changes. With regard to capital-C constitutional amendments, consider the relevant provisions in the constitutions of Tunisia and Turkey:

> The Constitution shall be amended upon the approval of two-thirds of the members of the Assembly of the Representatives of the People. After an amendment by two-thirds of the members of the Assembly has been approved, the President may submit the amendment to referendum in which case it will be adopted if it receives an absolute majority of votes cast.[62]
>
> A law on the Constitutional amendment adopted by a two-thirds majority of the total number of members of the Grand National Assembly of Turkey ... may be submitted to a referendum by the President of the Republic.[63]

It is not immediately clear why either the Tunisian or Turkish president would choose to hold a referendum on a constitutional amendment that the

[62] Constitution of the Tunisian Republic, 2014, article 144.
[63] Constitution of the Republic of Turkey, 1982, article 175(5).

legislature has already enacted. It might seem foolish for a president to take the risk of submitting to referendum an amendment that has already won the necessary legislative majorities. In both cases, however, the discretionary referendum allows the president to play the same role that Dicey saw for the British House of Lords: a kind of democratic life preserver for a representative system that has drifted away from the people. This discretion is especially valuable in semi-presidential systems like Tunisia, where the president and the legislature are elected separately and may be political or ideological rivals.[64]

Richard Albert's contribution to this volume presents a typology of non-obligatory referendums and considers their implications. He suggests, for example, that having held a non-obligatory referendum on constitutional change once, a referendum may become politically obligatory in the future even if it remains non-obligatory in a strictly legal sense.[65] And even though discretionary referendums may not be binding in a strictly legal sense, once a government commits to holding one its results become difficult to ignore. The Canadian Supreme Court has recognised this political reality:

> Although the Constitution does not itself address the use of a referendum procedure, and the results of a referendum have no direct role or legal effect in our constitutional scheme, a referendum undoubtedly may provide a democratic method of ascertaining the views of the electorate on important political questions on a particular occasion. . . . Our political institutions are premised on the democratic principle, and so an expression of the democratic will of the people of a province carries weight.[66]

C. Confirmatory and consultative referendums

The mandatory and discretionary referendums we discuss above all show up as the last step in the constitutional amendment process. Once elected representatives have done the work of drafting and enacting constitutional amendments,

[64] Zach Elkins and Alexander Hudson suggest in previous work that mandatory constitutional referendums are less likely to succeed than discretionary referendums: 'The constitutional referendum in historical perspective' in David Landau and Hanna Lerner (eds), *Comparative Constitution Making* (Northampton: Edward Elgar, 2019) 142, 157–58.

[65] See also Richard Albert, 'The Conventions of Constitutional Amendment in Canada' (2016) 53 *Osgoode Hall Law Journal* 399, 419, Aude Bicquelet and Helen Addison, 'Are Discretionary Referendums on EU Integration becoming "Politically Obligatory"? The Cases of France and the UK' (2018) 71 *Parliamentary Affairs* 219, and Laurence Morel, 'The Rise of "Politically Obligatory" Referendums: The 2005 French Referendum in Comparative Perspective' (2007) 30 *West European Politics* 1041, 1055–57.

[66] Reference re Secession of Quebec, [1998] 2 SCR 217, para 87.

the people are asked to confirm—or veto—those changes. In contrast to these confirmatory referendums, a referendum could also be used to gauge a population's openness to constitutional change before the government takes any legislative action. Instead of the referendum coming at the end of the process, after the legislature has enacted an amendment statute, the referendum may be a first, consultative, or facultative step in the process.

Croatia's constitution provides for both consultative and confirmatory referendums, empowering the president or the legislature to call a referendum on either a proposal to amend the constitution or a bill amending the constitution.[67] In 2013, following a citizen initiative, the Croatian legislature (Sabor) called a referendum on 1 December in which it asked voters 'Are you in favour of the constitution of the Republic of Croatia being amended with a provision stating that marriage is matrimony between a woman and a man?' Nearly two-thirds of voters said yes. Although it is not clear that the Sabor was bound to uphold this result, a two-thirds majority of the Sabor did amend the constitution in January 2014, inserting a clause into article 61 defining marriage as 'a living union between a woman and a man'. Australia's postal survey about same-sex marriage, although not relating to a constitutional amendment, was also consultative.

What distinguishes these consultative referendums from confirmatory referendums is that the impetus for change comes from the people rather than from government. Instead of going through the process of drafting constitutional amendments only to have them rejected at referendum, the government need only act if the people express a desire for constitutional change. In both Australian and Croatia, voters were asked for their views in the abstract, before the legislature went forward with making a change.

One implication of this approach is that voters will not have a chance to consider the precise text of the amendment, even though they approve an amendment in principle. In some cases, the distance between referendum question and statutory text will be small, as in Australia's and Croatia's same-sex marriage referendums. The question Australia's postal survey asked was 'Should the law be changed to allow same-sex couples to marry?'. Although voters had little information about how the definition of marriage would be changed or

[67] Article 87 of the Constitution of the Republic of Croatia, 1990, provides:

(1) The Croatian Parliament may call a referendum on a proposal for the amendment of the Constitution, on a bill, or any other issue within its competence.
(2) The President of the Republic may, at the proposal of the Government and with the counter-signature of the Prime Minster, call a referendum on a proposal for the amendment of the Constitution or any other issue which he considers to be important for the independence, unity and existence of the Republic of Croatia.

how that change might affect marriage celebrants with religious objections to same-sex marriage, the statutory change was ultimately well within what could have been anticipated at the outset.[68]

In other cases, though, the gap between the abstract question posed at the beginning of a constitutional reform process and the full implications of that change is much wider. Achieving the outcome that the answer to a simply phrased question demands can be difficult, complicated and come with unforeseeable costs. This lack of information means that voters might not really know at the outset what they are voting for.[69]

Brexit is the prime example of this. The simplicity of the question, 'Should the United Kingdom remain a member of the European Union or leave the European Union?' belied both the complexity of withdrawal negotiations over the course of the following three years, and the ultimate costs to Britons of withdrawal.[70] Trueblood's chapter in this volume considers the Brexit experience and argues strongly in favour of using referendums only in a confirmatory role and, in contrast to Stephen Tierney, sees little place for consultative constitutional referendums.

D. An unconstitutional referendum

A third understanding of the phrase 'constitutional referendum' concerns the constitutionality of the referendum. A referendum that is authorised or allowed by the constitution is a constitutional referendum in this sense. Both the

[68] The 1961 Marriage Act was ultimately amended by changing the definition of marriage from between 'a man and a woman' to between '2 people' (Marriage Amendment (Definition and Religious Freedoms) Act 2017, section 3). The Marriage Amendment Act also allows ministers of religion and religious marriage celebrants to refuse to solemnise if their religious beliefs do not allow them to do so (ss 47 and 47A).

[69] One common argument against referendums in general is that the people do not have access to enough information, are unwilling or have insufficient time to educate themselves enough to make informed decisions, or are just too stupid to understand the full implications of the constitutional decisions they are making. See, for example, Stephen Tierney's discussion of the 'deliberation deficit' in referendums in *Constitutional Referendums* (above n 13), 27–39, and Qvotrup's essay 'The Stupidity of the People or the Wisdom of Common Folks?' in Qvortrup, *The Referendum and Other Essays* (above n 11), 80–93. See also Maija Setälä, 'On the Problems of Responsibility and Accountability in Referendums' (2006) 45 *European Journal of Political Research* 699, 717, Anthony McGann, *The Logic of Democracy: Reconciling Equality, Deliberation, and Minority Protection* (Ann Arbor: University of Michigan Press, 2006); Giovanni Sartori, *The Theory of Democracy Revisited* (London: Chatham House, 1987) 120; and Simone Chambers, 'Democracy, Popular Sovereignty, and Constitutional Legitimacy' (2004) *Constellations* 153.

[70] Reversing Ireland's approach, efforts to educate and inform Britons through citizens assemblies about how withdrawal from the EU might happen only began after the referendum. See Alan Renwick et al, 'What kind of Brexit do Voters Want? Lessons from the Citizens' Assembly on Brexit' (2018) 89 *The Political Quarterly* 649.

mandatory referendums and the discretionary referendums we discuss above fit into this category. Beyond these constitutional, or constitutionally permissible referendums, we are interested in the referendums that the constitution actually prohibits: the unconstitutional referendums.

Perhaps the best-known example of an unconstitutional referendum is France's 1962 referendum, which transformed the Fifth Republic from a parliamentary system with an indirectly elected president into the semi-presidential system it has today. As Richard Albert points out in this volume, changing the mechanism of presidential election required an amendment to the 1958 Constitution, but no amendment according to the procedures set out in article 89 of the Constitution was ever passed by Parliament. Rather, knowing that he could not assemble the necessary legislative support for the amendment, President Charles de Gaulle put the question to the people in a referendum. Article 11 of the Constitution empowers the president to call a referendum under some circumstances, but it does not provide for a referendum on constitutional amendment.

Nevertheless, De Gaulle pressed ahead and held his referendum. With around 62 per cent of voters supporting the change, with a 77 per cent electoral turnout, the result was politically difficult to ignore regardless of its legality. When asked about the validity of the referendum result, the Conseil Constitutionnel concluded that because the people had approved the change and the people are sovereign, the constitutional limit on the referendum was essentially meaningless.

Catalonia's regional referendum on secession from Spain in 2017, as described by Antoni Abat's chapter in this volume, is a similar example. It too was a referendum with no constitutional authorisation, but an important difference between it and the French case is that the Spanish Constitutional Court suspended the Catalan law authorising the referendum and later declared it to be unconstitutional.[71] Unlike in France, not even the significant vote in Catalonia in favour of secession—92 per cent—swayed the Court to overlook the unconstitutionality of the referendum. Of course, the Court's suspension of the referendum law before the vote may well have biased turnout in favour of voters who already felt alienated from Madrid's authority. Indeed, voter turnout was only 43 per cent.

The difference in these two judgments raises an interesting question about the relationship among a sovereign people, the desires they express in a referendum, and a constitution. The limitation on the referendum in the French case

[71] Pleno Sentencia 114/2017, 17 October 2017.

was procedural: that is, the president was not empowered to call a referendum about the mechanism of presidential election. But nothing in the substance of the constitution suggested that the mechanism of presidential election was sacred. An amendment establishing a directly elected president could easily have been passed through the processes outlined in article 89.

What about a situation where a referendum is procedurally constitutional, but where voters support a change that is substantively inconsistent with a constitution's fundamental principles? The Spanish Constitution, for example, provides in article 2 that it 'is based on the indissoluble unity of the Spanish Nation, the common and indivisible homeland of all Spaniards'. The same article goes on, however, to recognise and guarantee 'the right to autonomy of the nationalities and regions that make it up and solidarity between all of them'.

The Spanish Constitution does not contemplate the break-up of Spain or the secession of any of its regions, but it does recognise that its regions have distinct identities and may wish to exercise a degree of autonomy from Madrid. Autonomy within a federal state, though, is a quite different matter to independence. The Spanish Constitution does not appear to contemplate the latter. Rather, territorial integrity has been understood as a fundamental, defining and unamendable principle of the Spanish Constitution.[72]

The idea that some elements of a constitution are unamendable is not new, and the doctrine of unconstitutional constitutional amendments has seen plenty of attention in recent decades.[73] The logic here is that even though most constitutions provide for their own amendment, they are built on a set of norms and principles that, if abandoned, would undermine the integrity of the entire constitutional system. Amending a constitution in a way that departs from or is inconsistent with these norms and principles would effectively abrogate the entire constitution and would in that light be unconstitutional and invalid in light of the existing constitution.

The doctrine is usually discussed in the context of purported amendments enacted by the legislature. A constitution is meant to ensure, at least in part,

[72] Montserrat Guibernau 'Secessionism in Catalonia: After Democracy' (2013) 12 *Ethnopolitics* 368, 374–79, 389. See also the Spanish Constitutional Court decision on the 2006 Statute of Autonomy, 31/2010, 28 June 2010.

[73] See, for example, Yaniv Roznai, *Unconstitutional Constitutional Amendments: The Limits of Amendment Powers* (Oxford: Oxford University Press, 2017), Gary Jeffrey Jacobsohn, 'An Unconstitutional Constitution? A Comparative Perspective' (2006) 4 *International Journal of Constitutional Law* 460, Richard Albert, Malkhaz Nakashidze and Tarik Olcay, 'The Formalist Resistance to Unconstitutional Constitutional Amendments' (2019) 70 *Hastings Law Journal* 639, Gabor Halmai, 'Unconstitutional Constitutional Amendments: Constitutional Courts as Guardians of the Constitution?' (2012) 19 *Constellations* 182, Aharon Barak, 'Unconstitutional Constitutional Amendments' (2011) 44 *Israel Law Review* 321, Richard Albert, 'Nonconstitutional Amendments' (2009) *Canadian Journal of Law and Jurisprudence* 5, Virgilio Afonso da Silva, 'A Fossilised Constitution?' (2004) 17 *Ratio Juris* 454.

that elected representatives do not threaten the fundamental principles to which a political community has agreed. The situation may be different when the body seeking to make the change is the political community itself, rather than its elected representatives. Little of the academic attention to unconstitutional constitutional amendments has considered the implications of a referendum. But if De Gaulle's referendum was politically difficult to ignore, would the same not be true for a substantively unconstitutional constitutional amendment supported in a referendum?

One way to approach this question is to consider that constitutions often claim to express a people's most fundamentally held beliefs and desires, and that the referendum appears to be the most direct way for a people to express their beliefs and desires. If we take this relationship between the people and the constitution seriously, it is meaningless to think of the constitutionality or unconstitutionality of an amendment by referendum.[74] It is always open to the very people in whose name the constitution is made to fundamentally alter that constitution or make an entirely new one, even though such changes would amount to unconstitutional amendments were the legislature to make them. Inverting this logic, as Carlos Bernal does in the arguments he presents in this volume, it may well be unconstitutional for a legislature to ignore or repudiate the results of a referendum, even where the referendum is not formally binding.

On one hand, this is axiomatic. A constitution that is meant to codify the principles and norms in term of which a group of people agree to live together must continue to do so. If those principles and norms change—that is, if the group of people come to agree on different principle and norms as the basis of their community—the constitution must change accordingly.

On the other hand, it remains unclear whether the referendum is the best or the only way for the people to express the principles and norms on the basis of which they agree to live.[75] Richard Stacey argues in this volume both that there are substantive limits to what principles and norms a people can democratically agree to, and that a referendum is in turn neither necessary nor sufficient for a constitution to make a meaningful claim to the authority of popular

[74] Yaniv Roznai and Silvia Suteu argue that entrenching a nation's territorial indivisibility as an unamendable provision in the constitution is in tension with a commitment to popular sovereignty and the referendum as a mechanism of expressing sovereignty: 'The Eternal Territory: The Crimean Crisis and Ukraine's Territorial Integrity as an Unamendable Constitutional Principle' (2015) 16 *German Law Journal* 542. See also Mark Tushnet, 'Peasants with Pitchforks and Toilers with Twitter: Constitutional Revolutions and the Constituent Power' (2015) 13 *International Journal of Constitutional Law* 639.

[75] See, for example, Glen Staszewski, 'Rejecting the Myth of Popular Sovereignty and Applying an Agency Model to Direct Democracy' (2003) 56 *Vanderbilt Law Review* 395.

sovereignty.[76] Does a commitment to designing a constitution through the democratic mechanism of referendum impose substantive limits on what can go into the constitution? If the answer is yes, then there might be such a thing as an unconstitutional constitutional referendum, not due to the content of a particular constitution, but due to the democratic foundations of referendum itself.

VI. Conclusion—The future of referendums

We are in the midst of the age of the referendum. And that age will not soon end. The time is right to examine anew what democracy requires for a referendum to be legitimate when it is used in complex, diverse, modern states. The contributions in this book make good progress on this front—a challenge that it is not unlikely to be faced by every modern state in the years ahead.

Questions nonetheless remain for future research, particularly in the design of referendums. How should referendums be organised? Should they continue to require a single vote on a single day, the winner securing a simple majority by carrying 50 per cent plus one of the ballots? Or should they entail some assurances to give us confidence that the vote has been democratic in a fuller sense of the term, yet without imposing liberal outcomes as a limiting reagent in the vote?

Some possibilities for constitutional designers and legislators to consider include: offering voters' opportunities to learn about the stakes of their choice; giving resources to the electorate to become properly informed; and creating fora for the people to engage in a deliberative exchange of views and also to hear rigorous debates by opposing sides. Other possibilities include guaranteeing public funding to camps advocating for or against the ballot question to ensure that one side does not drown out the other due to an imbalance in available campaign financing. Still another possibility involves requiring a heightened supermajority threshold for winning a referendum, beyond the conventional rule of a simple majority vote, in the interest of yielding settlements that are

[76] See also Ludvig Beckman, 'Democratic Legitimacy does not Require Constitutional Referendum: On "The Constitution" in Theories of Constituent Power' (2018) 14 *European Constitutional Law Review* 567(arguing that a legal system's democratic legitimacy does not depend on approval at constitutional referendum, and that a referendum is not always sufficient for democratic legitimacy), and Aurel Croissant, 'Ways of Constitution-Making in Southeast Asia: Actors, Interests, Dynamics' (2014) 36 *Contemporary Southeast Asia* 23, (arguing that in eleven Southeast Asian systems, people's acceptance of a legal order (the 'day-to-day plebiscite') is more important to legitimacy than referendal approval at some point in the past).

more likely to be durable and reflective of broad popular support. One additional design option for referendums of the future draws its inspiration from the Scandinavian model of constitutional reform: to require a second confirmatory vote after an initial approval vote. The options for innovating the design of referendums are virtually endless, but there is a powerful simplicity to the conventional referendums that we commonly see today. Is there room for experimentation in referendum design? In all states and all circumstances? Or only in certain cases? And how to introduce these innovations in referendum design without gaming their uses?[77]

The next generation of constitutional change will see continued use of referendums. Referendums of all kinds are here to stay, and we should continue to build the theoretical justifications and practical solutions for holding them freely, fairly, deliberatively and consistent with the highest expectations of electoral integrity.

[77] For a discussion of one creative answer to this temporal problem in constitutional reform, see Daniel E Herz-Roiphe and David Singh Grewal, 'Make Me Democratic, But Not Yet: Sunrise Lawmaking And Democratic Constitutionalism' (2015) 90 *New York University Law Review* 1975 (discussing sunrise amendments as a solution).

PART I
WHY REFERENDUMS?

1

The Strange Case of the Package Deal

Amendments and Replacements in Constitutional Reform

Zachary Elkins and Alexander Hudson

I. Introduction

Discussions of formal constitutional change in the United States often run into two related obstacles. The first is the idea that the formal amendment process in Article V raises such a high threshold for amendments that it is "next to impossible" to change the constitution this way.[1] The second is a deep-seated fear[2] of a "runaway convention" that would go far beyond its mandate and alter the constitution in ways not envisioned by those who moved for amendment.[3] It is likely that both of these pieces of folk wisdom are myths.[4] In the case of amendment difficulty, Mexico has an almost identical amendment procedure to the US, and has passed more than 700 amendments in the last century.[5] The fear of a "runaway" convention grows out of the fact that the constitutional convention that met in 1787 (and eventually drafted the current US Constitution) was originally charged only with revising the Articles of Confederation. Legal scholars (and indeed the protagonists themselves) have long debated whether or not the convention actually had the legal authority to opt for replacement

[1] Sanford Levinson, *Our Undemocratic Constitution: Where the Constitution Goes Wrong (and How We the People Can Correct It)* (Oxford University Press 2008) 160; Donald S Lutz, "Toward a Theory of Constitutional Amendment" (1994) 88 The American Political Science Review 355.

[2] Perhaps first raised by Thomas Jefferson as he opposed the convening of a new constitutional convention to formally propose the Bill of Rights. See Walter E Dellinger, "The Recurring Question of the 'Limited' Constitutional Convention" (1979) 88 The Yale Law Journal 1623.

[3] Michael B Rappaport, "Reforming Article V: The Problems Created by the National Convention Amendment Method and How to Fix Them" (2010) 10 Virginia Law Review 1509, 1528–1531.

[4] Vicki C Jackson, "The (Myth of Un) Amendability of the US Constitution and the Democratic Component of Constitutionalism" (2015) 13 International Journal of Constitutional Law 575; Paul J Weber and Barbara Ann Perry, *Unfounded Fears: Myths and Realities of a Constitutional Convention* (Greenwood Press 1989).

[5] Mariana Velasco-Rivera, "Constitutional Rigidity: The Mexican Experiment" (2021) 19(3) International Journal of Constitutional Law 1042–1061 <https://doi.org/10.1093/icon/moab087>.

Zachary Elkins and Alexander Hudson, *The Strange Case of the Package Deal* In: *The Limits and Legitimacy of Referendums*. Edited by: Richard Albert and Richard Stacey, Oxford University Press. © Zachary Elkins and Alexander Hudson 2022. DOI: 10.1093/oso/9780198867647.003.0002

instead of amendment.[6] Whatever the historical truth of the matter, the idea of the "runaway convention" in Philadelphia in the summer of 1787 provides us with a fascinating opportunity for considering a counterfactual process of constitutional change in US history that we explore further below.

In a recent study of constitutional texts, David Law and Ryan Whalen have found that the difference between a package of amendments and a complete constitutional replacement is in many cases essentially semantic. The same larger political purposes could be in either type of revision, and identical changes in the constitutional text could be achieved through either method.[7] This suggests, of course, that drafters could simply market their changes differently. For example, Donald Lutz has argued that it is more accurate to describe the US Constitution as an amended version of the Articles of Confederation, a reframing that presumably would have changed future Americans vision of the document.[8] These accounts suggest that the choice between *amendment* and *replacement* may be of little consequence for the content of the constitution. However, it could be that the choice between presenting a revision of the constitution as an amendment (or series of amendments), and presenting a full replacement matters quite a lot for how voters view the changes, and whether or not they approve them in a referendum. [9]

Indulge us in a thought experiment for a moment: what if the convention in Philadelphia had proposed a series of amendments to the Articles of Confederation instead of its replacement? Following both Lutz and Law and

[6] Akhil Reed Amar, "Philadelphia Revisited: Amending the Constitution Outside Article V" (1988) 55 University of Chicago Law Review 1043; Robert N Clinton, "A Brief History of the Adoption of the United States Constitution Essays" (1989) 75 Iowa Law Review 891; Bruce Ackerman and Neal Katyal, "Our Unconventional Founding" (1995) 62 University of Chicago Law Review 475; Robert G Natelson, "Proposing Constitutional Amendments by Convention: Rules Governing the Process" (2010) 78 Tennessee Law Review 693; Michael Farris, "Defying Conventional Wisdom: The Constitution Was Not the Product of a Runaway Convention" (2017) 40 Harvard Journal of Law & Public Policy 61.

[7] David S Law and Ryan Whalen, "Constitutional Amendment Versus Constitutional Replacement: An Empirical Comparison", *Routledge Handbook of Comparative Constitutional Change* (Routledge 2020). They write (p. 8): "Any attempt to compare formally labeled 'amendments' with formally labeled 'replacements' will merely be a comparison of what certain drafters chose to label as 'amendments' with what other drafters chose to label as 'replacements.'"

[8] Donald S Lutz, "The Articles of Confederation as the Background to the Federal Republic" (1990) 20 Publius 55, 65.

[9] There is no easy answer for the plural of referendum. Both "referenda" and "referendums" are grammatically defensible, and each sound wrong to one camp or the other. Fortunately, the *Daily Edge* has conducted a rolling online referendum on the topic, which we check periodically. Since our last publication on the topic, the electorate has expanded to 5,901 voters, but the results have remained the same: 60 percent prefer "referenda," followed by 22.4 percent "have we nothing better to be voting on," and only 17.5 percent "referendums." The people, apparently, have spoken—or at least some people. Vote and view online at <https://www.dailyedge.ie/lets-figure-this-out-whats-the-real-plural-of-referendum-261522-Oct2013/> (accessed 16 January 2022). Our preference is mostly to avoid the plural whenever possible, though the people's choice is attractive to us, and seems appropriate in work on the referendum.

Whalen, we grant that the possibility that the important changes could have been considered in either manner. And it seems that, but for Madison's urging and initiative, an approach of discrete amendments may well have been preferred. Regardless, our theory and evidence lead us to think that a series of line-item amendments would have been highly risky—if not disastrous—for the Philadelphia delegates. Our descriptive contention is a simple one: discrete amendments are likely to receive considerably less support than will package deals. The constitution that emerged from that convention has been called a "bundle of comprises,"[10] and perfectly illustrates the choices that drafters have to make between bundling issues into a single choice or offering voters control over the individual elements.

The implications of the counterfactual are, in some sense, rather wide ranging. It is probable that a sequence of amendments would have meant fewer changes, that the Articles would remain as the controlling document (at least for a while longer), and that the US would have proceeded as a confederation, albeit a more coordinated and centralized one. We suspect that many of the proposed amendments would have failed even with a supermajority threshold, much less with the unanimity rule, which would have been fatal. In the immediate historical context, perhaps this highly constrained reform would have precipitated many of the political conflicts around slavery and state sovereignty that the US avoided confronting for many decades. One of the obvious limitations of this analogy—given our focus on the public referendum—is the fact that the US constitution was ratified through state conventions, rather than direct popular vote. Yet the choices made at the Philadelphia convention usefully illustrate the strategic calculations that extend from negotiations over content, to the specifics of how the constitutional text will be presented to voters. For the purposes of this chapter, the key idea is that while the full constitution was able to muster sufficient (though certainly not overwhelming) support to become law, the law would have been very different if the method of change had been a discrete series of amendments.

With these sorts of counterfactuals in mind, we explore the empirical difference between the probability of success of a referendum on replacement versus that on a discrete amendment. The historical data we have collected on constitutional ratifications demonstrate a marked difference in the success rate of votes on full constitutions in comparison with those on amendments. The difference between amendments and replacements speaks to a more general problem of *bundling* in the market of ideas, whether in the context of

[10] Max Farrand, "Compromises of the Constitution" (1904) 9 The American Historical Review 479.

legislation, constitutional politics, or negotiation scenarios more generally. We theorize about the exchange of ideas between constitutional designers and citizens and how and whether bundled ideas are effective. We close with a discussion of something we call the *intitialed* referendum, which combines some of the virtues of line-item and bundled constitutional appraisal.

II. Why a Referendum Anyway?

These days it seems almost required that democratic lawmakers would put a constitutional reform to the public for approval—even in cases where a referendum is not actually part of the legal process for constitutional reform (e.g. Canada 1992, Iceland 2012, Russia 2020). And if the presentation of the content of the ballot affects the outcome of the vote, as we will suggest that it does, it makes sense to remind ourselves of the rationale for the very exercise in the first place. After all, the process should be consistent with the purpose.

The chief virtue of a referendum is the opportunity to give citizens a decisive role in the crafting of law. Although we make the case below that the referendum is increasingly common, it is still quite something that a citizen might decide the content and structure of higher law. In many implementations, the referendum offers back-gate protections for representation: laws should not pass that strike a majority of the public as flawed. Importantly, the symbolic, expressive value of such participation is powerful—maybe even more powerful than its intrinsic value. Legitimation may well be the principal *raison d'etre* of the referendum, for better or worse.

Alongside this central purpose of representation and legitimation, the referendum also likely allows voters to speak to a more complete and substantive set of political concerns (as compared to voting in partisan elections). As used, for example, in many US states, the referendum (and the closely related citizen's initiative) provides opportunities for citizens to influence policy and legal change in a wide variety of areas—from marijuana laws, to gay marriage, to electoral systems. The referendum is also thought to support some fundamental democratic values, such as transparency, accountability, and efficacy.[11] Empirical evidence for these arguments is mixed, but it seems that at least under some conditions, a referendum can have these positive effects.[12] Iris Bohnet and

[11] Mads Qvortrup, *A Comparative Study of Referendums: Government by the People* (Palgrave 2002).

[12] Matthew Mendelsohn and Fred Cutler, "The Effect of Referendums on Democratic Citizens: Information, Politicization, Efficacy and Tolerance" (2000) 30 British Journal of Political Science 669.

Bruno Frey have argued that such votes give citizens strong incentives to form opinions, demand information, and ultimately develop trust. They write:

> If alternatives are created, shaped and decided in a representative body, outcomes reflect strategic decision-making, i.e., there is less chance to solve social dilemmas which results in an underprovision of public goods or an undesirably low amount of redistribution. On the other hand, if initiatives and referendums induce citizens to talk to one another, creating new choice environments, they are more likely to produce efficient and morally accepted results.[13]

Seen in this light, the referendum would seem to be a central tool for democrats.

However, the referendum has its detractors, and the potential risks and dysfunctions of this mechanism of direct democracy are periodically on display. There are, of course, a number of high-profile examples (such as the Brexit referendum of 2016) that have left one or the other side deeply embittered. However, beyond the anecdotes, many scholars have warned of the dangers of referendum on more substantive and scientific grounds. The older critiques of the referendum focused on the potential for the votes to undermine representative democracy. Direct democracy often means an end run around legislatures and can create divisions within the body politic—divisions that may be more muted if debate is restricted to congressional chambers.

David Butler and Austin Ranney also note the possibility that the practical usefulness of the referendum might be limited by lack of knowledge or interest on the part of citizens, the inability of a referendum to measure the intensity of preferences (though this would be true of most systems of voting), and the possibility that the votes result in decisions that harm the interests of minorities.[14] More recently, scholars have noted the connection between the use of the referendum and other democracy-harming outcomes. For example, both Simone Chambers and Stephen Tierney have argued that poorly-designed ballots might stifle democratic deliberation.[15] And some have observed elements

[13] Iris Bohnet and Bruno S Frey, "Direct-Democratic Rules: The Role of Discussion" (1994) 47 Kyklos 341, 351.

[14] Butler David and Austin Ranney (eds), *Referendums: A Comparative Study of Practice and Theory*. AEI Studies 216 (American Enterprise Institute for Public Policy Research 1978); Giovanni Sartori, *The Theory of Democracy Revisited* (Chatham House Publishers 1987) 115.

[15] Simone Chambers, "Constitutional Referendums and Democratic Deliberation" in Matthew Mendelsohn and Andrew Parkin (eds), *Referendum Democracy: Citizens, Elites, and Deliberation in Referendum Campaigns* (Palgrave 2001); Stephen Tierney, *Constitutional Referendums: The Theory and Practice of Republican Deliberation* (Oxford University Press 2012).

of direct democracy often go hand in hand with a concentration of power in the executive.[16]

While the device may have some inherent advantages and disadvantages, in practice it seems that the substantive democratic quality of the referendum owes much to the political context in which it takes place. As we know, there is a great deal of variation in setting. Perhaps the best example of a meaningful public vote is the process in the US state of Oregon, where an institutionalized mini-public (Citizens' Initiative Review) provides voters with some guidance on ballot propositions.[17] This procedure is, however, far from the norm. In fact, a majority of jurisdictions in our data on constitutional ratifications are at best marginally democratic. Of the 644 national votes on constitutional questions included in our sample, the mean Polity2 score (which ranges from −10 to 10) is 1.8 (which Polity reads as "anocracy") and the distribution is skewed toward autocracy. More than one hundred votes took place in a country with a Polity2 score of −5 or below (autocracy). A counter example to Oregon is the use of the referendum to ratify amendments to the constitution of Azerbaijan. Since 2002, Azerbaijan has approved 66 constitutional amendments by referendum, with an average "yes" vote of 93 percent. We find it difficult to believe that such high approval votes are the product of careful decision-making on the part of a free and well-informed electorate.

Indeed, the fondness that some authoritarians have shown for the referendum has not escaped the noticed of scholars of direct democracy. In some of the early work on this subject, Butler and Ranney wrote, "Perhaps it should be seen as a tribute to the power of democratic ideology that countries which lack the reality of open discussions and freely voted consent should embrace its forms."[18] Historical examples of autocrats expanding their powers or adding to their tenure through the referendum are multitudinous. In his comprehensive study of direct democracy, David Altman especially notes the use of such votes by Nicolae Ceauşescu, Alexander Lukashenko, "Baby Doc" Duvalier, and Ferdinand Marcos. Qvortrup adds Napoleon Bonaparte, Adolf Hitler, and Benito Mussolini to the list of authoritarians who have used or abused the referendum.[19] The Duvaliers in Haiti are particularly noteworthy in this regard,

[16] Zachary Elkins, "Constitutional Revolution in the Andes" in Rosalind Dixon and Tom Ginsburg (eds), *Comparative Constitutional Law in Latin America* (Edward Elgar Publishing 2017).

[17] Katherine R Knobloch, Michael L Barthel, and John Gastil, "Emanating Effects: The Impact of the Oregon Citizens' Initiative Review on Voters' Political Efficacy" (2019) 68(2) Political Studies 426–445.

[18] Butler and Ranney (n 14) 9.

[19] Matt Qvortrup, "Two Hundred Years of Referendums" in Matt Qvortrup (ed), *Referendums Around the World: With a Foreword by Sir David Butler* (Springer International Publishing 2018) <https://doi.org/10.1007/978-3-319-57798-2_9> accessed 16 June 2020.

having successfully altered the constitution via a manipulated referendum in 1971, but precipitating their own overthrow through their manipulation of another constitutional referendum in 1985.[20]

It is not hard, then, to understand an alternative view of the referendum as a tool available to cynical elites seeking an expeditious path to their preferred policy outcome. Mark Walker describes this view quite well:

> Political actors use referendums to achieve their goals. They do so deliberately and sometimes manipulatively with respect to the general public… Actors in nondemocratic regimes have used referendums for the same purpose. Indeed authoritarian states have developed a fondness for referendums because they grant legitimacy to a policy position and the implementers of the device by utilizing the vote of the people.[21]

The use of the referendum in non-democracies may be particularly worthy of our attention with regard to processes of constitutional change, as the imprimatur of public approval could be seen to legitimize actions that alter core aspects of a constitution in what Richard Albert has called "constitutional dismemberment,"[22] or other kinds of perceived mischief.

Yet, even in ostensibly well-functioning democracies, ratification elections are vulnerable to various kinds of manipulation. In a wide-ranging study of the theory and practice of the referendum, Maija Setälä suggests that the votes are open to manipulation in at least three areas: procedural manipulation, manipulation of the public agenda, and manipulation of public preferences.[23] In more recent work, Setälä and Maija Jäske noted in particular the potential for manipulation in "government initiated referendums, which are often organised, rather purposefully, to strengthen the government's position, or to promote a particular law."[24] This concern about *when* manipulation is more likely to happen is especially relevant to the constitutional referendum.

[20] Peter Emerson, "The Dictators' Referendums" in Peter Emerson (ed), *Defining Democracy: Voting Procedures in Decision-Making, Elections and Governance* (Springer 2012) <https://doi.org/10.1007/978-3-642-20904-8_8> accessed 16 June 2020.

[21] Mark Clarence Walker, *The Strategic Use of Referendums: Power, Legitimacy, and Democracy* (Palgrave Macmillan 2003) 1.

[22] Richard Albert, *Constitutional Amendments: Making, Breaking, and Changing Constitutions* (Oxford University Press 2019) 84–90.

[23] Maija Setälä, *Referendums and Democratic Government: Normative Theory and the Analysis of Institutions* (Springer 1999) 161.

[24] Jäske Maija and Maija Setälä, "Referendums and Citizens' Initiatives" in Stephen Elstub and Oliver Escobar (eds), *Handbook of Democratic Innovation and Governance* (Edward Elgar 2019) 90–104.

III. The Referendum and constitutional reform

In most jurisdictions, a referendum is reserved for matters of high importance, and few aspects of governance are more important than foundational, higher law. It may be that ideal-typic use of a referendum is that for constitutional reform. Certainly, foundational ideas in constitutional theory support the appropriateness of referendum as a means of ratifying constitutional change, whether for replacements or amendments to a constitution. A crucial concept in this body of thought is that of *constituent power*, which has organized the thoughts of scholars and practitioners of the referendum since at least the writings of Emmanuel Joseph Sieyès during the French revolution (which, handily, corresponds to the first empirical observation in our sample below). Constituent power provides the normative and conceptual justification for a "people" establishing a set of constitutional laws, from what otherwise may seem an unlawful basis. Two related distinctions are helpful: that between constituent power and constituted power, and that between original constituent power and derived constituent power.[25]

The second distinction suggests a reasonable way to think about amendments as against replacements. And at some level, much like the distinction between amendments and replacements more generally, the distinction between original and derived is somewhat artificial, but a useful fiction perhaps. So it is in some cases useful to stipulate that replacements can only happen through an *original* act of constituent power. Amendments that are effected through the official process of constitutional revision set out in the constitution then rely on *derived* constituent power. Adopting slightly different terminology, Stephen Tierney (citing Andreas Kalyvas) describes votes on amendments as operating within the "command sovereignty" of the existing constitution, while those on replacements "transcend the existing order" and thus rely on "constituent sovereignty."[26] The key claim here is that the moral and legal power to change a constitution rests on different foundations in amendments and replacements. It is this distinction that competes with Law and Whelan's claim that the difference between amendments and replacements is in most cases one that exists in name only.[27] Whether this theoretical difference affects voter behavior is an open question.

[25] Yaniv Roznai, *Unconstitutional Constitutional Amendments: The Limits of Amendment Powers* (Oxford University Press 2017) 113.

[26] Tierney (n 15) 11–12; Andreas Kalyvas, "Popular Sovereignty, Democracy, and the Constituent Power" (2005) 12 Constellations 223.

[27] Law and Whalen (n 7).

IV. Historical Patterns in the Use of the Constitutional Referendum

In order to understand the historical deployment of the constitutional referendum (and its outcomes), we have collected (mostly from published data handbooks and datasets) a new dataset with 644 observations of constitutional ratifications between 1789 and 2016.[28] Much of our interest is in understanding how "automatic" they are: do citizens accept the proposed reforms or are they predisposed to the status quo? The number of ratification votes and the diversity of contexts in which they have taken place is itself striking. Much of the scholarly attention to the constitutional referendum has been focused on relatively few cases, in particular Ireland, Switzerland, Australia, and Canada, with some serious glances to Turkey and Colombia. In other words, most of the prominent analyses in this field have not gone very far beyond the countries that Ran Hirschl has referred to as the "usual suspects."[29] In our earlier work, we described the incidence of referendum votes across time and space and theorized and tested a set of risk factors for referendum failure.[30]

The increased use of the referendum in constitutional change is indeed striking, though perhaps not surprising given the research in this area over the past few decades. As we note briefly above, there are some distinct trends in the inclusion of ratification as a mechanism of change in national constitutions. The actual *use* of the referendum follows similar patterns. As Figure 1.1 shows, the trend in the occurence of ratification votes has been increasing for both amendments and replacements.[31] Plots of the proportion of amendments and replacements that use ratification look similar to the event-count trend we include here. It happens that 1992 set the record for most constitutions put to the voters in a referendum in one year, at twelve, a wave that is seemingly unrelated to the dissolution of the Soviet Union.[32] The high point for amendments came in 1996, when ten states held eleven referendum-events. The slight downward trend in the case of replaced constitutions is true for both the number of events and the proportion of replaced

[28] This was the first year that we considered, but the first observation is not until 1793.

[29] Ran Hirschl, *Comparative Matters: The Renaissance of Comparative Constitutional Law* (Oxford University Press 2014) 4, 241.

[30] Zachary Elkins and Alexander Hudson, "The Constitutional Referendum in Historical Perspective" in David Landau and Hanna Lerner (eds), *Comparative Constitution-Making* (Edward Elgar 2019).

[31] Note that the points here represent "events" in which voters address a referendum, many of which (especially in the case of amendments) may include more than one question.

[32] While the timing might imply a connection to the fall of the USSR, the new constitutions that year were primarily found in Africa. Burundi, Comoros, Djibouti, Estonia, Ghana, Lithuania, Madagascar, Mali, Niger, Republic of the Congo, and Togo all approved a new constitution through a referendum. The referendum on a new constitution in the Seychelles failed.

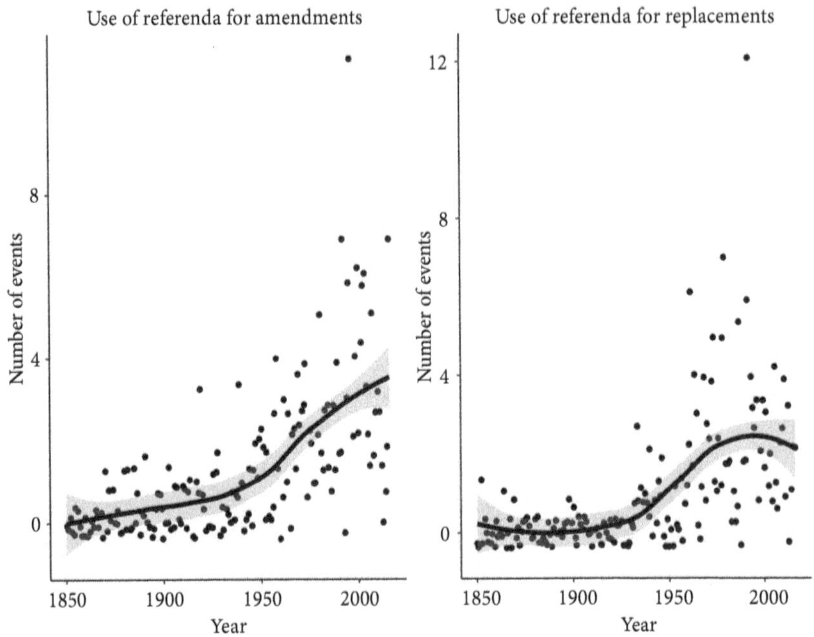

Figure 1.1 Referendum events, 1850 to 2016

constitutions. There is little to go on here yet, of course, but this could be an early indication of a move away from the referendum as a ratification mechanism.

A. Outcomes: replacements versus amendments

Political theory suggests a difference in the legitimating logic between amendments and replacements, but one might wonder whether there is a real difference in the rate of success between votes on amendments and those on replacements. After all, revisions through both modalities can enact fundamental legal change that, while important to voters, may not capture the voters' imagination or attention. This particular question was not our main motivation as we set out to collect data on constitutional ratifications, but the starkness of the answer provoked us. Our sample, which we believe to be a large percentage of the universe of cases, includes records on 193 votes on new constitutions (and associated sub-questions), and 451 on individual amendments. The differences between modalities with respect to both success and margin of success are eye-opening. As shown in Table 1.1, ratification votes on new constitutions were successful in all but 11

Table 1.1 Success and failure in constitutional ratification (1789–2016)

	New constitutions			Amendments		
	Ratified	Rejected	Total	Ratified	Rejected	Total
Number	168	11	179	277	174	451
Percent	93.9%	6.1%	100%	61.4%	38.6%	100%

cases (93.9 percent approval). In contrast, amendments pass only 61.4 percent of the time. If it really is the case that there can be little textual difference between amendments and replacements, we would expect to find that the two forms of constitutional revision have roughly similar success rates. The clear difference in referendum outcomes that we find here suggests that whatever the content of the constitutional text, voters react to these different forms of constitutional change in different ways. It is this remarkable difference in outcomes that we seek to explain in the sections that follow.

Beyond the top-line results, there is also substantial variation between amendments and replacements with regard to the closeness of the vote. As Figure 1.2 illustrates, the distributions of "yes" votes are remarkably different

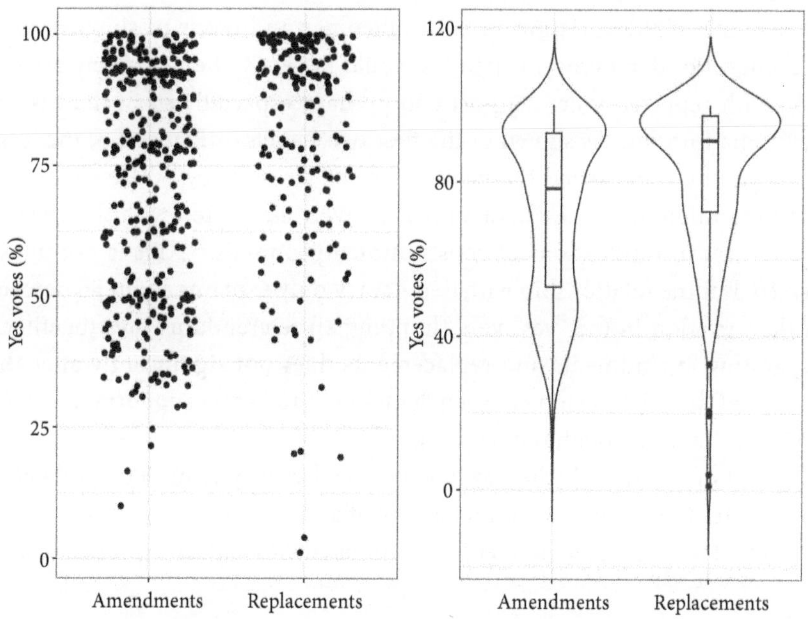

Figure 1.2 Distribution of "yes" votes in amendments and replacements

between the two kinds of constitutional votes. Most of the new constitutions in our dataset passed with ease, often with "yes" votes in excess of 90 percent. The median "yes" vote share for ratification of replacements is actually an astonishing 91.8 percent. In contrast, the median "yes" vote share for votes on amendments is only 78.3 percent. But this statistic misses the real story in the difference. Rather, it is the bimodal nature of the vote distribution for amendments that is illustrative of the potential for failure in votes on amendments. While there is still a high degree of yea-saying—in many support approaches 100 percent support—we find a large cluster located right around 50 percent (see the right panel in Figure 1.2), which suggests that many amendments pass or fail by a very small margin. This stark difference between the level of support for replacements and that for amendments suggests that there is something fundamentally different in the way that voters interact with these different forms of constitutional change.

B. Contextual explanations

The most obvious explanation for the difference in outcomes that we observe might be that these kinds of votes happen in very different political contexts. In our view, there are two major contextual factors that could explain some of the variation in both outcomes and levels of support. One is the level of democracy, which we would expect to be negatively associated with reported voter support and perhaps especially so in the case of new constitutions. As shown in the first two panels of Figure 1.3, the level of polyarchy as measued by the Varieties of Democracy (V-Dem) dataset (here standing in for democracy) is negatively associated with the level of "yes" votes in ratifications of constitutional proposals.[33] This is not unexpected, but the relationship with democracy only explains about 36 percent of the variation in the "yes" vote (lumping all referendum votes together). Separating amendments and replacements does not significantly alter the picture of the relationship between democracy and voter support for constitutional change through referendum.

To test more precisely the way in which the larger systemic level of democracy relates to the differential probability of success in a referendum on a replacement versus an amendment, we estimated two logistic regressions with

[33] See Coppedge and others "V-Dem Codebook V10" [2020] Varieties of Democracy (V-Dem) Project. <https://doi.org/10.23696≥.

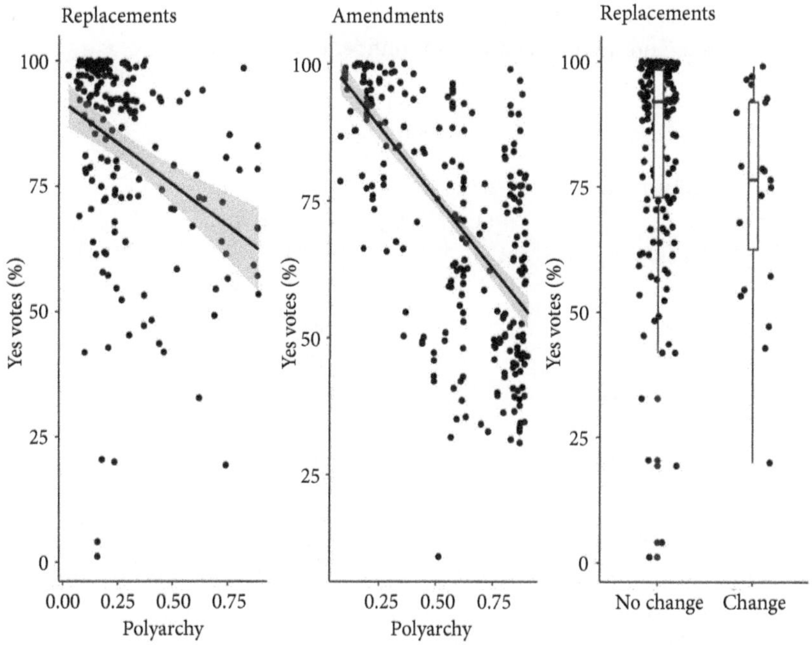

Figure 1.3 Relationships with democracy and regime change (all referendum votes)

the binary outcome of the referendum as the dependent variable (Table 1.2). Looking at the difference between amendments and replacements in isolation (no control variables), we would conclude that replacements are almost 600 percent more likely to pass than are amendments. In our view, a more appropriate specification should also control for (1) the number of years since the last constitutional revision, (2) the overall level of democracy (polyarchy), (3) whether or not a referendum is required to ratify constitutional changes,[34] and (4) the degree to which a referendum represents a credible threat of legal change. We collected data on the time since the last constitutional revision from the CCP Chronology of Constitutional Events,[35] and the other variables come from V-Dem.[36] Even after controlling for the level of democracy (and other contextual factors), we find that replacements are more than 150 percent more likely to pass than are amendments. The systemic level of democracy

[34] Simplified to a binary coding where 1 indicates that a referendum is at least sometimes required.

[35] Zachary Elkins, Tom Ginsburg, and James Melton, "Chronology of Constitutional Events Version 1.3" [2019] Comparative Constitutions Project <http://www.comparativeconstitutionsproject.org>.

[36] Coppedge and others (n 33).

Table 1.2 Predictors of success of a constitutional referendum (odds ratios and confidence intervals)

	Dependent variable: Result (pass/fail)	
Replacement	6.95***	2.54**
	(4.14, 12.43)	(1.27, 5.36)
Years since last rev.		1.03
		(0.99, 1.08)
Polyarchy		0.01***
		(0.00, 0.02)
Ref. required		1.88
		(0.72, 4.71)
Ref. credible threat		2.03*
		(0.98, 4.38)
Constant	1.592***	16.58***
	(1.319, 1.927)	(7.02, 43.23)
Observations	644	491
Log Likelihood	-355.90	-195.05
Akaike Inf. Crit.	715.81	402.11

Note: *p < 0.1; **p < 0.05; ***p < 0.01

itself, of course, has a very large and negative relationship with the likelihood of success in a referendum (also illustrated in Figure 1.3). Interestingly, we also find that ratifications are more likely to pass when they are a required part of the process for constitutional revision (though this is not statistically significant; $p = 0.18$).

A second theoretically plausible explanation for the difference in outcomes is that replacements are more common in cases where there is a significant change in the larger political system, and that democratizing processes in particular might predict a higher probability of referendum success. This is not supported by the data we have collected. We operationalize the concept of "regime change" by creating a binary variable that records whether or not there was a shift in the V-Dem polyarchy measure of greater than 0.3 (equivalent to moving from the first quartile to the third quartile). While (in a bivariate regression) we do find a statistically significant effect of regime change on the "yes" vote in votes on replacements, it is in the opposite direction, and regime change is associated with a lower "yes" vote. We cannot repeat the analysis for amendments, as we find very few amendments accompanying regime change events. This statistical relationship suggests at the very least that the difference we describe between amendments and replacements cannot be explained by regime-change or democratizing events.

However, there is more that should be said about the importance of the political context. To this point, we have described the constitutional referendum in a rather homogenizing way. While we noted the possible roles of both democracy and democratizing moments, there are other layers of political context that can matter in determining the outcome of a referendum. The best way to proceed here may be a short comparative study of two referendum votes that had similar features in terms of the distinctions that we highlight in this chapter, and radically different outcomes.

The first case is the Canadian referendum on a package of constitutional reforms called the Charlottetown Accord in 1992. The decade that followed Canada's patriation of the constitution and adoption of the Charter of Rights and Freedoms in 1982 had been dominated by attempts to revise the constitution further in a way that would assuage Canada's regional divisions and especially gain the support of the province of Quebec. The first major effort (the Meech Lake Accord) began with elite-level negotiations in 1987 and ended in legislative defeat in several provincial legislatures in 1990. A new process began shortly thereafter, and involved public consultations across the country, negotiations between the federal and provincial governments, and a non-binding referendum on a package of proposed constitutional changes. All the pieces seemed to be in place for a successful revision of the constitution. The nationally unprecedented level of public participation should have legitimated the proposed changes, and (according to our theory) bundling the proposed changes into a single vote on a larger package should have increased the "yes" vote. However, on the day, Canadians voted against the constitutional changes with a vote of 55 percent against.[37] This referendum effectively closed the door to major revisions to Canada's constitution for at least a generation.[38]

The Canadian experience in 1992 contrasts with the 2020 referendum on constitutional revisions in Russia. These recent constitutional changes in Russia comprise a large and diverse series of issues. The most political salient was a "reset" on the term limits for the current president, Vladimir Putin. However, this change was accompanied by more than 200 others, including alterations to

[37] R Johnston, "An Inverted Logroll: The Charlottetown Accord and the Referendum" (1993) 26 PS: Political Science and Politics 43

[38] P H Russell, *Constitutional Odyssey: Can Canadians Become a Sovereign People?* (University of Toronto Press 2004) 190.

pensions, the minimum-wage, and increased discrimination against same-sex families.[39] As in Canada, the vote was in legal terms merely consultative, and offered voters a single yes/no choice on the entire package of constitutional amendments. The political strategy here is open for all to see, as the changes to the constitution that do not deal with presidential terms seem calculated to capture support from large segments of the Russian population.[40] Unlike Canada, the referendum passed by a wide margin, with a reported 78 percent of voters supporting the changes.[41]

The comparison of the two cases highlights the role of the broader political context in shaping the outcomes of constitutional referendum. While the substance of the proposed constitutional amendments was quite different between the two cases, they share potential important institutional features in the design of the referendum. Here we have two very large federal countries each voting on a large package of amendments with a single (merely consultative) vote. The differences between them include both the larger level of democracy, and the order of operations. In Canada, a vote in parliament would have followed the referendum, while in Russia the amendments were actually legally completed (having been approved by both the national and regional legislatures) before the public vote. Yet, despite the clear importance of political context that appears in individual case studies, we argue that a systemic explanation of the difference in outcomes between amendments and replacements will heavily rely on this issue of combining (or not) a number of different issues into a single choice.

V. Theorizing the Effects of Bundling

As we have seen, the broader political context (e.g. in terms of the level of democracy, or regime change) does not account for the difference between amendments and replacements that we have observed. How should we then understand these different public reactions to replacement versus amendment propositions? We proceed by way of analogy, developing two accounts that

[39] Holly Ellyatt, "Russia Holds One of Its Most Important Votes in Years — but the Result Is Seen as a Foregone Conclusion" (*CNBC*, 1 July 2020) <https://www.cnbc.com/2020/07/01/russia-constitutional-vote-what-it-means.html> (accessed 1 July 2020).

[40] A Higgins, "The Theatrical Method in Putin's Vote Madness" *The New York Times* (New York, 1 July 2020) 18.

[41] Deutsche Welle, "Russia's Putin Wins Referendum on Constitutional Reforms" *Deutsche Welle* (2 July 2020) <https://www.dw.com/en/russias-putin-wins-referendum-on-constitutional-reforms/a-54018337> accessed 2 July 2020.

relate the choices individual voters make in constitutional change to more quotidian choice environments. We follow this theory-developing exercise with more concrete explanations that relate to elite-level political strategies.

A. Product Bundles

It is probably not too far-fetched to think of voters as consumers. Certainly, political campaigns for a referendum can feel like a sales pitch. If we adopt that sales frame, it is relevant to consider how "real" consumers respond to bundled products as against itemized ones. Generally, marketing scholars assume that individuals would prefer the flexibility of buying individual products, and that producers prefer to bundle. Bundling allows producers to "upsell" by adding ancillary products, many of which may have high margins and/or low popularity. Together, these added items represent increased value for consumers, but only if consumers would prefer to add these items anyway, and at the same or higher cost. But most fast-food consumers, it turns out, prefer not to order a drink or side dishes when they are unbundled from a sandwich.

Bundling, however, reduces complexity considerably for consumers, especially when the options are dizzying. Ordering lunch or a phone plan can now be as easy as asking for "Meal #1" or "Plan A." Once the menu identifies one option as "our most popular," the choice is even easier. One implication is that the components of the bundled product receive less scrutiny than they would if offered singly. And what if a bundle is the only way to purchase the product?

Taken this way, we can understand positive responses to bundled constitutional provisions. Deciding on whether to "buy" each particular amendment in a series of them can be just as hard as deciding what to have for lunch, and maybe less important to voters, sadly. In contrast, a larger bundle obscures some of the hard choices and can have the allure of a pre-selected, well-curated package. It may dawn on the voter that the bundle is a *package* of provisions that already balances well, in that the various provisions complement one another and that the requisite bargains have been struck. Surely, his or her side must have gotten *something* out of the deal.

We know, also, that faced with difficult decisions, individuals tend towards acquiescence. Such yea-saying can be a response based on politeness or deference to authorities, but it is also a natural response to task difficulty. The ballot, we know, is quite similar to a survey. And what we know from survey research is that most respondents often act in a "satisficing" manner to get through the survey protocol as conscientiously and sincerely as possible, but also with the least amount of effort.[42] Agreeing with proposals is one way to "get through" the survey with minimal friction. Deferring to authorities is another method. Both of these methods should push responses towards the "yes" camp, on a proposed referendum. But a third response effect, a status-quo bias, might cut the other direction, if the referendum is framed as disrupting business as usual. Our assumption—which deserves empirical testing, admittedly—is that acquiescence overrides the status-quo bias, as long as authorities are in agreement, which they generally are if the proposal found its way to the voters.

But any of these response biases are, naturally, conditional on aspects of the task (especially its difficulty) as well as those of the respondents (in particular, their knowledge and motivation). In the case of task difficulty, constitutional replacements differ quite markedly, *on average*, from referendum questions. Asking someone for their opinion of, say, the Bible is different from their opinion of the edict to "love thy neighbor." The respondents' opinion of the aggregated work, if we take it seriously, is just that—an aggregation of many, sometimes multi-dimensional, opinions. But note that "on average" is an important qualifier in this difference. Surprisingly, some referendum questions can present an extraordinarily difficult cognitive task and have multiple meanings or dimensions. For example, in another essay, we puzzle over the state of Texas' penchant for presenting voters with up-or-down questions such as the following, which was put to Texas voters in 2013:

> [the amendment] authorize[s] a political subdivision of this state to extend the number of days that aircraft parts that are exempt from ad valorem taxation due to their location in this state for a temporary period may be located in this state for purposes of qualifying for the tax exemption.

This question was *not* some sort of joke on the part of the Texas legislature. In fact, it is only a slightly more complicated version of the kinds of questions that the legislature puts to Texans every two years. (By the way, 58 percent of voters favored the exemption for aircraft parts—only one of several things that make the question look like a coin flip.) We wondered, among other things, about the effect of acquiescence bias in these kinds of difficult questions. In a 2019 survey of voters, we found that opinions can shift as much 40 percentage

[42] Jon A Krosnick, "Response Strategies for Coping with the Cognitive Demands of Attitude Measures in Surveys" (1991) 5(3) Applied Cognitive Psychology 213–236.

points, depending upon which direction the proposal is framed.[43] There is a good chance that a majority would have been *against* exempting aircraft parts if the proposal were to *remove* the exemption. All of this starts to seem like a giant game of "Simon Says."

These sorts of vexing and perhaps, stultifying, referendum questions may not be the norm. Easier questions, such as the one in 2019 that asked Texans whether or not to forbid the legislature from imposing an income tax (87 percent say yes) may be more common. And in general, such questions are far easier to answer than it would be to conjure an opinion of an entire constitutional text that in all likelihood respondents have never read.

B. Terms of service agreements

Consider another analogue. Have you either read through the privacy notice or terms of service agreement for a software application, or decided not to install the software because of the agreement? If you answered yes to either of these questions, you are in rare company. In one experiment, researchers found that three-quarters of respondents skipped through these agreements without reading them, and those who read them spent roughly 30 seconds doing so. 97 and 93 percent, respectively, agreed to the privacy policy and the terms of service, and therefore agreed to some interesting provisions planted by the researchers, which included turning over both their first-born children to the experimenters, and their email inboxes to the National Security Administration.[44] We should note that the level of agreement for these kinds of contracts is almost exactly comparable to the average level of agreement on full constitutions. The percentage of those that reject either kind is in the single digits.

In the case of products' terms of service, it is probable that respondents view these agreements as relatively benign, or at least standard, and that actually reading them is burdensome. Complicated legislation and full constitutions might represent something similar. If a text makes its way through the legislature and then to the voters, we must think that it has been approved by at least

[43] Joseph Francesco Cozza, Elkins Zachary, and Hudson Alexander, "Reverse Mortgages and Aircraft Parts: The Arcane Referendum and the Limits of Citizen Competence" (2021) 74 Electoral Studies <https://doi.org/10.1016/j.electstud.2021.102408> (1 December 2021).

[44] Jonathan A Obar and Anne Oeldorf-Hirsch, "The Biggest Lie on the Internet: Ignoring the Privacy Policies and Terms of Service Policies of Social Networking Services" (2020) 23(1) Information, Communication & Society 128–147.

some people who care about such things and/or that it is standard practice in some other jurisdiction.

But of course privacy on the internet increasingly matters to more and more people. Does it make sense to bundle the various components of the agreement in a single document? In some ways, yes. Producers benefit from masking a favorable policy (to them), and consumers incur those costs in exchange for the convenience of a single up or down question and use of the product. But what if the producers un-bundled the policy and asked consumers for their approval on each of the critical elements? Consumers would understand their trade-offs better, and fewer might agree to them. This is, of course, the approach that consumer advocates suggest, and that some companies have taken. It is also why important contracts include approvals for sub-components of the contract. But more on that suggestion in Section VI "Discussion" below.

C. A Matter of Gestalt and "Emergence"

It is intriguing to think that the bundles of constitutions represent something more than the sum of their parts, which may be another factor pushing their approval. We note above that bundles are sometimes attractive in that they represent a certain balance, in that the inevitable compromises are already settled and competing elements are harmonized, perhaps in the sense of Jacobsohn.[45]

The idea reminds us of the concept of *emergence*, which seems to describe many phenomena. The concept has its origins in the context of biological evolution and is associated with Lloyd Morgan[46] and Ernst Mayr.[47] Mayr describes emergence in the following way:

> Systems almost always have the peculiarity that the characteristics of the whole cannot (not even in theory) be deduced from the most complete knowledge of the components, taken separately or in combinations. This appearance of new characteristics in wholes has been designated as emergence.[48]

[45] Gary J Jacobsohn, *Constitutional Identity* (Harvard University Press 2010).

[46] Conwy Lloyd Morgan, *Emergent Evolution: The Gifford Lectures* (Williams and Norgate 1923).

[47] Geoffrey M Hodgson, "The Concept of Emergence in Social Science" (2000) 2(4) Emergence 69–70; Ernst Mayr, *The Growth of Biological Thought: Diversity, Evolution, and Inheritance* (Harvard University Press 1982).

[48] Ibid, 63.

In a review of the concept, Hodgson suggests that emergence is everywhere, if we are willing to look for it: "We find emergent properties in any complex, evolving system, throughout the natural and social realm."[49] It seems quite natural then, to think of constitutions as having emergent properties. These properties are intuitively understood by students of particular constitutions, and most likely also by voters as they consider their options in an up-or-down vote on a new constitution.

Some (maybe most) constitutions communicate something in their entirety. Think about "The Castle," one of the better films that feature constitutions—an admittedly narrow and undistinguished genre. The character Dennis Denuto is a hapless small-time attorney who, in a key moment, finds himself arguing a case at the high court. Interrogated by a justice as to which part of the constitution has been violated, Dennis stammers and cites the "uh, *vibe?*" of the constitution. It is an unwittingly apt characterization of such documents, and it is quite possible that citizens detect exactly that—a vibe. Think of the Brazilian constitution, a rambling mix of social and economic promises and everything in between. But it is not the components that led to a resounding vote in favor of the document. It was its "vibe" as the "citizens' constitution." So too with the Mexican and US constitutions. They all represent transitions from the country's past to its glorious future, or so we might think. And citizens may be voting on exactly those terms.

D. A political aspect of bundling: party mobilization of voters

Beyond the effect of bundling on voters' assessments of the relative attractiveness of a constitution, bundling may have more strategic political importance as well. In the context of a legislature, gaining support from a multi-partisan coalition may be necessary to pass legislation. In order to gain this support, it is often necessary to add new issues to a piece of legislation, creating a package of issues that may go far beyond the original intention of a bill's author.[50] Does the same inter-party dynamic apply in the case of the constitutional referendum? We expect that it might. One reason that the kind of bundling of issues that we find in the case of a complete constitution would predict a higher likelihood

[49] Hodgson (n 47) 75.

[50] Thomas Stratmann, "The Effects of Logrolling on Congressional Voting" (1992) 82 The American Economic Review 1162; Raya Kardasheva, "Package Deals in EU Legislative Politics" (2013) 57 American Journal of Political Science 858.

of support in a referendum is the opportunity to gain support from a larger number of political parties.

The endorsements of political parties are not a guarantee of increased votes, but they are in many cases a vital part of success in a referendum. Influential research on votes on initiatives and referendums in the US has pointed to the possibility that even non-party endorsements can provide cues that could inform vote choice.[51] Partisan endorsements can be even more powerful. In some contexts, political parties explicitly endorse a particular vote option, and put the force of the party machinery behind a campaign to drive the vote. There is strong empirical evidence from a number of European countries that political parties and leaders can often affect the outcomes of ratification by mobilizing their supporters to vote. For example, Sara Binzer Hobolt's research on Denmark's votes on the Maastricht Treaty has shown that political party endorsements (and the extent of their mobilization) can have a strong impact on the outcome.[52] Similarly, Ben Crum has shown that in the votes on the ratification of the EU Constitutional Treaty in 2005, opposition party support was crucial to success for the "yes" side.[53] Despite the ultimate failure of the initiative, there is strong evidence from Italy's 2016 referendum that government endorsement of the proposal was a strong influence on voter behavior.[54] Going beyond the yes/no vote choice, Nemčok, Spáč, and Voda have shown that political parties can also exert a strong influence on outcomes by encouraging their supporters to boycott a vote and thus prevent the "yes" side from achieving a statutorily required threshold of support.[55] However, not all parties are equally successful in influencing outcomes in this way. Claes de Vreese has shown that the effects of party endorsements vary both with the characteristics of the party and the individual characteristics of voters.[56]

[51] Arthur Lupia, "Shortcuts Versus Encyclopedias: Information and Voting Behavior in California Insurance Reform Elections" (1994) 88 American Political Science Review 63.

[52] Sara Binzer Hobolt, "How Parties Affect Vote Choice in European Integration Referendums" (2006) 12 Party Politics 623.

[53] Ben Crum, "Party Stances in the Referendums on the EU Constitution: Causes and Consequences of Competition and Collusion" (2007) 8 European Union Politics 61.

[54] Andrea De Angelis, Céline Colombo, and Davide Morisi, "Taking Cues from the Government: Heuristic Versus Systematic Processing in a Constitutional Referendum" (2020) 43 West European Politics 845.

[55] Miroslav Nemčok, Peter Spáč, and Petr Voda, "The Role of Partisan Cues on Voters' Mobilization in a Referendum" (2019) 25 Contemporary Politics 11.

[56] Claes H de Vreese, "Political Parties in Dire Straits?: Consequences of National Referendums for Political Parties" (2006) 12 Party Politics 581.

VI. Discussion: Bundled, Unbundled, and Initialed Constitutions

Of course, this stark difference between the success of replacements and that of amendments invites pragmatic and normative questions. Tight vote margins seem more democratic; nothing says "authoritarian" like a landslide vote. But should voters have the line-item veto power over the work of constitutional drafters? The strategic answer, for legislators at least, is clear: no. A wrapped, package deal is the shortest path to enactment. But of course, such a *fait accompli* may well defeat some of the idealized rationale for the referendum. Suppose that, in addition to legitimating their product, leaders want to learn something from, and teach something to, voters. For example, leaders might want to settle an argument over competing proposals, secure approval over core elements, or educate citizens about institutional choices. For those purposes, a package deal may not be optimal.

Of course, the choice between a package deal on the one hand, and a series of discrete amendments on the other, does not represent the only set of options. Like most things institutional, a hybrid solution is available. Consider, for example, Iceland's famous constitutional experiment of 2012, which was roundly lauded for its participatory (even crowdsourced) elements.[57] Most scholars of the affair focused on the recruitment of citizens and their web-mediated deliberation. But another singular Icelandic element was the ballot; voters were asked to weigh in not only on the full document, but also on a set of individual provisions, such as the official religion clause and the one on the ownership of natural resources. Voters approved of the new constitution (66.9 percent), and also each of the various components, but by varying degrees (ranging from 57 percent for official religion to 87 percent for natural resources).[58] The result was something of a package-level *and* line-item veto for the public. We call this kind of referendum—a joint vote for the full constitutions *and* several key provisions from it—the *initialed* referendum. We derive the term from the practice in contracting of requiring signatories to initial individual pages and/or important components.[59] Some parts of the contract matter more than others, and it is critical sometimes to establish consent over the important sub-components. One would not rent a car without initialing the insurance provision; why

[57] Alexander Hudson, "When Does Public Participation Make a Difference? Evidence From Iceland's Crowdsourced Constitution" (2018) 10(2) Policy & Internet 185–217.

[58] Despite passing in this referendum, the constitution was never approved by the parliament, and has not become law.

[59] There may be a term for this practice in the contracting literature, though we have not found one.

agree to a constitution without initialing, say, the official religion provision? Our sense is that initialing is worthy of consideration, and it makes sense to sift through any evidence of its use.

In fact, Iceland is not alone in the practice of *initialing*, though almost so. We count five cases in this category; the others are Benin 1990, Bolivia 2009, Chile 1925, and Ecuador 1979. Undoubtedly, other historical cases exist. The advantages of this sort of referendum are many, for both voters and leaders. For one thing, the added comprehension benefits are significant. Discrete questions about particular aspects of the "deal" are more cognitively manageable for voters, in that they focus attention and distill language. As such, the line-item questions *educate* the voters about the critical elements of a deal, in the same way that sign-off for insurance on a car rental contract clarifies that core element for drivers. Voters, then, learn something about their constitution. But so too do leaders, who can validate their hunches about the body politic with real data. Are voters committed to the right to health, to ranked-choice voting, to an official religion? There is nothing like a specific referendum—and its campaign—on such issues to demonstrate legitimation or repudiation.

Of course, it is the repudiation part that worries constitution drafters. Once the voters have had their say on, say, whether to leave or remain in the European Union, it is hard to put the genie back in the bottle. Just ask David Cameron. But Brexit offers some useful lessons. What does it mean when a referendum fails? Do voters need to agree to all line-items for them to remain in the document? Perhaps not. A constitution might specify an income tax—something that might prove unpopular at the ballot box (think of our Texas example above). But there is no reason to write ballot questions that pander to base instincts. A more constructive approach might ask voters to choose between two coherent options in order to clarify the alternatives. In the case of taxation, one could ask the voters whether they would prefer to fund the government with income taxes, sales taxes, or property taxes—or some combination thereof. A relevant historical example is the case of Benin's 1990 referendum, in which voters could choose to ratify the constitution with an age limit for the president, ratify the constitution without an age limit, or reject the proposed constitution.

One objection to selective line-item votes might be that it provides another opportunity for some sort of partisan manipulation of the constitution-making process. However, we suggest that a principled approach to this could be agreed upon before the drafters begin to put pen to paper. One potentially relevant precedent was the decision in the South African constitution-making process of 1994–1996 that if the Constitutional Assembly was unable to muster at least two-thirds support for the constitution, it would be placed before the voters in a referendum the following year. It could be that a similar rule would provide that individual articles of the constitution that failed to reach some specified supermajority support would then be placed before the voters as a sub-question in the ratifying referendum. Another relevant example was the referendum on the system of government that Brazil held in 1993. The choice between presidentialism and parliamentarism was one of the hardest-fought battles in the Constituent Assembly in 1986–1988. The presidentialists ultimately won the day, in a dramatic come-from-behind victory, but the bitter parliamentarists secured an agreement to put the question to the voters five years later. Despite the delay, the Brazilian approach also supports the idea of allowing the voters to decide on the issues that were most contentious in the constitution-making process.

The strongest argument against line-item decision making, including an *initialed* ballot, might be that the provisions in question are interdependent. Constitutions may be "designed," in the sense that they are coherent and one provision builds upon another.[60] Or they may represent a set of compromises, carefully balanced. In either or both of these cases, subjecting provisions to line-item consideration potentially ignores that interdependence. But it is also the case that the possibility of a future line-item vote by the public can grease the wheels for agreement about the package. In that sense, the agreement between parliamentarists and presidentialists in Brazil to administer a subsequent referendum on their positions sweetened some of the bitterness of the loss for the parliamentarists and gave them hope that a public might one day vindicate their position (alas, no).

We call this mechanism a *downstream inducement*, which we see as the corollary to Jon Elster's understanding of the referendum as providing *downstream constraints* on the work of drafters.[61] Elster's observation is that delegates take into account the reality of a later public vote on their work and modify their creation in anticipation of resistance. But it is also the case that recognition of a public vote can facilitate and even liberate drafters. Knowing that an idea will be subjected to a vote—especially under the scrutiny of an initialed ballot—takes *some* of the pressure off of settling things in the legislative chamber. There was something like this at work at the US founding. Elster's point is undeniable: "In the United States, the fact that the Constitution had to

[60] Donald L Horowitz, "Constitutional Design: Proposals Versus Processes" in Andrew Reynolds (eds), *The Architecture of Democracy* (Oxford University Press 2002) 15–36 <https://doi.org/10.1093/0199246467.003.0002>.

[61] Jon Elster, "Forces and Mechanisms in the Constitution-Making Process" (1995) 45 Duke LJ 364.

be ratified by the states meant that the framers were not free to ignore the interests of the states."[62] But it is also likely that the drafters sensed they could work more freely knowing that their critics in state legislatures would let them know if they went too far. And of course many states did exactly that. We may forget how close the ratification votes were in some states, including the pivotal jurisdictions of Massachusetts (187–168), New York (30–27), and Virginia (89–79). And in these states, the constitution would not even have been approved at all without the explicit stipulation that the vote was contingent upon the Congress tacking on a set of amendments regarding rights. Think of those stipulations as another variant of a downstream inducement. In both kinds, the thinking is similar: we can pass this thing, unsatisfactory as it is, only because we will have another bite at the apple.

This brings back to our opening paragraphs, and the conundrum that is constitutional reform in the US then and now. Our counterfactual from 1789 seems pretty clear, based on the evidence: the "bundle of compromises" approach was the one most likely to secure the passage of the constitutional revisions. Bundling also likely had positive effects in terms of the coherence and durability of the constitution. As calls grow from both left and right for comprehensive reform of the US Constitution, our research here provides some cautionary notes. First, while the idea of individual amendments might be more politically palatable in the current environment of widespread constitutional veneration (contra the founding era views of the Articles), constitutional change in this manner would be unlikely to result in success for more than two-thirds of the proposed changes. Second, even if a series of amendments is the chosen method, the fewer and more capacious these amendments are, the more likely they are to be ratified. Given both the US precedents and our broader comparative analysis, we would not be surprised to find that a process intended to produce amendments instead resulted in a proposal for constitutional replacement. Damn the veneration, full speed ahead, will likely be the only way to reform US institutions. For better or worse.

[62] Ibid, 374.

2

Discretionary Referendums in Constitutional Amendment

Richard Albert

I. Introduction—The Constitution as an incomplete code

Recent referendums around the world have produced surprising results. Voters in the United Kingdom decided in June 2016 to withdraw from the European Union,[1] Colombians rejected the historic peace pact with the Fuerzas Armadas Revolucionarias de Colombia (FARC) in October 2016,[2] Italians foiled a package of major reforms in December 2016,[3] and Turkish voters ratified a significant expansion of executive power in April 2017.[4] Referendums on questions just as controversial had been promised for France and the Netherlands: Marine Le Pen and Geert Wilders, respectively, pledged to hold votes on membership in the European Union had they won their elections. Both were defeated, and for now the tides of EU exit referendums have subsided.

The unexpected results of these recent referendums have highlighted an important similarity among many of them: they were not constitutionally required, neither at the stage of proposal nor ratification. Constitutional actors around the globe have often felt compelled by political imperatives to forego the formal rules of constitutional change in order to bring their proposals for

[1] Steven Erlanger, "Britain Votes to Leave E.U.; Cameron Plans to Step Down", *The New York Times* (June 23, 2016), online: <https://www.nytimes.com/2016/06/25/world/europe/britain-brexit-european-union-referendum.html?_r=0>.

[2] Sibylla Brodzinsky, "Colombia Referendum: Voters Reject Peace Deal with Farc Guerrillas", *The Guardian* (October 3, 2016), online: <https://www.theguardian.com/world/2016/oct/02/colombia-referendum-rejects-peace-deal-with-farc>.

[3] Stephanie Kirchgaessner, "Italian PM Matteo Renzi Resigns After Referendum Defeat", *The Guardian* (December 5, 2016), online: <https://www.theguardian.com/world/2016/dec/04/matteo-renzis-future-in-the-balance-amid-high-turnout-in-italy-referendum>.

[4] Patrick Kingsley, "Erdogan Claims Vast Powers in Turkey After Narrow Victory in Referendum", *The New York Times* (April 16, 2017), online: <https://www.nytimes.com/2017/04/16/world/europe/turkey-referendum-polls-erdogan.html>.

Richard Albert, *Discretionary Referendums in Constitutional Amendment* In: *The Limits and Legitimacy of Referendums*. Edited by: Richard Albert and Richard Stacey, Oxford University Press.
DOI: 10.1093/oso/9780198867647.003.0003

major constitutional change directly to the people in referendums that are not required by the constitution. This is not a rare practice: it has occurred historically and recently. As Stephen Tierney has shown, we are witnessing increasing recourse to referendums where the constitution does not mandate their use.[5] This use of non-obligatory referendums raises foundational questions about the modalities of constitutional change, the legitimizing sources of constitutional reform, as well as the limits of codifying constitutional rules in a single master-text.

Recourse to non-obligatory referendums in constitutional reform involves constitutional actors departing from the established rules of constitutional change in order to alter the very constitution that presumably binds them. This is not an irreconcilable tension, though, since no constitution, whether codified or not, is an exhaustive catalogue of all official rules, nor can it reasonably purport to be comprehensive.[6] The tension may instead reflect the inescapable truth of constitutional change located within the interstices of constitutional time: where constitutional actors make a fundamental break with the rules of constitutional change to formally amend some part or principle in the constitution, constitutional actors do more than alter that part of the constitution they formally propose to change—they alter the nature of the constitution itself.[7]

In this chapter, I draw from non-obligatory referendums held around the world to develop a typology of discretionary referendums in constitutional amendment. I focus in Section II specifically on non-obligatory popular votes in Canada (1992), Colombia (2016), France (1962) and the United Kingdom (2016). The successful French referendum on direct presidential elections illustrates the category of a *reconstructive* referendum while the Canadian referendum on the failed Charlottetown Accord is an example of what I define as an *obstructive* referendum. I classify the failed Colombian plebiscite on the FARC peace pact as an instance of an *inoperative* referendum while the successful Brexit referendum in the United Kingdom is an example of what I identify as a *revertive* referendum. I explain these categories and their interrelations in Section III.

I examine in Section IV why leaders deploy discretionary referendums and I situate recourse to them against the backdrop of an increasingly observable

[5] Stephen Tierney, *Constitutional Referendums: The Theory and Practice of Republican Deliberation* (Oxford: Oxford University Press, 2012) at 7.

[6] *See generally* John Gardner, "Can there be a Written Constitution" in Leslie Green & Brian Leiter, eds, *Oxford Studies in Philosophy of Law, Volume 1* (Oxford: Oxford University Press, 2001) (probing the limits of writtenness).

[7] For more on this point, *see* Richard Albert, *Constitutional Amendments: Making, Breaking, and Changing Constitutions* (Oxford: Oxford University Press, 2019).

phenomenon in constitutional democracies around the world: the circumvention of the recognized rules of constitutional change. This phenomenon occurs when incumbents deliberately bypass the accepted rules of constitutional change in order to amend the constitution, with recourse not only to referendums but to other modalities of constitutional change. At its weakest, a single instance of circumventing the rules of change is a non-precedential departure from the otherwise strong constitutional norms that should structure the rules of constitutional change. In contrast, the strongest effect of circumventing the rules of constitutional change amounts to an informal amendment to the amendment rules themselves—and this could in some cases undermine the democratic legitimacy of the constitution.

II. Four discretionary referendums

The number of national referendums around the world has grown steadily over the past century, from fewer than 50 in 1901–1910 to roughly 600 in 1991–2000, though the number dropped to about 440 in 2001–2010.[8] Constitution have sometimes required referendums for a constitutional amendment. But at other times incumbents have exercised their discretion to hold a referendum in connection with a constitutional amendment where the constitution has not required one. In a subsequent section of this chapter, I will explore why constitutional actors have sometimes used discretionary referendums to validate a constitutional amendment.[9] But first, in this section, I illustrate four cases where constitutional actors around the world have used discretionary referendums—some successfully and others not—as a vehicle for constitutional change.

A. Two successful referendums

Constitutional actors have sometimes held successful discretionary referendums to change a constitution whose amendment rules do not expressly contemplate the legal validity of a referendum. In some cases, as in the recent Brexit referendum in the United Kingdom, successfully passing the referendum does

[8] Matt Qvortrup, "Conclusion" in Matt Qvortrup, ed, *Referendums Around the World* (Houndsmills, UK: Palgrave Macmillan, 2014) at 247.

[9] *See infra* Section IV.A.

not end the matter. More steps are needed before the constitutional change takes effect. In contrast, in other cases, for example the French referendum on direct presidential election in 1962, some referendums are enough by themselves to authorize a constitutional amendment even though an amendment-by-referendum defies the constitution's own rules of change.

Consider first the French case. The 1958 Constitution, which remains in force today, originally created an electoral college for presidential selection.[10] The electoral college consisted of members of Parliament, mayors, some municipal councillors and other designated officials numbering almost 80,000.[11] The only president ever elected by this electoral college was Charles de Gaulle, in the first election held under the new Constitution. Since then, the president has been elected by direct universal suffrage. The switch from an electoral college to a direct election was controversial because it was accomplished by a national referendum described at the time as "unconstitutional."[12]

The rules of constitutional amendment in France are relatively straightforward. The Constitution codifies detailed procedures in Article 89 that specify how to initiate and ratify an amendment. Either the president or a member of Parliament may initiate an amendment,[13] after which both chambers of Parliament must pass identical versions of the amendment bill within certain time limits in order for the proposal to proceed to the next step.[14] That next step—ratification—requires approval by national referendum.[15] There is only one explicit exception to this procedure: an amendment proposal need not be ratified by a national referendum where the president chooses to submit a government amendment bill to Parliament convened in Congress. In that case, the proposal becomes official if it is approved by a three-fifths vote of parliamentarians.[16]

After his election as president, De Gaulle wanted to undertake a major constitutional reform but he could not assemble the parliamentary support needed to achieve it via constitutional amendment. He therefore organized a referendum using his authority in Article 11 of the Constitution, which reads as follows:

[10] Constitution of France, tit II, art 6 (1958) (later amended in 1962).
[11] Stanley H Hoffmann, "The French Constitution of 1958: I. The Final Text and Its Prospects" (1959) 53 *American Pol Sci Rev* 332 at 342.
[12] *See François Mitterand, Le Coup d'État permanent* (Paris: Plon, 1964) at 113.
[13] Constitution of France, tit XVI, art 89(1).
[14] *Ibid* at art 89(2).
[15] *Ibid*.
[16] *Ibid* at art 89(3).

> The President of the Republic may, on a recommendation from the Government when Parliament is in session, or on a joint motion of the two Houses, published in the Journal Officiel, submit to a referendum any Government Bill which deals with the organization of the public authorities, or with reforms relating to the economic or social policy of the Nation, and to the public services contributing thereto, or which provides for authorization to ratify a treaty which, although not contrary to the Constitution, would affect the functioning of the institutions.[17]

Article 11 authorizes the president to petition the people directly without parliamentary authorization. It appears to authorize referendums only for limited purposes unrelated to constitutional amendment, which has its own process and exceptions outlined in Article 89.

De Gaulle's referendum polled the people on whether they wished to move from presidential election by electoral college to direct popular vote—a possibility Parliament feared would divest it "of its role as the sole bearer of national sovereignty."[18] De Gaulle resorted to this procedure instead of Article 89 precisely because it allowed him to bypass Parliament. At the time, parliamentarians did not support his plan to move from indirect to direct elections because presidential election by direct universal suffrage would have eroded Parliament's power over the president and given him an independent mandate from the people.[19] In the end, the referendum passed with 61.75 percent of voters in favour of the change. The Conseil Constitutionnel later heard a challenge to this unusual amendment-by-referendum. The Conseil concluded that the will of the people as expressed in the referendum had to be respected because, in France, the people are sovereign.[20] The French Constitution was therefore amended—its text formally altered—by this irregular constitutional referendum.

The Brexit referendum in June 2016 was both similar to and different from the French direct election referendum. As in the French case, voters in the United Kingdom approved the referendum; but unlike it, the Brexit referendum vote was not sufficient on its own to validate the change the referendum had

[17] *Ibid* at art 11(1).

[18] Henry W Ehrmann, "Direct Democracy in France" (1963) 57 *Am Pol Sci Rev* 883 at 883.

[19] *See* Jean-Philippe Derosier, "The French People's Role in Amending the Constitution" in Richard Albert, Xenophon Contiades & Alkmene Fotiadou, *The Foundations and Traditions of Constitutional Amendment* (Oxford: Hart, 2017) at 321.

[20] Décision no 62-20 DC, novembre 6, 1962, online: <http://www.conseil-constitutionnel.fr/conseil-constitutionnel/francais/les-decisions/acces-par-date/decisions-depuis-1959/1962/62-20-dc/decision-n-62-20-dc-du-6-novembre-1962.6398.html>.

proposed. The proposed constitutional change was of course the withdrawal of the United Kingdom from the European Union (EU). The Conservative Party had pledged to hold a referendum on membership in the EU as part of its 2015 election manifesto:

> We will legislate in the first session of the next Parliament for an in-out referendum to be held on Britain's membership of the EU before the end of 2017. We will negotiate a new settlement for Britain in the EU. And then we will ask the British people whether they want to stay in on this basis, or leave. We will honour the result of the referendum, whatever the outcome.[21]

The Conservative Party's pledge had two parts: first, to pass a referendum law; and second, to "honour the result of the referendum, whatever the outcome." The Party made good on the first by passing the European Union Referendum Act 2015,[22] which declared that "a referendum is to be held on whether the United Kingdom should remain a member of the European Union"[23] and that the ballot question would be "should the United Kingdom remain a member of the European Union or leave the European Union?"[24] The Party honoured its second pledge when, after the Brexit referendum produced a 52 percent vote in favour of leaving the European Union, the prime minister resigned from office in order to make way for a new leader to begin exit negotiations with the EU.[25]

Holding a referendum was not required by the Constitution of the United Kingdom. The rule famously remains that Parliament has the power to make or unmake any law, and that its laws are immune from override or repeal by another body.[26] The referendum was instead a choice of the prime minister of the day, who felt compelled as a political matter to promise a referendum in order to placate the strong anti-EU forces in his party and also to keep at bay the rival UK Independence Party, which at the time was growing in strength at the expense of the Conservative Party.[27] Facing pressure from within his party and

[21] *The Conservative Party Manifesto 2015: Strong Leadership; A Clear Economic Plan; A Brighter, More Secure Future*, p 73 (2015) (copy on file with author).

[22] European Union Referendum Act 2015, c 36 (Dec 17, 2015).

[23] *Ibid* s 1(1).

[24] *Ibid* s 1(4).

[25] Steven Erlanger, "Britain Votes to Leave E.U.; Cameron Plans to Step Down", *NY Times*, June 23, 2016, online: <https://www.nytimes.com/2016/06/25/world/europe/britain-brexit-european-union-referendum.html?_r=0>.

[26] AV Dicey, *Introduction to the Study of the Law of the Constitution* (London: Macmillan 8th ed, 1915) at 3–4.

[27] *See* Steven Erlanger & Stephen Castle, "In 'Brexit' Vote, David Cameron Faces Problem of His Own Making", *NY Times*, June 21, 2016, online: <https://www.nytimes.com/2016/06/22/world/europe/david-cameron-brexit-european-union.html>.

outside of it, the prime minister conceded that "My backbenchers are unbelievably Eurosceptic and UKIP are breathing down my neck."[28]

The UK Supreme Court later suggested that the referendum had been not only unnecessary but ineffective. The question before the Court was whether the United Kingdom could give notice of its intention to withdraw from the EU—as required by Article 50 of the Treaty on the European Union—on the strength of a governmental declaration alone informed by the political result in the referendum, or whether the government needed the legal validation of statutory authorization. The Court held that the government needed statutory authorization in order to give notice of its intention to withdraw the United Kingdom from the EU.[29] For the Court, then, the result of the Brexit referendum on its own was legally invalid despite its high political salience.

B. Two failed referendums

Constitutional actors have sometimes incorporated discretionary referendums in their amendment sequence only to see them fail. Yet the failure to pass a discretionary referendum has not always entailed the failure of the amendment itself. In some cases, the amendment effort has come to an end because the failed referendum made it politically unpalatable for constitutional actors to proceed any further. In other cases, however, constitutional actors nonetheless proceeded with their plans for constitutional amendment even in the face of a popular rejection of their amendment proposal. Consider examples of both, the former from Canada and the latter from Colombia.

In Canada, the federal government decided in 1992 to send a major package of constitutional reforms known as the Charlottetown Accord to the people for their approval despite there being no requirement of a referendum in the Constitution's formal amendment rules.[30] In order to make the discretionary referendum possible, Parliament passed the *Referendum Act* authorizing the Governor General "to obtain by means of a referendum the opinion of electors on any question relating to the Constitution of Canada."[31] The law made

[28] Martin Kettle, "The Downfall of David Cameron: A European Tragedy", *The Guardian*, June 24, 2016, online: <https://www.theguardian.com/politics/2016/jun/24/david-cameron-downfall-european-tragedy>.

[29] R v Secretary of State for Exiting the European Union, [2017] UKSC 5 (Jan 24, 2017).

[30] *See* Procedure for Amending Constitution of Canada, Part V of the *Constitution Act, 1982*, being Schedule B to the *Canada Act 1982*, 1982, c 11 (UK) (hereinafter "*Constitution Act, 1982*").

[31] Referendum Act, s 3(1), SC 1992, c 30. In their study of the Charlottetown Accord, Richard Johnston, André Blais, Elisabeth Gidengill and Neil Nevitte explain that the referendum was indeed two separate votes: one organized by Quebec in the province; and the other organized by the federal

referendums purely consultative, not legally binding, though a majority vote for the Charlottetown Accord across the provinces would have legitimated the package of reforms and left constitutional actors with little choice as a political matter but to ratify it in the provincial assemblies according to the unanimity procedure that would have been used had the referendum passed.[32] But the formal amendment process came to a halt when Canadians rejected the Accord by a nation-wide tally of 54.3 percent to 45.7 percent.[33] The outcome of the Charlottetown Acord was peremptory in that it eroded the political will across most of the country to proceed any further with the formal amendment process.

The choice to put the Charlottetown Accord to a referendum was driven by the failure of the Meech Lake Accord just two years prior. The Meech Lake Accord would have introduced significant changes to the Constitution of Canada, formally amending both the *Constitution Act, 1867* and the *Constitution Act, 1982*, for instance by requiring annual constitutional conferences among Canada's first ministers,[34] transferring to provinces some power of immigration,[35] constitutionalizing the Supreme Court,[36] recognizing Quebec as a "distinct society",[37] and amending the Constitution's formal amendment rules themselves.[38] The entire package was subject to a three-year ratification deadline expiring in 1990—a deadline that constitutional actors failed to meet, leading to the defeat of the Accord and dimming the prospects for eventual reform.[39] As much as the content of the Meech Lake Accord drew criticism,[40] its design process prompted what could be seen as an over-correction in the

government in the rest of the country. *See* Richard Johnston, *The Challenge of Direct Democracy: The 1992 Canadian Referendum* (Montreal & Kingston: McGill-Queen's University Press, 1996) at 51–60.

[32] Part V of the *Constitution Act, 1982* entrenches five different formal amendment procedures, and each is designated to be used for amendments to an expressly identified set of provisions or principles. *See Constitution Act, 1982*, being Schedule B to the *Canada Act 1982* (UK), 1982, c 11, pt. V.

[33] *See The 1992 Federal Referendum—A Challenge Met: Report of the Chief Electoral Officer of Canada*, Part 2, at 58, January 17, 1994, online: <http://www.elections.ca/res/rep/off/1992/1992_Referendum_Part_2_E.pdf>.

[34] Meeting of the First Ministers on the Constitution, *The 1987 Constitutional Accord* (Ottawa: June 3, 1987), Schedule at s 13 [Meech Lake Accord].

[35] *Ibid* Schedule at s 3.

[36] *Ibid* Schedule at s 9.

[37] *Ibid* Schedule at s 1.

[38] *Ibid* Schedule at s 9.

[39] *See* Christopher P Manfredi, "Institutional Design and the Politics of Constitutional Modification: Understanding Amendment Failure in the United States and Canada" (1997) 31 *L & Soc'y Rev* 111 at 123.

[40] For a discussion of the major criticisms of the Meech Lake Accord, *see* Peter J Meekison, "The Meech Lake Accord: The End of the Beginning—or the Beginning of the End" (1990) 1 *Const Forum* 13 at 14.

decision to rest the fate of the Charlottetown Accord in the hands of the masses in only the third nation-wide referendum in Canadian history.[41]

The Meech Lake Accord had been negotiated and drafted in the paradigmatic model of executive federalism: out of sight and without public input. In their post-mortem of the process, Bruce Ellman and Anne McLellan stressed just how secretive it had been: "On the 30th of April, 1987, the eleven first ministers—gathered in a cabin by the shore of Meech Lake and, hidden from the prying eyes of aboriginal groups, women's groups, and special interest groups of all sorts, they struck a deal on the future of Canada."[42] For Beverley Baines the drafting process might well have been called the "men's round" both for the exclusion of explicit protections for women's rights and for the relative absence of women in the negotiating room.[43] Indigenous Persons also objected both to the secrecy of the process and to the content of the reforms themselves.[44] Even insiders have conceded that the fatal flaw of the Meech Lake Accord could well have been, as Mary Dawson describes, "that the deal had been cooked up behind closed doors by a group of men in suits."[45]

When constitutional actors tried to achieve peace in Canada with the Charlottetown Accord, the then-recent defeat of the Meech Lake Accord could not help but shape their strategy. Rather than negotiating the terms of agreement in secrecy, the federal and provincial governments created opportunities for public participation and consultation, both with individual citizens and groups formed around identity or interests.[46] Meeting doors were thrown open, there was frequent communication with the public through the press, and virtually everyone who wanted to give input in the proceedings could do so in the roving meetings the government held across the country.[47] But the centerpiece of the Charlottetown strategy was the referendum: Canadians across the country would be given an advisory vote on the package of reforms in a nation-wide referendum even though the Constitution's formal amendment

[41] *See* Benoît Dostie & Ruth Dupré, "'The People's Will': Canadians and the 1898 Referendum on Alcohol Prohibition" (2012) 49 *Explorations Econ Hist* 498 at 499.

[42] Bruce P Elman & A Anne McLellan, "Canada After Meech" (1991) 2 *Const Forum* 63 at 64.

[43] Beverley Baines, "An Alternative Vision of the Meech Lake Accord" (1988) 13 *Queen's LJ* 1 at 13.

[44] W H McConnell, "The Meech Lake Accord: Laws or Flaws?" (1988) 52 *Saskatchewan L Rev* 115 at 119.

[45] Mary Dawson, "From the Backroom to the Front Line: Making Constitutional History or Encounters with the Constitution: Patriation, Meech Lake, and Charlottetown" (2012) 57 *McGill LJ* 955 at 983. But it is important to ask whether assigning blame solely or even primarily to the process failures of the Meech Lakes Accord might not mistake effects for causes, specifically that the ultimate source of the failure of the Accord could have been Patriation itself. *See* Patrick J Monahan, "After Meech Lake: An Insider's View" (1990) 22 *Ottawa L Rev* 317 at 328.

[46] *See* Richard Albert, "The Conventions of Constitutional Amendment in Canada" (2016) 53 *Osgoode Hall LJ* 399 at 410.

[47] *Ibid.*

rules do not require a referendum nor even consultation in connection with a constitutional amendment. Holding a referendum for all Canadians was therefore a political choice, not a legal obligation. In the end, the referendum failed, and with it the prospects of formally remaking the Constitution died. And they have yet to be revived.

A more recent instance of a failed popular vote occurred in Colombia in October 2016. We must begin with Colombia's Constitution in order to understand the significance of the failed vote—a failure that ultimately did not inhibit the change that had been proposed directly to the people. The Constitution codifies three methods for amendment: by legislative act, by referendum and by constituent assembly.[48] In addition, the Constitution creates a number of avenues for the people to participate in the elaboration of public policy, including via plebiscite,[49] whose result the Constitution makes mandatory on the president.[50] According to law, a plebiscite is a mechanism by which the people endorse or reject a decision made by the president.[51] In order for its result to be valid, the plebiscite must attract the participation of at least half of all registered voters, and a majority of voters must vote in favour.[52] These are Colombia's basic rules of constitutional change.

Congress took two controversial actions in anticipation of an eventual plebiscite on a peace deal with the FARC. It passed a constitutional amendment—known as the fast-track amendment—establishing an abbreviated procedure for implementing the peace deal if the people ultimately approved the agreement in a plebiscite.[53] It also passed a new law setting a minimum turnout of 13 percent of registered voters in order for the plebiscite to be valid.[54] The law was promulgated in August 2016, just one month after the Constitutional Court had upheld its validity in draft form.[55] On the day the law was promulgated, the president announced a plebiscite on an eventual peace deal with the FARC,[56] which was finally achieved the following month.[57]

[48] Constitution of Colombia, tit XIII, art 374 (1991).

[49] *Ibid* art 103.

[50] *Ibid* art 104.

[51] Law 134/1994, art 7 (May 31, 1994).

[52] Law 1757/2015, art 41 (July 6, 2015).

[53] *See* Gaceta de Congreso 706, at p 3 (Sept 15, 2015) (recognizing that the capacity to activate the fast-track procedure will depend on popular endorsement).; Gaceta de Congresso 943, at p 7 (Nov 18, 2015) (same).

[54] Law 1806/2016, art 2 (August 24, 2016). This law was passed under Congress's power to regulate plebiscites and other mechanisms of popular participation. Constitution of Colombia, tit VI, ch III, arts 152-53.

[55] Constitutional Court of Colombia, Judgment C-379/2016 (July 18, 2016).

[56] "'Todo está acordado, el texto definitivo es inmodificable': Santos", *El Tiempo* (Aug 25, 2016), online: <http://www.eltiempo.com/politica/proceso-de-paz/fecha-de-plebiscito-por-la-paz-sera-el-2-de-octubre-57063>.

[57] *See* Nicholas Casey, "Colombia Signs Peace Agreement with FARC After 5 Decades of War", *NY Times* (Sept 26, 2016), online: <https://www.nytimes.com/2016/09/27/world/americas/colombia-farc-peace-agreement.html?_r=0>.

The plebiscite on the peace deal failed in October 2016 by a less than one percent.[58] Later asked whether he would hold a second plebiscite, the president replied no.[59] Instead, he and the government agreed to terms with the FARC on another deal. But out of fear of popular rejection a second time, the parties decided not to send the new agreement to the people for their approval, contrary to what they had chosen to do for the first deal.[60] Congress endorsed this new agreement the following week,[61] and the Court approved it shortly thereafter on the theory that the public endorsement required to activate the fast-track process had been fulfilled by the congressional ratification of the second peace deal in lieu of direct popular approval in a plebiscite.[62] Since then, Congress has used the fast-track procedure to implement the peace deal. In contrast to the failed advisory referendum in Canada marking the end of the amendment effort, here in Colombia the defeat of the advisory plebiscite did not deter constitutional actors from taking further action.[63]

III. A typology of discretionary referendums

These four popular votes in Canada, Colombia, France and the United Kingdom represent four different types of discretionary referendums in constitutional amendment. In this section, I introduce a four-part typology of discretionary referendums: the French and Canadian referendums illustrate what I define respectively as *reconstructive* and *obstructive* referendums, while the UK and Colombian votes illustrate what I identify as *revertive* and *inoperative* referendums, respectively. This typology cuts across civil and common law, and both codified or uncodified constitutions. It is an effort to map the possibilities of discretionary referendums in constitutional amendment.

[58] Julia Symmes Cobb & Nicholas Casey, "Colombia Peace Deal is Defeated, Leaving a Nation in Shock", *NY Times* (Oct 2, 2016), online: <https://www.nytimes.com/2016/10/03/world/colombia-peace-deal-defeat.html>.

[59] "Santos descartó otro plebiscito para avalar nuevo acuerdo con Farc", *El Colombiano* (Nov 2, 2016), online: <http://www.elcolombiano.com/colombia/acuerdos-de-gobierno-y-farc/santos-descarta-otro-plebiscito-para-implementar-acuerdo-final-con-farc-XL5287541>.

[60] Nicholas Casey, "Colombia and FARC Sign New Peace Deal, This Time Skipping Voters", *NY Times* (Nov 24, 2016), online: <https://www.nytimes.com/2016/11/24/world/americas/colombia-juan-manuel-santos-peace-deal-farc.html?_r=0>.

[61] "Refrendado el acuerdo de paz; el Día D ha llegado", *Semana* (Nov 30, 2016), online: <http://www.semana.com/nacion/articulo/refrendado-el-nuevo-acuerdo-de-paz/507536>.

[62] Constitutional Court of Colombia, Judgment C-699/2016 (Dec 13, 2016).

[63] "La histórica votación a la refrendación del acuerdo en el Congreso", *El Tiempo* (Dec 1, 2016), online: <http://www.eltiempo.com/politica/proceso-de-paz/como-fue-la-votacion-en-congreso-para-refrendar-nuevo-acuerdo-de-paz-31402>.

A. Mapping discretionary referendums

Combining two pairs of distinctions yields four types of discretionary referendums. Whether the referendum succeeds or fails controls the first of two inquiries in mapping discretionary referendums. The second question focuses on the legal consequence of the referendum in light of whether it has succeeded or failed. Two possibilities follow here: either the result of the referendum compels constitutional actors to credit the discretionary, non-obligatory referendum procedure as equally valid to—and therefore as a substitute for—the conventional procedure used for constitution amendment; or they ignore the result of the discretionary referendum and return to the conventional procedure recognized as legally valid under the constitution of the jurisdiction.

In the French case, for example, De Gaulle held a referendum in an overt effort to circumvent the formal rules of constitutional amendment. He would have failed using the ordinary procedure of amendment because that route required congressional approval—and parliamentarians were not ready to cooperate with him, and therefore blocked that path to amendment. De Gaulle's won his referendum, and its result was credited as equally valid to a formal amendment. The referendum therefore substituted for the formal amendment rules in the Constitution, in the process informally amending the formal rules of change. We can describe De Gaulle's referendum as *reconstructive* in that it effectively rewrote the procedures of formal constitutional change in the French Constitution. The referendum rebuilt the formal rules of change, though not without controversy since the constitutional text did not then recognize the legal validity of this amendment-by-referendum as a path to president-initiated constitutional amendment. The ruling of the high court—in favour of De Gaulle—ended the legal debate on the validity of this constitutional reconstruction.

In the UK, the successful Brexit referendum did not exert the same transformative legal effect on the Constitution that De Gaulle's referendum had in France. In the French case, the unconventional procedure used to change the Constitution ultimately proved legally valid, as the domestic high court refused to call its use into question and indeed interpreted the popular support for the change as legitimately overriding the legal constraints on constitutional amendment. But the constitutional culture of popular sovereignty in France made the referendum result too compelling to ignore. In contrast, the Brexit referendum itself did not end the matter. Although the referendum passed and the government of the day was prepared to proceed on the basis of its outcome alone, the UK Supreme Court did not credit the referendum as a valid mechanism of constitutional reform and instead focused on the procedural question. The UK Supreme Court denied the legal sufficiency of the outcome of the referendum as the basis for issuing notice under Article 50 of the jurisdiction's intent to withdraw from the EU. The principle of popular sovereignty that had so animated the Conseil Constitutionnel in France did not have the same moral force. What mattered for the UK Supreme Court was instead legal validity, and that could not come without parliamentary consent. The referendum was *revertive*: it pressed actors to return to the conventional process of constitutional change in order to legally break the link to the EU.

The Canadian and Colombian cases are examples of failed referendums that each had different effects in the larger practice of constitutional reform. In Canada, the failure of the Charlottetown referendum put an immediate end to the constitutional amendment process. The definitive vote against the major package of constitutional reforms prevented actors from engaging the formal process of constitutional change ordinarily required. The failed referendum did not create a legal impediment to proceeding with the formal amendment process; as a matter of constitutional law, actors could still have tried to pass the amendment package using the formal procedures of change. But they chose against going any further. Their refusal to proceed suggests that the failure of the referendum raised a political barrier to even trying to pass the amendment package using the ordinary rules of constitutional change. We can understand the Charlottetown referendum as an *obstructive* referendum: its failure doomed the constitutional amendment process because it was seen as a substitute for it. The failure of the discretionary referendum was treated as a failure of the formal amendment process, and constitutional actors saw no reason to proceed any further.

In Colombia, in contrast, the plebiscite on the peace pact might as well not been held because it was credited as neither legally nor politically valid. It was an *inoperative* vote. Although voters rejected the peace deal in the plebiscite, actors nonetheless proceeded to ratify it in modified form, ignoring the referendum result despite the president's earlier commitment that he would respect the voice of the people. Politically, then, the referendum was treated as both legally and politically invalid. The Constitutional Court subsequently ruled the referendum legally unnecessary. In the Court's view, as long as there was some measure of popular consent for the deal, actors could legally proceed with its ratification under the fast-track procedure. In the end, the Court credited congressional support for the deal as satisfying this requirement of popular consent.

Table 2.1 A typology of discretionary referendums

	Successful Referendum	Failed Referendum
Substitution	France (1962) Reconstructive Referendum	Canada (1992) Obstructive Referendum
Reinforcement	United Kingdom (2016) Revertive Referendum	Colombia (2016) Inoperative Referendum

Each of the types of referendums described above—reconstructive in France, revertive in the UK, obstructive in Canada and inoperative in Colombia—is depicted in a typology (Table 2.1).

B. The supremacy of the people?

These four types of discretionary referendums suggest that the people are not always supreme. They are supreme in France, of course, as even the Conseil Constitutionnel accepts that its own reading of the French Constitution is inferior as a legal and political matter to the people's own. The answer is more complicated in Canada, where constitutional actors recognized the political supremacy of the will of the people, though the legal basis for that position is unclear. If confronted with the same question before the French Conseil Constitutionnel—was the referendum constitutional?—the Canadian Supreme Court could well return to its judgment in the *Secession Reference*, which made clear that "the results of a referendum have no direct role or legal effect in our constitutional scheme."[64] The Court could alternatively recognize that the Charlottetown referendum set a precedent that has since matured into a convention, following its reasoning in the *Patriation Reference* to hold that any major constitutional change must now be put to an advisory referendum.[65] The UK and Colombian referendums are unequivocal in their implications

[64] Reference re Secession of Quebec, [1998] 2 SCR 217 at para 87. One would be right to ask whether this is the proper role for a Court. Its involvement in this dispute on the political future of a subnational entity has been described in the global context as "unprecedented." *See* Ran Hirschl, "The Judicialization of Mega-Politics and the Rise of Political Courts" (2008) 11 *Ann Rev Pol Sci* 93 at 103.

[65] Albert, *supra* note 46, at 419–33.

and in the contrasts they raise with France and Canada: in each of those cases, the people are not supreme.

And yet in the conventional theory of constitutional change, there is no greater source of legitimacy than the people themselves. The Lockean formation of constitutional consensus to legitimate a new constitution or a major constitutional change emerges most directly from popular appeals to the people.[66] The consent of the people to a constitutional event insulates constitutional actors against charges of misuse of the forms of constitutional change. There are, then, both instrumental and intrinsic reasons for holding referendums in particular, or more generally some method of collective decision-making, to whose outcome constitutional actors can point as reflecting the will of the people.

The theory of constituent power is the source of these conventional views on constitutional change. Drawn from French revolutionary theorist Emmanuel Joseph Sieyès, the theory posits a division of labour between the people as principals and their agent representatives in government.[67] Only with the approval of the principals may the agents transform the constitution or write a new one altogether; without it, the agents may alter the constitution but only if the content or form of the change remains consistent with the constitution's existing values or architecture.[68] The people are supreme; they are the constituent power, which by its approval of or acquiescence to the creation of a constitution constitutes the constituted powers of government, namely the institutions the constitution sets to perform the specific tasks assigned to them by the constituent power. At its base, constituent power theory reflects a hierarchical relationship: the people as constituent power representing the highest source of legitimating authority, and the institutions of government as the inferior constituted power at least notionally bound by the commands of the people.

We can also understand the relationship between the constituent and constituted powers in topographical terms, which is to say how and where the constituent and constituted powers are located relative to the constitution. If we imagine a constitution represented by a circle, the constituent power stands

[66] John Locke, *Second Treatise of Government* (Indianapolis: Hackett Publishing Co, CB MacPherson ed 1980) at 47–48 (§89).

[67] Emmanuel Joseph Sieyès, *Qu'est-ce que le Tiers état?* (Paris: Éditions du Boucher, 2002) (originally published in 1789).

[68] For a discussion and critique of constituent power theory, *see* Joel Colón-Ríos, *Weak Constitutionalism: Democratic Legitimacy and the Question of Constituent Power* (Abingdon: Routledge, 2012); Mattias Kumm, "Constituent Power, Cosmopolitan Constitutionalism, and Post-Positivist Law" (2016) 14 *Int'l J Const L* 697; Richard Stacey, "Constituent Power and Carl Schmitt's Theory of Constitution in Kenya's Constitution-Making Process" (2011) 9 *Int'l J Const L* 587.

above and outside of it, the positioning reflecting the derivative quality of the constitution with respect to the will of the people. The constituted power, in turn, sits below the constituent powers directly inside the circle. The institutions and actors that we identify as the constituted powers are part of what the constituent power—the people—create when they converge in their agreement to found a new constitution. As the constituted powers carry out their constitutional duties and as they exercise their delegated discretion, they must remain within boundaries of the circle representing the constitution. Any change to the boundaries of the constitution must be authorized by the constituent power, which stands on watch above the constitution to police how the constituted powers exercise their limited delegated authority.

Delegation offers another way to understand the relationship. The constituent power creates a constitution, which in turn authorizes the constituted power created by the constitution to act in the people's name consistent with the constitution. The constituted power is authorized to alter the constitution provided that any alteration to it does not undermine the constitution as constructed by the constituent power. Only the constituent power has the competence to rewrite the constitution in a way that departs materially from what the constitution has established as law. The constituent power is therefore a pre-constitutional power that controls both how a constitution is made in the first place and also how the constituted power exercises its limited delegated authority to change the constitution in the name of the people.

Still another way to understand the relationship is the language of rights. Two pairs of ideas are useful here: inherent and delegated; and negative and positive. While the constitution-making power inheres in the constituent power, the constitution-changing power is held in trust by the constituted power and it may be exercised as a delegated power subject to the restrictions placed upon its exercise by the inherent right holder, here the constituent power. In the end, the constituent power holds both negative and positive rights: it possesses the inherent positive right to make a constitution but it also has the negative right to be free from intrusions on its constitution-making power by an overreaching constituted power. On this view, the constituted power holds only a narrow positive right to make ordinary laws and constitution-level changes within the delimited constitutional boundaries originally set by the constituent power when it authorized the creation of the constitution. These four renderings of constituent power theory—hierarchy, topography, delegation and rights—concretize the basic idea that the people are supreme.

IV. Stasis and catalysis in constitutional change

It is of course a legal fiction that the people are always supreme. Sometimes they are supreme in both constitutional law and politics, as in the French referendum of 1962, and sometimes they are supreme in constitutional politics alone, as in the Canadian referendum of 1992. But the views of the people may also be inferior to the choices of the constituted branches of government. The people's views were not supreme in either constitutional law or politics in the Colombian plebiscite of 2016. Nor were the supreme in constitutional law in the UK referendum of 2016. In this section, I explore the motivations driving discretionary referendums from a higher level of abstraction, informed by but detached from the particular experiences of Canada, Colombia, France and the United Kingdom, and I consider why constitutional actors might find it necessary or expedient to appeal directly to the people even where the constitution does not require it.

A. Why discretionary referendums?

The answer to the question "why discretionary referendums?" must begin with Tierney's analysis of what he labels "executive-led, extra-constitutional referendums" in reference to the 1962 French referendum on direct presidential election.[69] He suggests that constitutional actors might hold a discretionary referendum like this one in times of "crisis or of impasse, where constitutional change is difficult to achieve, where the temptation to surmount constitutional impediments can be great, and crucially where the constitutional culture pays homage—at least symbolically—to the resilience of a popular *pouvoir constituent* even within a formally entrenched constitutional structure."[70] Each of these conditions characterizes the French legal-political context in 1962. Each could on its own be sufficient to persuade constitutional actors to circumvent the ordinary rules of constitutional change in pursuit of an objective they thought worth the cost of illegality.

We can also identify other motivations behind an incumbent's choice to hold a discretionary referendum. The difficulty of satisfying the rules of constitutional change, for instance, might be an additional reason to hold a discretionary referendum.[71] Where the procedures of change are too onerous, or

[69] Tierney, *supra* note 5, at 131.
[70] *Ibid* at 131.
[71] *Ibid.*

perceived to be too difficult to satisfy, constitutional actors look for other ways to achieve their preferred policy objectives. We should therefore expect to see recourse to discretionary referendums or other non-obligatory procedures of change in jurisdictions with rigid constitutions. And indeed we can confirm our hypothesis with reference to the United States Constitution, one of world's most rigid constitutions.[72] There have been no constitutional referendums in the United States but the Constitution changes routinely without textual alteration, for example as a result of "constitutional moments",[73] super-statutes,[74] or authoritative interpretations.[75]

And yet the French Constitution is not particularly rigid. It reveals another reason why constitutional actors might hold a discretionary referendum: to overcome political resistance. Quite apart from the difficulty of constitutional amendment as a result of a high threshold for initiation, proposal or ratification, a constitution may be hard to change because of the unwillingness of constitutional actors to consent to the reform, even where the rules of change are relatively flexible. Here, then, actors might invoke the idea of a referendum as a threat to go over the heads of their opponents, or they might in fact hold a referendum in order to break the stalemate. Whether merely threatened or actually deployed, then, a discretionary referendum can be an effective offensive strategy to tear down political barriers.

Nor is the Colombian Constitution entrenched under especially onerous formal amendment rules. The local circumstances around the peace pact plebiscite suggest another reason for holding a discretionary referendum: as a defensive strategy to give constitutional actors political cover for an important or controversial choice. The use of a discretionary referendum can depoliticize a decidedly political choice by transforming the decision from a political one to a popular one. Where popular consent forms behind a choice, any negative consequences associated with the choice can become less pronounced as ownership for the choice is transferred from the constitutional actors who have made it to the people themselves in the case of a referendums victory. There is a non-trivial risk, however, in putting a choice before the people where the choice has already been made internally by the constitutional actors who decide to hold

[72] Donald S. Lutz, *Principles of Constitutional Design* (Cambridge: Cambridge University Press, 2006) at 170.

[73] Bruce Ackerman, *We the People—Volume 2: Transformations* (Cambridge: Harvard University Press, 1998) at 15–26.

[74] William N Eskridge, Jr & John Ferejohn, "Super-Statutes" (2001) 50 *Duke LJ* 1215 at 1230–31.

[75] Walter F Murphy, "Constitutions, Constitutionalism, and Democracy" in Douglas Greenberg et al, eds, *Constitutionalism and Democracy: Transitions in the Contemporary World* (New York: Oxford University Press, 1993) 3 at 13.

the referendum. Here the risk of popular repudiation of the choice can have serious consequences for constitutional actors who miscalculate their odds of winning the discretionary referendum.

The Canadian Constitution is also extraordinarily difficult to amend for major reforms, perhaps even more difficult than the United States Constitution.[76] Nonetheless, the Charlottetown referendum does not appear to have been motivated by amendment difficulty. This may suggest an additional reason why constitutional actors might hold a discretionary referendum: to attract popular approval for a major constitutional change. There is sometimes authentic interest in taking the pulse of the people on a matter of importance or controversy, though of course that interest may be payment for a debt incurred from a track record of insularity and lack of public consultation on similar prior policy choices. Seeking the views of the people may therefore be motivated by intrinsic or instrumental purposes: intrinsic where there is genuine interest in gauging where the people stand; and instrumental where the interest springs from an effort to right an earlier wrong, in which case we may fairly characterize the referendum as motivated by self-interest.

We can posit three other reasons why constitutional actors might hold discretionary referendums in connection with a constitutional change. For one, they might feel compelled to adhere to a custom of popular consultation, what to constitutional actors might feel like a convention that is politically binding though not legally required. The non-obligatory referendums on accession to and integration into the European Union may owe their frequency to this phenomenon.[77] Constitutional actors might also organize a discretionary referendum in order to entrench a choice more strongly than could be achievable using the ordinary rules of change. In this case, a referendum victory could reinforce the change and give it a greater measure of political durability since instead of its validation by constitutional actors alone—assuming there were no direct involvement of voters in making the change—it would now be bolstered by direct popular approval. An additional motivation for holding a discretionary referendum in constitutional amendment could conceivably be driven by a larger strategy to move the state toward a more popular consent-based regime. Prioritizing popular choice in this way could reveal or more cynically conceal an effort to transform the ultimate source of legitimation in a given

[76] *See* Richard Albert, "The Difficulty of Constitutional Amendment in Canada" (2015) 39 *Alberta L Rev* 85 at 93–105.

[77] *See* Laurence Morel, "The Rise of 'Politically Obligatory' Referendums: The 2005 French Referendum in Comparative Perspective" (2007) 30 *W Euro Pol* 1041 at 1055–57.

jurisdiction from an institutional, elite, divine or hereditary source of authority to a more democratic basis of sovereignty and legitimacy.

B. A critique of the hydraulics theory of constitutional amendment

There is a universal truth behind the choice to hold a discretionary referendum whose outcome is taken as legally or politically valid despite its not being authorized by the ordinary rules of change in the constitution: no codified constitution is a complete code. Constitutional designers may intend their codification of formal amendment rules to cover the universe of possible forms and results of constitutional change, but moments, forces, and personalities intervene to modify by conduct the range of permissible action even if it creates a tension or outright disjunction with the constitutional text. The judge-made doctrines of the "basic structure" in India and the "substitution of the constitution" in Colombia both sit uneasily with the constitutions in which they are rooted since neither text contemplates the possibility that the substance of a constitutional amendment can depart so widely from the constitution as to be unconstitutional.[78] And yet the idea of an unconstitutional constitutional amendment has migrated across the globe.[79] There is evidence, then, of codified constitutions resembling uncodified constitutions insofar as the former are susceptible to changes we see in the latter by practice that mature into convention.[80]

One of the more compelling explanations for this phenomenon is the hydraulics theory of constitutional change advanced by Heather Gerken in the American context.[81] The United States Constitution has often been informally amended, its meaning having changed without a corresponding textual alteration. Gerken argues that where the path to formal amendment is blocked as a result of its difficulty, constitutional actors can nonetheless make significant

[78] For two works on these doctrines in India and Colombia, respectively, *see*Sudhir Krishnaswamy, *Democracy and Constitutionalism in India: A Study of the Basic Structure Doctrine* (New Delhi: Oxford University Press, 2009); Carlos Bernal, "Unconstitutional Constitutional Amendments in the Case Study of Colombia: An Analysis of the Justification and Meaning of the Constitutional Replacement Doctrine" (2013) 11 *Int'l J Const L* 339.

[79] *See* Yaniv Roznai, *Unconstitutional Constitutional Amendments: The Limits of Amendment Powers* (Oxford: Oxford University Press, 2017).

[80] *See* Richard Albert, "How Unwritten Constitutional Norms Change Written Constitutions" (2015) 38 *Dublin U LJ* 387.

[81] Heather K Gerken, "The Hydraulics of Constitutional Reform: A Skeptical Response to *Our Undemocratic Constitution*" (2007) 55 *Drake L Rev* 925.

changes to the Constitution, though without engaging the codified procedures of formal change. The difficulty of amendment forces constitutional actors intent on reforming the constitution to "effectively redirect[] those constitutional energies into different, potentially more productive channels"[82], for instance judicial interpretation, legislation and political practice. The predicate for this hydraulics theory is what Gerken regards as a causal connection between formal amendment difficulty and informal constitutional change: "[a]n informal amendment process exists because formal amendment is so difficult."[83] Hydraulics theory has applications all over the world where rigid constitutions have pushed actors to rely on sub-constitutional methods to make constitution-level changes.[84]

Yet hydraulics theory does not explain why constitutional actors choose the path of informal amendment where the constitution is relatively easy to amend.[85] Indeed, hydraulics theory denies that possibility since it holds that informal amendment occurs because of formal amendment difficulty. Nor does hydraulics theory explain the use of discretionary referendums to formally amend the constitution in cases where the constitution is either easy or hard to amend. We could resolve the matter by stating quite simply that the hydraulics theory applies only to informal constitutional changes. Yet the use of discretionary referendums in formal amendment does precisely what hydraulics theory predicts: it redirects constitutional energies to other channels.

The use of discretionary referendums in constitutional amendment suggests that we should amend the hydraulics theory of constitutional change both to narrow it and also to expand it. These refinements cluster around three themes we can describe as irregularity, political expediency and legitimacy.

First, the four cases of discretionary referendums discussed above highlight a broader trend in constitutional amendment: constitutional actors do not always regard formal amendment rules as the only permissible route to constitutional change. They sometimes engage extra-constitutional procedures to alter the constitution. Second, constitutional actors sometimes use discretionary referendums for reasons that may or may not be driven by constitutional rigidity. The constitution may in fact be relatively easy to amend using the formal procedures but the use of the referendum can yield important political returns

82 *Ibid* at 927.
83 *Ibid* at 933.
84 *See*Richard Albert, "Quasi-Constitutional Amendments" (2017) 65 *Buffalo L Rev* 739.
85 For a discussion of informal amendment in easy-to-amend state constitutions, *see* Michael Besso, "Constitutional Amendment Procedures and the Informal Political Construction of Constitutions" (2005) 67 *J Pol* 69 at 75.

that constitutional actors see as warranting a departure from the conventional rules of change. Therefore, the hydraulic pressure building in a constitutional regime behind recourse to extra-constitutional procedures of change may derive either from the practical impossibility of satisfying the legal requirements of constitutional change or from the political expediency of amending the constitution outside of the ordinary rules of change. Third, it may well be that the balance of authorities in a jurisdiction weighs in favour of engaging in formally illegal conduct where constitutional actors can claim their actions are nonetheless clothed in the superior democratic legitimacy of a referendum instead of a change made by legislators.

V. Conclusion—appealing to the people: early and modern applications

Appealing directly to the people in departure from the formal rules of amendment is nothing new. The United States Constitution was itself born of a formally unconstitutional though nonetheless democratically legitimate circumvention of the exceptionally onerous rules of change.[86] The Articles of Confederation required the consent of Congress and each of the thirteen state legislatures for an amendment to become valid,[87] quite literally an impossible threshold to satisfy as no amendment to the Articles was ever successful.[88] When the Philadelphia Convention gathered "for the sole and express purpose of revising" the Articles,[89] the Convention broke from the Articles and proposed an altogether new constitution that would become valid when ratified by nine out of the thirteen states—in the process creating a much lower threshold for constitutional creation than for constitutional amendment under the Articles.[90] The Constitution was ultimately approved in extraordinary conventions in the several states. These were popular assemblies convened for two purposes: to express the choice of the voting peoples and also to root the constitution, if a new one were to be adopted, in the consent of the governed, the

[86] *See* Richard Albert, "Four Unconstitutional Constitutions and their Democratic Foundations" (2017) 50 *Cornell Int'l LJ* 169.

[87] Articles of Confederation, art XIII (1781).

[88] Benjamin Fletcher Wright, "Consensus and Continuity—1776-1878" (1958) 38 *Boston U L Rev* 1 at 19.

[89] *Journal of the Continental Congress*, 1774–1789, Feb 21, 1787 at 74 (Washington C. Ford et al, 1904–37).

[90] Constitution of the United States, art VII ("The ratification of the Conventions of nine States, shall be sufficient for the Establishment of this Constitution between the States so ratifying the Same.").

highest authority possible.[91] The conventions were not referendums—there were closer to "deliberative plebiscites"[92]—but they were a forum for popular choice, much like referendums, though mediated through representatives.

This founding precedent may offer a model for the United States in the present moment. It is not uncommon to read today that Constitution is broken and in need of a serious makeover, whether by major amendment or replacement altogether.[93] In many cases these broken features—the Electoral College and the Senate's equal suffrage rule, to name only two—are "hard-wired" into the Constitution, meaning that they are resistant to change by informal amendment.[94] This raises a question: what progress is possible given that the formal path to constitutional amendment runs through Congress? Article V creates two pairs of procedures to amend the Constitution, but each requires the consent of Congress: both houses of Congress may propose an amendment, by a two-thirds vote, which must then be ratified by three-quarters of the states either in legislative votes or conventions in order to be valid; or two-thirds of the states may petition Congress to call a convention of states and the amendments proposed in Convention must be ratified by three-quarters of state legislatures or conventions in order to be valid, the choice of ratification procedure in both procedures being up to Congress.[95] Congress is today effectively paralyzed from partisan division so it seems unlikely that it could reach two-thirds agreement on much of anything let alone something like an amendment—not to mention that Congress is unlikely to endorse any substantial changes to its composition, for instance the admission of a new state. Congress has an obvious conflict when it convenes to vote on constitutional amendments that implicate its own powers.

Return for a moment to 2010. In his first State of the Union Address,[96] then-president Barack Obama urged Congress to take action to reverse the Supreme Court's judgment in *Citizens United*, a case holding in relevant part that corporations are not restricted in how much they can lawfully spend independently in federal elections.[97] The president later pressed for a constitutional

[91] Richard S Kay, "The Illegality of the Constitution" (1987) 4 Const Comment 57 at 75.

[92] Bruce Ackerman & Neal Katyal, "Our Unconventional Founding" (1995) 62 *U Chicago L Rev* 475 at 562.

[93] *See* Sanford Levinson, *Our Undemocratic Constitution: Where the Constitution Goes Wrong (And How We the People Can Correct It)* (New York: Oxford University Press, 2006) at 27.

[94] *Ibid* at 29.

[95] Constitution of the United States, art V.

[96] Barack Obama, "The 2010 State of the Union Address", *The Obama White House Archives*, Jan 27, 2010, online: <https://obamawhitehouse.archives.gov/photos-and-video/video/2010-state-union-address#transcript>.

[97] Citizens United v Fed Election Comm'n, 558 US 2010 (2010).

amendment.[98] Although many amendments were proposed in Congress—some driven not by an honest effort to actually reform the constitution but by narrow parochial interests like position taking, credit claiming and advertising[99]—unsurprisingly none of them succeeded.[100] Neither Congress as an institution nor most of its members have an interest in reversing the ruling in *Citizens United*. The path to formal amendment through Article V was therefore closed from the beginning. What, then, could the president have done then, or could a president do now, to pass an amendment overturning *Citizens United* in the face of congressional resistance or inaction?

The founding precedent suggests that the tradition of American popular sovereignty credits expressions of popular will as legally valid but more importantly politically binding where the views of the people are clear. An American president, then, could perhaps legitimately make an end-run around the strictures of Article V—much like the Philadelphia Convention circumvented the rule of unanimity in the Articles of Confederation—to hold a referendum inviting all eligible voters to answer a yes/no question on whether an amendment should be passed reversing *Citizens United*. There would of course be important details to work out including how the question would be phrased, where the vote would be held, and who would tabulate the ballots since elections are ordinarily conducted by state officials. Here, in light of the Supreme Court's federalism case law, the federal government could not commandeer the states to run a nationwide referendum.[101]

A failed referendum on *Citizens United* would put an end to the question for the near- to mid-term. But were the referendum to return a convincing vote in favour of reversal, it could have the effect of a reconstructive referendum as in the French referendum of 1962—in which case the Constitution would be declared formally amended even though the process had not conformed to the textually entrenched rules of change—or a revertive referendum in the spirit of the UK referendum on Brexit, compelling Congress to act in deference to expressed popular will, with the ratifying states soon

[98] *See* Fredreka Schouten, "President Obama Wants to Reverse Citizens United", *USA Today*, Feb 9, 2015, online: <https://www.usatoday.com/story/news/politics/onpolitics/2015/02/09/president-obama-wants-to-reverse-citizens-united/81582308>.

[99] *See* David R Mayhew, *Congress: The Electoral Connection* (New Haven: Yale University Press, 1974) 73.

[100] *See* Richard Albert, "The Unamendable Core of the United States Constitution" in András Koltay, ed, *Comparative Perspectives on the Fundamental Freedom of Expression* (Budapest: Wolters Kluwer, 2015) 13 at 37.

[101] *See* Printz v. US, 521 US 898 (1997).

to follow. Nothing in Article V, after all, purports to prescribe an exclusive method of formal constitutional change, as Akhil Amar has theorized in his work on referendums.[102]

The late Walter Murphy was right: "to think that words can constrain power seems foolish."[103] The rules of formal amendment cannot on their own withstand claims that they are suppressing the will of the people or that the popular will has expressed in another form—whether legally valid or not but in either case with democratic legitimately—its preferences for how to reallocate powers, rebalance rights or redesign institutions of government. Appeals to the people resonate with us because for now the consent of the governed remains today an important determinant in both constitutional law and politics. Yet it is less clear whether the consent of the governed will remain tomorrow "the only legitimate fountain of power,"[104] as it was when James Madison wrote these words at the founding. The national model of American constitutionalism is on the decline around the world,[105] and other sources of legitimacy may soon gain primacy, no longer rooting legitimacy in majoritarian democratic politics but rather in moral values, contested though they inevitably are.

In this chapter, I have developed a typology of discretionary referendums in constitutional amendment. Drawing from non-obligatory popular votes in Canada (1992), Colombia (2016), France (1962) and the United Kingdom (2016). I have suggested four categories of discretionary referendums in constitutional amendment: reconstructive, obstructive, revertive and inoperative referendums. I have also explored why constitutional actors might choose to deploy discretionary referendums in circumvention of the established rules of change. This chapter has sought moreover to reinforce an unalloyed truth we have long known to be true but that is worth stressing once more: no constitution is a complete code of its own rules—and even where they are written in precise language those rules are in a constant state of evolution, interpretation, and contestation.

102 Akhil Reed Amar, "Philadelphia Revisited: Amending the Constitution Outside Article V" (1988) 55 *U Chicago L Rev* 1043.

103 Walter F Murphy, "Constitutions, Constitutionalism, and Democracy" in Douglas Greenberg et al, eds, *Constitutionalism and Democracy* (New York: Oxford University Press, 1993) 3 at 7.

104 Jacob E Cooke, ed, *The Federalist* No 49 (Middleton: Wesleyan University Press, 1961) 339.

105 David Law & Mila Versteeg, "The Declining Influence of the United States Constitution" (2012) 87 *NYU L Rev* 762 at 854.

3

The Unnecessary Referendum

Popular Sovereignty in the Constitutional Interregnum

Richard Stacey

We are the Egyptian people, sovereigns in a sovereign homeland. This is our will and this is the Constitution of our revolution.
Preamble to the Constitution of the Arab Republic of Egypt, 2014

We, the people of Kenya … adopt, enact and give this Constitution to ourselves and to our future generations.
Preamble to the Constitution of Kenya, 2010

I. Introduction

The relationship between constitutions and popular sovereignty is a close one, at least textually. Many of the world's constitutions make the preambular claim to having been adopted and enacted by the people themselves in an exercise of sovereign self-government. Once the people have spoken in adopting a constitution, the constitution becomes the authoritative statement of the nation's sovereign will,[1] and it remains the only marker of popular sovereignty until the people come together to exercise popular sovereignty anew, abrogate the old constitution and establish a fresh constitutional foundation for political authority.[2]

[1] Stephen Tierney, 'Constitutional Referendums: A Theoretical Inquiry' (2009) 72(3) *Modern Law Review* 360, at 365–66; Stephen Tierney, *Constitutional Referendums* (Oxford: Oxford University Press 2012), at 133; Stephen Gardbaum, 'Revolutionary Constitutionalism' (2017) 15 *International Journal of Constitutional Law* 173, at 182; Martin Loughlin, *The Idea of Public Law* (Oxford: Oxford University Press, 2003), at 84; Thomas Hobbes, *Leviathan*, Edwin Curley (ed) (Indianapolis and Cambridge, Mass: Hackett, 1994), ch XVII at para 13; ch XVIII at paras 6–7.

[2] John Locke, *Second Treatise of Government* (1689), ch XIX §§ 221-2; ch IV § 22. See also Mark Tushnet, 'Peasants with pitchforks, and toilers with Twitter: Constitutional revolutions and the constituent power' (2015) 13 *International Journal of Constitutional Law* 639, at 641; James A Gardner, 'Consent, Legitimacy and Elections: Implementing Popular Sovereignty under the Lockean Constitution' (1990) 52 *University of Pittsburgh Law Review* 189, at 200–205.

Richard Stacey, *The Unnecessary Referendum* In: *The Limits and Legitimacy of Referendums*. Edited by: Richard Albert and Richard Stacey, Oxford University Press. © Richard Stacey 2022. DOI: 10.1093/oso/9780198867647.003.0004

The referendum is a handy mechanism for aggregating a political community's preferences. Referendums are frequently used to gauge public opinion on non-constitutional questions,[3] and are increasingly used to ratify new constitutions.[4] The constitutional referendum has thus emerged as a vehicle for popular sovereignty, allowing a political community to speak as one to approve the basic rules of the legal system that will bind it. My objective in this chapter, however, is to chill the enthusiasm for constitutional referendums by rejecting two arguments about the connection between referendum and popular sovereignty during moments of constitutional change.

One argument is that a referendum is necessary for a new constitution to make a claim to the authority of popular sovereignty. The argument is most compelling in circumstances of 'constitutional interregnum,'[5] where a new constitution replaces an old one and in doing so removes all existing markers of popular sovereignty. In the absence of any markers of the people's sovereign will, a new expression of that will is required—and the referendum is that expression.[6] The second argument is that referendal approval is sufficient to infuse a constitution with the authority of popular sovereignty, and that any constitution approved at referendum carries the imprimatur of popular sovereignty. I set out these arguments in Section II of the chapter, noting briefly how they were deployed during constitution-making processes in Kenya in the mid-2000s and Egypt after the Arab Spring.

I make the case for rejecting these arguments in Section III. I argue that a referendum by itself is not sufficient to imbue a constitution with popular sovereignty because certain conditions must be in place, independent of the

[3] See, e.g., Lawrence LeDuc, *The Politics of Direct Democracy: Referendums in Global Perspective* (New York: Broadview, 2003); Matt Qvortrup, *A Comparative Study of Referendums: Government by the People* (Manchester: Manchester University Press, 2002); Matthew Mendelsohn and Andrew Parkin (eds), *Referendum Democracy: Citizens, Elites and Deliberation in Referendum Campaigns* (New York: Palgrave, 2001); Rich Braunstein, *Initiative and Referendum Voting: Governing through Direct Democracy in the United States* (New York: LFB Scholarly Publications, 2004).

[4] Comparative Constitutions Project, Chronology of Constitutional Events (v. 1.2); Zachary Elkins and Alexander E Hudson, 'The Strange Case of the Package Deal: Amendments and Replacements in Constitutional Reform' (*in this volume*).

[5] Richard Stacey, 'Popular Sovereignty and Revolutionary Constitutionalism', in David Dyzenhaus and Malcolm Thorburn (eds), *Philosophical Foundations of Constitutional Law* (Oxford: Oxford University Press, 2016).

[6] For summaries of this position, see, e.g., Tierney 'Constitutional Referendums' (n 1), at 363; Eoin Daly, 'A Republican Defence of the Constitutional Referendum' (2015) 35 *Legal Studies* 30, at 38, 44–47; Richard Albert, 'Constitutional Amendment and Dismemberment' (2018) 43 *Yale Journal of International Law* 1, 11–13. Much of this work emerges from Carl Schmitt's theory of constituent power—see especially *Constitutional Theory*, Jeffrey Seitzer (trans) (Durham: Duke University Press, 2008). Although Schmitt himself says very little about the referendum as a mechanism of constituent power, he does say that the identity of the people is represented to the fullest extent through a referendum (at 240; see also at 287–88, 133–34 and 304–305).

constitution or the referendum, in order for popular sovereignty to flow from the referendum to the constitution. If we understand popular sovereignty as the idea that a society establishes rules for its own governance—as opposed to constituent power, where any person or institution can establish constitutional rules—then each member of that society must enjoy the freedom to form an opinion about how they want to be governed. Moreover, each person must be assured that their opinion will be considered in constituting the new system of government. Popular sovereignty involves something other than just majoritarian decision-making or a form of 'constitutional positivism'.[7] The claim to popular sovereignty brings with it a prior commitment to substantive principles of moral autonomy and political equality that do not depend on the outcome of any referendum that follows.[8]

Moreover, I argue that this substantive commitment to equality is by itself sufficient to make meaningful a constitution's claim to popular sovereignty. The result of any referendum that follows is irrelevant to the constitution's claim to popular sovereignty. What matters is that the constitution is drafted and presented to the people for their approval in a way that respects their equal moral autonomy. The referendum itself is an unnecessary afterthought.

In Section IV, I consider what a referendum can bring to a constitution if it does not bring the authority of popular sovereignty. I distinguish between popular sovereignty on one hand, and sociological legitimacy on the other hand. A constitution that has the referendal support of a majority of citizens may be legitimate, but it may not claim the authority of popular sovereignty because of that referendal support. I end by warning that referendums can bring a veneer of legitimacy to abusive or illiberal constitutional arrangements that are established under conditions of inequality and oppression that make nonsense of any claim to popular sovereignty.[9]

[7] See, e.g., Frederick Schauer, 'Constitutional Positivism' (1992-1993) 25 *Connecticut Law Review* 797, at 806–807; and David Dyzenhaus, 'The Incoherence of Constitutional Positivism' in Grant Huscroft (ed), *Expounding the Constitution: Essays in Constitutional Theory* (Cambridge, UK: Cambridge University Press, 2008).

[8] Stacey, 'Popular Sovereignty' (n 5), at 173–78; Andreas Kalyvas, 'Popular Sovereignty, Democracy, and the Constituent Power' (2005) 12 *Constellations* 223, at 234–35; Hannah Arendt, 'What is Freedom' in *Between Past and Future: Eight Exercises in Political Thought* (New York: Penguin, 1993): and Hannah Arendt, 'Some Questions of Moral Philosophy' (1994) 61 *Social Research* 739, at 741; and Joel Colon-Rios, *Weak Constitutionalism: Democratic Legitimacy and the Question of Constituent Power* (London and New York: Routledge, 2012).

[9] Bellamy, *Political Constitutionalism* (n 3), at 263. On the various ways that constitutional government can fail to uphold principles of liberal democracy, see, e.g., David Landau, 'Abusive Constitutionalism' (2013) 47 *UC Davis Law Review* 189; Fareed Zakaria, *The Future of Freedom: Illiberal Democracy at Home and Abroad* (New York: WW Norton and Company, 2003); Steven Levitsky and Lucan Way, *Competitive Authoritarianism; Hybrid Regimes after the Cold War* (Cambridge: Cambridge University Press, 2010); Mark Tushnet, 'Authoritarian Constitutionalism' (2015) 100 *Cornell Law Review* 391.

II. The case for referendum: constitution-making by the people

A constitution plays a key role in modern legal systems by serving as a marker of legal validity. The principle of constitutional supremacy means that any law that is inconsistent with the constitution is of no legal force in that system, and no ordinary law can supersede the provisions of the constitution.[10] The principle of constitutionalism recalls HLA Hart's account of a legal system as the union of primary rules of conduct and secondary rules of rulemaking.[11] On this account, a constitutional system emerges from the union of constitutional rules and ordinary laws which depend for their validity on congruence with those constitutional rules. For Hart, a society's secondary rules and in particular the 'rule of recognition' allow its members to conclusively identify commands that carry the force of law, and to distinguish them from social conventions, customs, rules of etiquette, or presidential tweets that do not.[12] Constitutions provide secondary rules for rulemaking by establishing 'manner and form' procedures, according to which laws are made by legislative bodies specifically constituted for the purposes of making law, and by setting substantive limits to the laws a legislature can pass.[13]

For Hans Kelsen, the validity of the ultimate secondary rule on which the validity of all other law depends is determined by its social acceptance.[14] We can tell that a new legal order is valid, even when it replaces an existing legal order, when 'individuals whose behaviour the new order regulates actually behave, by and large, in conformity' with it.[15] Hart, too, sees the validity of the rule of recognition as a matter of sociological fact flowing from its acceptance by society as an appropriate standard of legal validity.[16]

[10] See, for example, section 2(4) of the Kenyan Constitution, 2010: 'Any law, including customary law, that is inconsistent with this Constitution is void to the extent of the inconsistency, and any act or omission in contravention of this Constitution is invalid'; and section 2 of the South African Constitution, 1996: 'This Constitution is the supreme law of the Republic; law or conduct inconsistent with it is invalid'.

[11] HLA Hart, *The Concept of Law* (New York and London: Oxford University Press, 1961), ch 5.

[12] Id, at 92. Hart never mentioned tweets, of course, but he did point out that the rules of recognition allow people to distinguish a lawmaker's private orders to his wife or mistress from formal announcements of law (id, 66).

[13] Hart, id, at 66–70. Kent Greenawalt cautions against conflating the constitution with Hart's rule of recognition, because most constitutions provide for their own amendment. In turn, Greenawalt suggests that constitutional amendment rules might amount to a rule of recognition in constitutional democracies: 'The Rule of Recognition and the Constitution' (1987) 85 *Michigan Law Review* 621, at 632–33.

[14] Hans Kelsen, *General Theory of Law and State* (New York and London: Routledge, 2005), at 120.

[15] Id, 118. See also Tushnet, 'Peasants with Pitchforks' (n 2), at 647, 654.

[16] Hart, *The Concept of Law* (n 11), at 105–107.

If the validity of secondary rules depends on their acceptance by members of a political community, then there is no reason that those same people cannot define the secondary rules. Just as there is a distinction between primary and secondary rules, there is a distinction between primary and secondary rulemaking. Policing a society by making primary rules—in the form of statutes, regulations, and bylaws, for example—is an exercise of 'command sovereignty' that is made possible and controlled by secondary rules. Making secondary rules, however, is an exercise of 'constituent sovereignty'.[17] Constituting a legal system, then, involves making the secondary rules by which officials can make primary rules and by which society can recognise primary rules as valid law. In this sense, sovereignty means the capacity to 'determine the constitutional form, the juridical and political identity, and the governmental structure of a community in its entirety'.[18]

Popular sovereignty, making a very short leap here, implies that the people hold the constituent power to define the constitutional, political, and legal contours of their community by directly controlling second-order lawmaking.[19] While command sovereignty is embodied in an already constituted legislator or legislative institution, and constituent sovereignty might conceivably be exercised single-handedly by a people's conqueror (the US-led coalition imposing the Transitional Administrative Law in Iraq in 2003, say, or Daenerys Targaryen and her dragons abolishing slavery in Meereen in season 4 of *Game of Thrones*), the challenge of popular sovereignty is that all of the individuals who would form a political community have to exercise that power. As a vehicle for popular sovereignty, the constitutional referendum claims to 'encapsulate a real-world manifestation of the notion of the people as the ultimate source of legitimate power'.[20]

Majoritarian decision-making plays a part in Hobbes's social contract theory too. Hobbes starts with the premise that a multitude of individuals threatened by the infelicity of the state of nature will choose to erect a common power to 'conform the wills of them all to peace'. All the members of this multitude agree with one another to submit to the lawmaking authority of this common power.[21] The social contract is an exercise of constituent sovereignty, then,

[17] Tierney, 'Constitutional Referendums' (n 1), at 363. The distinction between periods of ordinary lawmaking and exceptional moments of constitutional lawmaking is made by Bruce Ackerman, *We the People: Foundations* Cambridge, Mass: Belknap Press, 1991), ch 1. See also Joel Colon-Rios and Allan C Hutchinson, 'Democracy and Revolution: An Enduring Relationship?' (2011-12) 89 *Denver University Law Review* 593.

[18] Kalyvas, 'Sovereignty' (n 8), at 226.

[19] Tierney, 'Constitutional Referendums' (n 1), at 364.

[20] Tierney, 'Constitutional Referendums' (n 1), at 363.

[21] Hobbes, *Leviathan* (n 1), ch. XVII at paras 13–14.

because it is the act by which a power to make laws binding on all the members of a new political community is established and assigned to a lawmaker. For Hobbes, it is also an act of popular sovereignty because the people (or a majority of them) exercise this power:

> A commonwealth is said to be instituted, when a multitude of men do agree and covenant, every one with every one, that to whatsoever man or assembly of men shall be given *by the major part* the right to present the person of them all (that is to say, to be their representative) every one, *as well as he that voted for it as he that voted against it*, shall authorize all the actions and judgments of that man or assembly of men, in the same manner as if they were his own.[22]

Once Hobbes's multitude has come together to exercise their sovereignty and authorise a sovereign to rule over them, they are reduced to mere subjects of the sovereign's authority and no longer hold sovereign power themselves. They are in no position to complain about any of the sovereign's commands, because having authorised the sovereign to govern them they are themselves author of those commands.[23] Further, since the people give up their sovereignty at the moment they confer authority on the sovereign to govern over them, they cannot lawfully make a new contract to replace the sovereign.[24] Like drone bees that die after fertilising their queen, popular sovereignty withers once exercised to empower a sovereign.

A society governed by Hobbes's sovereign rests on an unwritten constitution containing but one secondary rule: whatever commands the sovereign issues are laws that must be obeyed. Although most constitution making results in constitutions with more detailed rules of lawmaking than this, both processes share at least one common outcome. Once an exercise of popular sovereignty has produced a constitution setting out secondary rules according to which valid laws are made, the constitution itself assumes this sovereign authority. The people's constituent power is effectively 'replaced by the representational force of constitutional authority'.[25] The paradoxical implication is that popular sovereignty is eventually limited and controlled by the very constitution to

[22] Hobbes, *Leviathan* (n 1) ch. XVIII at para1 (my emphasis). See also ch. XVI at paras 14-15; ch. XVIII at para 5.

[23] Hobbes, *Leviathan* (n 1), ch XVII at para 13; ch XVIII at paras 6–7.

[24] Id, ch. XVIII at para See also Schmitt, *Constitutional Theory* (n 6), at 125.

[25] Tierney 'Constitutional Referendums' (n 1), at 366; see also Gardbaum, 'Revolutionary Constitutionalism' (n 1), at 182.

which its initial exercise gives rise.[26] Abraham Lincoln fully committed to this paradox in his inaugural address. 'A majority, held in restraint by constitutional checks and limitations,' he said, 'is the only true sovereign of a free people'.[27]

A constitution thus limits a people's sovereignty. While constitutional amendments are of course possible, they are possible only to the extent that the constitution itself contemplates and according to rules the constitution itself sets out. Making a distinction between constitutional amendment and constitutional replacement, Carl Schmitt and others suggest that it is not possible to change the fundamental substance of a constitution through the amendment procedures.[28] On this view, the replacement of a constitution changes the second-order rules of lawmaking and amounts to an act of constituent sovereignty which, if popular sovereignty is be respected, cannot happen without the intervention of the people.[29]

This does not mean, however, that a constitution can never be replaced once adopted. One difference between Hobbes and Locke is that Locke sees the people retaining a right to reassert sovereignty. In Locke's view the people delegate sovereignty through a social contract, but they do not irrevocably alienate it.[30] Whenever the sovereign acts in foolish or wicked ways, the bond of obedience legal subjects owe is severed and sovereign power reverts 'into the hands of those that gave it, who may place it anew where they think best for their safety and security'.[31] From a Lockean perspective, a people who expend sovereign power to enact a constitution as the foundation of their political community nevertheless retain a residual sovereign power to replace that constitution.

[26] Martin Loughlin and Neil Walker, 'Introduction' in Loughlin and Walker (eds), *The Paradox of Constitutionalism: Constituent Power and Constitutional Form* (Oxford: Oxford University Press, 2007), at 1.

[27] Abraham Lincoln, First Inaugural Address, 4 March 1861, quoted in Herman Belz, *Abraham Lincoln, Constitutionalism, and Equal Rights in the Civil War Era* (New York: Fordham University Press, 1998), at 86.

[28] Schmitt, *Constitutional Theory* (n 24), at 79, 72–74 and 150–55. For academic commentary, see also Gary J Jacobsohn, 'An Unconstitutional Constitution: A Comparative Perspective' (2006) 4 *International Journal of Constitutional Law* 460; for judicial consideration, see the Indian Supreme Court in *Kesavananda Bharati v State of Kerala*, AIR 1973 SC 1469 and the South African Constitutional Court in *United Democratic Movement v President of the Republic of South Africa (No 2)* 2003 (1) SA 495 (CC).

[29] Schmitt, *Constitutional Theory* (n 6), at 152. Stephen Gardbaum sees the people' hand in 'revolutionary constitutionalism', to the extent that raw constituent power must be exercised through a 'genuine form of mass mobilization' ('Revolutionary Constitutionalism' (n 1), at 177).

[30] Loughlin, *Public Law* (n 1), at 103.

[31] Locke, *Second Treatise of Government* (n 2), ch. XIII at para 149. Carl J Friedrich calls this 'a right to revolution': *Constitutional Government and Democracy; Theory and Practice in Europe and America* (Boston: Ginn, 1950), at 129. George Lawson, in the 1660 work *Politica Sacra et Civilis or, A Modell of Civil and Ecclesiastical Government*, Conal Condren (ed) (Cambridge: Cambridge University Press, 1992) at 47), distinguishes between the King's 'inferior, delegated, and constituted "personal majesty"' and the 'real majesty' to 'constitute, abolish, alter, reform forms of government'. See also Loughlin, *Public Law* (n 1), at 85; and Tierney, *Constitutional Referendums* (n 1), at 135–37.

From this discussion I make two observations. First, replacing one constitution with another necessarily involves a constitutional interregnum. I do not use the phrase to suggest that there is a perceptible moment in time when no constitution is in force (although this might happen, as it did for a period in Egypt). Rather, I use the phrase to highlight the idea that a constitution that replaces an old constitution in its entirety cannot look to the old constitution as the source of its authority. Even a self-consciously temporary constitution which foresees and sets out procedures for its own replacement, like South Africa's 1993 interim Constitution, cannot imbue the new constitution with authority because any authority vanishes at the moment the old constitution is no longer law.[32] As soon as the old constitution is abrogated, a nation occupies a 'legal no-man's land' until the new constitutional order is in place.[33]

The second observation is corollary to the first: making a new constitution extinguishes the previous constitution's claims to sovereignty. The makers of a new constitution cannot rely on whatever claims to popular sovereignty the previous constitution made, as a basis for claiming that the new constitution is backed by the authority of popular sovereignty. Each new constitution, therefore, must make a new claim to popular sovereignty. It does not follow, in my view, that each new constitution's claim to popular sovereignty requires, or would be satisfied by, a referendum. This, however, is precisely the line of reasoning behind the constitutional referendums in Kenya and Egypt, and it is this line of argument that is my target in this chapter.

A. Constituent power in Kenya

In March 2004, the Kenyan High Court temporarily derailed the country's progress towards constitutional reform. In *Njoya v Attorney General*,[34] the

[32] Section 73(1) of the Constitution of the Republic of South Africa Act 200 of 1993 provided: 'The Constitutional Assembly shall pass the new constitutional text within two years as from the date of the first sitting of the National Assembly under this Constitution.' Section 73(13) provided: 'A new constitutional text adopted in terms of this Chapter shall be assented to by the President and shall upon its promulgation be the Constitution of the Republic of South Africa.' A referendum was to be held only in the event that the Constitutional Assembly approved a constitutional text with a majority of members rather than a two-thirds supermajority (s. 73(6)–(8)).

[33] David Landau, 'The Importance of Constitution-Making' (2011-12) 89 *Denver University Law Review* 611, at 612: 'Virtually all new constitution-making happens this way, because it is rare for an existing constitution to have a provision allowing for its own replacement'. For the contrary view that constitutional revolutions can happen without any break or rupture, see e.g. John Finnis, 'Revolutions and the Continuity of Law' in AWB Simpson (ed), *Oxford Essays in Jurisprudence (2 series)* (Oxford: Clarendon Press, 1973), 44, at 52–53.

[34] *Njoya and Others v Attorney General and Others* [2004] eKLR; [2004] LLR 4788 (HCK).

Court found that the process for enacting a new constitution, set out in the Constitution of Kenya Review Act 13 of 1997, was fatally flawed because it did not require a referendum on a new draft constitution. Taking a Lockean rather than a Hobbesian line on sovereignty, the Court said that the sovereignty of the people 'betokens that they have a constituent power—*the power to constitute and/or reconstitute*, as the case may be, their framework of government'.[35] The Court emphasised the connection between constitutionalism and popular sovereignty in an important line in the judgment, concluding that 'the Constitution is supreme because it is made by they in whom the constituent power is reposed, the people themselves'.[36]

The Court recognised that while practical limitations require a representative body to draft the new constitution ('there is neither a stadium large enough to accommodate them nor expertise on the part of their body as a whole to process a Constitution'[37]), constituent power requires the popular ratification of any new draft constitution such a body produces. The Court's resort to referendum as a vehicle of popular sovereignty recalls Schmitt's sense that some form of political decision is necessary if a people is to exercise popular sovereignty.[38] A process by which a new constitution replaces an old one must cut as closely as possible to an ideal of popular sovereignty, despite the practical limitations.[39] Schmitt insists that 'the people's constitution-making will always expresses itself only in a fundamental yes or no',[40] and while he does not say much about the referendum as a mechanism of decision he does recognise at one point that the identity of the people is represented to the fullest extent possible by referendum.[41]

The Kenyan High Court accordingly held that a constitutional referendum is a fundamental right of the people in the exercise of their constituent power, and that the constituent power requires nothing less than a compulsory referendum on a proposed new constitution.[42] The legislature amended the Review Act to require a referendum on the new constitution, echoing the High Court's rhetoric and affirming that 'the people of Kenya have the sovereign right and power to replace the Constitution with a new Constitution'.[43] In a referendum held in November 2005, 57 per cent of voters rejected the draft.

[35] Id, at 15 (my emphasis).
[36] Id.
[37] Id, at 16.
[38] Schmitt, *Constitutional Theory* (n 6), at 132–35.
[39] Colon-Rios and Hutchinson, 'Democracy and Revolution' (n 17), at 608.
[40] Schmitt, *Constitutional Theory* (n 6), at 132.
[41] Id, at 240; see also at 287–88, 133–34 and 304–305.
[42] *Njoya*, (n 34), at 16–17.
[43] Constitution of Kenya Review Act, 13 of 1997 (as amended), section 26.

When the constitutional reform initiative was restarted after the bloody national elections in 2007, the new statute contemplated a referendum:[44] Kenya's Constitution of 2010 became law in August 2010 after approval by 67 per cent of voters.[45]

B. Constitutional reform in Egypt

The end of Hosni Mubarak's 30-year rule in Egypt in early 2011, following months of popular protests, was the dramatic centrepiece of the regional uprisings known as the Arab Spring. The Supreme Council of the Armed Forces (SCAF) assumed power after Mubarak's resignation and made a number of statements indicating their commitment to the 'legitimate demands of the people'.[46] On 13 February, the SCAF issued a declaration suspending the operation of the 1971 Constitution, arrogating lawmaking and executive authority to itself and indicating that amendments to the 1971 Constitution would be made in due course and submitted to referendum.[47] The 2011 interim Constitution took effect on 30 March.

It would be wrong to conclude that because no formal constitution was in force between 13 February and 30 March, these 45 days were a period of constitutional interregnum. On the contrary, the SCAF's 13 February rules themselves constitute a constitutional document, setting out the Hobbesian secondary rule that the SCAF 'shall issue laws during this transitional

[44] See the Constitution of Kenya Review Act, 2008, Act 9 of 2008, part V.

[45] For a fuller account, see Richard Stacey, 'Constituent Power and Carl Schmitt's Theory of Constitution in Kenya's Constitution-making Process' (2011) 9 *International Journal of Constitutional Law* 587.

[46] *New York Times*, 'Egypt's Supreme Council of the Armed Forces: Statements and Key Leaders' <http://www.nytimes.com/interactive/2011/02/10/world/middleeast/20110210-egypt-supreme-council.html?_r=0> (accessed 3 August 2017).

[47] The relevant provisions of the 13 February declaration read:

> *First*: The Constitution is suspended.
> *Second*: The Supreme Council of the Armed Forces shall temporarily administer the affairs of the country for a period of 6 months or until People's Assembly, Shura Council and Presidential elections are held.
> *Third*: The Chairman of the Supreme Council of the Armed Forces shall represent it internally and externally.
> *Fourth*: The People's Assembly and the Shura Council are dissolved.
> *Fifth*: The Supreme Council of the Armed Forces shall issue laws during this transitional period.
> *Sixth*: A committee to amend a number of articles of the constitution shall be established, and a popular referendum shall be held.

period'. But the declaration of new constitutional rules on 13 February effected a constitutional interregnum even as it put new constitutional rules in place. Since the declaration at once suspended the 1971 Constitution and replaced it with new rules, no pre-existing constitutional rules authorised the declaration. The SCAF made the declaration in a vacuum of constitutional law. And while this make the SCAF's declaration an exercise of constituent sovereignty, it is far from clear that it was an act of popular sovereignty.[48]

Compare the 13 February declaration with the 2011 interim Constitution, the short-lived 2012 Constitution, and the 2014 Constitution. All were ratified by referendum and were seen as a result to carry an authority that not even the SCAF could controvert. In 2012 the SCAF tried to reassert control over the drafting of the 2012 Constitution by imposing a set of 'supra-constitutional principles' on the drafting committee. Opposition politicians objected that because the people had ratified the 2011 interim Constitution by referendum, including its rules for constitution-making, the SCAF had no authority to supersede those rules.[49]

Egypt's experience illustrates the distinction between constituent power and popular sovereignty, in that a set of secondary rules for rulemaking need not claim popular sovereignty in order to succeed in authorising primary lawmaking. But Egypt's experience also indicates how the referendum is seen as an unassailable indicator of popular sovereignty. A referendum is required for a constitution to assume the authority of popular sovereignty, and once approved by referendum, no power other than the people's can supplant it. I question below whether a referendum is either necessary or sufficient to transform an exercise of constituent sovereignty into an act of popular sovereignty.

III. The flaws in constitutional positivism

The core of popular sovereignty is the idea that when it comes time to constitute or reconstitute the legal system, the people to be governed by that system will select the secondary rules of lawmaking. A commitment to

[48] Stacey, 'Popular Sovereignty' (n 5), at 178: 'Where a constitution-making body assumes the authority to enact a constitution simply by having defeated all other competitors by force, and is unconcerned with representing the sovereignty of the people, then popular sovereignty is simply not in play'.

[49] Kristen Stilt, 'The End of "One Hand": The Egyptian Constitutional Declaration and the Rift between the "People" and the Supreme Council of the Armed Forces' (2010-2011) 16 *Yearbook of Islamic and Middle Eastern Law* 43, at 43–44; Landau, 'The Importance of Constitution-making' (n 33), at 615.

popular sovereignty could be taken to imply a kind of constitutional positivism, in that the validity of a society's constitutional rules depends only on their source in the people's constituent power, rather than on their substantive merit. Constitutional positivism has its roots in Hart's 'sources thesis', which holds that the validity of primary rules of conduct depends only on whether they are generated in accordance with the secondary rules of lawmaking. The law's provenance, not its moral goodness, is what makes it valid.[50] Where the people are sovereign, the principle that they are bound by only those rules they have themselves agreed to be bound by emerges as the rule of recognition. As Schmitt says, 'law is everything that the people intends'.[51]

The constitutional referendum fits neatly into this this scaled up, constitutional version of the sources thesis, providing a mechanism by which the people can accept a set of secondary rules for lawmaking and government. In turn, constitutional rules will be valid if, and only if they have been accepted by the people. The normative content of the rules, as for Hart's legal positivism, does not matter to the constitution's validity. Schmitt endorses constitutional positivism when he declares that 'a constitution is not based on a norm whose justness would be the foundation of its validity' but on 'a political decision concerning the type and form of its own being'.[52] The constituent power of the people is, accordingly, an 'unmediated will' that exists prior to any constitutional rules and procedures.[53]

There are reasons we should be sceptical of this positivist understanding of popular sovereignty. I argue that a constitution's claim to the authority of popular sovereignty does not depend on the outcome of the referendum that approves it, but rather on whether, at the moment at which the referendum occurs, every would-be legal subject of the new legal system is treated as equally important. This condition of equality requires, at least, that everyone has an equal opportunity to consider the content of the proposed constitution, is able to participate in the process of formulating the constitution and is represented to the extent that they cannot participate.

[50] Hart, *The Concept of Law* (n 11). See also John Gardner, 'Legal Positivism: 5½ Myths' (2001) 46 *American Journal of Jurisprudence* 199.

[51] Schmitt, *Constitutional Theory* (n 6), at 286.

[52] Schmitt, *Constitutional Theory* (n 6), at 125.

[53] Id, at 132. See also the comments of the Colombian Constitutional Court in 1990, saying that because the people of Colombia are 'the primary constituency which takes on a sovereign character ... it cannot have any limits other than those it imposes on itself, nor can the constituted powers revise its acts' (quoted in Landau, 'The importance of Constitution-making' (n 33), at 617.

A. Asking the people what they think means you have to let them think first

A common question about the voluntarist virtues of social contract theories is whether the people ever actually enter into a contract. And if they do not, can it be said that popular sovereignty is the foundation of the system? Locke insists on one hand that a deliberate and voluntary act of consent is required if the members of a polity are to establish a political community,[54] but admits on the other hand that tacit consent, identifiable in people's acquiescence to being governed and their continued use of public goods, is sufficient.[55] But for subjects of a legal system to tacitly consent to it by continuing to allow themselves to be governed by it, they must be able to assess the system as it is and decide that it is good enough for them not to oppose. It follows that a society's tacit consent to a constitutional system is the product of a qualitative assessment of a system's normative content rather than the product of a contracting procedure.

If even tacit consent rests on the people's assessment of an existing legal system's normative quality, then surely a referendum on a proposed legal system must depend at least as much on voters' qualitative assessment of its normative quality. For a referendum to make the claim that it is an exercise of popular sovereignty, and for a constitution to make the claim that it bears the authority of popular sovereignty because it has been approved at referendum, the people must first be given an opportunity to consider the content of the constitution and form an opinion about whether they agree with it or not.

Recognising that would-be legal subjects must be able to assess the normative quality of a constitutional proposal before they vote on it implies a commitment to the view, first, that people are morally autonomous agents capable of assessing the normative strength of the rules meant to govern their lives, and second, that they are equally capable of doing so. Moreover, every person's normative assessment warrants consideration. Only if everyone's view is taken into account can the constitution make a claim to the authority of popular sovereignty. If the constitution-approving process fails to take into account the views of some people, we are only a little better off than with a conqueror asserting constituent power over a people.

[54] Locke, *Second Treatise* (n 2), ch. VIII at para 99. See also ch. VIII at para 122; ch XI at paras 140-41; and ch XV at para 173.

[55] Id, ch. VIII at para 119.

Of course, people will disagree in their assessments of the constitution, and some views will be in the minority. While not all views will be equally valued at the end of the process, what matters is that everyone has an equal opportunity to present their views and to contribute to the formation of the people's sovereign will. Republican theorists are generally wary of referendums precisely because their simple majoritarianism, single-issue focus, and reductivist questions tend to undermine deliberation.[56] One way to mitigate this concern is to ensure that voters are able to explore ideas as equals before the vote. The referendum is important to the concept of popular sovereignty not because of what its result says about any particular constitution, but because of what the decision to hold a referendum says about how a society values its legal subjects. The claim to popular sovereignty is made meaningful by the fact that every putative member of the new legal system is treated as equally valuable in the process by which the constitution is approved. The result of the referendum, where a condition of equal moral autonomy is secured beforehand, is largely irrelevant to the claim to popular sovereignty. It is the condition of equality that makes the claim possible.

B. From consideration to participation

Equality's centrality to popular sovereignty has important implications for constitution-makers. Whoever makes the claim that a constitution bears the authority of popular sovereignty because it was approved at referendum is bound, by that claim, to recognise in the first place that people are morally autonomous agents whose views about the content of the constitution matter, and to take positive steps in the second place to protect every person's opportunity to voice their opinion about the constitution. Even if it is true, as the sources thesis holds, that whatever constitutional rules the people approve are valid, the people's exercise of sovereign power to make constitutional rules is nevertheless subject to the constraints of equality.

Even Carl Schmitt's advocacy of constitutional positivism is tempered by his admission that a democratic constitution is bound to uphold certain substantive principles. A 'merely formal concept of law such as that the law is anything

[56] See, e.g., Phillip Pettit, *Republicanism: A Theory of Freedom and Government* (Oxford: Clarendon Press, 1997), at 8; Richard Bellamy, *Political Constitutionalism: A Republican Defence of the Constitutionality of Democracy* (Cambridge: Cambridge University Press, 2007); Sherman J Clark, 'A Populist Critique of Direct Democracy' (1998) 112 *Harvard Law Review* 434; and Erwin Chemerinsky, 'Challenging Direct Democracy' (2007) *Michigan State Law Review* 293.

that the lawmaking bodies ordain', he says, merely transforms a legal system from the tyranny of a despot or the absolutism of a monarchy into the 'absolutism of the legislative office'.[57] Constitutional democracy is different, Schmitt continues, because the 'constitutional regulation of legislative authorizations *presupposes* a substantive concept of law'.[58] Although Schmitt thinks that 'law is everything the people intends',[59] he concedes that the people are constrained when they intend a certain kind of legal system: 'Equality before the law is immanent to the *Rechtsstaat* concept of law.'[60]

Similarly, where the claim is made that a referendum is a certain kind of referendum—i.e. one that delivers the authority of popular sovereignty to a constitution—the referendum is bound to recognise and uphold principles of moral equality. The point is not so much that equality is an immanent principle of any constitutional democracy that makes a claim to the authority of popular sovereignty (although I think that is true[61]), but rather that the constitutional referendum must take place in circumstances of equality if it is to be the basis of that claim.

It is possible at this point to illustrate the irrelevance of the sources thesis, and in turn to point out that an affirmative referendum result is not sufficient by itself to imbue a constitution with popular sovereignty. Notice, first, that the obligation to respect and uphold a commitment to equality does not arise because the people say so. Indeed, a condition of equality must be in place before referendum voting even begins. Even if the referendum is the source of the constitution's validity, it cannot be the source of the principles that regulate the referendum. Consequently, the principle of equality is valid regardless of what the people think about it. Even if the people approve a constitution that makes no substantive commitment to equality, or worse, entrenches inequality,[62] a constitution can make no claim to the authority of popular sovereignty unless the process of its adoption respects the basic idea that everyone must have an equal opportunity to express their considered view about whether the constitution should bind them going forward.

As soon as it becomes clear that equality is important in principle, it follows that institutional mechanisms must protect and promote equality in practice.

[57] Schmitt, *Constitutional Theory* (n 6), at 191.
[58] Id, at 189. (Schmitt's emphasis).
[59] Id, at 286 (see also above, n 52).
[60] Id, at 194.
[61] Stacey, 'Popular sovereignty' (n 5). See also Pasquale Pasquino, 'The Un-constituent Power of the People: Article 138 of the Italian Constitution and Popular Referendum' (2017) *Italian Law Journal* 139, 143.
[62] Schmitt, *Constitutional Theory* (n 6), at 286: 'There are no limitations on this *will* stemming from democratic principles. Injustices and even inequalities are possible.'

Affording every person a vote in the referendum is a fairly uncontroversial consequence of a commitment to equality. However, ensuring people can participate in formulating the content of the constitution before it goes to referendum may be just as important. Contemporary societies are increasingly diverse and characterised by widespread disagreements about how people should behave, what rights we have or do not have or should or should not have, and what those rights allow us to do or prevent others from doing.[63] Without input from the people in whose name the constitution claims to speak, it is unlikely that a constitution will adequately reflect everyone's views on these contentious matters. The success of a constitution at referendum, then, depends on its congruence with people's preferences.

Consequently, constitution makers have to take disagreement seriously in designing constitutional frameworks and recognise that there is no single view to which they can give voice in claiming to speak for the people. Indeed, failing to recognise the diversity of a plural society and attempting to shoehorn divergent views into a single voice seems to undermine any real commitment to popular sovereignty.[64] Popular sovereignty can no longer be thought of as all of the people 'intoning a shared political catechism', but must recognise that the sovereign people is composed of numerous competing and contradictory voices.[65]

Upholding a commitment to the idea that this multi-throated people are sovereign means that the people in its numerous opinions and identities must be involved in the process of drafting the constitution. Simone Chambers argues in this regard that even if hypothetically agreeable and suitably universal constitutional principles are able to get us some of the way towards popular sovereignty, it is just as important that people be given a chance to make their views known and to actively participate in formulating the content of a new constitution. She points to South Africa's extensive public consultation during the drafting of the 1996 Constitution and to debates in post-unification Germany about whether a new constitution should be drafted for a unified Germany.[66] Similarly, the Committee of Experts who revised Kenya's draft constitution in 2009 invited and received tens of thousands of comments during their work in drafting the text.[67]

63 Jeremy Waldron, *Law and Disagreement* (Oxford: Oxford University Press, 1999); Waldron, 'The Core of the Case Against Judicial Review' (2006) 115 *Yale Law Journal* 1346, at 1366–69.

64 Simone Chambers 'Democracy, Popular Sovereignty, and Constitutional Legitimacy' (2004) 11 *Constellations* 153. See also Tierney, 'Constitutional Referendums' (n 1), at 375–76.

65 Chambers, id, at 158.

66 Id, at 161–68.

67 Christina Murray and Coel Kirkby, 'Constitution-Making in Anglophone Africa—We the People?', in Muna Ndulo and Mamaoudou Gazibo (eds), *growing Democracy in Africa; Elections, Accountable*

The inevitability of disagreement means that a constitution's claim to the authority of popular sovereignty cannot rest exclusively on the fact that it was approved in a referendum. In order for a referendum's result to make good that claim, two conditions must be met: First, the referendum must have been held under conditions that respect and protect a basic conception of participatory equality; and second, the constitution must reflect to at least some extent the concerns and desires of those whose lives it will eventually govern.

C. Representation on top of participation

A third condition that makes possible a referendum's claim to popular sovereignty is the people's representation in the institutions that draft the constitution. No matter how extensive a people's participation in a constitution-drafting exercise, it remains very difficult to make the case that 'the people themselves' have actually authored the constitution.[68] On a practical level, some degree of representation is unavoidable at the constitutional moment because the people cannot collectively draft their new constitution, as the Kenyan High Court has helpfully pointed out. Since it is never 'the people' who write the constitution, there must be a distinction between authoring a constitution and authorising its drafting.[69]

There is also a distinction, however, between a people authorising a body to draft a constitution and acquiescing to the constitution that some non-representative body thrusts upon them. A referendum held on a constitution drafted by a person or a group unconnected to a people's political identity allows the people to do no more than confirm or reject constitutional proposals formulated independently of them.[70] Popular sovereignty, however, involves the people selecting for themselves the rules that will bind them. It cannot be reduced to the post-hoc majoritarian approval of a constitutional proposal. Rather, the content of the constitution presented to the people at referendum

Governance and Political Economy (Newcastle upon Tyne: Cambridge Scholars Publishing, 2016) 86, at 102.

[68] On perhaps the closest the world has come to a people-authored constitution, see Iceland's unsuccessful experiment with massive public participation: Alex Hudson, 'When Does Public Participation Make a Difference? Evidence from Iceland's Crowdsourced Constitution,' (2018) *Policy & Internet* 10, 185.

[69] Pasquino, 'Un-constituent Power' (n 61), 143.

[70] Daly, 'A Republican Defence' (n 6), at 39.

must be formulated in a manner representative of the people's constitution-making power. Where the people cannot participate as author of the constitution, the constitution must at least be drafted by persons or institutions that represent the people.

The Kenyan High Court said as much in the *Njoya* case, faulting the composition of the National Constitutional Conference that produced the final draft constitution in 2004 because most of its members were appointed rather than elected.[71] In contrast, Tunisia's 2014 Constitution was drafted by an elected constitutional assembly and went into force without ever being subjected to referendum. In a departure from most other constitutions' preambles, the Tunisian Constitution's preamble provides: 'We, *the representatives of the Tunisian people*, members of the National Constituent Assembly ... *in the name of the Tunisian people* ... draft this Constitution (emphasis added).'

So far in this chapter I have argued that referendal approval alone is not sufficient for a constitution's claim to popular sovereignty, because a referendum must take place under pre-existing conditions of equality. Further, I have suggested that the referendum is unnecessary to a constitution's claim to popular sovereignty because securing conditions of equality is sufficient to support that claim. The strongest counter-case that a constitutional referendum is in fact necessary for popular sovereignty arises in cases like Egypt in February 2011, where there are no institutions in place that can secure conditions of equality and where a post-hoc referendal affirmation of the constitution appears to be the only available route to the authority of popular sovereignty.

My response to this counterargument builds on the distinction between authority and acquiescence. What the referendum delivers in these cases, however, is not authority or popular sovereignty. Where the people are not represented in the process of drafting the constitution, even if they approve the referendum after the fact, the constitution can claim neither that the people are authors of the constitution nor that they authorised its drafting. Not even a referendum, in these circumstances, can infuse a constitution with the authority of popular sovereignty. If not popular sovereignty, what does follow from referendal approval in cases like Egypt's? I take up that question in the final section of this chapter.

[71] *Njoya v Attorney General* (n 34), at 16.

IV. The constitutional referendum, popular sovereignty, and popular legitimacy

My thesis is that for a constitution to make a claim to the authority of popular sovereignty, it is necessary and sufficient that it be drafted and adopted in conditions of moral, participatory, and representative equality. A referendum is not necessary to that claim. What, then, do we make of the situation where a proposed constitution is defeated at referendum? The Kenyan people rejected the proposed 2004 constitution, even though the circumstances under which the constitution was drafted and the referendum conducted were, broadly speaking, consistent with conditions of equality. Surely no constitution can make a claim to popular sovereignty, no matter the circumstances of its adoption, if the people reject it. A constitutional referendum might not be sufficient to make the claim to popular sovereignty, but the possibility of a 'no' vote certainly suggests that it is necessary.

My response to this conundrum is to identify more specifically what a referendum brings to a constitutional system, and to separate the idea of a constitution's acceptance, as a sociological or empirical matter, from the authority that flows from substantive conditions of equal moral autonomy. I argue there is a conceptual distinction between a constitution's claims to popular sovereignty and to legitimacy, between its authorship and its acceptance, which revolves around the fact that a multi-throated people will inevitably disagree about what details a constitution should include in much the same way that they will disagree about whether primary laws of conduct are right or wrong.[72]

Where the people governed by a legal system accept that the state is justified in taking steps to ensure that everyone complies with the law, including those people who hold a reasonably defensible view that some of these laws are simply wrong, the state can be said to enjoy a measure of de facto or sociological legitimacy.[73] People may complain that a specific law is morally bad, wrongheaded, ill-advised, misguided and so on, without those complaints necessarily calling into question the legitimacy or 'respect-worthiness' of the broader legal system in which those laws are situated.[74] Some people will

[72] Jeremy Waldron, *Law and Disagreement* (n 64), at 7, 105–106, 112–13, 152–58. See also Waldron, 'Moral Truth and Judicial Review' (1998) 43 *American Journal of Jurisprudence* 75, at 77–79 and *Law and Disagreement*, at 176–80.

[73] Frank I Michelman, 'Is the Constitution a Contract for Legitimacy?' (2003) 8 *Review of Constitutional Studies* 101, at 103; and Richard Fallon, 'Legitimacy and the Constitution' (2005) 118 *Harvard Law Review* 1787, at 1795–1801, distinguishing between legal, sociological, and moral legitimacy.

[74] Michelman, id, at 105–106.

consider some laws good that others consider bad, but until a law turns out to fall foul of the constitutional rules that determine the validity of primary rules, it requires obedience. One of the ways of assessing the respect-worthiness of a legal system as a whole, is to look to the constitution that sets out the secondary rules from which all other rules derive their force as law.[75]

On what basis can a constitution claim legitimacy, then? Where does its respect-worthiness come from? Even where the people bound by a constitution agree that it is respect-worthy, they will continue to disagree about what it actually means. In the United States, debates persist as to whether same-sex couples should be allowed to marry even though the US Constitution extends the equal protection of the laws to all, and whether the criminal justice system should allow sentences of death even though the Constitution prohibits cruel and unusual punishment. And yet, there can be no doubt that the US Constitution and dozens of others all around the world are legitimate and are workable in fact, despite the persistence of these disagreements about their content.

How does a constitution get to a position of legitimacy and workability despite these deep and irresolvable disagreements about its content? Post-hoc acceptance of the terms of the constitution by referendum is one possibility. A people may choose to adopt a constitution as binding on them even though people continue to disagree with one another as to what the constitution actually says. Another route to legitimacy, however, is a claim to popular sovereignty, made meaningful by a people having been treated as morally autonomous equals and having had an opportunity to participate in or be represented in the constitution-making process.

Popular sovereignty and referendum thus offer two quite distinct routes to constitutional legitimacy, but this does not establish any necessary connection between popular sovereignty and referendum. The failure of a constitution to win approval from the voting public at referendum means only that it cannot claim the legitimacy of social acceptance, but there is nothing in that failure that undermines an independent claim to the authority of the people. There is no contradiction in a constitution whose author makes a reasonable claim to represent the people at the moment of its drafting but which the people, being a multi-throated and internally inharmonious thing, nevertheless chooses not to endorse when put to referendum. To make a facile analogy, I am the author of this chapter and I was the author of a much different first draft. Having returned to the first draft after some time I found it unsatisfying and revised

[75] Michelman, id, at 107–109; Gardbaum, 'Revolutionary Constitutionalism' (n 2), at 189–92.

it into its current form. While I remain the author of the first version of this chapter, I nevertheless chose, on reflection, not to approves its publication.

The possibility of authorial revision is entirely consistent with the model of popular sovereignty I present here: the disagreement, pluralism, and diversity made visible in an unsuccessful constitutional referendum presupposes a commitment to and celebration of the moral autonomy and political equality from which disagreement springs in the first place. And no meaningful claim to representing the people as author of the constitution can be made without recognising the moral autonomy and political equality of each of the people. Indeed, the Lockean understanding of popular sovereignty, which reserves the right of revolution to the people, assumes that the people may approve of or accept a constitution at one moment, and yet change their minds and reject that same constitution at some later time.

Put at its simplest, my position is that popular sovereignty concerns the authorship of a constitution, while the outcome of a referendum goes to its acceptability or sociological legitimacy. The challenges involved in having the people themselves draft the new constitution mean that if those charged with drafting the constitution are to adequately represent the people as authors of the constitution, the process must be built on guarantees that everyone has just as much of an opportunity to contribute to the text of the constitution as anyone else. Approval of the text at referendum makes the claim to legitimacy a little easier. But the important point remains that the substantive constraints that popular sovereignty imposes make possible a meaningful claim to the people's authorship of a constitution, regardless of whether or not the people subsequently accept the constitution at referendum. The cogency of a constitution's claim to popular sovereignty, to growing directly out of the people's constituent power, is independent of its sociological legitimacy.

V. Conclusion: the danger of 'yes'

The distinction between authorship and acceptance discloses another permutation of constitutional transition. We need not look very far around the world to find constitutional transitions that fail to uphold the principles of moral autonomy and political equality that I argue here are necessary and sufficient for a meaningful claim to popular sovereignty. Some of these constitutional systems nevertheless claim legitimacy from their approval at referendum: the system established under Egypt's 2014 Constitution is an example,[76] while Erdogan's

[76] For the illiberal character of Egypt's legal system, see, e.g., Zaid al Ali, 'Egypt's Third Constitution in Three Years: A Critical Analysis' in Bernard Rougier and Stéphane Lacroix (eds), *Egypt's Revolutions: Politics, Religion and Social Movements* (Houndmills: Palgrave MacMillan, 2016) 123.

Turkey is another.[77] The legitimacy that flows from a 'yes' vote provides a veneer under which an otherwise illiberal constitutional system operates.

In societies already characterised by permanent minorities or historically disenfranchised groups, the likelihood that referendum will solidify the advantages of the politically privileged or socially better-off is something of a self-fulfilling prophecy. A distribution of socio-political goods (civil and political rights, access to the mass media, or social capital) that is already skewed towards certain groups makes it more likely that those groups' views will prevail in a referendum, whether or not they constitute a numerical majority. 'The use of a referendum in this type of situation is particularly dangerous', Stephen Tierney warns,

> because this clear act of hegemony is presented as being democratic, offering a spurious constitutional legitimacy for political power play. The referendum is paraded as a self-evidently democratic device. It asks 'the people' to speak, and each person can do so with an equal say. But this simplistic notion of fairness is based upon … 'undifferentiated equality'. Voters as individuals are decontextualised from their discrete communal settings. Their votes are then aggregated across communities and the total is taken to be the voice of one demos.[78]

A constitution clothed in the legitimacy of a positive referendum result has a seductive appeal to proponents of democracy.[79] But there is a great danger in equating popular sovereignty with referendum results. It is undeniable that a constitution acclaimed by a majority of the people bears a certain legitimacy because of the 'yes' vote; but it is far from clear that this legitimacy amounts to popular sovereignty.

The argument I have sought to make here is twofold. In the first place, I reject the claim that a constitutional referendum is sufficient to make a constitution's claim to popular sovereignty meaningful. A substantive commitment to principles of moral autonomy and political equality must precede any reliance on

[77] The rules for constitutional amendment in Turkey allow the President to put constitutional amendments to a referendum if proposals for amendment do not win sufficient support in the legislature (Constitution of the Republic of Turkey, 1982, article 175). President Recep Erdogan's government proposed constitutional amendments in 2017 to centralise power in the office of the president, which failed to win the necessary majorities in the legislature but were subsequently approved at referendum.

[78] Tierney, *Constitutional Referendums* (n 1), at 71. The quote comes from Avigail Eisenberg, 'The Medium is the Message: How Referenda Lead Us to Understand Equality for Minorities' in Mendelsohn and Parkin (eds), *Referendum Democracy* (n 3), at 149.

[79] Bellamy, *Political Constitutionalism* (n 3), at 132.

referendum as a marker of popular sovereignty. Second, I have sought to dispel the idea that a constitutional referendum is necessary to the claim to popular sovereignty by drawing a distinction between authorship as a matter of popular sovereignty, and acceptance as a matter of sociological legitimacy.

Accordingly, we should be wary of the false positives that constitutional referendums may produce. In a world where new democratic governments are increasingly susceptible to backsliding into illiberal democracy, competitive authoritarianism, or abusive constitutionalism, the referendum is just one more device by which constitution-makers can claim the legitimacy of popular sovereignty even as they undermine the conditions that popular sovereignty implies.

PART II
WHO ARE THE PEOPLE?

4

Referendums in Federal States

Territorial Pluralism and the Challenge of Direct Democracy

Stephen Tierney

I. Introduction

This chapter addresses the use of referendums within federal systems. The aim of the chapter is to bring together two developing areas of constitutional theory: that focused upon the recent proliferation in the use of direct democracy as a mechanism of constitutional change on the one hand, and federal theory which is a surprisingly neglected area of constitutional thinking on the other.

The main question that referendum democracy poses for constitutional theory is: how should change be managed within a constitutional system? There is already a long-standing debate about the ideal relationship between change and stability within constitutional systems: the extent to which institutions and constitutional values or principles should be embedded versus the democratic imperative of leaving political decision-making open to political debate. This leads to a second debate about *how* constitutional change, when it is permissible, should be made and how to achieve the optimal balance between the role of representatives on the one hand and the self-determining power of a politically active citizenry on the other. In practice constitutions tend to approach the first issue in a way that encompasses also the second. Constitutional systems which entrench amendment processes generally leave these in the hands of representative institutions, most obviously parliaments, with popular input filtered through elected officials. The referendum as a tool of constitutional change is therefore a radical shift from the norm. It involves the people directly, giving effect in practice to popular self-determination. It is no surprise that few constitutions entrench the referendum as a routine tool of constitutional change, but some do and the trend seems to be in this direction.

Stephen Tierney, *Referendums in Federal States* In: *The Limits and Legitimacy of Referendums*. Edited by: Richard Albert and Richard Stacey, Oxford University Press. © Stephen Tierney 2022. DOI: 10.1093/oso/9780198867647.003.0005

As the referendum proliferates within constitutional politics it is timely to take stock of its usage.

The issue of constitutional change is also a useful prism through which to examine federalism as a discrete form of government. Despite several decades in which constitutional theory has undertaken broad and searching reappraisals of many areas of constitutional practice,[1] federalism has been surprisingly neglected. In particular, it has tended not to be treated as a distinctive site of constitutional practice with such a fundamentally different foundational purpose from unitary constitutionalism that it merits its own conceptualisation as a particular genus of constitutional rule. There is not scope in this chapter to develop such a systematic reappraisal of federalism, but focusing only upon the issue of constitutional change will serve to indicate the need for such a reconsideration.

The chapter begins by summarising the parallel rise of federalism as a template for government and of the use of the referendum within constitutional practice, in particular for the making of fundamental constitutional decisions (Section II). It is not suggested that constitutional turns towards both federalism and direct democracy are in any way connected, but it is notable that a number of significant recent referendums have taken place at sub-state level, and that the proliferation of federalism does of course provide an increased number of territorial sites within which referendums might be organised. This background leads to the core case study of the chapter: the application of the referendum to constitutional change in federal systems which I address by way of several steps. First, I consider criticisms of referendums in general by those who question their compatibility with constitutionalism. Here we focus upon the ways in which the referendum challenges how we think about the legitimacy of change in constitutional settings (Section III).

I then turn to the developing discipline of constitutional theory and how we might apply this to reassess the growth of federalism both as a system of government and as a constitutional idea. This will in turn allow us better to understand the theoretical issues surrounding constitutional change as they

[1] J Tully, *Strange Multiplicity: Constitutionalism in the Age of Diversity* (Cambridge: Cambridge University Press, 1995); Ran Hirschl, *Towards Juristocracy The Origins and Consequences of the New Constitutionalism* (Cambridge, Mass.: Harvard University Press, 2004); Sujit Choudhry (ed.), The Migration of Constitutional Ideas (Cambridge: Cambridge University Press, 2006); Martin Loughlin and Neil Walker (eds.), *The Paradox of Constitutionalism* (Oxford: Oxford University Press, 2007); J Tully, *Public Philosophy in a New Key: Volume I: Democracy and Civic Freedom* (Cambridge: Cambridge University Press, 2008); Michel Rosenfeld, *The Identity of the Constitutional Subject: Selfhood, Citizenship, Culture and Community* (Routledge, 2010); David Dyzenhaus and Malcolm Thorburn (eds.), *Philosophical Foundations of Constitutional Law* (Oxford: Oxford University Press, 2016); Alison Young, *Democratic Dialogue and the Constitution* (Oxford: Oxford University Press, 2017).

pertain specifically to the federal context (Section IV). In Section V I explore how the dramatic intervention of 'the people' in constitutional change upsets general understandings of the balance between change and stability in mainstream constitutional theory. From here we can then confront how direct democracy poses a particular test for federal constitutional theory which is itself predicated upon a conceptual pluralisation of 'the people' for constitutional purposes. Federal constitutional systems often come with deep entrenchment, whereby formal constitutional change, dependent upon multiple majorities, can be very difficult to bring about: the USA, Australia and Canada are obvious examples. In such a setting the referendum, which supplants representative democracy by way of a majoritarian appeal to 'the people', can appear particularly incongruous. The Australian constitution has managed to accommodate the referendum as part of its amendment process, as I discuss. Canada has held very few national referendums and the United States none at all. Finally, it is argued that the tensions which are exposed in the relationship between federalism and the referendum serve as a dramatic exemplar of how, more generally, the singular nature of federalism as a highly particular form of constitutional ordering has not been given the theoretical attention it requires.

II. Federalism and referendums: two developing fields of constitutional practice

The spread of federalism as a form of government is one of the most significant constitutional developments of the past 70 years. Since 1945 it has been estimated that approximately one-third of states have adopted or are moving towards a federal constitutional system.[2] Many of the most vivid developments have occurred recently, with federalism being adapted to accommodate complex territorial pluralism in many of the world's most troubled locations, such as Bosnia-Herzegovina and Iraq. The proliferation of direct democracy has been more recent but nonetheless even more dramatic. Before turning to recent trends it should of course be noted that the referendum has been a prominent feature of certain federal states for over a century. In both Switzerland and Australia direct democracy is part of the fabric of constitutional change.[3]

[2] Michael Burgess calls this the 'federal tendency.' Michael Burgess, *In Search of the Federal Spirit: New Theoretical and Empirical Perspectives in Comparative Federalism* (Oxford: Oxford University Press, 2012), 2.

[3] Federal Constitution of the Swiss Confederation, 18 April 1999 Title 4, Chapter 2; Commonwealth of Australia Constitution Act 1901, s.128.

Table 4.1 Categories of constitutional referendum

4 types of referendum in the 'new wave'	Examples
Founding of new states	New states emerging from the former USSR and SFRY Also: Eritrea (1993), East Timor (1999), Montenegro (2006), South Sudan (2011). Scotland (unsuccessful) 2014. Catalonia—ongoing pressure
Creation and amendment of new constitutions	Again former republics of the USSR and SFRY Iraq—ratification of the Constitution of 2005 Egypt—constitutional reforms 2011
Sub-state autonomy	Spain referendums: e.g. Basque Country 1979, Catalonia 1979, Galicia 1980 United Kingdom referendums: Scotland 1997, Wales 1997 and 2011, Northern Ireland 1998
European Union: treaty-making processes in respect of both integration and accession; and exit	2004: Malta, Slovenia, Hungary, Lithuania, Slovakia, Poland, Czech Republic, Estonia, Latvia 2012: Croatia 2016: UK 'Brexit' decision

The USA has also seen the referendum become an increasing part of state—although not national—politics, while in Canada it has come to play a prominent role in the national machinations over the status of Quebec,[4] and subsequently in relation to provincial electoral systems in British Columbia and Ontario.[5]

A significant turn towards the use of referendums in constitutional decision-making came after 1989. The referendum had been attractive, particularly to sub-state nationalists and colonised peoples long before this,[6] but it is in the past three decades that we see a significant expansion in the use of referendums in four main areas of constitutional development (Table 4.1). Across the board the interplay between the referendum and federalism is evident in this process of proliferation. First, referendums have been used in the founding of new states. A major factor in the early '90s was the collapse of the federal USSR and Yugoslavia which each dissolved in the face of popular revolt expressed

[4] Robert A Young, *The Struggle for Quebec: From Referendum to Referendum?* (McGill-Queen's University Press: Montreal/Kingston, 1999)

[5] A Blais, R K Carty and P Fournier, 'Do Citizens Assemblies Make Reasoned Choices' in M E Warren and H Pearse (eds.), *Designing Deliberative Democracy: The British Columbia Citizens' Assembly* (Cambridge: Cambridge University Press, 2008)

[6] J Mattern, *The Employment of the Plebiscite in the Determination of Sovereignty* (Baltimore: John Hopkins Press, 1920).

through direct democracy. The referendum has since become the default mechanism leading to the emergence of most new states, for example Eritrea (1993), East Timor (1999), Montenegro (2006) and South Sudan (2011), each of which emerged from troubled and ultimately unsuccessful attempts to build federal structures. In each case the referendum was held specifically in the territory of the nascent state rather than the whole territory of the existing state. The referendum in each case was also about the principle of statehood itself rather than the system of government that would be constituted within the new state. Secondly, and relatedly, the referendum helped bring about devolved models of government, putting formerly unitary states such as Spain and the United Kingdom on a decentralising trajectory, in the direction of federalism itself.[7] Ironically, the referendum has also become the focus of separatist nationalism in Scotland, where an independence referendum was held in 2014, and in Catalonia where on 1 October 2017 nationalists staged a referendum on independence. This was declared unconstitutional by the Constitutional Court of Spain before it took place and was afterwards declared void. These situations give an indication of the potentially incendiary nature of the referendum, and of how difficult it is to contain it within a constitutional plan or apparently self-contained federal trajectory.

Thirdly, referendums were once very rarely used in the creation or amendment of constitutions, but throughout Central and Eastern Europe and more recently in Iraq and Egypt we see the referendum emerge both in the founding of new constitutions and within the text of these constitutions as part of future amendment procedures. It is notable that a number of these constitutions ratified by referendum, such as that of Iraq, have sought to embed a federal form of government. But it is equally noticeable that many have not and that the referendum is also a key device in unitary or monist nation-building processes: a popular reassertion of the identity of a distinctive demos, particularly where, as in Central and Eastern Europe, territories emerged from a period of undemocratic government or foreign influence. Again this brings to the fore the symbolic but also homogenising potential of the referendum, which will be a key consideration as we turn to federal constitutionalism.

Fourthly, referendums have played a very significant role in the recent history of the European Union (which is in the view of many an essentially

[7] In Spain a national referendum was held in 1978 to ratify the new constitution. The draft constitution included provision for devolution. By contrast, devolution referendums in the United Kingdom in 1979 and 1997 were held only within the Scotland and Wales (another was held in 1998 in Northern Ireland). See M Keating, *Nations Against the State—The New Politics of Nationalism in Quebec, Catalonia and Scotland* (London: Palgrave Macmillan, 2nd edn 2001).

federalising polity) in three ways: the accession of new states,[8] the ratification of new treaties[9] and the exit of a Member State itself, set in motion by the 'Brexit' referendum in the United Kingdom in June 2016.

Across all of these sites, the rise of referendum democracy brings its own set of challenges for constitutional theory. In the next two sections I will address respectively the democratic problems associated with referendums, particularly the problem of majoritarianism which is most pertinent to the federal context, and the neglect of federalism as a discrete area of enquiry by constitutional theory. I will in due course situate the use of the referendum in federal context, taking account of how the democratic challenges referendums pose lead to particular issues for the constitutional theory of federal democracy.

III. Referendums and the democratic paradox

One simple question seems to encapsulate the very premise of this volume: are referendums democratic? This very question can appear paradoxical. For some it is an intuitive assumption that referendums represent an ideal model of democracy. Voters are called upon to speak as one unified people, deciding on an issue directly without the mediation of politicians. What could be more democratic? The referendum gives a directly determining voice to the demos in a way that captures neatly both the people's popular sovereignty and the political equality of all citizens. The promise of government *by* the people is seemingly fulfilled. As one advocate of referendum democracy (Vernon Bogdanor) once stated, 'arguments against the referendum are also arguments against democracy.'[10]

But in fact among many constitutionalists and political historians, referendums have a bad name. In addressing the history of referendum practice it is the very mobilisation of direct popular rule that is the problem since it unleashes dangers which constitutions are specifically designed to prevent. If, as we discuss below, the core purpose of modern constitutionalism is the regulation and management of political power, domesticating it through the concept of constitutional authority, the referendum may in fact be a threat: it has the

[8] Of the first 15 countries to join the EU only Ireland and Denmark held referendums to ratify the decision. Of the 10 accession countries in 2004 only Cyprus did not. This trend continued in January 2012 with Croatians voting in a referendum for accession in 2013.

[9] Particularly in Denmark and Ireland which guarantee constitutionally the use of referendums in this context.

[10] V Bogdanor, *The People and the Party System* (Cambridge: Cambridge University Press, 1981), 93.

potential to release raw political power as a potential trump card in relation to the otherwise careful conditioning of that power by the constitution.

There are three main objections that inform the scepticism behind this position: that referendums lend themselves by definition to elite control and hence manipulation by the organisers of the referendum (the elite control syndrome); that there is an in-built tendency of the referendum process merely to aggregate pre-formed opinions rather than to foster meaningful deliberation (the deliberation deficit); and that referendums consolidate and even reify simple majoritarian decision-making at the expense of minority and individual interests (the majoritarian danger).[11] These objections are highly salient but it is my contention that the first two are largely problems of practice which can be overcome by careful referendum design and adequate regulation.[12]

The majoritarian danger is more problematic and it is also the issue that has the greatest potential to bring the referendum into direct conflict with constitutionalism, federal or otherwise. Unlike the other two criticisms, the issue of majoritarianism is one that unavoidably leads to competing positions based upon ideology. Those who oppose the use of referendums in constitutional change will often cast it as a threat to the carefully-crafted counter-majoritarian provisions of the constitution. Superimposed upon this can be a form of moral constructivism which considers the constitution itself to be an instrumental vehicle for the protection of substantive political values. This approach to constitutionalism is of course commonly associated with liberalism, which views the constitution in large measure as an instrumental vehicle designed to insulate rights, in particular individual rights, from the risk that majorities will simply vote to harm minorities or individuals. The referendum can be seen as a particular threat because, by definition, it operates by way of majority decision-making. It can therefore act to homogenise the electorate in a way that ignores a plurality of views. It can make specious claims to speak as the voice of 'the people', asserting a legitimacy founded upon constituent power, which purports to rival or even transcend the validity of the constitution itself.

Those who, on the other hand, advocate or at least defend the use of the referendum for constitutional change, tend to bring to the debate a different ideological disposition. It is too simplistic to counterpoise 'liberal' and 'civic republican' constitutionalism in a Manichean way.[13] But in order to bring out a difference in disposition over the issue of direct democracy, it is useful to draw

[11] S Tierney, 'Constitutional Referendums: A Theoretical Enquiry' (2009) 72 *Modern Law Review* 360.
[12] S Tierney, 'Constitutional Referendums' (n 11).
[13] A Tomkins, 'What's Left of the Political Constitution?' (2013) 14(12) *German Law Journal* 2275–2292.

a fairly quick caricature that does identify some underpinning differences between these approaches. A 'civic republican' attitude to constitutionalism tends to be sceptical of entrenching externally constructed moral values. Republican approaches consider it better if political values are left open to the public sphere and to political contestation. Constitutionalism is important to protect the institutions of the constitutional system, but decision-making around political ideals should be made through the cut and thrust of political debate. Building upon this, it is accepted that majoritarian decision-making is an inevitable fact of constitutional life and is usually the fairest way to reach decisions. Furthermore, a civic republican perspective tends to emphasise the good of an active, engaged demos, which has the democratic right to make important constitutional decisions and which should be assisted to do so by the polity. The citizen has the opportunity to grow as a politically knowledgeable and engaged actor through the responsibility of active engagement, particularly in fundamental decisions, including decisions about constitutional change.

There is of course no automatic mapping of a general republican outlook onto a specific conclusion that referendums are a good mechanism with which to engage the public in making decisions about constitutional change: the elite control syndrome and, in particular, the deliberation deficit would first have to be addressed by careful referendum design. But there are two features specific to important constitutional decision-making which, from a civic republican perspective, make direct democracy potentially attractive. The first concerns the significance of the issues at stake. When matters involving the very framing or re-framing of a democratic system of government, whether in whole or in part, are in play, the direct engagement of the people either supplementing, or indeed in place of, representative institutions may be considered by civic republicans to be a good way to ratify and hence fully legitimise the process. This argument builds upon work within the republican revival by scholars such as Bruce Ackerman who argue that constitutional politics is distinct from ordinary politics and that in relation to the former there is a particularly compelling case for citizen engagement.[14] That is not to say a referendum follows automatically from this point but it is an obvious way of achieving such ratification. The second argument is that in the making of such decisions, particularly where they are truly constitutive of a new or transforming legal order, a constitution can also be 'self-constituting' for the people involved, embodying

[14] Bruce Ackerman, *We the People: Foundations* (Cambridge, Mass.: Harvard University Press, 1991). See also more recent publications: Gary Jeffrey Jacobsohn and Yaniv Roznai, *Constitutional Revolution* (New Haven: Yale University Press, 2020); Richard Albert (ed.), *Revolutionary Constitutionalism: Law, Legitimacy, Power* (Oxford: Hart Publishing, 2020).

their political selfhood. In this sense, as well as serving the functional purpose of framing a system of government, by being 'popular' in orientation, the constitution can also take on a symbolic representational role, encapsulating the very identity of the people, while also embodying emblematically its collective settled will.[15] In turn, individuals come reflexively to identify with one another through their shared commitment to this constitution. Again the referendum is by no means an automatic building block with which to help construct this dimension of the constitution, but when its totemic nation-building potential comes to be understood it is no surprise that it is seen as one way by which significant constitutional decisions ought to be reached.

In Section V we will address how these features of the referendum in constitutional democracy impact upon federalism in a highly particular way, raising specific issues for the majoritarian danger. Before doing so it is necessary to consider how federalism has been neglected by constitutional theory and, in doing so, to begin to draw out its specific character as a constitutional idea.

IV. Constitutional theory and the neglect of federalism

Constitutional theory embodies a discrete discipline of constitutional inquiry which is concerned with analysing and evaluating a particular area of social activity: the framing, founding, practice and changing of constitutions, operational through internationally comparable institutions and rules.[16] While related to political theory and political science, constitutional theory offers a distinctive approach with which to understand the specific nature of constitutional practice and how that practice establishes a specific form of path dependency. Constitutional theory is defined by the 'functional normativity' inherent in its methodology.[17] The constitutional scholar assesses the specific constitutional (as opposed to political) purposes of the constitution as the facilitator of governmental practice, and it is these purposes which provide constitutionalism with a normative essence. In this way constitutional theory seeks to explain the anatomy of 'good' or 'prudential' government.[18] This is by

[15] Rosenfeld discusses how modernist constitutionalism has played the role of constructing a form of collective self that builds upon but is, in its unitary and unifying functions, also different from diverse pre-constitutional cultural and ethnic attachments. Rosenfeld 2010 (n 1).

[16] Tierney, 'Constitutional Referendums' (n 11) 2–4.

[17] Peter Oliver and Stephen Tierney, 'Book Review/Response, Constitutional Referendums: The Theory and Practice of Republican Deliberation', *Int'l J. Const. L. Blog*, 25 February 2014, available at: <http://www.iconnectblog.com/2014/02/book-reviewresponse-stephen-tierney-and-peter-oliver> accessed on January 28, 2022.

[18] Martin Loughlin, *The Idea of Public Law* (Oxford: Oxford University Press, 2003).

definition a normative turn but it is a normativity grounded in the *functions* of constitutional government; a form of constitutional ethics rather than political morality, which elicits principles immanent within lived constitutional reality that can, for that very reason, all the better guide the further instantiation of effective constitutional practice.

Significant progress has been made by contemporary constitutional theory in illustrating how constitutionalism takes on its own dynamics, different from, and in many ways shaping, the political conditions and purposes of any polity.[19] There are essentially five elements in the anatomy of contemporary constitutional analysis which have been the focus of extensive analysis and debate: constitutional foundations, the inherent purpose of constitutionalism, the subjects of the constitution, its design, and the dynamics of constitutional change through formal amendment or gradual development.

However, despite the growth in constitutional theory and the advances it has made in assessing constitutional practice in general, it has tended to operate on the basis of one implicit code, a conception of the polity in unitary or monist terms which in turn implies that all democratic constitutions serve essentially the same set of constitutional purposes for one constitutional people. As a result, unitary or monist constitutionalism which presupposes a singular relationship between one unitary polity and one undifferentiated body of citizens, has become the default canvas from which constitutional theory construes generalisable analysis.[20]

It may seem odd to suggest that federalism is under-explored. There has been, since the Second World War, a renewed focus upon federalism across the social sciences. But most of this work has been conducted by empirical political scientists and political sociologists, addressing either particular federations or engaging in broader comparative study. Within the literature there is a strong emphasis upon the behavioural underpinnings of federal systems,[21] empirical institutional analysis,[22] attempts (largely of a lexical nature) to arrive at definitions of terms such as federal, federation and federal state,[23] analysis of

[19] Martin Loughlin, 'Constitutional Theory: A 25th Anniversary Essay' (2005) 25 *Oxford Journal of Legal Studies* 183.

[20] J Tully, 'Federations, Communities and their Transformations: An Essay in Revision' in André Lecours and Geneviève Nootens (eds.), *Dominant Nationalism, Dominant Ethnicity: Identity, Federalism and Democracy* (Brussels: Peter Lang, 2009), 195–212.

[21] William S Livingston, *Federalism and Constitutional Change* (Oxford: Clarendon Press, 1956).

[22] This emerged as part of broader, heavily empirical turn in political science in the 1960s. William Riker offered an early, seminal study that applied rational choice theory in a dense experimental and observational account of federalism. William Riker, *Federalism: Origin, Operation, Significance* (Boston: Little, Brown, 1964). For a modern revival of this tradition see Jan Erk, *Explaining Federalism* (London: Routledge, 2010).

[23] K C Wheare, *Federal Government* (New York: Oxford University Press, 1947). Wheare was a pioneer in the legal analysis of federalism. His work brought to federalism what Burgess calls a 'somewhat

the political and constitutional structures of particular states[24] (often in comparative relief[25]) and assessments of how federal relations play out in practice through party politics,[26] political attitudes and identities.[27]

Much of this work has broadened our understanding of federalism and, in particular, the extent to which it varies in practice. But as we map this scholarship and, more importantly, reflect upon federalism's proliferation as a form of government, it remains something of a surprise that federalism has not been the subject of more widespread theoretical analysis by political and, especially, constitutional theorists, particularly in light of the revival of constitutional theory in relation to so many areas of constitutional practice. The lack of comprehensive theoretical interventions is often noted by political scientists themselves. Burgess for example recently argued that as yet there is 'no fully fledged theory of federalism.'[28] Kyle Scott in another book contends that federal theory lacks a 'normative theory that is prior to policy making and implementation.'[29] Indeed he goes so far as to say 'there is no theory of federalism.'[30] When we look to the canon of political theory, federalism has rarely featured except in discussions about the constitutional design of a particular state.[31] And this omission

narrow legalistic focus that dwelled largely in the language of constitutional law.' Burgess, *In Search of the Federal Spirit*, 1. A modern development of this definitional approach can be seen in R Watts, *Comparing Federal Systems* (Montreal/Kingston: McGill-Queens University Press, 2nd edn 1999).

[24] E.g. I Morgan, P Davies (eds.), *The Federal Nation: Perspectives on American Federalism* (USA: Palgrave MacMillan, 2008); M Umbach (ed.), *German Federalism: Past, Present and Future* (London: Palgrave MacMillan, 2002); A-G Gagnon (ed.), *Contemporary Canadian Federalism* (Toronto: University of Toronto Press, 2009); N Aroney, *The Constitution of a Federal Commonwealth: The Making and Meaning of the Australian Constitution* (Cambridge: Cambridge University Press, 2007).

[25] R Watts, *Comparing Federal Systems* (Montreal/Kingston: McGill-Queens University Press, 2nd edn 1999); Michael Burgess and Alain-G Gagnon (eds.), *Comparative Federalism and Federation: Competing Traditions and Future Directions* (Hemel Hempstead, UK: Harvester Wheatsheaf, 1993); Michael Burgess, *Comparative Federalism: Theory and Practice* (London: Routledge, 2006); T O Hueglin and A Fenna, *Comparative Federalism: a Systematic Enquiry* (Peterborough, Ont.: Broadview Press, 2006).

[26] B Truman, 'Federalism and the Party System', in Aaron B Wildavsky (ed.), *American Federalism in Perspective* (Boston: Little, Brown, 1962), 81–109; Riker 1964 and Michael Burgess, *Comparative Federalism: Theory and Practice* (Abingdon: Routledge, 2006), 150

[27] Livingston, *Federalism and Constitutional Change* (n 21);Carl J Friedrich, *Trends of Federalism in Theory and Practice* (London: Frederick A. Praeger Publishers, 1968).

[28] He continued: 'At best there is partial theory based upon rigorous conceptional analysis and the pursuit of terminological precision. At worst there is crass empiricism rooted in the failure to develop concepts and define the key terms.' Burgess, *Comparative Federalism: Theory and Practice*, 1.

[29] Kyle Scott, *Federalism: A Normative Theory and its Practical Relevance* (New York: Continuum, 2011), preface vii.

[30] Scott, *Federalism: A Normative Theory and its Practical Relevance*, 1. See also Alfred Stepan, 'Federalism and Democracy: Beyond the U.S. Model' in D Karmis, and W Norman (eds.), *Theories of Federalism* (New York: Palgrave-Macmillan Publishing, 2005), 256 and T O Hueglin and A Fenna, *Comparative Federalism: a Systematic Enquiry* (Peterborough, Ont.: Broadview Press, 2006), 113.

[31] Clinton Rossiter (ed.), *The Federalist Papers* (New York: New American Library, 1961), being the obvious exception.

has not been corrected in the past few decades despite federalism becoming such a significant feature of constitutional practice.[32] For example, federalism is rarely if ever discussed in the work of contemporary political philosophers as a factor which might impact upon their notions of justice. This is so even for scholars such as John Rawls or Jürgen Habermas who have lived and worked within federal states.

This neglect has subsisted despite the erstwhile revival in constitutional theory more broadly. The default approach to constitutional theory has served to overlook the fact that federalism, as a model of government, is fundamentally different from the monist or unitary default model of constitution against which contemporary constitutional theory operates.

My contention is that, as constitutionalists, we need to understand federalism in the first instance as an *idea*: a structural concept underpinning a particular form of government. The functional normativity of constitutionalism leads us to understand this federal idea as one which develops over time through its instantiation in practice, and which is sufficiently capacious to accommodate a range of constitutional forms.

Federalism therefore requires to be re-examined by way of a detailed analysis of the five elements of contemporary constitutional theory mentioned above: foundations, purposes, subjects, design, and dynamics. The key characteristic of constitutionalism, and in turn the key purpose of constitutional government, is the regulation and management of political power. Constitutional theory understands this purpose of regulation and management against the default framework. In this way the relationship between citizen and government is conceived in unitary terms, and therefore ancillary purposes and the institutional management of political power are also conceived in a universalistic way in relation to this template. A federal constitution differs and it does so radically. Like all forms of constitutionalism, federal constitutionalism is geared towards the regulation and management of political power, but in a federal constitution this is primarily geared towards a specific core, territorially oriented purpose. The essential purpose of a federal constitution is to give constitutional recognition to a plurality of territories, to entrench this recognition and to ascribe to the governments of those territories discrete and significant constitutional authority. It is upon this basis that we can summarise the core purpose of federalism as being the constitutional accommodation of territorial pluralism.

[32] E.g. Deiter Grimm, *Constitutionalism Past, Present, and Future* (Oxford: OUP, 2016).

It is therefore necessary that contemporary constitutional thought should broaden its horizons to appreciate fully how federalism introduces deep diversity into constitutional practice and to accept that default theorising can serve to superimpose a general universality upon constitutional theory that fails to reflect a plurality of constitutional realities. Federalism in fact marks a radical fork in the road, offering a fundamentally different register through which to understand the nature of constitutional authority, from where this authority derives and who constitute its fundamental subjects. This is a major lacuna in constitutional theory and not one that can be unpacked here. One dramatic dimension of this gap in theory, however, is the dynamics of change within federal systems to which we now turn in the context of direct democracy.

V. The dynamics of constitutional change in federal systems

From the five constitutive elements of modern constitutionalism we will concentrate upon dynamics. Constitutional change has been a focal-point of recent constitutional theory with studies in how change is effected through constitutional amendment;[33] the transformation of constitutions over time without, or in addition to, formal amendments;[34] the role of the courts in developing constitutional interpretation;[35] and the growing trend, either by way of formal entrenchment or judicial protection, towards the creation of 'unamendable' constitutional provisions.[36]

If the core constitutional purpose of federalism is the constitutional accommodation of territorial pluralism, what does this in turn tell us about how constitutional change ought to be managed? There are two dimensions to this. The first in relation to constitutional amendment and the second concerned with constitutional interpretation. I will limit discussion here to the former. There has been little attention given within constitutional theory to the specific implications of federalism for how formal processes of constitutional change ought to be structured. There are many important issues that lie under-explored in relation to both entrenchment and subsequently to constitutional change in

[33] Richard Albert, 'Amending Constitutional Amendment Rules' (2015) 13 *International Journal of Constitutional Law* 655–685.

[34] Ackerman (n 14).

[35] Hirschl (n 1).

[36] S Suteu, *Eternity Clauses in Democratic Constitutionalism* (Oxford: Oxford University Press, 2021);; Y Roznai, *Unconstitutional Constitutional Amendments: the Limits of Amendment Powers* (Oxford: Oxford University Press, 2017); Richard Albert and Bertil Emrah Oder (eds.), *An Unamendable Constitution? Unamendability in Constitutional Democracies* (Switzerland: Springer, 2018).

the federal context. As building blocks to a discussion of referendums within federal systems, let us address two: the general issue of how entrenchment fits with federal design, and whether particular aspects of design require special protection within federal constitutionalism.

Federal constitutions are certainly consistent with the modern trend of written constitutions, entrenched by way of particular and often complex amendment processes. There is even evidence to suggest that even when analysed within the broader category of constitutionalism in general, federal constitutions can be particularly difficult to change, entrenched as they are through especially demanding levels of counter- or super-majoritarian constraint. Older constitutional systems, each in their own way, have proven to be difficult to amend. The American requirement of amendment ratification by three-fourths of the states, the Australian system of a double majority (parliament and referendum) and Canada's complex model with a default of seven provinces representing over 50% of the population, and, for very significant changes the unanimous consent of the provinces, each have left constitutional reformers frequently frustrated. From the perspective of constitutional theory we need to ask what justifies this level of entrenchment?

In asking this we must return to the foundational purpose of federalism—the protection of territorial pluralism. We have noted in relation to the liberal versus civic republican constitutionalist debate that the liberal justification for constitutional entrenchment tends to focus upon individualism and the protection of individual rights. The arguments from legitimacy for this position tend to interweave with liberal contract theory and the conditional surrender of pre-constitutional prerogatives by free individual agents in some form of conceptually contrived state of nature or veil of ignorance. However, since a federal constitution is established through the foundational recognition of, and the giving of mutual commitments by, a plurality of territorially based political communities, the whole way in which constituent power is understood in federal context requires special treatment. Federalism indeed is established upon a conception of foundational legitimacy very different from that which is the focus of standard contract theory. There is not space to explore this here but it seems clear that in the creation of constitutional form the principled resistance to simple majoritarianism finds a different basis within federal thinking. In a federal context the focus of the majoritarian debate is not upon the potential endangerment of individual rights (although of course liberal political debates can and do elide with federal debates and federal constitutions can emerge also as liberal constitutions), but rather upon the protection of territorial prerogatives, in particular, autonomy on the one hand and shared rule on the other.

This leads to a second issue, namely what in institutional terms therefore becomes the focus of entrenchment in a federal system and how might this differ from the approach taken within the monist default model of constitutionalism? One key point is that federal constitutionalism is primarily institution-focused and is not an approach to constitutional embeddedness founded upon moral constructivism or externally derived values. A related issue is that federalism as a model of constitutional government is, despite its pactual nature and entrenched institutional arrangements, something of a contingent or uneasy constitutional settlement. It is often noted that federalism is, by definition, in a state of constitutional tension, with self-rule coexisting with what can be the contradictory concept, shared rule.[37] This has led a number of federal theorists to note that in fact avenues of open deliberation and political decision-making are essential in order constantly to defuse these tensions. This might suggest that a constitutional system that is flexible and easier to change may in fact be imperative for federal systems, possibly more so than for unitary systems.

Can we resolve this conundrum? The fact that federal constitutions are often very inflexible on the one hand, rubbing up against the structural need to keep them flexible on the other? It would seem that one possible answer lies in the fact that within a federal system it is only necessary to entrench the institutional fabric of the system. Good federal design should be able on the one hand to create the institutional apparatus for the coexistence of multiple territorial communities but at the same time leave space for this cohabitation to operate by way of open political cooperation or competition. The institutional structure of the state needs to be entrenched to make sense of the initial federal constitutional commitment, but policy choices thereafter should be open and negotiable across the polity, and in particular should, through principles such as subsidiarity, be left to the regional level where possible. The very fact that the polity has been constituted on the basis of plural communities represented by plural governments suggests that behind this decision, at least in some cases, is a need to recognise cultural and value-based difference.[38] In other words, the sort of value-based entrenchment we find in monist constitutionalism is arguably less suited to and less workable in a federal constitution. Certainly patterns in federal constitutional practice indicate that the territorial character is particularly fundamental in federal systems in terms of entrenchment and procedures for amendment. We see this for example in the 10th amendment to the US

[37] Daniel J Elazar, *Exploring Federalism* (Alabama: University of Alabama Press, 1987), 12.

[38] There is an argument flowing from this that insofar as rights regimes may be entrenched, decisions as to which values to embed should be negotiated in reference to the multiple political communities of the state.

Constitution which reserves residual powers 'to the States respectively, or to the people', or in the fact that the federal character of the German constitution is one of the few unamendable provisions of that constitution.[39]

Given therefore that federalism seems, at least at the level of constitutional theory, to approach the issue of constitutional entrenchment differently from a unitary system, how then does it deal with the process of constitutional change? Again we see in federal constitutions that the territorial dimension is invariably central to the detail of such processes. Constitutional amendment within federal constitutions tends to require special majorities, either within the central legislature, such as in Germany where the approval of two-thirds of both legislative chambers is required (bearing in mind that the second chamber is a territorial chamber selected directly by the lander), or by a direct role for the states as in the United States (in addition to that for Congress where again one house is a territorial chamber). This can even lead to unanimity provisions which, as discussed, we find for example in the constitution of Canada and which proved fatal to the Meech Lake constitutional process of 1987. Going further, we can find territorially based *asymmetry* in levels of entrenchment and processes of change. This for example is enjoyed by Quebec in certain respects within the Canadian constitution, giving constitutional recognition not only to the salience of provinces but also to their demotic specificity.

What then can we say about the use of referendums in processes of constitutional change? We have seen that referendums are often considered to sit very uncomfortably within liberal constitutionalism due in large part to the counter-majoritarian position taken within this tradition in relation to rights. But simply saying that the foundational purpose of federal constitutionalism prioritises the institutional entrenchment of territorial prerogatives above the entrenchment of 'national values', does not make federalism automatically more amenable to referendum democracy. If anything the simple majoritarianism seemingly inherent within referendum democracy becomes even more problematic in federal context. A federal system may not take a value-based approach as its fundamental justification for entrenchment but it has entrenchment none the less. Simple majoritarianism still runs up against the carefully crafted federal constitutional order, designed to entrench the institutional authority of territories, possibly in an asymmetrical way, and entrenching also modes of amendment that may require super-majority approval upon a territorial rather than individual basis. Again asymmetry can even be a feature

[39] Basic Law, Article 79(3).

of the amendment process, giving certain territories a particular role in the amendment issues for certain purposes.

This leads to another major difficulty with referendums in federal context which is less of an issue, or indeed not a problem at all, for a monist conception of the constitution: namely the role the referendum plays, even implicitly, as a nation-affirming or nation-building tool, allowing a sense of popular constituent power to emerge at seminal constitutional moments. I have discussed how federal constitutionalism presents a radically different foundation upon which to conceptualise the constitution and in particular the nature of constituent power that undergirds its legitimacy. One interesting feature of the liberal–republican debate concerning constitutional entrenchment/constitutional change is that, despite the heat which it has generated, it is a debate that is founded upon mutual agreement as to the core identity of the constitution's demotic subjects. Liberal constitutionalists may favour strong entrenchment, civic republicans may be more inclined to leave more decision-making to the political arena, but both accept that the debate about how a democracy ought to organise itself constitutionally revolves around a monist conception of the constitutional people.

The referendum of course brings to the fore the notion of 'the people' and it does so in singular terms. However, the very notion of the demos is handled in complex and subtle ways within the federal idea. When a referendum is introduced into a federal system, how can it cope with what may be a very subtle constitutional navigation around this very first question of democracy—who are the people? Certainly a federal polity is one founded upon territorial pluralism but it is also one polity. It creates a potentially uneasy coexistence between the territories and the central state: as Albert Dicey famously said, in a federal system 'the inhabitants... must desire union, and must not desire unity ... '.[40] Those who join together to form the federation relinquish some degree of their own discrete peoplehood, while the new polity makes a more attenuated claim upon their demotic attachment than can a unitary state. But the result can be a delicate and inchoate relationship between territorial and state attachments in which relative patterns of loyalty and identity between the two levels will vary from federal state to federal state, and even within each state itself. Indeed, federal states, even after centuries, can struggle to pin down the notion of demotic identity. For example, the fundamental question of whether

[40] A V Dicey, *Introduction to the Study of the Law of the Constitution* (London: MacMillan, 1915), 141. Dicey's interest in and views about federalism were shaped by his wider concerns with Irish Home Rule. Alvin Jackson, 'The Failure of British and Irish Federalism, circa 1800–1950' in R Schütze and S Tierney (eds.), *The United Kingdom and the Federal Idea* (Oxford: Hart Publishing, 2018), 29–47.

American federalism is characterised by one people or the several peoples of the several states is an occasional source of dispute before the US Supreme Court.[41]

If we take territorial pluralism seriously, there are therefore two opposing dangers in using constitutional referendums within a federal polity. One is unwarranted homogenisation: positing the entire people of the state as one determining group when the constitution has in fact been crafted in a way that builds in complex and pluralised models of decision-making to reflect the territorial pluralism of the polity. An example is arguably the Brexit referendum in the UK. The UK of course is usually not characterised as a federal state but it does appear to be set upon a federal trajectory with the effective constitutional entrenchment of 'self-rule' for Scotland and Wales[42] and developing levels of shared rule through more formalised intergovernmental relations.[43] In the end the referendum result was a vote for Leave by 52%–48% across the UK, but there were majorities for Remain in Northern Ireland and Scotland—the latter by 62%–38%. This raised the issue of whether the UK was simply one demos and indeed whether important constitutional change should be effected in a unitary way—one undifferentiated people voting on a straight majority basis, or whether implicit in the gradual federalisation of the UK was an implicit commitment to pluralised decision-making among the constituent territories of the state. It is notable that the First Minister of Scotland argued for example that majorities for Leave in the four 'nations' of the UK should have been secured in order for the decision to be legitimate. This dispute has continued, with the Scottish Government continuing to oppose Brexit-related legislation as it passes through the UK Parliament.

The other danger with referendums in federal systems is the accentuation of demotic difference: overriding what can be a fluid system of shared and overlapping identities and interposing a mode of decision-making that makes people choose binary either/or identities. An example is how referendums can act as a destabilising force in federal states by bringing to the surface the existence of multiple political communities within the state, and by giving each of these the capacity to make constitutional demands with the force of popular support. Certainly the referendum story of the former Union of Soviet Socialist

[41] U.S. Term Limits, Inc. v. Thornton, 514 U.S. 779 (1995).

[42] Scotland Act 2016 s.1; Wales Act 2017, s.1.

[43] S Tierney, 'Drifting Towards Federalism? Appraising the constitution in light of the Scotland Act 2016 and Wales Act 2017' in Robert Schütze and Stephen Tierney (eds.), *The UK and Europe: Federalism Within and Without* (Oxford: Hart Publishing, 2018), 101–122; and 'The Territorial Constitution and the Brexit Process' (2019) 72 *Current Legal Problems* 59–83.

Republics (USSR) and Socialist Federal Republic of Yugoslavia (SFRY) is one of collapse as nationalists in numerous republics used direct democracy to validate secessionist aspirations.[44]

It is unsurprising that the referendum remains the favoured constitutional tool of sub-state nationalists. This is clear from the Quebec experience and evidenced more recently in Scotland and Catalonia. It can in fact be hard to square the tendency of a referendum to make unilateral decisions with the more pluralistic mode of decision-making that tends to characterise a federal constitution. In a federal system, territories come together in a complex bond of multi-dimensional relationships which operate through a complex matrix of divided and shared powers. The notion of ending that relationship unilaterally is conceptually problematic. It is notable that the Supreme Court of Canada in addressing the issue of secession did so by articulating how Canadian federalism is a broad mosaic. Accordingly it concluded that Quebec had no right under the constitution to secede by way of an entirely unilateral process; this could only come about in constitutional terms through negotiations with its partners in confederation.[45] In the UK unionists took a similar view in relation to the Scottish independence referendum. Within the union a complex web of shared and mixed identities and patterns of loyalty had built up over centuries. This was being challenged by a referendum process that would produce a binary outcome between belonging and not belonging to the state. Regardless of how one views the rights of national minorities within federations, which is a much broader issue, these examples serve simply to show how the referendum can prove to be deeply incendiary within the context of a long-lived and deeply interwoven multi-level system of government. It institutionalises a binary approach to identity in place of more complex patterns and in doing so gives to a 'self-determining' group a unilateral power that seems to run counter to the careful institutional design of the federal model which is specifically designed to dilute such powerful unilateralism.

All of that said, in Section III we discussed the intuitive attractiveness of direct democracy within the civic republican tradition in terms of engaging people in vital constitutional decisions. We also noted the potential of such major constitutional moments to foster identification with the polity.

[44] S Tierney, *Constitutional Law and National Pluralism* (Oxford: Oxford University Press, 2004). The issue of sovereignty and direct democracy has remained a vexing subject in the former Soviet lands, as the Crimean crisis of 2015 demonstrates. See S Tierney, 'Sovereignty and Crimea: How Referendum Democracy Complicates Constituent Power in Multinational Societies' (2015) 16 *German Law Journal* 523–541.

[45] Reference Re Secession of Quebec [1998] 2 SCR 217, para 88.

Therefore, is there a way to keep the participatory and deliberative advantages of direct democracy within a federal system while avoiding the problems of either homogenisation or separatism? Certainly referendums can be held at sub-state level on issues other than separatism without any threat to the federal system. Referendums on matters that are within the competence of the regions are not uncommon: I have alluded to the American states' experience but other examples are the referendums on electoral reform in British Columbia and Ontario in 2004/2009 and 2007 respectively.

But it is also the case that 'national' or federation-wide referendums can and do work. Federal systems are built upon a nuanced approach to the demos but it is still accepted that there is a national federal people, whatever other identities exist below the level of the state. We must not forget that even by Dicey's formulation, 'union' is part of the deal even if 'unity' is not. And referendums do operate within federal systems at the national level. Few federal systems use them systematically in processes of constitutional change but the two key exceptions do so by adapting direct democracy to the principle of territorial pluralism. The constitution of the Commonwealth of Australia is a case in point. Constitutional amendments require to be ratified by referendum, but a double majority is required: a majority of all citizens across the country and a majority of the six states. Switzerland operates on a similar basis.

It is notable however that other federal systems seem deeply suspicious of national referendums. The USA and Germany do not use them for pan-state constitutional decision-making. One fear is that a referendum could overturn the federal system itself. We have noted that federalism in Germany is one of the few features of the constitution protected by an eternity clause. We also need to take account of the fact that the entrenchment of liberal values in both constitutions coexists with the federal dimension of the constitution, and therefore liberal counter-majoritarianism and federal counter-majoritarianism intertwine in ways that cannot be fully separated.

I am not therefore presenting an argument for or against the use of national referendums in federal systems as a point of constitutional principle. Instead the goal has been to show that referendums, by implicating and requiring the articulation of the demos which often lies unexplored in constitutional practice, raise fundamental questions about the 'constitutional self.' When deployed in federal systems this in turn exposes the fundamentally different purpose of federal constitutionalism and the radically different way in which constituent power acts to legitimise federal constitutionalism. This is an important new area for exploration and one that requires far more detailed and comparative analysis than I have been able to accord it in this chapter.

VI. Conclusion

Both federalism as an idea and a template for government, and the referendum as a mechanism of constitutional change are on the rise. Although there is no clear connection between the two, it is inevitable that the interaction between the two will also grow as the number of referendums within federal states over the past three decades demonstrates. This chapter has shown how this raises a number of theoretical problems. Referendums in general challenge traditional constitutional theory, in particular a default approach to constitutionalism that is moving towards more elaborate forms of constitutional entrenchment which serve to insulate from politics an ever-wider collection of purportedly universal political values. In this respect the long-standing debate between republican and liberal constitutionalism is given a new playing field.

But into this mix we also see the rise of a specific form of government—federalism—which also depends upon constitutional entrenchment as a way to bind territories together in a common political project. It does this often by putting into abeyance the notion of 'the people' as constitutional legitimiser in favour of a more pluralised notion of the demos, which can also encompass in certain federations and for certain purposes a sense of multiple demoi within the state. The older certainties of federalism in countries such as Switzerland, the USA, Canada, Australia and Germany were in some sense, although in my view ultimately unsuccessfully, accommodated within a general default, and essentially monist, template for constitutional theory. But we see now ever more radical, imaginative and deeply pluralist manifestations of the federal idea in states such as South Africa, Ethiopia, Bosnia-Herzegovina and Iraq. These states have required to take account of deep territorial pluralism by for example asymmetrical accommodation of sub-state national particularity which, of the older federations, was only really a feature of Canadian constitutional development. In this setting the referendum poses new and dramatic challenges. We have explored how it can act as a crude device in the way it defines the 'self' for the purpose of constitutional 'self-determination', serving either to be over-inclusive or homogenising in its demotic reach, or crudely binary and hence centrifugal, jarring against a more complex reality of mixed and shared identities across the state.

In earlier work I have argued that the position of the referendum need not in fact be treated as an outlier by contemporary constitutional theory. That the democratic problems it presents are largely those of practice not principle, and that by good constitutional design the issues of elite control and deliberation deficit can be overcome.[46] But the issue of the majoritarian danger is the most difficult challenge to resolve largely because rival approaches to it are in many ways ideologically informed. When looked at through the prism of federalism we see just how significant a challenge this is to constitutional theory. Constitutionalism as a theoretical framework for thinking about the legitimacy of authority in the modern state has tended to construct a narrative of counter-majoritarianism that takes insufficient account of the salience of plural territories and their societal specificities. When we challenge modern thinking about constitutional authority and legitimacy through the prism of the referendum we see more clearly the extent to which federalism itself, as a discrete and proliferating form of constitutional government, requires the renewed attention of detailed, systematic and rigorous constitutional theory.

[46] S Tierney, 'Direct Democracy in the United Kingdom: Reflections from the Scottish Independence Referendum' [2015] *Public Law* 633–651.

5

Referendum and Self-Determination in Catalonia

Antoni Abat i Ninet

I. Introduction

On 9 June 2017, the Government of Catalonia announced the celebration of a referendum on self-determination to be held the next 1 October 2017. Catalan citizens were asked to decide their political future against the volition of the Spanish Government that had vowed to use all possible means to stop the voting. The Catalan call triggered a new political and legal quarrel with the Spanish Government that was inexorably opposed to recognising the right of self-determination of Catalonia. The political clash between the State and the autonomous community opened several questions on the use of referendum on self-determination without the authorisation of the State.

After this brief introduction, section two of the chapter scrutinises the Catalan referendum on independence analysing in detail both the Spanish arguments to abort the voting (considered as an unconstitutional act that breached the rule of law and a criminal offense) and the Catalan thesis to hold the plebiscite (democratic principle and the exercise of the human right of self-determination). The section focuses on the events after the Spanish Constitutional Court ruling on the Statute of Autonomy of Catalonia in 2010, a decision that took four years to produce and that rejected all the most significant and symbolic portions of the Statute of Autonomy. Catalan institutions alleged this Constitutional Court decision as an unacceptable grievance and the trigger of the current territorial dispute. The section goes further by describing the Catalonia–Spain political tension that the unilateral referendum has caused.

The third section is devoted to the referendums in self-determination as a legal instrument, and it analyses the use of referendums from a comparative and historical perspective. The section examines the institution of referendums

Antoni Abat i Ninet, *Referendum and Self-Determination in Catalonia* In: *The Limits and Legitimacy of Referendums*. Edited by: Richard Albert and Richard Stacey, Oxford University Press. © Antoni Abat i Ninet 2022.
DOI: 10.1093/oso/9780198867647.003.0006

as a democratic instrument and its suitability or not to settle territorial disputes where national minorities are involved. It also notes the problems that referendums have as an instrument of political decision-making, such as the so-called plebiscitary deviation, the increase of political polarisation, populist instrumentalisation and the deviation of responsibilities. And, how all these aspects may be conditioning the appropriateness of its use in territorial conflicts.

The chapter continues in section four by critically analysing the legitimacy of secession referendums in constitutional democracies. There is a legal penumbra in international law on referendums in secession, meaning that there is no legal body regulating the exercise of this kind of referendum to channel and legitimise a process of external self-determination (Cassese). Therefore, the section examines advisory opinions (International Court of Justice on Kosovo), the United Nations Security Council Resolutions 1244 (1999) and 1203 (1998) and the applicable international standards of the European Commission for Democracy through Law (Venice Commission) on referendums. In this sense, in a context of a unilateral referendum on secession, as happened in Catalonia, these set of norms may be more relevant to provide a legal framework and guidance to the organisers of the voting. The chapter ends with a short conclusion that summarises the main arguments and raises questions for future research on secession referendums.

II. The Referendum in Catalonia

The Spanish-Catalan political conflict highlights many legal and political dilemmas; such as the boundaries of federalism; the undesirable clash between democracy and the rule of law; the limits of the principle of non-interference in domestic affairs and the principle of self-determination. This section analyses the origins, standing and potential outcome of this political conflict within the Spanish–Catalan scenario.

A. The Spanish–Catalan Political Conflict

A chronology of the most outstanding events of the current Spanish–Catalan conflict must begin with the ruling of the Constitutional Court against the Statute of Autonomy of Catalonia in 2010. In 2005, Catalonia proposed a new Statute of Autonomy that aggressively asserted an integrated set of very strong and interactive distinctive identity claims.[1] The Preamble provided that "Catalonia's self-government is founded on the Constitution, and also on the historical rights of the Catalan people, which, in the framework of the Constitution, give rise to recognition in this Statute of the unique position of the Catalan Government." It claimed that "Catalonia (is) a nation"; that Article 2 of the Spanish Constitution "recognises the national reality of Catalonia as a nationality"; and that the new Statute of Autonomy fulfils "the inalienable right of Catalonia to self-government".[2]

Article 1 of the Statute provides that "Catalonia, as a nation, exercises its self-government by constituting itself as an Autonomous Community."[3] Article 3 declares that "The relations between the Generalitat (Government of Catalonia) and the State are founded on the principle of mutual institutional loyalty and are governed by ... the principle of autonomy, that of bilateralism and also that of multilateralism."[4] It goes on to state that "Catalonia has its geographical and political space of reference in the State and the European Union and incorporates the values, principles and obligations that derive from the fact of being part of them."[5] Article 5 asserts that Catalan "self-government ... is also founded on the historical rights of the Catalan people."[6] These were considered as strong, provocative assertions.

The Statute goes further and creates a "Council of Justice of Catalonia," which it deems "the governing body of the judicial power in Catalonia".[7] Another provision declares that in areas marked by the Spanish Constitution for shared national and subnational power, ultimate authority to interpret the scope of subnational authority lies with the Catalan legislature and executive, relegating the national government and the Spanish Constitutional Court to establishing only basic or minimal rules.[8] The proposed Statute, in short, offered a considerably different vision of the status of Catalonia within Spain than the 1979 Statute of Autonomy, one that at a minimum proceeded to the very outermost limits of subnational autonomy authorised by the Spanish Constitution.[9] Notwithstanding the ambitious scope of the proposed alterations, the Spanish

[1] Antoni Abat Ninet and James Gardner, "Distinctive Identity Claims in Federal Systems: Judicial Policing of Subnational Variance" (2016) 14 International Journal of Constitutional Law 378, 410.
[2] Ley Orgánica 6/2006 de 19 Julio de 2006, Preamble (hereinafter Catalan Statute of Autonomy 2006).
[3] Ibid Art. 1.
[4] Ibid Art. 3(1).
[5] Ibid Art. 3(2).
[6] Ibid Art. 5.
[7] Ibid Art. 97.
[8] Ibid Art. 111.
[9] Abat and Gardner (n 1) 380–390.

Government in Madrid approved the changes, and in 2006 Parliament passed a law bringing them into effect.[10]

Almost immediately, a politically fraught lawsuit was brought in the Spanish Constitutional Court challenging the constitutionality of the new Statute.[11] In a decision that took four years to be issued, the Court decisively rejected most significant portions of the Statute.[12] Rather than take the Statute for what it transparently was i.e. a rewriting of the constitutional relationship between national and subnational power, approved by the central government following bilateral negotiations with Catalonia, the Court chose instead to take the view that the Statute was the complete opposite: a well-intentioned and altogether minor alteration to prevailing norms and practices that suffered from clumsy drafting.[13]

Thus, the Court chose repeatedly to rely on a rule of interpretation under which it construed the language in the Statute, no matter how significant and challenging to the existing constitutional order, in a way that rendered it consistent with existing constitutional principles. A "maximalist conception", the Court said early in its ruling, "must always be opposed".[14]

The Court's approach was evident from the beginning. Constitutional challenges to strong language in the Preamble were rejected on the ground that preambles have no binding legal effect.[15] Similarly, the Court sustained Article 5, which declared "the self-government of Catalonia" to be "based on the historical rights of the Catalan People". This provision, the Court said, "would be clearly unconstitutional if it attempted to gain for the Statute of Autonomy a foundation outside the Constitution".[16]

The decision of the Court goes on in this vein for another 137 paragraphs, interpreting contextually significant language to have no significance, and very occasionally invalidating a provision of the Statute when it is susceptible to no saving interpretation. While the Court's hostility to Catalonia's claim—and its official recognition by Spain—is thus covered by a thin veneer of polite condescension, it is hostile

[10] And on 18 June of 2006, the people of Catalonia voted in favour in a referendum with a participation rate of 49.41 per cent.

[11] The plaintiffs included the opposition Partido Popular and the governments of Aragon, Valencia, Murcia, la Rioja, and the Balearic Islands. On the political context of these challenges, see James Gardner and Antoni Abat Ninet, "Sustainable Decentralisation: Power, Extraconstitutional Influence, and Subnational Symmetry in the United States and Spain" (2011) 59(2) American Journal of Comparative Law 491, 519–520

[12] Sentencia Tribunal Constitucional, STC (8045-2006) de 16 Junio 2010.

[13] Abat and Gardner (n 1).

[14] Ibid 6.

[15] Ibid 7.

[16] Ibid 10.

'nonetheles'.[17] The decision of the Constitutional Court had a widespread rejection in Catalonia. A massive demonstration was held on 10 July 2010, "Som una Nació: Nosaltre decidim" (We are a Nation: We decide) against the ruling of the Constitutional Court.[18]

After that, Catalonia has experienced large political demonstrations to claim for secession and, in 2012, the political parties that claimed for the holding of a referendum on secession won the elections.[19] In that sense, the new pro-referendum Parliament passed a "Declaration of Sovereignty and the Right to decide of the People of Catalonia". In that document, the Parliament of Catalonia recognised the people of Catalonia, based on the principle of democratic legitimacy, as a sovereign political and legal entity. The document remarked that the process of exercising the right to decide would be scrupulously democratic, transparent, and Catalonia will engage in dialogue and negotiations with the Spanish State, the European institutions and with international organisations.

After massive demonstrations, regional elections and the official Parliamentary elections won by secessionist parties, the institutions of Catalonia were placed in a different scenario and put forward on different occasions the beginning of a constructive dialogue to approach the subject of the referendum. The channels used to reach an agreed solution with the Spanish Government were both formal (sending to the Spanish Parliament a delegation of the Catalan Parliament; official letters of the Catalan President to the Spanish President; sectorial meetings where representatives of both sides were present); and informal (public statements of the speakers of each government; media presences; informal debates; opinion articles).

From the Presidency of the Catalan Government, it was stated that following point four of the Declaration of Sovereignty on Dialogue, if the State accepted to dialogue, the negotiation would not have limits, including the question of threshold and date.

The Spanish Government refused to negotiate on an agreed referendum, which was considered an illegal proposal and a political fraud that aimed to legalise an unconstitutional demand. The first factual response by the Catalan institutions to the silence of Madrid was the organisation of a popular symbolic consultation on independence on 9 November 2014. The non-binding

[17] Interestingly, provisions similar to those invalidated in the Catalan Statute of Autonomy had not previously been thought to present constitutional problems in the Statutes of Autonomy of other Autonomous Communities. See Gardner and Abat (n 11) 519.

[18] <www.bbc.com/news/10588494> accessed 25 June 2020.

[19] <www.gencat.cat/governacio/resultats-parlament2012/09AU/DAU09999CM_L2.htm> accessed 25 June 2020.

consultation was opposed by the Spanish Government that challenged the Catalan Government's decree calling for the consultation vote in Spain's Constitutional Court. The Highest Court decided that two articles of the decree were unconstitutional.[20]

When the Constitutional Court overruled the decree the Catalan President and the Government, against the advice of the political parties that supported him, decided to accept the decision and transformed the query into something radically different: a participatory process left to the public with minimal support from the Government.[21] Later, the Spanish Constitutional Court also banned this popular consultation formula and did not answer a request of the Catalan Government on what Catalan institutions were allowed to do. Receiving no answer, the Catalan Government organised the symbolic voting (popular consultation) anyway.[22] More than 80.8 per cent of those who cast their vote in the popular non-binding consultation organised by thousands of volunteers did so in favour of independence, with a participation rate of approximately 37 per cent of the people with the right to vote.[23]

The answer to this challenge to the constitutional authority resulted in the condemnation of Former Catalan President (Artur Mas), the former vice-President (Joana Ortega), former Minister of the Presidency (Francesc Homs) and former Minister of Education (Irene Rigau) of one year of ineligibility and a fine of five million euros.

However, judicial action did not intimidate public and institutional behaviour in Catalonia. The refusal of the Spanish institutions to open a process of dialogue on an agreed referendum led to new regional elections in Catalonia that secessionist political parties and their stakeholders understood as a plebiscite for independence. Voters gave separatist parties a majority in the parliamentary seats (72 of 135 seats) and 49.2 per cent of the total voting.

Even that the new Government and Parliamentarian majority updated the political road map towards independence; in changing a unilateral declaration of independence by a referendum the escalation of tension increased. On 31 July 2017, the two secessionist parties in the Catalan Parliament registered a draft Bill on the referendum of self-determination.[24] The draft was followed by

[20] Antoni Abat i Ninet, *Catalan Political Representatives Stand Criminal Trials*, International Journal Constitutional Law <www.iconnectblog.com/2017/02/catalan-political-representatives-stand-criminal-trials> accessed 25 June 2020.

[21] Ibid.

[22] Ibid.

[23] Ibid.

[24] <https://drive.google.com/file/d/0Bxrh_sv1paPsdFNiRDhrSndvTTA/view> accessed 25 June 2020.

the approval of the Law of legal transition to afford legal certainty and transparency to the transitional period. This Bill (according to the Catalan political parties) will endow the Catalan institutions with the necessary legal means to exercise the right of self-determination.

B. The Catalan referendum of self-determination

Catalan institutions expected to hold the referendum on self-determination on 1 October 2017. However, the Spanish Government reiterated that this would not happen. So far, the Spanish Government had never disclosed which measures it would take in order to prevent Catalans from unconstitutional voting.

The unilateral referendum in Catalonia was going to be conducted based on the law on the Referendum of Self-determination registered in the Catalan Parliament. The Preamble of the law grounded its legitimacy on the international legal corpus on self-determination ratified by Spain. It also quoted the advisory opinions of the International Court of Justice and mentioned Articles 96 and 10.2 of the Spanish Constitution (on the validity of international treaties ratified by the State). The explanatory memorandum of the draft went further, mentioning the multiple resolutions of the Catalan Parliament (never challenged by the Spanish Constitutional Court) on the right of Catalonia to exercise self-determination.[25] The legal corpus providing legitimacy to the referendum (according to the Catalan Government) was completed by the Declaration on Sovereignty and the right to decide of the People of Catalonia of 2006.

The Bill, according to the Catalan institutions, met the vast majority of recommendations and good conducts that the Venice Commission prescribe in its doctrine. On the rule of law condition the law of the referendum created an exceptional legal regime to regulate and guarantee the referendum of self-determination in Catalonia.[26] The final disposition Number One afforded legal supremacy to the law (including the state norms and the Constitution) in matters related to the referendum, an act which is considered unconstitutional and void (iuris et de iure) under the Spanish law.

Despite this fact, the Catalan institutions followed the strategy expressed by the International Court of Justice in its Advisory Opinion on Kosovo, where there was an implicit recognition of the legitimacy of the Assembly of Kosovo to

[25] Catalan Statute of Autonomy 2006, Preamble.
[26] Ibid Art. 3.

establish new legality, hierarchically superior to the still applicable Serbian legality.[27] The law on the referendum also established the general conditions and principles of the electoral law according to prescriptions of the Commission of Europe, including the role of political parties and other political associations, the political campaign and the proportionate and fair appearance in media of supporters and detractors of secession.

The Catalan Bill also created the Electoral Syndicate of Catalonia an ad hoc and independent organ of the Catalan Parliament in charge of the electoral administration of the referendum. The tasks of this syndicate consisted of validation of the electoral census, validation of ballots, early voting, the exercise of the disciplinary jurisdiction, supervision of the political campaign, accreditation of the international observers, general scrutiny, certification of the official results and publication of them in an Official Journal.

The (precise and not suggestive) question to be asked in the referendum was: "Do you want Catalonia to be an independent state in the form of a republic?"[28] There was no mention of a valid threshold of participation to legitimatise the outcome. This omission seems to oppose the recommendations of the Venice Commission. However, these recommendations are contradictory because on the one hand, in its report on the compatibility of the existing legislation in Montenegro concerning the organisation of referendums with applicable international standards, the Commission states that the requirement that the majority of the electorate voted in the referendum for it to be valid is consistent with international standards. On the other hand, point 7 of the Code of Good Practice on Referendums recommends not establishing a threshold of participation.[29]

In other recent laws on self-determination processes, such as the "Clarity law" passed by the National Assembly of Quebec, a threshold is established.[30] In the Catalan case, the omission aimed to void a possible boycott of part of the population.

[27] Accordance with International Law of the Unilateral Declaration of Independence in Respect of Kosovo (Request for Advisory Opinion), General List No. 141, International Court of Justice (ICJ), 22 July 2010, available at <https://www.refworld.org/cases,ICJ,4c5151002.html> accessed 29 June 2020.

[28] Ibid Art. 4.

[29] Venice Commission, CDL-AD (2005)041 on the compatibility of the existing legislation in Montenegro concerning the organisation of referendums with applicable international standards and CDL-AD (2007)008 Code of Good Practice on Referendums.

[30] Act respecting the Exercise of the Fundamental Rights and Prerogatives of the Québec people and the Québec State, (*Décret 37-2016 du 28 janvier 2016*), Art. 4.1, states: "When the Québec people is consulted by way of a referendum under the Referendum Act (chapter C-64.1), the winning option is the option that obtains a majority of the valid votes cast, namely 50% of the valid votes cast plus one". Available at: <http://legisquebec.gouv.qc.ca/fr/ShowDoc/cs/E-20.2> accessed 25 June 2020.

As we approached the celebration of the unilateral self-determination referendum in Catalonia, the Spanish Government agreed to assume control of Catalonia's essential spending —education, health, social services and payrolls. At the same time, other complementary measures were under consideration, ranging from the suspension of Catalan autonomy (Article 155 Spanish Constitution), the enforcement of the state of exception (Article 116 Spanish Constitution) to the use of force (Article 8 Spanish Constitution) and the continuing detention and prosecution of Catalan political representatives.

In addition to these constitutional measures, Spanish institutions and stakeholders warned and requested to public officers in Catalonia not to collaborate with the organisation of the referendum. Police actions and judicial interrogatories to the members of the Catalan Government suspected to be collaborating or organising the referendum were intensified in the days before the voting.

After repressing the voting of 1 October with the use of non-proportional force, the Spanish Government implemented, for the first time in Spanish constitutional history, the punitive measures established in Article 155 of the Constitution (a sort of nuclear provision) suspending the Catalan autonomy and resuming direct rule over Catalonia.

The members of the Catalan Government and Catalan representatives' grassroots activists were arrested and jailed. After 500 days of pre-trial detention, the Spanish Supreme Court found guilty former Catalan representatives and grassroots activist of crimes of sedition (a political crime) and embezzlement that carries from 9 to 13 years in prison.

The legal and extra-legal aggressive response on the part of the power structure of the State had not a response of any kind on the Catalan counterpart, which naively expected a "divine" intervention of the European Union against a Member State, wishful thinking that never materialised.

III. The referendum in self-determination

The Venice Commission states that instruments of direct and participatory democracy should be seen as complementing representative democracy.[31] It follows defining: "Parliamentary democracy supported by free and fair elections ensuring representatives, (political) pluralism, and the equality of citizens, as

[31] Venice Commission, CDL-PI (2017)001, "Compilation of Venice Commission Opinions and Reports concerning referendums" 5.

the core, but not the only aspect of the democratic process".[32] The truth is that there is no universal and general accepted definition of the meaning of direct democracy. A literal interpretation of the term does not really help to clarify the current political and legal meaning of the development. A first approach in an epistemological sense of the term indicates that "direct democracy" is a subtype of democracy exercised directly, meaning without intermediaries or representatives, by the people themselves. Again, this allows multiple interpretations.

With the foundation of the modern constitutional State, representative democracy effectively undertakes the legitimacy of direct democracy based on the fiction of power delegation and the discredit of direct democracy. The Federalist papers 10 and 49, with the lack of any reference to democracy in Article XVI of the Declaration of the Rights of Man and of the Citizen 1789, are good examples of this fact.

According to deflectors, (direct) democracy cannot work qualitatively because the people are considered incompetent and incapable to satisfactorily influence public policies, legislate or even judge.[33] Quantitatively, direct democracy is not workable because a great number of people taking decisions necessarily implies uncertainty, instability and an extreme additional difficulty concerning making decisions.

Referendums do not escape either of this same criticism because it gives to the people the capacity of decision-making. Even so, constitutions and constitutional practices give referendums a prominent role.[34] The vast majority of constitutions of the world contain institutions related to direct democracy, but they accommodate differently the concepts, denominations and institutions under the label of direct democracy. As of 2008, only 20 per cent of 193 countries deemed independent had no provision at all for referendums at the national or subnational level, liberal democracies have more often provisions for referendums (only 13 per cent have no provisions of any kind at any level).[35]

Constitutions vary in the extent to which they specify the process and organisation of direct democracy mechanisms in the constitutional text. Defining such matters as the timing of referendums, the turnout and majority requirements, the organisation of the referendum and the rules for campaigning in the Constitution may protect the neutrality of these rules and ensure that referendums are less likely to be abused by incumbent majorities. Failure to do

[32] Ibid.
[33] Giovanni Sartori, *The Theory of Democracy, The Contemporary debate* (CQ Press 1987).
[34] Ibid 4.
[35] Laurence Morel, "Referendum" in Michel Rosenfeld and András Sajo, *The Oxford Handbook of Comparative Constitutional Law* (OUP 2012), 509.

this may undermine the neutrality of the referendum process and weaken the legitimacy of the result.[36] Somehow, to include these set of rules in a constitutional norm is to constitutionalise the procedure of constitutional amendment, which according to Richard Albert are the most important norms of the constitution.[37]

The more consolidated the constitutional democracy is, the greater the confidence in the ability of the people, and mechanisms that allow the people to decide are established. Referendums improve the quality of our mixed or representative democracies and new constitutions seem to follow Nino's statement: "that it is essential to widen the ways of direct participation of the people whose interest are at stake, be general procedures such as plebiscites or popular consultations, or by decentralising decisions into smaller ambits in which the people concerned can affect them ...".[38]

In the twenty-first century, with the lower illiteracy rate and in the midst of the information age and the network society, some of the critiques of democracy and by extension to referendums are consigned to the past. Other concerns on the viability of referendums need to be addressed seriously. Some of this criticism can be summarised as follows: whether the referendum is a truly democratic device; whether the referendum reflects the will of the people because voters do not answer the actual referendum question; the plebiscitary deviation; and whether the referendum increases political polarisation.[39] These critical aspects are developed further in other chapters of this book.

A decision taken by a referendum, even if it fulfils all the standard requirements and good practices, does not exhaust per se all the democratic requests. A referendum needs to be conducted in accordance with the minimum standards of legality (rule of law), respect for human rights and good electoral practices. Some of these standards are not mandatory or based on *jus cogens* regulations, and they need to be adapted to each national/local situation. The question is whether can we impose additional requirements to consider legitimate a referendum that does not breach any *jus cogens* norm.

If the referendum fulfils these requirements and good practices, some of the criticisms discussed above can be satisfactorily dismissed, despite there is no authorisation of the State to conduct such a plebiscite in a part of its territory.

[36] Elliot Bulmer, "Direct Democracy" (2017) International Institute for Democracy and Electoral Assistance" (International IDEA) 18.

[37] Richard Albert, *Constitutional Amendments: Making, Breaking, and Changing Constitutions* (OUP 2019).

[38] , Vicki C. Jackson and Mark Tushnet, *Comparative Constitutional Law* (Foundation Press 2006).

[39] Laurence Morel (n 35) 505.

IV. The legitimacy of a referendum in self-determination

The dimensions and repercussions of an independence referendum may be well represented by some of the vicissitudes that Ulysses faced in his return journey from Troy to Ithaca. Among the vicissitudes that Ulysses found in his ten-year journey home, he fought the Cyclopes, Polyphemus; Circe, a witch-goddess converted half of his men into swine; he crossed the Strait of Messina between two horrible monsters, Scylla and Charybdis; and so did Poseidon.[40] A referendum as a political instrument of decision-making has its problems that could affect not only the appropriateness of the holding of a referendum in secession but also its legitimacy.

The intrinsic worth as an exercise of direct democracy does not avoid some of the cons that the institution of the referendum has (plebiscitary deviation; polarisation increased by the binary nature of referendums; unrealistic beliefs on the outcome; opportunistic use by political actors deviating the assumption of responsibilities). With this in mind, it is necessary to remark that a referendum is not always the best instrument to channel and conclude a political conflict. This fact is even more pressing in very polarised societies. Therefore, the referendum cannot always be associated with a Heroic Ulysses struggling against monsters and vicissitudes.

The stress to the constitutional textures of the State happens only if the demand of a referendum meets some requirements and constraints, and the State is a constitutional democracy, or it aims to be so. The first requirement to consider the demand to hold a self-determination referendum is certainty, which needs to be supported by majoritarian democratic support and legitimacy. A demand to hold a self-determination referendum is "certain" when there is a complete conviction that the plebiscite is going to happen. This complete conviction needs to be firm and majoritarian in the territorial entity that claims the celebration of the referendum. The conviction is more than a simple act of faith; it is normally supported by political and legislative manifestations and acts in that direction.

A second requirement to consider the claim is that it needs to have majoritarian support in the territorial unit. This support is expressed generally by the established political channels, that is, voting in regular elections for the different political parties that aim for the secession or the celebration of the referendum; for example, when the electoral results (in the different levels, Supra-State (European), State, Federal, or Local) show majoritarian support

[40] Homer, *The Odyssey* (Trends in Classics 2018).

for a political party or political coalition that openly claims for secession. The firmness and majoritarian character of that choice can also be expressed in different ways (surveys, polls or analysis of opinions).

Obviously, this is not a very reliable methodology because it departs from a voting deviation; to vote for a secessionist party in an electoral context does not imply necessarily support for a referendum on secession. The vote can be motivated by very different factors, among others, to support more federal powers for the territorial unit, to aim for a different political pact, to exercise a vote-protest against some State policies, or to express support or opposition to a particular candidate.

Therefore, to assume that all the voters of a secessionist party necessarily support the secession or the celebration of a referendum is not accurate, but it has been the only measure to evaluate the popular support for the celebration of a referendum. This methodology can be defined as opportunistic because it extrapolates a consequence from a question that is not clearly posed. That was the case in Quebec for the *Parti Québécois*, in Scotland for the Scottish Nationalist Party and in Catalonia for the political and civil society coalition *Junts pel Sí*. The lack of certainty on the real support for secession weakens the secessionist claim and the clarity of the demand.

The element of popular support is essential to consider the demand as certain and legitimate. It is not possible to compare the challenge and pressure in Catalonia, where the popular support to hold a referendum is around 82 per cent,[41] to the one that exists in Bayern (Germany) with an estimated popular support of 2.1 per cent.[42] One might well wonder, where are the millions of citizens of Texas or Bayern demonstrating and claiming independence every year? Was there ever a "Baltic way"[43] in Padania or Bavaria? A third element which defines a referendum as real and suitable is legitimacy. Legitimacy is the key question, and when, as happened in Spain or Italy, the Constitution or the interpretation that the Constitutional Court provides on the text denies the possibility of holding a political referendum, the legitimacy needs to be essentially democratic.

[41] <www.publico.es/politica/encuesta-catalunya-82-catalanes-creen-solucion-referendum-independencia-pactado.html> accessed 26 June 2020.

[42] <www.wahlrecht.de/umfragen/landtage/bayern.htm> accessed 29 June 2020.

[43] The Baltic Way was a peaceful political demonstration which took place on 23 August 1989 when approximately two million people joined hands forming a 600 km long human chain through the Baltic countries (Lithuania, Latvia and Estonia), thus demonstrating their unity in their efforts towards freedom. See <www.thebalticway.eu/en/history/> accessed 20 June 2020. The Catalan Way was a political demonstration that took place in Catalonia in 2013. At least 1.6 million people, according to official estimates, took their places in a massive human chain for independence, spanning over 400 kilometres, inspired by the Baltic Way

A. Rule of law in terms and legitimacy of a self-determination referendum

The proposed Law of the Self-Determination of Catalonia shows that the demand was grounded in international law, human rights (including self-determination) and the communitarian acquis that the State (Spain) is part of.[44] It also claimed for a different interpretation of the Spanish Constitution, more open and friendly to popular decision-making.

The requirement that the rule of law and legality imposes on a referendum opens broader debates, such as the hierarchy and primacy of international law, European Union Law or the Constitution. The conception of the rule of law expressed by Catalan institutions advocates for the ending of a holistic interpretation of the Constitution. The relations between two of the foundational principles of constitutional democracies, democracy and the rule of law should not collide but complement each other. Ideally, the relationship is complementary, coordinate and symbiotic, one limits and strengthens the other and vice versa. In contemporary constitutional democracies, there is no democracy without the rule of law and no rule of law without democracy.

On that point, the paramount Opinion of the Canadian Supreme Court in secession and self-determination is illuminating, in its paragraph 67: "Yet democracy in any real sense of the word cannot exist without the rule of law. It is the law that creates the framework within which the 'sovereign will' is to be ascertained and implemented ... in a political system must also possess legitimacy, and in our political culture, that requires an interaction between the rule of law and the democratic principle."; also in paragraph 78: "Viewed correctly, constitutionalism and the rule of law are not in conflict with democracy; rather, they are essential to it" or in Question 1: "Democratic rights under the Constitution cannot be divorced from constitutional obligations. Nor, however, can the reverse proposition be accepted."[45] Now, it is a paradox that a Supreme Court, a non-elected institution and of dubious democratic nature, in an act of judicial activism, defines the boundaries and limits of the democratic system and the relations of the democratic principle with other constitutional principles. Among the attributions of the Canadian Supreme Court, the Spanish Constitutional Court or the Italian Constitutional Court does not define and limit the democratic principle.

[44] Llei 19/2017 del 6 de Setembre, del Referèndum d'autodeterminació.
[45] Supreme Court of Canada, "Reference Re Secession of Quebec" (1998) 2 SCR 217.

On the relation between the rule of law and the Principle of Democracy in the concrete case-scenario of self-determination, the International Court of Justice (ICJ) in its advisory opinion on Kosovo, explicitly recognised the legitimacy of the authors of the declaration of independence (Assembly of Kosovo) as a representative democratic institution and acting outside the framework of the interim administration.[46] The demand of a referendum of external self-determination threatens, under some circumstances, the principle of territorial integrity and territorial protection. The ICJ recalls that the Principle of Territorial Integrity is an important part of the international legal order and is enshrined in the Charter of the United Nations, in particular in Article 2, paragraph 4.[47] However, the ICJ in its advisory opinion on Kosovo expressly limits the scope of the principle of territorial integrity to the sphere of relations between states.[48]

A completely different approach to the doctrine is expressed by the Commission of Venice, who noted that: "The principle of territorial integrity commands very widespread recognition—whether express or tacit—in constitutional law. On the other hand, constitutional law just as comprehensively rules out secession or the redrawing of borders. This should come as no surprise since that branch of law is the very foundation of the State, which might be deprived of one of its constituent parts if such possibilities were provided for."[49] Despite the scope of the principle of territorial integrity, some requirements to measure the legitimacy of an external self-determination referendum are understandable.

The rule of law requirement is materialised by demanding the referendum to comply with the legal system as a whole, and especially with the procedural rules. The Venice Commission remarks that referendum in a broader sense cannot be held if the Constitution or a statute in conformity with the Constitution does not provide for them.[50] In this sense, it bans any possible unilateral referendum prioritising the principle of territorial integrity to self-determination.

In the report on the referendum of the Autonomous Republic of Crimea, the experts of the Council of Europe concluded that the Constitution of Ukraine provided for the indivisibility of the country and therefore it does not allow the holding of any referendum on secession.[51] It also affirms that

[46] ICJ (n 27), para. 109.
[47] Ibid para. 80.
[48] Ibid.
[49] See CDL-AD (2014)002.
[50] CDL-AD (2007) 008, III, 1 on the specific rules.
[51] CDL-AD (2014)004, paras. 16, 17 and 27.

self-determination is understood primarily as internal self-determination within the framework of the existing borders, and not external self-determination through secession.[52] This limitative interpretation is exposed without further explanation or justification. The experts of the Venice Commission did not mention any of the international treaties that Ukraine is a signatory to and that recognise self-determination, nor the constitutional crisis and situations that the country has faced since 1996.

It this sense, the Venice Commission in two previous reports on Ukraine considered that, "in order to bring the Law on amendments into compliance with the principles of pluralist democracy and the rule of law, the Law should be further discussed and some improvements made."[53] It also remarked after a constitutional amendment in 2004: "taking the time necessary for finding a real consensus among all political forces and the civil society on a well-balanced and coherent constitutional reform would secure legitimacy of the new Constitution and the political system in Ukraine."[54] This kind of consensus has not been reached in Ukraine.

According to this limitating and Westphalian interpretation, the "rule of law" means that national rule of law and human rights are also valid only as part of the state constitutional structure of the State. A different and less state-centred reading of the rule of law and public international law is possible without justifying the Russian annexation of Crimea.

The conclusion of the report on the Crimean referendum has an additional point that seems contradictory to the final, decisive and holistic condition of "national" rule of law interpreted by the Commission. Its second concluding point reads: "circumstances in Crimea did not allow the holding of a referendum in line with European democratic standards. Any referendum on the status of a territory should have been preceded by serious negotiations among all stakeholders. Such negotiations did not take place."[55] Following the rationale of the same Venice Commission, is now asking for negotiation of something illegal, unconstitutional and against the rule of law? Why should the stakeholders' opponents of the referendum negotiate on the status of a territory?

The principle of the rule of law also generates procedural requirements that vary according to the specificity of each referendum. In the case of a referendum of self-determination, these procedural and substantive conditions will be conditioned by the agreement or not with the State and the way that the

[52] Ibid para.18.
[53] CDL-AD (2010)126, Draft Opinion on the Constitutional Situation in Ukraine, para.16.
[54] CDL-AD (2005)015, Opinion on the Amendments of the Constitution of Ukraine, para. 53.
[55] Ibid para 28.

referendum is conducted. An additional requirement is the existence of an effective system of appeal through judicial review.[56] In a case of a non-agreed referendum on self-determination, (as the cases of Slovenia, Croatia, Kosovo or Catalonia) an international body is desirable to grant credibility to the whole process. This body will be competent in granting the respect of electoral principles and the results of the balloting. However, whether this is a realistic enquiry is another question because any international body participating in a non-authorised referendum is going to be considered as an illegal interference in the domestic affairs of the State.

In this sense, the ICJ Opinion on Kosovo is also enlightening when it remarks: "the illegality attached to the declarations of independence thus stemmed not from the unilateral character of these declarations as such, but from the fact that they were, or would have been, connected with the unlawful use of force or other egregious violations of norms of general international law, in particular those of a peremptory character (*jus cogens*)."[57]

A referendum of self-determination will not controvert the international law if it is conducted without an unlawful use of force or other egregious violation of norms of general international law. Even when the referendum is held without the authorisation or consent of the State. In fact, the celebration of the referendum can be considered already as an act of self-determination by itself.

B. Dialogue

Dialogue is mandatory, and a breach of this requirement by one the parties might justify unilateral actions as response. This mandatory dialogic imperative must be conformed to some requirements and norms. It is not enough to allege the predisposition and acceptance of dialogue to settle an agreement and the principle of good faith. A calendar must be established, possible solutions must be proposed, and opportunities and difficulties that self-determination might cause to the parties must be clarified.

The settlement negotiations are mediated by an impartial international third party, which will have the power to rule whether any party fails to comply with the dialogic binding mandate. The consequences of breaching the imperative mandate imply ensuring the recognition of the holding of a unilateral referendum conducted by the sub-state entity with international support and

[56] CDL-AD (2007) 008, para.22.
[57] ICJ (n 27), para. 81.

recognition. In case of non-completion by the sub-state entity, the breach will mean the denial of any international support or recognition and the international acceptance of state policies to avoid the potential holding of the self-determination referendum.

According to the ICJ advisory opinion on Kosovo and the Security Council Resolutions 1244 (1999) and 1203 (1998), the "dialogic imperative" requirement is essential, or in terms of the ICJ: "to enter without preconditions into a meaningful dialogue on political status issues".[58]

C. Unilateral Referendums of Self-Determination in Liberal democracies

If the State is not a constitutional democracy, the response to the demand for a referendum will end as any other demand of democratic improvement or political openness, that is, repression, violence, political persecution and violation of Human Rights. Strict authoritarian regimes react to these political demands as China did in Tibet, or as Saddam Hussein's regime did in Iraq Kurdistan.[59] When a credible claim of holding a referendum of self-determination appears, the political pressure to the democratic foundations of the State is high. Only mature democracies can successfully resist this demand, not even the illiberal but non-authoritarian constitutional systems would pass the stress test.[60]

The processes of secession of Slovenia and Croatia from the Socialist Federal Republic of Yugoslavia in 1991 are good examples and relevant to the Catalan–Spanish conflict. Both (Croatia and Slovenia) held legally contested referendums on the issue of self-determination and secession and, justified or not, the spectre of a potential disintegration as happened in Yugoslavia, looms over Madrid. Let us accept, for the sake of this theoretical example, that the Socialist Federal Republic of Yugoslavia in 1990–1991 was an illiberal democracy

Croatia and Slovenia claimed that self-determination was a constitutional right granted to the "Nations of Yugoslavia" in the Constitutional Principles of Yugoslav Constitution of 1963 and in Tito's Constitution of 1974. Both territories held a referendum unilaterally and with fierce opposition from the

[58] Ibid para. 116.

[59] Ben Hillman and Gray Tuttle, *Ethnic Conflict and Protest in Tibet and Xianjiang* (Columbia University Press 2016); Payam Akhavan, "Lessons from Iraqi Kurdistan: Self-Determination and Humanitarian Intervention Against Genocide" (1993) 11(1) Netherlands Quarterly of Human Rights 41, 62

[60] Antoni Abat Ninet and Mark Tushnet, *The Arab Spring, An Essay on Revolution and Constitutionalism* (Edward Elgar 2015) 15

Yugoslav institutions, that finally consented to the voting with no international support.[61] The Yugoslav Presidency viewed Slovenia's plebiscite as an illegal act of secession, arguing other constitutional dispositions (Article 203 YC, that precluded the use of constitutionally granted rights in ways which threaten the existence of the State; Article 244 YC guaranteeing Yugoslavia its territorial integrity),[62] secession was considered a unilateral act that ignored the interests of other Yugoslav nations.[63] Regardless of the validity and legitimacy of the arguments of each of the parties, the disproportionate and authoritarian bias of the federation merged when the Yugoslav army carried out military action in Slovenia in 1991, in what is known as the ten-day war.

Spain is not Yugoslavia and Catalonia is not Croatia or Slovenia. The young Spanish constitutional democracy is a member of the European Union and can be compared with any democratic system in the world. Spain's democracy, built for 40 years, has endured and overcome major challenges (a coup attempt in 1981; terrorism and episodes of State terrorism; and systemic political corruption, which has come to affect even the Royal Family). Spanish had an elite fascist and democrat transitional pact. The transitional period started with the death of Dictator Francisco Franco in 1975 and ended with the democratic elections in 1982.

However, the bargained way to democracy had huge burdens to the democratic system in Spain. A clear example of this was the draft of Article 2 of the Spanish Constitution proscribing that the Constitution is based on the indissoluble unity of the Spanish nation imposed by the Military Command.

After 40 years of democratic regime these burdens are pressing. The Spanish State is the second country in the world, only surpassed by Cambodia, with more mass graves containing disappeared victims.[64] None of the political leaders, military or police of the Francoist regime have been prosecuted for alleged universal crimes against humanity.

Now, the self-determination claim in Catalonia questions and opens some of these pressing issues. As evidence of this fact, the Catalan Parliament

[61] In Slovenia, in the plebiscite conducted on 23 December 1990, 88.5 per cent favoured autonomy and the independence of Slovenia. Croatia conducted a plebiscite on 19 May 1991 in which 94 per cent voted in favour of independence. It is estimated that 83 per cent of the population voted. See Richard F Iglar, "The Constitutional Crisis in Yugoslavia and the International Law of Self-Determination. Slovenia's and Croatia's Rights to Secede" (1992) 15(1) Boston College International and Comparative Law Review 218.

[62] Richard F Iglar (n 61) 219.

[63] Ibid 220.

[64] In 2008, Judge Baltasar Garzón Real received a list with the names of 143,353 missing in the Civil War and during the Francoist dictatorship, delivered by the Platform for Victims of Enforced Disappearances by the Franco regime. Baltasar Garzon, *En el Punto de Mira* (Planeta, 2016).

passed Law 11/2017 of 14 July 2017 that annuls all the summary trials that occurred in Catalonia between 1939 and 1980.[65] Previously, in 2009, the Catalan Assembly also passed Law 10/2009 on the location and identification of disappeared people during the Civil War and the Francoist dictatorship, and the dignification of the common graves.[66]

These Bills seem to be justified because they are seeking restorative justice and dignity to the victims of a dictatorial regime. However, at the same time they introduce more elements of friction with the State. Although they can also create sympathies in sectors that demand reparatory justice, democrats and human rights activists, and others sectors of the population considered the claim as a new element of political confrontation.

To sum up, our Ulysses (Spain) is a young constitutional system that aims to become a mature one, which needs to take a decision to avoid the two horrible sea monsters. If the constitutional democratic State accepts the holding of a self-determination referendum, based on a democratic, non-violent and legitimate demand, it risks losing a part of its territory and eventually the disintegration of the State.

If our Ulysses (State) responds to the demand by not tolerating, prohibiting or with repression, its democratic essence will be called into question. A repressive reaction will probably increase the supporters of the self-determination claim in the sub-state entity, will generate sympathies of the secessionist movement in the international arena, it potentially opens the case for international intervention, and finally, it might create the opposition of sectors of the own state's population aiming for a dialogic solution.

The truth is that when a demand of secession is on the table, the vessel cannot continue sailing through the Strait of Messina as if the monsters do not exist.

V. Conclusion

Regrettably, with the Catalan voting on independence from Spain on 1 October, the fears of violence came true. Instead of a carnival of democracy (symbolic or effective), or a tense stand-off between protesters and police, we witnessed scenes of police repression on the streets of Catalonia.[67] Unlike in

[65] *Llei* 11/2017, de 4 de juliol, de *reparació jurídica de les víctimes del franquisme.*

[66] Llei 10/2009, de 30 de juny, sobre la localització i la indentificació de les persones desaparegudes durant la Guerra Civil i la dictadura franquista, i la dignificació de les fosses comunes.

[67] Zoran Oklopcic, "Introduction to I-CONnect Symposium: The Independence Vote in Catalonia: 'introduction'" <www.iconnectblog.com/2017/10/introduction-to-i-connect-symposium-independence-vote-in-catalonia/ > accessed 25 June 2020.

other countries that call themselves liberal democracies (Canada, United Kingdom, Denmark), the Catalan referendum on self-determination was held in very critical, almost unimaginable conditions.

Unlike in other constitutional democracies that claim to cherish the ideals of democratic self-government, the Spanish Government made it necessary for the ordinary citizens to protect the safety of their polling stations themselves, risking, in the process, their physical safety. Together with the officials of the Catalan Government, political representatives and private enterprises, many Catalan citizens were made the target of unlawful violence, unleashed by the repressive apparatus of the Spanish State.[68]

Some may argue that the referendum did not fulfil the basic requirements to be considered valid. However, the circumstances of repression, obstruction and police brutality need to be considered. As Stephen Tierney states: "Canada and the United Kingdom came slowly to accept the dramatic capacity of the referendum to instantiate and give voice to the popular force that underpins the very legitimacy of the multinational State, but in doing so they may have saved their states from a painful loss. Whether this lesson that will or can be learned by the Spanish State, and perhaps in time also by the European Union, remains to be seen."[69]

From a general point of view, a potential solution to the political conflict that the demand for a referendum of self-determination generates is a preventive regulation, at least of the institution of referendum. The empirical evidence shows that a constitutional accommodation of the principle of self-determination is not sufficient; the accommodation of a mechanism to enforce this right is needed.

When the self-determination demand comes into force, arguments such as unconstitutional constitutional norms, constitutional incongruences and sudden constitutional incompatibilities arise. Therefore, a procedure to face the claim, safeguarding the democratic principle (in a broad sense), the legality and other constitutional identity elements of the State is required. Nonetheless, it is necessary to acknowledge that this is an extremely complicated task and a stress test for mature constitutional democracies.

[68] Antoni Abat i Ninet, I-CONnect Symposium: The Independence Vote in Catalonia: "!Aidez la Catalogne et l'Espagne" <http://www.iconnectblog.com/2017/10/i-connect-symposium-the-independence-vote-in-catalonia-aidez-la-catalogne-et-lespagne/> accessed 14 February 2022.

[69] Stephen Tierney, I-CONnect Symposium: The Independence Vote in Catalonia: "Sovereignty Referendums: Constitutionalism in Crisis?" <http://www.iconnectblog.com/2017/10/i-connect-symposium-the-independence-vote-in-catalonia-aidez-la-catalogne-et-lespagne/> accessed 25 June 2020.

A Clarity Law, a constitutional pact on self-determination, or a special procedure would probably attenuate the stress that the democratic institutions and the rule of law are experiencing in Spain because of this political/constitutional crisis. These measures require political will and deconsecrate the principle of national unity and the borders of the State. The State's reticence to accommodate this kind of "self-destruction or segmentation" procedure is obvious, and the incentives are low. Only when there is a clear, constant and majoritarian demand of secession of a territory do these regulations make sense.

Eternal constitutional clauses prescribing territorial unity do not make the unit everlasting. On the contrary, the constitutional accommodation of the Westphalian principles to impose unity evidence fragility and that constitutional force might be required some day before a claim of secession. Constitutional identity based on the principle of unity and territorial integrity (as happens in Spain) does not make the State united forever, because at the end of day, what it is eternal? Who, in this day, still believes in Zeus, Polyphemus or Poseidon?

6

Referendums and Autocratization

Explaining Constitutional Referendums in the Post-Soviet Space

Anna Fruhstorfer

I. Introduction

Why do autocratic leaders use referendums to amend a constitution, and what is the purpose of these amendments? While the goal of autocratic leaders to stabilize their rule follows a rational motive, we know relatively little about the different strategies to achieve such stability. Scholars have emphasized a number of tactics that significantly increase autocratic survival, most importantly legitimacy, repression, and cooptation; these are described as the main 'pillars' that support autocratic regimes.[1] With the resurgence of studies interested in autocracies, dictatorships and, in particular, what is often referred to as 'competitive authoritarianism',[2] research has returned to the classic debate about legitimacy, with the notion of stability of autocratic regimes, the hegemonic power of the ruling elite and with this also autocratic survival.[3] One of the tools to legitimize the power of the ruler is a referendum, the direct consent from the demos, particularly when it comes to changing the fundamental rule of the political entity.

[1] Johannes Gerschewski, 'The three pillars of stability: Legitimation, repression, and co-optation in autocratic regimes' (2013) 20 Democratization 13; See also Fiona Shen-Bayh, 'Strategies of repression: Judicial and extrajudicial methods of autocratic survival' (2018) 70 World Politics 321; Joseph Wright, Erica Frantz and Barbara Geddes, 'Oil and autocratic regime survival' (2015) 45 British Journal of Political Science 287; Joseph Wright and Abel Escribà-Folch, 'Authoritarian institutions and regime survival: Transitions to democracy and subsequent autocracy' (2012) 42 British Journal of Political Science 283; Michael Albertus and Victor Menaldo, 'Dictators as founding fathers? The role of constitutions under autocracy' (2012) 24 Economics & Politics 279.

[2] Steven Levitsky and Lucan A. Way, 'The rise of competitive authoritarianism' (2002) 13 Journal of Democracy 51, 52: 'In competitive authoritarian regimes, formal democratic institutions are widely viewed as the principal means of obtaining and exercising political authority. Incumbents violate those rules so often and to such an extent, however, that the regime fails to meet conventional minimum standards for democracy.'

[3] For a more detailed discussion, see Johannes Gerschewski, 'Legitimacy in autocracies: Oxymoron or essential feature?' (2018) 16 Perspectives on Politics 652

Anna Fruhstorfer, *Referendums and Autocratization* In: *The Limits and Legitimacy of Referendums.* Edited by: Richard Albert and Richard Stacey, Oxford University Press. © Anna Fruhstorfer 2022. DOI: 10.1093/oso/9780198867647.003.0007

In this chapter, I show that almost all public referendums pursued in this region were constitutionally mandated. I argue that referendums in these autocracies are primarily used to legitimize the organization or preservation of the hegemonic power of the ruling elite—in the post-Soviet context, the *nomenclature*.[4] More specifically, in line with previous findings, my central argument is that the existence of a hegemonic party, fully supporting the autocratic leadership, reduces the potential of intra-elite competition and therefore reduces the need for the autocratic leader to resort to a referendum to pursue his/her agenda.[5] Hence, I expect to find a negative relationship between the level of party institutionalization and the attention that autocratic leaders devote to constitutional change via a referendum. Furthermore, following the insights of research on populist constitutionalism,[6] I hypothesize that the level of deliberation and participation during constitution making establishes a path-dependent pattern and increases the responsiveness of the public to populist rhetoric.

The results show that referendums are pursued almost exclusively when the codified rules of constitutional change make a referendum mandatory. The results of the comparative analysis as well as the case studies show that autocratic leaders choose to follow the treacherous path of citizen involvement when they cannot rely on a clear party system dominated by a hegemonic party. The fact that these referendums are used to justify an autocratic rule is surprising enough. While the process is often fraught with extensive voter fraud and repression, the degree of public support for the strong and powerful leader that referendum results reveal is surprising.[7]

The arguments developed in this chapter open the door to a more accurate understanding of how constitutions are changed and what impact institutional rules and partisan actors have in autocratic societies. The results narrow the gap in our understanding of constitutional politics that opened up with the

[4] Autocracy here is used as a term that includes several subtypes of authoritarian and hybrid regimes that can be thought of as the opposite of a consolidated democracy.

[5] Jason Brownlee, *Authoritarianism in an Age of Democratization* (Cambridge University Press 2007); Jennifer Gandhi and Adam Przeworski, 'Authoritarian institutions and the survival of autocrats' (2007) 40 Comparative Political Studies 1279; Anna Fruhstorfer, 'Paradoxes of constitutional politics in the post-Soviet space' (2017) 2 Illinois Law Review; Anna Fruhstorfer, 'Autocratic Leadership and Constitutional Change in the Post-Soviet Space' (forthcoming).

[6] Abrak Saati, 'Participatory constitution-making as a transnational legal norm: Why does it "stick" in some contexts and not in others?' 2 UC Irvine Journal of International, Transnational, and Comparative Law 113; Todd A. Eisenstadt, A. Carl LeVan and Tofigh Maboudi, 'When talk trumps text: The democratizing effects of deliberation during constitution-making, 1974–2011' (2015) 109 American Political Science Review 592.

[7] David S. Law, David S. and Mila Versteeg 'Constitutional variation among strains of authoritarianism' in Tom Ginsburg and Alberto Simpser (eds), *Constitutions in Authoritarian Regimes* (Cambridge University Press 2014) 165.

autocratic backsliding that has characterized the resurgence of populist politics in recent years and the instrumental role of constitutional politics in these events. This has important implications for autocratic stability, which cannot be achieved simply via repression and violence, and for our understanding of constitutional development under varying conditions.

In the paragraphs that follow, I summarize the expectations that one can draw from the existing literature, outline the hypotheses, describe the data and statistical models, and discuss what the statistical analysis as well as the two case studies presented here can teach us about the relationship between party institutionalization and constitutional referendums in the hybrid and autocratic regimes in the post-Soviet countries.

II. Theoretical Arguments

In this section, I explain the theoretical basis of this chapter and develop the main argument aimed at answering the research questions of why autocratic leaders use constitutional referendums to pursue their goals and what the purpose of these amendments is.

A. Public vote under autocracy

The literature on democratic regimes identified incentives for referendums, ranging from the normative idea of engaging citizens to the strategic use of the public to ratify the position of the referendum's sponsors.[8] Conversely, in autocratic regimes, the use of any popular vote is primarily associated with an effort to legitimize the prevalent rule, both at home and abroad.[9] A distinction is usually made between referendums and plebiscites,[10] signalling that the former is binding and the latter is advisory. This distinction, however, does not really apply to autocratic regimes, hence I shall use the term 'referendums' to refer to both types of popular vote on policy issues. Both follow a top-down

[8] Matthew Mendelsohn and Andrew Parkin, 'Introduction: referendum democracy' in Matthew Mendelsohn and Andrew Parkin (eds), *Referendum Democracy: Citizens, Elites and Deliberation in Referendum Campaigns* (Palgrave Macmillan 2001) 3.

[9] Stephen Tierney, 'Sovereignty and Crimea: how referendum democracy complicates constituent power in multinational societies' (2015) 16 German Law Journal 523; Mads Qvortrup, 'The rise of referendums: Demystifying direct democracy' (2017) 28 Journal of Democracy 141.

[10] Matt Qvortrup, Brendan O'Leary, and Ronald Wintrobe, 'Explaining the paradox of plebiscites' (2020) 55 Government and Opposition 202–219, 203.

mechanism that does not differentiate between autocracy and democracy. While the means to push the favoured results through and the chances of success obviously vary dramatically between autocracy and democracy, the underlying mechanism does not. Although normatively designed to include the people, top-down referendums are, in their most basic sense, a tool used by the initiating party to achieve the goal of institutional change. Although autocratic and democratic regimes clearly differ, the disparities are not always a black-or-white issue; rather, they fall at different points on a spectrum of genuine popular support and political interests. Hence, referendums are defined here quite broadly as popular votes on legislation—whether bills or initiatives - with or without binding effect.

Despite the variety of roles referendums can play in different political systems, there are also commonalities. The shared purpose of all referendums is to gain legitimacy, not only genuine sociological legitimacy won by seeking the support and approval of the citizens, but also ostensible legitimacy gained through referendums as a form of manipulation, a point emphasized for various referendums on secessionist movements and territorial conflicts.[11] We know from previous research on referendums in autocratic regimes that they are 'an instrument of choice by repressive governments',[12] or what has also been described as 'the recourse of the prince'.[13] Some argue that they serve the 'universal acclamation of the autocrat',[14] while another author refers to the 'power consolidation referendum'.[15] Others have described referendums in autocratic contexts as 'a favoured tool of tyrants and dictators seeking to legitimize and sustain their rule'[16] and as a 'political weapon'.[17]

Studies have also shown that the importance of these referendums as instruments or weapons varies according to type of autocratic regime. Case studies suggest that personalist regimes in particular seek the comfort of a referendum to prove their control over the people. One comprehensive study of referendums in autocratic regimes argues that a referendum is three times more likely

[11] Tierney (n 9). Stephen Tierney, *Constitutional Referendums: The Theory and Practice of Republican Deliberation* (Oxford University Press 2012).

[12] Qvortrup, O'Leary, Wintrobe (n 10) 4.

[13] Hamon, Francis, Le référendum: étude comparative (LGDJ 1995).

[14] Qvortrup, O'Leary, Wintrobe (n 10) 3.

[15] Jonathan Wheatley, 'A problem or a solution? The referendum as a mechanism for citizens' participation in constitution making' in Saskia Ruth, Yanina Welp, and Laurence Whitehead (eds), *Let the People Rule? Direct Democracy in the Twenty-First Century* (ECPR Press 2017) 41.

[16] Lawrence LeDuc and Larry LeDuc, *The Politics of Direct Democracy: Referendums in Global Perspective* (Broadview Press 2003).

[17] Fredrik Uggla, '*Bolivia: Referéndums como Armas Políticas*' (20 Congreso Internacional sobre Democracia Directa en América Latina, 2008).

to take place in so-called sultanistic regimes[18] than in other autocratic regimes.[19] This is in line with the assumption that sultanistic regimes use plebiscites to assure the loyalty of their people.[20] This becomes particularly salient in times of transition: studies have emphasized that the majority of referendums in non-democratic regimes occur within the first months following a leadership change.[21]

Based on these empirical observations, a number of arguments have been raised to explain the use of constitutional referendums in autocratic societies. Two arguments have been particularly prevalent in post-Soviet contexts: first, the autocratic populism argument; and second, the persistence of a post-Soviet legacy that is rooted in the use of referendums during the transition period of *glasnost*.[22]

B. The initial constitution making

The idea of referendums is an important aspect of constitutional development in the region of the former Russian Empire (after World War I). We can observe significant differences in the early Bolsheviks' enthusiasm for referendums, the Communists' reluctance to use them, and the important role referendums played in bringing about the fall of the Soviet Union. Early Soviet enthusiasm for referendums was, unsurprisingly, not sustainable. Lenin and Stalin initially supported referendums as tool to exercise national self-determination, yet without any actual translation into political reality.[23] The Second Soviet Constitution (1936) allowed for calling referendums on the initiative of the presidium of the Supreme Soviet of the Union of Soviet Socialist Republics (USSR) or of one of the Union republics.[24] This was never actually implemented in the Soviet Union, and the use of a so-called approval by popular vote

[18] A personalist ruler, ruling without any ideological restraint and often dealing with arbitrary decisions.

[19] Qvortrup, O'Leary, Wintrobe (n 10) 11.

[20] Houchang E. Chehabi and Juan J. Linz, 'A theory of sultanism 1: A type of nondemocratic rule' in Houchang E. Chehabi and Juan J. Linz (eds), *Sultanistic Regimes* (John Hopkins University Press 1998) 3.

[21] Qvortrup (n 9) 151.

[22] In Anna Fruhstorfer and Michael Hein (eds), *Constitutional Politics in Central and Eastern Europe. From Post-Socialist Transition to the Reform of Political Systems* (Verlag für Sozialwissenschaften 2016).

[23] Stephen White and Ronald J. Hill, 'Russia, the former Soviet Union and Eastern Europe: The referendum as a flexible political instrument' in Michael Gallagher and Pier Vincenzo Uleri (eds), *The Referendum Experience in Europe* (Palgrave Macmillan 1996) 153.

[24] Art. 49 Sec. d.

was extremely rare. By way of comparison, 19 countrywide referendums were held in the region until 1989.[25]

These top-down provisions of the Second Constitution of the Soviet Union could be found in the Moldovan Constitution of 1978,[26] the 1976 Albanian constitution,[27] and the 1947 Bulgarian Constitution.[28] White and Hill also describe a certain openness to ideas of public engagement throughout the period of Khrushchev's rule.[29] A genuinely effective political role for referendums was, however, never enabled until the restructuring envisioned by the *perestroika* movement under the slogan of *glasnost* ('openness'). Accompanied by popular uprisings, the 1990 referendum law of the Soviet Union became a 'tool for refashioning authority'[30] designed to help maintain the diminishing authority of Mikhail Gorbachev. Despite overwhelming support within Russia for Gorbachev's initial 1991 referendum on the preservation of the USSR as a federation, authorities were not able to stanch the growing influence of the newly elected Russian president Boris Yeltsin, and the dissolution of the Soviet Union became inevitable.

Despite the rather ambiguous history of referendums in the region, they nevertheless became an important source of legitimacy for decisions regarding constitution making after the fall of Communist rule. Strong, direct involvement of the people realized not only the question of independence, but sometimes also the adoption of new post-Soviet constitutions. Of the twelve constitutions that were enacted in former Soviet republics shortly after the fall of the USSR, four were by a referendum (in Armenia, Belarus, Kazakhstan, and Russia). Seven out of twelve countries voted for national independence from the Soviet Union in a referendum (Armenia, Azerbaijan, Georgia, Moldova, Turkmenistan, Ukraine, and Uzbekistan).

The impact of this public participation on democratic transition is at best ambiguous. A populist strategy and the rise of—more or less—charismatic leadership figures, linked 'the revolutionary street protests in city squares across the former Communist countries to the creation of binding constitutional law'.[31] Yet this use of plebiscitary engagement in constitutional design is controversial. In particular, Bruce Ackerman argues for using 'these fleeting

[25] Henry E. Brady and Cynthia S. Kaplan, 'Eastern Europe and the former Soviet Union' in David Butler and Austen Ranney (eds), *Referendums Around the World: The Growing Use of Direct Democracy* (Basingstoke 1994), 174.
[26] Art. 5, 46, 106.
[27] Art.67 and Art. 77.
[28] Art. 17 and Art. 35.
[29] White, Hill (n 23) 154–155.
[30] Brady, Kaplan (n 25) 175.
[31] William Partlett, 'The dangers of popular constitution-making' (2012) 38 Brook. J. Int'l L. 193, 200.

moments to build new and stronger foundations for liberal politics before the opportunity for self-conscious transformation is lost in the centrifugal whirl of liberal society'.[32] Other authors also emphasize the positive effects on the development of democracy,[33] while some warn about the dangers this process poses for democracy.[34] In hindsight, we know that the effects were not positive. With regard to the outcome in the post-Soviet context, the assessment of the effect of this public involvement is unambiguous: '[T]he greater [sic] role granted to popular referenda and extra-parliamentary authorities, the less constitutionalism matters as a political force.'[35] What is even worse is the behavioural pattern that has been established with this process: elites see the constituent power as a revolutionary and ultimate legitimizing force. At the first moment of challenge after the initial transition, these same elites used the established populist rhetoric to protect their rule from contenders. The cry for the strong leader and the institutionalization of his[36] charisma was heard,[37] and presidents such as Yeltsin and Lukashenko imposed their autocratic ideas on the society—either with a constitution or a swift constitutional amendment.[38] This observation leads me to the following hypothesis:

H1: Popular constitution making increases the probability that autocratic presidents will resort to referendums to amend the constitution.

What we observe with the use of constitutional referendums does not resemble an autocratic populism in the narrow sense. According to this disputed concept, the autocratic leader garners support as an anti-establishment, outsider figure.[39] Abandoning the realm of parties is a particularly important element of

[32] Bruce Ackerman, *The Future of Liberal Revolution* (Yale University Press 1992) 27.

[33] Sabine C. Carey, *Protest, Repression and Political Regimes and Empirical Analysis of Latin America and Sub-Saharan Africa* (Routledge 2009); Todd A. Eisenstadt, Carl A. LeVan & Tofigh Maboudi, 'When talk trumps text: The democratizing effects of deliberation during constitution-making, 1974–2011' (2015) 109 American Political Science Review 592, 600.

[34] Abrak Saati, *The Participation Myth: Outcomes of Participatory Constitution Building Processes on Democracy* (Umeå University 2015); Wheatley (n 15).

[35] Stephen Holmes and Cass Sunstein, 'The politics of constitutional revision in Eastern Europe' in Sanford Levinson (ed), *Responding to Imperfection: The Theory and Practice of Constitutional Amendment* (Princeton University Press 1995) 290.

[36] I use the male pronoun here.

[37] Thomas A. Baylis, 'Presidents versus prime ministers. Shaping executive authority in Eastern Europe' (1996) 48 World Politics 297, 319. Krzysztof Jasiewicz, 'Poland: Walesa's legacy to the presidency' in Raymond Taras (ed), *Postcommunist Presidents* (Cambridge University Press 1997) 130; Ackerman (n 32).

[38] Luis Lopez Guerra, 'The application of the Spanish model in the constitutional transitions in central and eastern Europe' (1997) 19 Cardozo L. Rev. 1937.

[39] See for this conceptualization Kurt Weyland, 'Clarifying a contested concept: Populism in the study of Latin American politics' (2001) Comparative Politics 1; Steven Levitsky and James Loxton, 'Populism and competitive authoritarianism in the Andes' (2013) 20 Democratization 107.

autocratic populism. Examples such as the Belorussian President Lukashenko, a self-styled outsider, might fall into this category of populist behaviour, but most post-Soviet leaders were firmly embedded in the ruling Communist elite and survived the transition quite comfortably. Nevertheless, they could not rely on an all-encompassing and all-powerful ruling party immediately after the fall of the USSR.

Parties are relevant institutions in modern political systems, and increasingly we see their importance in the survival of autocratic regimes.[40] In particular ruling parties co-opted by autocratic leaders contribute to the stability of the hegemonic power distribution.[41] Scholars have argued that autocratic leaders indeed rely heavily on classic institutions, most notably partisan legislatures, to broaden the basis of their support.[42] Yet, for this to be effective, the legislature has to be dominated by a more or less hegemonic party, and the party system should have reached a certain level of institutionalization. Without that, and despite an already low level of democracy, the legislature is a potential source of opposition to the autocratic leader and his hegemonic rule. When it comes to the role of parties within the organization and preservation of a hegemonic elite, the institutionalization and dominance of one party is a key variable that differs markedly in the countries of the post-Soviet space. With regard to the research question at hand, i.e., why do autocratic leaders try to amend the constitution through a referendum, the answer might be related to the way power is consolidated. Ideally, their parties should help to avoid confrontations and institutional struggles with parliament, ensuring 'the loyalty of parliamentarians.'[43]

Considering these assumptions, what we expect to see is a process of hegemonic preservation. Within the frame of competitive authoritarianism[44] and the idea of having institutions that mimic democratic procedures, the question still arises as to what the goal of constitutional amendments is, in particular via the difficult route of referendums. Ran Hirschl has argued that the initiation of constitutionalization processes can be related to threats to the hegemonic power of the ruling elite and possible problems their supremacy might face within a genuinely democratic decision-making process.[45] In particular,

[40] Steven Levitsky and Lucan A. Way, *Competitive Authoritarianism: Hybrid Regimes After the Cold War* (Cambridge University Press 2010).
[41] Jennifer Gandhi, *Political Institutions under Dictatorship* (Cambridge University Press 2008); Jason Brownlee, *Authoritarianism in an Age of Democratization* (Cambridge University Press 2007).
[42] Jennifer Gandhi and Adam Przeworski, 'Authoritarian institutions and the survival of autocrats' (2007) 40 Comparative Political Studies 1279.
[43] Wheatley (n 15) 48.
[44] Levitsky and Way (n 2) 52.
[45] Ran Hirschl, 'Preserving hegemony? Assessing the political origins of the EU Constitution' (2005) 3 International Journal of Constitutional Law 269, 281.

he emphasizes that 'facing possible threats to their hegemony, elites possessing disproportionate access to and influence over the constitutional arena may initiate a constitutionalization process in order to lock in their worldviews and policy preferences against unfavourable developments in the political sphere'.[46] Yet, while Hirschl points to the power transfer from the classic majoritarian institutions that are responsible for political decision making to courts, usually the supreme or constitutional court,[47] this chapter describes a different strategy of hegemonic preservation, namely via 'plebiscitarian acclaim'.[48] The core of the strategy, initially described for the entrenchment of competitive authoritarianism in Latin America, is first to use the 'disproportionate access'[49] or 'unfettered control'[50] of the ruling elite, and second, to manipulate the outcome of these Potemkin plebiscitary procedures so as to entrench the leadership. This extreme form of 'discriminatory legalism'[51]—that is, applying legal rules to opponents while not adhering to them themselves—is a common phenomenon in modern autocratic regimes.[52] In addition, resorting to the direct legitimization of the people when increasing his power makes the president more or less immune to threats both from opponents within the *nomenclature* and from the outside. This leads to a second hypothesis:

> H2: The more dominated the party system is by one party, the lower the probability that leaders in autocratic and hybrid regimes will use public involvement to change the constitution.

III. Empirical Analysis

In this section, I first discuss the dataset and then the operationalization of the dependent and the independent variables. First, to answer the research question 'Why are constitutional amendments pursued as constitutional referendums?', this chapter relies on a stepwise approach. I start with a rare-events logistic regression on an original dataset of constitutional amendments in 12 of

[46] ibid.
[47] ibid.
[48] Kurt Weyland, 'The threat from the populist left' (2013) 24 Journal of Democracy 18, 23.
[49] Hirschl (n 45) 281.
[50] Weyland (n 48) 23.
[51] ibid 24.
[52] But it is also important to clarify that the presence of what is here described as an instrument for organizing and preserving power does not necessarily identify an autocratic regime as hegemonic; see, e.g., Marc Morjé Howard and Philip G. Roessler, 'Liberalizing electoral outcomes in competitive authoritarian regimes' (2006) 50 American Journal of Political Science 365.

the 15 successor states of the Soviet Union (excluding the three Baltic states). This step is primarily aimed at understanding the structural variables that make a constitutional amendment via referendum more probable. This is followed by a most-dissimilar cases design describing the constitutional referendums in Azerbaijan and Tajikistan. These two case studies aim at gaining more insight into the additional motivations of leaders in autocratic and hybrid regimes to pursue an amendment via referendum.

A. Data

The 12 successor states of the Soviet Union (excluding the three Baltic states) are the focus of this contribution. They share a constitutional and political history; they were severely influenced by the breakup of the Soviet Union; and all face fundamental problems with features of democratic rule to varying degrees. Despite these important historic and contextual similarities, their constitutions have developed in surprisingly different forms; nevertheless, some core features remain constant, in particular the elevated position of the presidency.[53] Since the fall of the Soviet Union, the post-Soviet space has seen 19 constitutional amendment attempts via referendum (out of 88 adopted constitutional amendments), with 16 of those referendums being successful (see for an overview Table 6.1 and Figure 6.1). The original dataset includes all constitutional amendments from the implementation of the first post-Soviet constitution in 1992 until those implemented in 2016. Kyrgyzstan is the frontrunner in the area when it comes to the number of referendums held to amend a constitution. All six constitutional amendments in this country dealt with provisions concerning the presidency.

B. Operationalization

The dependent variable is the occurrence of a constitutional amendment via referendum in a respective year. It is coded as a binary variable of yes or no. The universe of cases for the models is country-years for all countries in the post-Soviet region that require a referendum for a constitutional amendment (Armenia, Azerbaijan, Belarus, Kyrgyzstan, Tajikistan, Turkmenistan). This

[53] Petra Stykow, 'The devil in the details: constitutional regime types in post-Soviet Eurasia' (2019) Post-Soviet Affairs 122, 123.

Table 6.1 List of constitutional referendums

Armenia 2005, Armenia 2015
Azerbaijan 2002, 2009, 2016
Belarus 1995, 1996, 2004
Kyrgyzstan 1996, 1998, 2003, 2007, 2010, 2016
Moldova 1999, 2010
Tajikistan 1999, 2003
Ukraine 2000

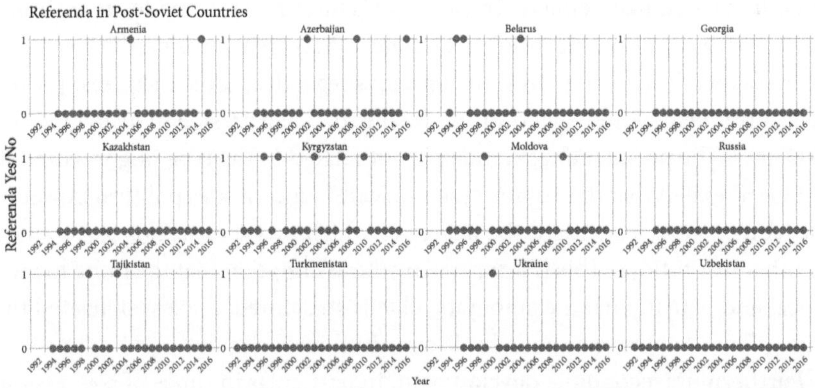

Figure 6.1 Constitutional referendums: country overview (referendum "yes" or "no", in the respective year)

selection is required as we are interested in why autocrats pursue an amendment despite the constitutional obligation to face the path of public involvement, which clearly runs the risk of failure.

The main variables of interest are the level of institutionalization of the party system and the way the constitution was originally enacted. Party institutionalization is an aggregated measure by V-Dem[54] that includes measures of party organization, depth of organization, and the degree to which a single larger party dominates the political system. It is coded from 0-1, with a higher value indicating a more institutionalized party system. The role of referendums in the implementation of the constitution after the fall of the Soviet Union is coded as a binary variable of 1 (with referendum) and 0 (without referendum).

[54] Michael Coppedge, John Gerring, Carl Henrik Knutsen, and others, 'V-Dem [Country-Year/Country-Date] Dataset v8' (2018) Varieties of Democracy (V-Dem) Project.

I also include different control variables. As some of these are highly correlated, I use them in separate models. At the national level, I include various measures that represent different concepts of democracy. First, I control for a more general measure of the level of polyarchy as provided by V-Dem,[55] and alternatively control for the level of freedom, a measure based on the additive index of civil and political liberties.[56] The measures provide a control for the intuitive assumption that less authoritarian regimes have more constitutional amendments.

To better understand the different spheres of a political entity that are relevant for a categorization as democracy or autocracy, an additional measure for the level of violence is included.[57] This controls for how respected the physical integrity of a human being is. This control is informed by the ideational argument that the more physical violence a state inflicts on its citizens, the lower will be the level of political interest in conscious legal decisions. I also test for the concentration of power. To do so, we use the so-called presidentialism index by V-Dem.[58] The presidentialism index is not related to the type of government, but to the extent that the regime systematically concentrates political power in the hands of one leader and the degree to which this actor is not constrained by other institutions. This is informed by the assumption that the more hierarchical and patrimonial the autocratic elite is structured, the less obligated the elite will feel to pursue an agenda via constitutional solutions.

Furthermore, economic development, in particular in times of a recession, often leads to a fundamental change in political structures, as well as more questioning of the political leadership and its institutional context. Wealth has to be distributed, but poverty has to be dealt with—the link between economic success and democratic development is thus empirically solid, yet not necessarily distinguishable from cultural and societal conditions.[59] I assume that a deterioration of prices or a recession could also trigger a constitutional referendum. Therefore, I include the level of economic development (as measured in GDP/capita in USD).[60]

[55] ibid.

[56] Freedom House, 'Freedom in the World' < https://freedomhouse.org/report/freedom-world/freedom-world-2019> accessed 28 June 2020.

[57] Coppedge and others (n 54).

[58] ibid.

[59] José Antonio Cheibub, *Presidentialism, Parliamentarism, and Democracy* (Cambridge University Press 2007); L. Diamond, 'Economic development and democracy reconsidered' (1992) 35 American Behavioral Scientist 450; Adam Przeworski, '*Democracy and the Market. Political and Economic Reforms in Eastern Europe and Latin America* (Cambridge University Press 1991).

[60] The World Bank, World Development Indicators, <http://data.worldbank.org/indicator/NY.GNP.PCAP.PP.CD.> accessed 10 January 2020.

Finally, war and various forms of civil unrest have the potential to recalibrate the most basic institutional configurations in the concerned states. In these times of crisis, presidents and more generally the executive become more dominant. This can 'put pressure on constitutional bargains'.[61] The constitution could be amended as a reaction to violent circumstances (for example by increasing presidential power), but also to eventually deal with unresolved issues (in the regional context that could be so-called frozen conflicts and so-called de facto states). To control for this possible effect, I include a binary indicator of organized violence, where at least one involved party was the government of the state. I draw these data from the Uppsala Conflict Data Program.[62]

C. Results

To understand the reasons why autocratic leaders choose to amend the constitution despite having to follow the challenging path of a mandatory referendum to do so, I employ a rare events logistic regression. The empirical strategy takes the data structure into account, in particular as the event of interest is rare: 19 of the 88 constitutional amendments in the post-Soviet region up to 2016 were pursued via referendum and, as described earlier, in the vast majority of cases only then by a referendum when the constitution required it of the political elite. I have not come across any other successful amendments that were put to a referendum without the explicit requirement to do so. I am only aware of three amendment drafts (in Moldova and Ukraine) that were pursued via a referendum when it was not required by the constitution, and they failed in the process.

I estimate the influence of the two main explanatory variables introduced earlier (party institutionalization and the process whereby the constitution was initially adopted following the break-up of the Soviet Union) on the probability that a referendum for a constitutional amendment is pursued. I rely first on the relogit estimator by King and Zeng, who show that ordinary logistic regression underestimates the probability of these events. They propose the relogit

[61] Z. Elkins, T. Ginsburg, and J. Melton. *The Endurance of National Constitutions* (Cambridge University Press 2009) 118.

[62] N. P. Gleditsch, P. Wallensteen, M. Eriksson, M. Sollenberg, and H. Strand, 'Armed conflict 1946–2001' (2002) 39 Journal of Peace Research 615–637; see for the definition of de-facto states Anna Fruhstorfer and Silvia von Steinsdorff, 'Post-Soviet de facto states in search of internal and external legitimacy' (2012) 45 Communist and Postcommunist Studies 117.

command in STATA 15, which accounts for the occurrence of rare events by estimating bias-corrected coefficients instead of logit coefficients (see Table 6.2).[63] I also present the results of the conventional logistic regression analysis (Table 6.3). Because the variables of interest are measured at the country level while the dependent variable is measured at the referendum level, I clustered the standard errors in the conventional logistic regression analysis at the country level.

The results presented in Tables 6.2 and 6.3 serve to explain the conditions under which autocratic leaders amend the constitution despite having no choice but to do so via referendum. To begin with *H1*, I assumed that popular constitution making increases the probability that autocratic presidents will also resort to referendums to amend the constitution. But against this expectation, the results notably suggest that having held a public referendum to adopt a given constitution does not make autocratic leaders more inclined to attempt a constitutional amendment via a referendum. At least from the comparative perspective, we do not observe the subsequent development of a populist strategy. While only part of the concept of public participation in constitution making, the involvement of the public in the drafting of a constitution fails to consistently predict a systematic increase in the use of referendums to amend the constitution, all else being equal. This also applies when we vary the control variable 'democracy' in both the relogit model and in the conventional logistic regression analysis.

The analysis does, however, confirm *H2*, one of the two core theoretical expectations. I hypothesized that the more the party system is dominated by one party, the lower the probability that leaders in autocratic and hybrid regimes will resort to public involvement to change the constitution. Controlling for confounding factors, I find significant negative coefficients (Table 6.2) and odds ratios (Table 6.3) for the variable 'institutionalization of the party system'. In line with the expectation in the second hypothesis and confirming the findings from existing literature,[64] parties and partisan legislatures are a significant factor in autocratic regimes. When parliament is dominated by a more or less hegemonic party in a party system, the legislature is not a potential adversary of the autocratic leader and his hegemonic rule. When it comes to the role of parties within the organization and preservation of a hegemonic elite, the institutionalization and dominance of one party is a key issue. The results in Tables

[63] Gary King and Langche Zeng, 'Logistic regression in rare events data' (2001) 9 Political Analysis 207.

[64] Gandhi (n 41); Brownlee (n 41); Gandhi and Przeworski (n 42).

Table 6.2 Regression results (relogit command in STATA 15)

	(1)	(2)	(3)	(4)
	Referendum (Coef.)	Referendum (Coef.)	Referendum (Coef.)	Referendum (Coef.)
Party Institutionalization	−2.21 (0.85)***	−2.42 (0.82)***	−2.20 (0.76)***	−2.32 (0.80)***
War	−0.05 (0.73)	−0.13 (0.81)	−0.05 (0.76)	−0.07 (0.78)
GDP/capita	−0.20 (0.22)	−0.21 (0.21)	−0.02 (0.23)	−0.21 (0.22)
Adoption via Referendum	0.65 (0.77)	0.69 (0.75)	0.62 (0.79)	0.72 (0.82)
Polyarchy (V-Dem)	0.22 (0.38)			
Level of Freedom		0.09 (0.19)		
Physical Violence			0.94 (1.26)	
Presidentialization				−0.38 (0.92)
Constant	−0.72 (0.13)***	−1.06 (0.96)	−1.17 (0.63)*	−0.38 (0.81)
Observations	273	273	273	273

Clustered standard error in parenthesis. * p < 0.10, ** p < 0.05, *** p < 0.01

Table 6.3 Regression results (conventional)

	(5)	(6)	(7)	(8)
	Referendum (OR)	Referendum (OR)	Referendum (OR)	Referendum (OR)
Party Institutionalization	0.10 (0.09)***	0.08 (0.07)***	0.10 (0.08)***	0.09 (0.07)***
War	0.62 (0.46)	0.55 (0.46)	0.63 (0.49)	0.60 (0.48)
GDP/capita	0.78 (0.18)	0.78 (0.16)	0.77 (0.18)	0.78 (0.17)
Adoption via Referendum	2.04 (1.01)	0.62 (0.79)	1.96 (1.57)	2.17 (1.72)
Polyarchy (V-Dem)	1.30 (0.51)			
Level of Freedom		1.10 (0.22)		
Physical Violence			2.88 (3.71)	
Presidentialization				0.68 (0.64)
Constant	0.49 (0.06)***	0.35 (0.34)	0.30 (0.19)	0.70 (0.58)
Observations	273	273	273	273
Goodness of fit (Hosmer and Lemeshow) χ^2 (8)	2.12 (p=.98)	8.14 (p=.42)	5.83 (p=.67)	10.68 (p=0.22)
C-Statistic	0.75	0.76	0.75	0.75

Clustered standard error in parenthesis. * p < 0.10, ** p < 0.05, *** p < 0.01

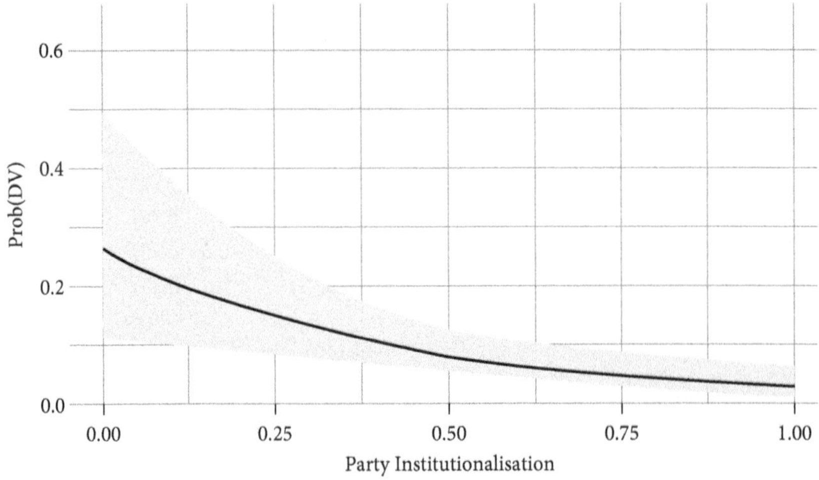

Figure 6.2 Relationship of referendums and party institutionalization

6.2 and 6.3, as well as Figure 6.2, suggest that the higher the institutionalization of the party system, the less likely a constitutional amendment will be pursued via referendum. The effect varies only slightly with a change in the measure of democracy/autocracy used in the respective models. Overall, a one-unit increase in the party institutionalization variable (scale from 0-1) decreases the odds of the occurrence of a constitutional referendum by 90 per cent.

To illustrate the importance of these mechanisms of hegemonic organization and preservation, I describe the two 'most dissimilar' cases that follow the schematic explanation of popular democratic engagement to legitimize hegemonic preservation: Azerbaijan and Tajikistan. The two cases exhibit some differences in the level of repression and how secure the presidency was for the incumbent. At the same time, both resort to a constitutional amendment via referendum to first organize and then preserve the hegemony of the ruling elite. A key issue in these two cases is a similarly low level of partisan hegemony supporting the president prior to the important constitutional amendment. Thus, the nomenclature had to resort to the public to start to establish their hegemonic power. Once that power was established, a referendum became a useful tool to further legitimize the power of the ruling elite.

1. The case of Azerbaijan

Azerbaijan is a paradigmatic case of a country deciding to hold a referendum to amend the constitution to guarantee the preservation of a hegemonic elite. Recall that the essential feature of the hegemonic preservation concept described earlier, that is, constitutionalization is initiated when the ruling elite is threatened and uses its constitutional possibilities to preserve its power against unfavourable developments. This is precisely the situation in Azerbaijan. The ruling nomenclature prior to but also after the important constitutional amendment in 2002 is not as coherent as one might assume, given the rather poorly developed state of democracy in the country. This incoherence of the elite is one important reason that the executive had to rely on pseudo-democratic referendums to guarantee lubricant power. Laporte counted three separate, powerful groups that drive Azeri politics and occupy all relevant political positions: the so-called old guard, the oligarchs, and the family of the president (in large part represented by the family foundation).[65] This was more so the case in 2002 when Laporte conducted her research, but the observation is still true today. These three groups are in competition, although their memberships are not necessarily mutually exclusive.

The 2002 constitutional amendment was a key reaction to the challenges that these competing groups represented, guaranteeing that the ruling Aliyev family kept power. The amendment was particularly aimed at increasing the influence of the ruling party. To help establish a more hegemonic party system with the New Azerbaijan Party (YAP) as the main beneficiary, one of the measures introduced with the 2002 amendment was the abolishment of the proportional election of 25 seats (out of 100) in the Milli Mejlis (the Azeri parliament), thus reducing the possibilities for smaller parties. Short-term considerations were also part of the amendment: the provisions that were changed stipulate that the prime minister becomes acting president (instead of the chairperson of the Milli Mejlis).[66] With the failing health of then-president Heydar Aliyev (who died in December 2003), this could have become important, so his son Ilham Aliyev was appointed prime minister in August 2003, at the same time that the older Aliyev travelled to the United States to seek medical treatment. Three months later, in October 2003, the younger Aliyev won the presidential election, much to no one's surprise.[67] This election was accompanied by severe

[65] Jody Laporte, 'Semi-presidentialism in Azerbaijan' in Robert Elgie and Sophia Moestrup (eds), *Semi-Presidentialism in the Caucasus and Central Asia* (Palgrave Macmillan 2016) 91 at 109–112.

[66] Art. 105 Sec. 1.

[67] Also, part of the 2002 amendment was Art. 101 Sec. II. of the Constitution, which allows for the election of the president with an absolute majority, and not a two-thirds majority as under the 1995 constitution.

measures against the opposition, which claimed voter fraud and, among other things, the detention of election officials.[68]

The 2009 amendment (which was, in fact, a referendum on 29 amendments) followed a similar logic of guaranteeing the influence and power of the Aliyev family, this time preserving the hegemony of the president himself. It was ostensibly pursued to put the country in compliance with requirements of the Council of Europe and the European Convention on Human Rights, but it was also a convenient occasion for the Aliyev family to tighten its grip on power, for example granting protection from investigation by journalists to government officials (guaranteeing their unwavering support).[69] The amendment also abolished the two-term limit for the president, replacing it with a section on term extension in a state of war.[70] The referendum was accompanied by intimidation and the occurrence of multiple voting, yet the turnout was only 71 per cent, with 88 per cent voting in favour of the amendment.[71] Although parts of the amendment were aimed at improving basic rights, the most likely underlying goal was to pre-empt unrest and to make the ruling elite more cohesive.[72] Any challenge to the rule of the Aliyev family was for the time being averted.[73]

In the course of 2014–2015, opposition groups started a campaign criticizing the government, while collecting the necessary signatures to be registered as candidates for the parliamentary elections. Interviews with Azeri oppositional activists have shown that interaction with voters while collecting the signatures was their 'only chance to spread their [oppositional] views undisturbed by the authorities. It is also a rare opportunity to gauge the level of support from the community.'[74] These observations are in line with the literature on the strategic behaviour of electoral authoritarian regimes. They aim to paralyze not to completely destroy any opposition,[75] a strategy that worked very efficiently for a long time in Azerbaijan. Yet, the role of the younger Aliyev as president was

[68] Freedom House, 'Azerbaijan 2010' <https://freedomhouse.org/report/freedom-world/2010/azerbaijan> accessed 10 January 2020

[69] Ronald J. Hill, Stephen White, 'Referendums in Russia, the Former Soviet Union and Eastern Europe' in Mads Qvortrup (ed), *Referendums Around the World: The Continued Growth of Direct Democracy* (Palgrave Macmillan 2014) 113,130.

[70] Art. 101 Sec V.

[71] Mads Qvortrup (ed), *Referendums Around the World: The Continued Growth of Direct Democracy* (Palgrave Macmillan 2014).

[72] Roger B. Myerson, 'The autocrat's credibility problem and foundations of the constitutional state' (2008) 102 American Political Science Review 125, 136.

[73] For a similar assessment, see Aser Babajew, 'Verfassungsänderung in Aserbaidschan' (2009) Friedrich-Ebert-Stiftung Fokus Südkaukasus.

[74] Sofie Bedford and Laurent Vinatier, 'Resisting the irresistible: "Failed opposition" in Azerbaijan and Belarus revisited' (2018) Government and Opposition 1 at 14.

[75] Andreas Schedler, *The Politics of Uncertainty: Sustaining and Subverting Electoral Authoritarianism* (Oxford University Press 2013) 374.

significantly more authoritarian than his father, also facing coup attempts as early as 2005. But the behaviour of the regime changed before the parliamentary election in November 2015 as it became more under pressure. Some international observers relate this to the economic conditions and the problems the paternalistic distribution of the Azeri wealth (in particular oil) had to face with the drop in the oil price.[76]

The action towards the opposition dramatically shifted, as paralysis was no longer sufficient, but the authorities reverted to classic repression and the arrest of a number of journalists, human rights activist, and oppositional representatives. This increased repression and more fraudulent parliamentary elections were then compounded by the 2016 constitutional amendment, which further preserved the Aliyev family's hegemonic grip on power. It provided a path for the family future, abolishing the age limit for the presidency[77] and establishing the office of vice-president, a position that was quickly assumed by Aliyev's wife. Again, the executive power stepped up repression, arrests, and violence, leaving no room for debate or controversy.

2. The case of Tajikistan

Tajikistan is a prime example of a window-of-opportunity argument and the idea that coups or civil wars are precursors to the consolidation of power via constitutional referendum.[78] After the end of the civil war in Tajikistan in 1997, the ruling elite was able to dominate the peace process as well as the amendment of the constitution in 1999. The then-president Emomali Rahmon—a former Soviet *apparatchik*—had been head of state since 1992. From the outset the 1994 constitution established a powerful presidency in a clear presidential system, with the president as the head of government (the presidential election and the referendum on the new constitution took place on the same day)[79]. The role of the president was quickly even further expanded when the civil war broke out, helping the president to fill any remaining voids in his control over the distribution of power. With a reported 97.6 per cent support for the 1999 constitutional referendum, the president and the supporting elite guaranteed their hegemonic hold on power, while co-opting the Islamic Renaissance Party by allowing religion-based parties to operate in the country (an important

[76] Laurence Broers, 'Parliamentary Election Highlights Aserbaijan's Change Dilemma' 29 October 2015 <https://www.chathamhouse.org/expert/comment/parliamentary-election-highlights-azerbaijan-s-change-dilemma> accessed 10 January 2020.

[77] Lower age limit of 35 years, Art. 100 Sec. 2.

[78] Wheatley (n 15).

[79] Broers (n 76).

provision to end the war that was abolished in 2016). While in 1995 we see no hegemonic party dominating the political system, following the 1999 constitutional referendum, the parliamentary elections in 2000 resulted in a majority for the People's Democratic Party of Tajikistan (PDPT) and a sound defeat for the Communist Party.

The amendment of 1999 prolonged the term of the president to seven years, but also instituted a one-term limit.[80] From an institutionalist perspective, the creation of a two-chamber parliament, with members directly appointed by the president or by local parliaments led by people appointed by the president, allowed for the decisive stabilization of Rahmon's rule.[81] The 2003 amendment, passed with 93.82 per cent in favour and an alleged turnout of 96.38 per cent of eligible voters, further strengthened autocratic rule in Tajikistan, maintaining the seven-year term but allowing for a maximum of two consecutive terms.[82] At the same time, President Rahmon announced that his first two terms would not be counted towards the newly established provisions. Since 2005, the PDPT has not only been the majority party, but has dominated the Tajik Parliament, consistently controlling around 50 of the 63 seats.[83]

The 2016 constitutional amendment—again via referendum—once again changed the article concerning term limits.[84] Roughly translated, the text of the amendment stipulated that the article's two-term limit does not apply to the 'Leader of the Nation', a new title conferred upon Rahmon. In addition, another article was amended to lower the age limit to become president, arguably to allow for a possible succession of his son or daughter.[85] Among other changes, Article 1 and Article 8 stand out. In the first article of the constitution, the presidential form of government is explicitly established. Religion-based parties, allowed according to the 1999 amendment, were once again prohibited, and the Islamist Party, one of the main challengers to the hegemonic rule of the PDPT, was characterized as a terrorist organization.[86]

After the civil war, Rahmon was able to quickly consolidate his power. The instruments he used to avert or to counteract threats against his hegemony included 'disproportionate access to and influence over the constitutional

[80] Art. 101 Sec. I.
[81] Freedom House, 'Tajikistan 1999' <https://freedomhouse.org/report/freedom-world/1999/tajikistan> accessed 7 May 2019.
[82] Wheatley (n 15) 46; again amending Art. 65.
[83] 49 seats in 2005, 55 seats in 2010, 51 seats in 2015; Election Archive, 'Tajikistan, Majlisi namoyandogon,' Inter Parliamentary Union,<archive.org/praline-e/reports/2309_A.htm> accessed 10 January 2020.
[84] Art. 65 Sec. 5.
[85] Art. 65 Sec. 1.
[86] Art. 8.

area … [to] initiate a constitutionalization process … against unfavourable developments in the political sphere'.[87] The scenario in 1998–1999 pointed to these unfavourable developments, in particular, the parliamentary election scheduled for June 1998. The president used his position to postpone the election and to get public endorsement for the formalization of his power. This fulfils both requirements of a 'power consolidation referendum' as described by Wheatley—a constitutional transfer of power from one institution to another, and a top-down approach.[88] Since then, President Rahmon's rule has gone unchallenged, but the constitutional changes were legitimized with a referendum (with a similarly incredible turnout and more than 90 per cent support).

These two case studies augment the perspective of the structural arguments provided in the comparative analysis by illustrating some of the possible motivations underlying the pursuit of a constitutional amendment via a referendum. Despite substantive differences in the Azeri and Tajik contexts, the ruling elite chose to pursue a change in the constitution by holding a referendum. As argued earlier, this is primarily a strategy of hegemonic preservation via 'plebiscitarian acclaim'.[89] While the contexts in which the presidents pursued these constitutional amendments were different (challenge to the leadership in Azerbaijan, desire to consolidate presidential power in Tajikistan), their common goal was to organize a hegemonic system and streamline parliament. In both cases the presidents successfully pursued this via a constitutional referendum, with long-lasting effects on the consolidation of their power.

IV. Conclusion

At the outset of this chapter I asked two research questions: Why do autocratic leaders use referendums to amend a constitution, and what is the purpose of these amendments? From the comparative analysis we see that constitutional amendments via referendums have been used as a tool to legitimize autocratic rule and as an attempt to first organize and then preserve the hegemonic power of a ruling elite. Both the statistical analysis and the case studies of referendums in Azerbaijan and Tajikistan provide evidence of the importance of the party system—particularly when the hegemonic party and the level of party institutionalization are not yet fully established—for the probability that a regime will

[87] Hirschl (n 45) 281.
[88] Wheatley (n 15) 41.
[89] Weyland (n 48) 23.

resort to a constitutional referendum. When the autocratic leader pursuing the amendment could not be sure of parliamentary cooperation to organize and preserve his autocratic rule, he took recourse to the people. In order to legitimize an illegitimate rule change, it is likewise a smart move to get the approval of the people, even if it requires pressure and fraud to do so. This choice is right in line with what research has described as 'veil of legitimacy'.[90] We also see that the majority of these referendums were successful in establishing a powerful presidency. In the rare cases where they were not successful, the institutionalized power of parliament to protect its own influence played an important role (Moldova is the prime example here). Belarus is also a particularly interesting case, as the opposition's proposed amendment in 1996, which lost out to the president's proposal, was also not aimed at democratizing measures, but rather at re-establishing the old Communist rule.

The mechanisms that lead to a constitutional referendum in the post-Soviet space are contingent on partisan organization. Efforts to first organize and then preserve hegemonic rule are frequent, and the manner in which such efforts are attempted is deeply affected by the amount of partisan support. The arguments developed in this chapter open the door to a more accurate understanding of how constitutions are changed and what role partisan actors and institutional rules play—even in autocratic societies. But we also see that constitutional politics can take many different forms and depends on varying national contexts. This calls for further interregional and large-n comparisons of autocratic regimes in order to better understand the interaction between party politics and constitutional politics. The findings of this study have important implications for the analysis of autocratic stability and how constitutional politics can be used to pursue specific goals. Building on these findings, future research should expand the partisan hegemony perspective and focus on the question of whether parties strategically emphasize the differences between themselves while being co-opted. Also expanding on the findings of this study, the question of how amendment attempts in autocracies become a salient issue should be addressed. Future research should look closely at the contextual factors that influence this salience and thereby explore the individual motivations that lead political actors to pursue constitutional referendums. This entails a closer look at interactions between government and legislature prior to these events. In terms of methodology, a mixture of comprehensive comparative analysis with

[90] David S. Law and Mila Versteeg, 'Sham constitutions' (2013) 101 California Law Review 171.

individual case studies focusing on key actors promises to be most productive. And while the post-Soviet space has seen constitutional referendums on various constitutional polities, the empirical examples are clearly skewed towards the role of the presidency. Hence, future research should emphasize and test more extensively for the role of referendums in resolving issues in other domains of constitutional politics.

PART III
ARE THE PEOPLE SOVEREIGN?

7

Brexit and Two Roles for Referendums in the United Kingdom

Leah Trueblood

I. Introduction

The 2016 referendum on the United Kingdom's membership of the European Union is a textbook example of how *not* to conduct a referendum. Further, the Brexit referendum was not an isolated democratic failing. It reflects a deeper structural weakness in the use of referendums in the United Kingdom. For decades in the United Kingdom before Brexit, referendums were used in an 'unplanned'[1] and *ad hoc* way[2] when it was politically convenient. This chapter will argue that the unprincipled use of referendums in the United Kingdom, at least in part, reflects an underlying disagreement about what referendums are for and their relationship with democracy. There are, broadly, two different accounts of the relationships between referendums and democracy in the United Kingdom. On the first view which I will call the 'referendums as limits' approach, referendums are a way for voters to act as a check on the actions of their representatives. This is the view taken by Dicey,[3] Qvortrup,[4] and Bogdanor.[5] The second approach is to see referendums as a way of temporarily substituting voters for representatives. On this view, drawing on the civic republican tradition, referendums are deliberative processes of expressing popular sovereignty. I will call this latter view 'referendums as substitutions.' This latter view of referendums is presented in its most effective form by Tierney.[6] It is also the view

[1] Vernon Bogdanor, *The People and the Party System* (CUP 1981) 66.

[2] Constitution Committee, 'Referendums in the United Kingdom' (2009) 12th Report 51.

[3] Albert V Dicey, *Introduction to the Study of the Law of the Constitution* (Roger E Michener ed, 8th Revised edition, Liberty Fund Inc 1982) cviii–cix.

[4] Matt Qvortrup, 'A.V. Dicey: The Referendum as the People's Veto' (1999) 20 History of Political Thought 531, 546; Matt Qvortrup (ed), *Referendums Around the World: The Continued Growth of Direct Democracy* (Palgrave MacMillan 2014) 1

[5] 'The referendum is an instrument of protection and not of change.' Bogdanor (n 1) 69.

[6] '[Referendums] can serve to supplant the two levels of representation that are present within democratic constitutionalism.' Stephen Tierney, 'Constitutional Referendums: A Theoretical Enquiry' (2009) 72 MLR 360, 383.

Leah Trueblood, *Brexit and Two Roles for Referendums in the United Kingdom* In: *The Limits and Legitimacy of Referendums*. Edited by: Richard Albert and Richard Stacey, Oxford University Press. © Leah Trueblood 2022.
DOI: 10.1093/oso/9780198867647.003.0008

of referendums that is increasingly reflected in law in the United Kingdom.[7] I will argue here that the 'referendums as limits' approach is the better view both in theory and in practice. The practical argument will focus in particular on the 2016 Brexit referendum. I will show that there were numerous failings with the Brexit referendum, but many came back to the same root: the attempt to use the referendum as a substitute for representatives rather than limits on the action of representatives. This attempt to use referendums to replace rather than guide representatives led to failings of process, content, execution, and accountability.[8] I will show that I do not think these failings would have occurred if referendums been used as limits on the actions of representatives to approve the Maastricht and Lisbon treaties, or if the 2016 Brexit referendum was clearly connected to new legislation or proposals for reform.

This chapter will fall into five further sections. I will begin in Section II by providing a brief history of the use of referendums in the United Kingdom. In Section III, I will outline two accounts of the relationship between referendums and representative democracy: (i) referendums as limits; and (ii) referendums as substitutions for representatives. In Section IV, I will show how the Brexit referendum was based on the view of referendums as temporary substitutions for representatives. In Section V, I will make a case for referendums as limits on the actions of representatives, both descriptively and normatively. Finally, in Section VI, I will show how this disagreement about two conceptions of democracy and, consequently, two conceptions of referendums, continues to cause disagreements about the meaning of Brexit.

II. Brief history of referendums in the United Kingdom

The failures of the Brexit referendums are a symptom of a deeper problem with the use of referendums in the United Kingdom: their use has always been '*ad hoc*.'[9] That the use of referendums has been *ad hoc* in the United Kingdom is not a novel point. Bogdanor says that 'Because the referendum was introduced in such an unplanned way ... there has been singularly little discussion as to its precise constitutional status: nor has there been any attempt to define its proper scope.'[10] Leyland warns that '... In the absence of ground rules governing

[7] Although it is not clear in law in the United Kingdom what the rationale for referendums is, I will argue in Section III that the 'referendums as substitutions' view is implicit in the statutes that make up the devolution settlement.

[8] These failings are the subject of Section VI.

[9] Committee (n 2) 51.

[10] Bogdanor (n 1) 66.

their application ... they have not only been used pragmatically but with an alarming lack of consistency.'[11] As the House of Lords Constitution Committee says, the use of referendums in the United Kingdom has evolved without 'constitutional principle.'[12] This *ad hoc* evolution, like the United Kingdom's constitution itself, has been a long time in the making. The use of referendums was first seriously considered after the introduction of the Great Reform Acts. As Bogdanor says, the question asked about referendums after the expansion of suffrage was: How were the 'people'—the newly enfranchised electorate—to exercise their power: solely through representative institutions, or through the machinery of direct democracy? This was the central issue in the constitutional debates of the years between 1890 and 1912.[13]

The debate was particularly salient in the wake of the Parliament Acts when the House of Lords was no longer a check on the House of Commons.[14] It was suggested by Conservatives that the referendum might serve as an alternative check on the House of Commons, but the Conservatives were unable to form a majority after the 1910 election, and this never came to pass.[15] While the possibility of referendums was entertained on issues such as membership of the League of Nations, women's suffrage, and tariff reform,[16] the use of referendums only began in earnest in the 1970s.[17] This reflected an uptick in the use of referendums that happened around the world.[18]

Starting in the 1970s, referendums were used across the United Kingdom in a variety of different ways. They performed a range of roles in the process of constitutional change. A referendum was held in 1973 in Northern Ireland on the question of whether Northern Ireland should remain part of the United Kingdom. While those who voted preferred to stay by a wide margin, the vast majority of Republicans boycotted the process.[19] The boycott was, in part, a result of the structural failings of the border poll itself. In a letter to *The Times* it

[11] Peter Leyland, 'Referendums, Popular Sovereignty, and the Territorial Constitution', *Sovereignty and the Law: Domestic, European and International Perspectives* (OUP 2014) 149.

[12] Committee (n 2) 48.

[13] Bogdanor (n 1) 11.

[14] 'When the House of Lords was stripped of its veto in 1911, removing the last institutional barrier against Home Rule, Conservatives argued that the referendum take over its functions.' Robert Saunders, *Yes to Europe!: The 1975 Referendum and Seventies Britain* (CUP 2018) 68.

[15] ibid. 68.

[16] Bogdanor (n 1) 33–35.

[17] 'Although there was prior experience, such as the Scottish referendum on prohibition in 1920 ... and local polls in Wales on the Sunday opening of pubs during the 1960s ... the modern history of referendums in the UK begin(s) in 1973.' House of Lords Committee (n 2). Report 7.

[18] Stephen Tierney, *Constitutional Referendums: The Theory and Practice of Republican Deliberation* (OUP 2012) 1.

[19] 'Turnout for "no" was 1.1% (the poll was subject to a widespread boycott by the Nationalist community.)' Committee (n 2) 9.

was warned that without connecting the border poll to the reforms outlined in the Government's White Paper, the vote would become a straightforward majoritarian headcount.[20] That is exactly what happened. The referendum in 1973 in Northern Ireland demonstrates that referendums are not magic wands. They cannot build political goodwill where none exists. On their own they cannot address division. Indeed, when used poorly, they can do exactly the opposite.

The first UK-wide referendum in 1975 endorsed continued membership of the European Economic Community (EEC) by a considerable margin.[21] Again, the relationship between the referendum and the reforms was complicated, not only by the referendum affirming the status quo rather than approving a constitutional change before it happened, but again the vote was shaped by negotiations and reforms. Harold Wilson had successfully secured reforms from the European Union on Commonwealth trade, aid and development, the Common Agricultural Policy, and the budget.[22] The approval of these reforms was central to the 1975 referendum.[23] Due to the *ad hoc* use of referendums in the United Kingdom, there have a been a wide range of relationships between proposals for reform and referendums. This relationship between referendums and reforms is important too in the Brexit context, as David Cameron did not succeed in casting the 2016 referendum as an affirmation of a successful renegotiation process.[24]

Referendums were also held concerning devolution in Wales and Scotland in 1979. In Wales, despite having the support of three of the four main political parties, proposals for reform were overwhelmingly rejected.[25] In Scotland, the requirement that 40% of the overall electorate[26] support the changes was not satisfied. While these proposals were rejected, they are important for the history of referendums in the in United Kingdom for two reasons. First, they began to establish the precedent that referendums would be used on devolution issues in the United Kingdom. As Leyland argues, over time this became a constitutional convention[27] and was then enshrined in law in the acts that make up the devolution settlement. Now, referendums are used as devices of

[20] *The Times* 16 January 1973.
[21] 67.2% for 'yes' to 32.8% for 'no' on a 64% turnout. Committee (n 2) 9.
[22] Saunders (n 14) 90.
[23] 'As *The Economist* put it, the "concessions which Mr Harold Wilson won ... are not in themselves significant. But the winning them, and the manner of winning them, were. The effect of all this was substantial. Unlike in 2016, the conclusion of the renegotiations produced a significant and enduring shift in the polls."' ibid. 93.
[24] ibid.
[25] 'Only 11.8% could be found to endorse the Wales Act.' Bogdanor (n 1) 51.
[26] Crucially, 40% of the entire electorate was required, not just those who cast votes.
[27] Leyland (n 11).

entrenchment to underline the 'permanence' of the devolution settlement. More will be said about the current law with respect to referendums in the United Kingdom in Section IV.

The three uses of referendums in the United Kingdom in the 1970s—The Northern Ireland border poll, EEC membership, and devolution—do have a unifying logic. The issues at stake: secession, European integration, and devolution fall into a similar category. The outlines of a set of constitutional changes that required referendums were beginning to come into focus. The difficulty is that while the three referendums in the 1970s considered similar types of constitutional questions, the form of the referendum questions was very different. This is important because the structure of referendum questions is illustrative of what role a referendum is taken to be playing in the process of constitutional change. The different uses of referendums in the 1970s reflect different accounts of the relationship between referendums and representative democracy.

Consider the structure of the three referendums held in the 1970s. The 1973 referendum asked a question about the status quo;[28] the 1975 question came at the end of a renegotiation;[29] and the 1979 referendum put forward a series of proposals for reform.[30] The contrast is starkest between the referendums in 1973 and 1979. The former was an open-ended question about the status quo. The latter performed an approval function for Acts of Parliament. The 1975 referendum sits uncomfortably between these types of referendums because voters were being asked to affirm membership of ECC, not to enter into it.[31] The renegotiated settlement with the European Union was also central to the 2016 Brexit referendum, and some voters saw themselves as approving those reforms, and other voters understood the point of the referendum to be something else entirely. This distinction between referendums as beginning and concluding processes of constitutional change is important. These different uses of referendums reflect two alternative views of the relationship between referendums and democracy. When referendums consider Bills or proposals for reform already passed by representatives, referendums are devices of approval. They are limits on the actions of those representatives. When referendums ask a question about the status quo, as in 1973, referendums are mechanisms of bypassing representatives. They do not approve constitutional changes but ask

[28] 'Do you want Northern Ireland to remain part of the United Kingdom? Or Do you want Northern Ireland to be joined with the Republic of Ireland outside the United Kingdom?'

[29] 'Do you think that the United Kingdom should stay in the European Community (the Common Market)?'

[30] 'Do you want the provisions of the Scotland/Wales Act 1978 to be put into effect?'

[31] Saunders (n 14) 80.

voters to choose whether to undertake them. The academic literature on referendums is driven by these sorts of distinctions and taxonomies.[32] A range of different labels are used to express the same idea.[33] A familiar distinction in these taxonomies is: are referendums devices of veto or are they a device of popular initiative? Put differently, should referendums initiate or conclude processes of constitutional change? This disagreement about the roles for referendums reflects deeper normative disagreement about the relationships between referendums and representative democracy. Consider now two accounts of the relationship between representative democracy and referendums.

III. Two accounts of the relationship between referendums and democracy

Disagreements about referendums tend to become disagreements about democracy. Bogdanor argues that arguments against referendums inexorably become arguments against democracy.[34] Bogdanor is right about this, but the arguments also flow in the other direction. Different views about democracy inform different accounts of referendums. Disagreements about referendums reflect different views about what makes democracy democratic and why. Here I will identify two broad traditions of thinking about referendums and democracy: (i) referendums as limits on the actions of representatives; and (ii) referendums as temporary replacements for representatives. The first view reflects the liberal tradition and the second the civic republican tradition. Consider first what I think is the more persuasive view, referendums as limits on the actions of representatives. In Riker's work on voting, he helpfully casts this debate between those who think voting is a negative limit on the actions of representatives, telling representatives what they cannot do, and those who think that votes can express a positive will.[35] Riker's two accounts of voting in

[32] Gordon Smith, 'The Functional Properties of the Referendum' (1976) 4 European Journal of Political Research 1.

[33] Gallager and Uleri, for instance, call this the difference between law-initiating and law-controlling referendums. Michael Gallager and Pier Uleri (eds), *The Referendum Experience in Europe* (Macmillan 1996) 4; the UK's independent commission on referendums makes the same point through the labels pre- and post-legislative referendums 'Independent Commission on Referendums' (Constitution Unit 2018) <https://www.ucl.ac.uk/constitution-unit/publications/tabs/unit-publications/182_-_Independent_Commission_on_Referendums> (accessed 30 July 2018).

[34] '... Arguments against the referendum are also arguments against democracy, while acceptance of the referendum is but a logical consequence of accepting a democratic form of government.' Bogdanor (n 1) 93.

[35] William Riker, *Liberalism Against Populism* (Freeman and Company 1982) 11–13.

democracies correspond to the two accounts of the relationship between referendums and democracy outlined here.

A. Referendums as limits on the actions of representatives

The first way of thinking about referendums in the United Kingdom is as limits on the actions of representatives. This is a tradition of thinking about referendums that can be tracked back to Dicey[36] (and before[37]) through Bogdanor and Qvortrup who write in his tradition. On this account referendums are small 'c' conservative processes, their impact is negative rather than positive.[38] Referendums were initially proposed to act as a 'shield rather than a spear.'[39] Referendums are a way to prevent major constitutional changes from happening that do not command broad public support. In Dicey's view, the core rationale for referendums is as 'the people's veto.'[40] He uses this label because 'It reminds us that the main use of the referendum is to prevent the passing of any important Act which does command the sanction of electors.'[41] As Qvortrup rightly argues in an analysis of Dicey's views on the referendum, it is clear that in Dicey's view the referendum is not a replacement for the actions of representative government but rather than an addendum to it.[42] Qvortrup also rightly argues that on this basis Dicey should be seen as offering an account of referendums squarely in the liberal democratic tradition.[43] Decades later Bogdanor writes largely in the tradition of Dicey arguing for a negative view of referendums, and he puts a gloss on Dicey's key propositions. Bogdanor specifically positions Dicey (and his) accounts of referendums in opposition to the view that they are freestanding expressions of popular sovereignty that replace

[36] Dicey was not the only one to take this view. 'Dicey was not the only British writer to advocate for the referendum. William E.H Lecky had advocated the referendum in 1899, and Henry Sidgwick... had supported the introduction of the referendum 'to avoid a deadlock resulting from a disagreement between the two chambers [of Parliament].' Qvortrup, 'A.V. Dicey' (n 4) 531.

[37] 'Dicey was not the only British writer to advocate the referendum. William E.H Lecky had advocated the referendum in 1899, and Henry Sidgwick... had supported the introduction of referenda "to avoid a deadlock resulting from a disagreement between the two Chambers [of Parliament]."' ibid. 532.

[38] 'The referendum is to have a 'purely negative effect.' Albert V Dicey, *Introduction to the Study of the Law of the Constitution* (Roger E Michener ed, 8th Revised edition, Liberty Fund Inc 1982) 382.

[39] 'It has been, in the words of Beaverbrook, "not a spear but a shield", an adjunct to representative government and not a replacement for it.' Bogdanor (n 1) 69.

[40] Dicey (n 3) cix.

[41] ibid.

[42] Qvortrup, 'A.V. Dicey' (n 4). 531.

[43] 'Dicey succeeded in developing an argument for the limited use of referendums in the Liberal tradition.' ibid. 531.

representatives.[44] This is all to say: there is a long-established tradition in the United Kingdom of treating referendums as limits on the actions of representatives rather than replacements for them.

This longstanding tradition of thinking about referendums as limits on the actions of representatives reflects the liberal approach to democracy. On the liberal or Madisonian approach, voting is a way of limiting the power of representatives.[45] Another way to make this point is that to say that for liberals voting is a tool; it is instrumentally valuable. As will be seen below, this is contrast to the civic republican view which sees the value of voting in procedural terms. Taking the liberal approach to voting does not mean accepting a view like Schumpeter's that democracy is the mere crass competition for votes.[46] Nor does it preclude the possibility that either democracy in general or voting in particular may have intrinsic value. Voting may well be many things and have many different types of value. The liberal conception of voting is not meant to downplay either the importance of voting or of many other acts of citizenship. The aim is only to identify what the mechanism of voting can achieve. The liberal approach to voting is merely committed to arguing that voting is a relative expression of preference given a finite set of options, and that expressing these preferences are a way of giving direction to representatives. While voting may well have many purposes and other sources of value, it should not be understood as an act of consent, the embodiment of political will, or making a decision directly. The real underlying difference between these two approaches is what makes democracy and voting valuable. For the civil republican, processes are principally procedurally valuable. For the liberal, the value is instrumental.

B. Referendums as temporary replacements for representatives

An alternative account of referendums is that they are temporary replacements for representatives. This case for referendums is in made in its most persuasive form by Stephen Tierney, and he grounds his argument in the civic republican

44 'The referendum is generally seen as an instrument of popular sovereignty, an institutional expression that the doctrine of political authority derives from the people. Yet as the history of the debate in Britain shows, the urge towards popular participation or self-government has not played a very important part in its advocacy. On the contrary, since first proposed by Dicey, the referendums has been suggested primarily as a means of checking disagreeable legislation.' Bogdanor (n 1) 69.

45 Riker (n 35) 12.

46 'The democratic method is that institutional arrangement for arriving at political decisions in which individuals acquire the power to decide by means of competitive struggle for the people's vote.' Joseph Schumpeter, *Capitalism, Socialism, and Democracy* (George Allen & Unwin Ltd 1943) 269.

tradition.[47] Tierney does not see referendums as a way of limiting the actions of representatives. While he thinks representatives are essential for a healthy democracy, and referendums cannot be separated from the representative context of which they are a part,[48] he nevertheless sees referendums as a way of temporarily supplanting representatives.[49] This is because he thinks there are some decisions that must be made by voters rather than by representatives. He argues that in constitutional referendums, '"... the people"... intervene directly to "produce" sovereign decisions in a way which affirms that legitimate democratic authority emanates from popular consent rather than the institutions of state.'[50]

Central to understanding Tierney's view is the distinction between legislative and constitutional referendums. Legislative referendums, he argues, are limits on the actions of representatives and consequently cannot properly be labelled 'direct democracy.'[51]

Constitutional referendums, on the other hand, he thinks in a different democratic category altogether. Constitutional referendums, Tierney argues, are opportunities for voters to intervene directly in the terms of their governance.[52] In contrast to the tradition of Dicey, Bogdanor, and Qvotrup, Tierney argues for referendums as positive interventions on political question rather than limits on the actions of representatives. Tierney writes that constitutional referendums: 'substitute the people directly for the representational role traditionally played by the democratic constitution.'[53] This is a different approach to referendums than the one taken in the conservative tradition outlined above. In the conservative tradition a referendum is another step in the process of legislating on a constitutional matter. Referendums are a part of the representative process itself. Tierney thinks this is a fair enough way to describe referendums on matters of policy; but not constitutional referendums. Constitutional referendums he says: 'Are a means by which representation itself is supplanted, returning direct power to the people; in other words as some kind of reversal of the original act of transference, or at least a temporary return of power to

[47] Tierney (n 18) 285.
[48] ibid. 302–303.
[49] 'We have observed that one way to understand the role of referendums is to envisage them as a means by which representation is itself supplanted, returning direct power to the people; in other words as some kind of reversal of the original act of transference, or at least a temporary return of power to the people.' Tierney (n 6) 367.
[50] ibid. 363.
[51] 'Therefore, even the categorisation of legislative referendums as an instance of *direct* as opposed to representative democracy is perhaps something of an over-simplification.' ibid. 364.
[52] ibid. 363.
[53] ibid. 361.

the people.'[54] Tierney envisages the act of voting as part of creating a 'collective body'[55] that temporarily replaces representatives this is only possible, however, under the sort of highly demanding conditions of deliberative democracy required by civic republicanism.[56] Tierney offers a sophisticated and effective case for referendums as instances of deliberative democracy. He lays out a stringent and persuasive set of conditions for what is required to conduct referendums in a deliberative way. Further, his view of referendums is the approach increasingly taken in the United Kingdom today. Consider now how the law governing referendums in the United Kingdom reflects Tierney's approach to referendums.

IV. Referendums in the United Kingdom

The law in the United Kingdom is not explicit about whether referendums are to be treated as limits on, or temporary replacements for, representatives. Nevertheless, Tierney's approach is implied given what the statutes say. There is no general law outlining the role of referendums in the process of constitutional change; there is only an administrative framework found in the Political Parties, Elections, and Referendums Act 2000.[57] Referendums are legally required for certain types of constitutional change including by the Wales Act 2017,[58] The Scotland Act 2016,[59] the European Union Act 2011,[60] and the Northern Ireland Act 1998.[61] None of these legal requirements for referendums requires proposals or Bills before Parliament. Indeed, all of these statutes

[54] Leyland (n 11) 367.

[55] Riker (n 35) 11.

[56] What is required is: '(i) Popular participation of the people within a broader system of representative government, (ii) public reasoning, reflection and discussion, (iii) Equality and parity of esteem, (iv) consent and collective decision-making.' Tierney (n 18) 56.

[57] s 101 of this Act stipulates the requirement of enabling legislation for referendums but does not specify how, when, or why referendums are to be used.

[58] '... it is declared that the Assembly and the Welsh Government are not to be abolished except on the basis of a decision of the people of Wales voting in a referendum.' The Wales Act 2017 s 1(3).

[59] 'the Scottish Parliament and the Scottish Government are not to be abolished except on the basis of a decision of the people of Scotland voting in a referendum.' The Scotland Act 2016 s 63A (3).

[60] s 6 Required a referendum on further European integration, but this has been repealed by the European Union (Withdrawal) Act 2018.

[61] 'It is hereby declared that Northern Ireland in its entirety remains part of the United Kingdom and shall not cease to be so without the consent of a majority of the people of Northern Ireland voting in a poll held for the purposes of this section in accordance with Schedule 1. (2) But if the wish expressed by a majority in such a poll is that Northern Ireland should cease to be part of the United Kingdom and form part of a united Ireland, the Secretary of State shall lay before Parliament such proposals to give effect to that wish as may be agreed between Her Majesty's Government in the United Kingdom and the Government of Ireland.' The Northern Ireland Act 1998 s 1, (1)–(2).

refer to a vote in a referendum as itself a 'decision.' This is much closer to the approach to referendums advocated by Tierney than the approach advocated by Dicey. That law in the United Kingdom is closer to the 'referendums as substitutions view' is seen most clearly in the Northern Ireland Act. The Act says, in section 1(2) that if a majority vote to cease to be a part of the United Kingdom, *then* proposals are required to that effect. In this way, in law in the United Kingdom votes in referendums are taken themselves to be decisions. They are not opportunities to veto the decisions taken by representatives.

These legal requirements for referendums do not exhaust the subjects on which they may be used, however. A referendum was used to consider the proposed change to the Alternative Vote system in 2011. This is an instructive referendum for purposes of this chapter. Contrast, for instance, the legislation for the Alternative Vote referendum in 2011 with that of the referendum on the United Kingdom's membership of the European Union in 2016. In the Alternative Vote referendum, section 8 of the Parliamentary Constituencies and Voting Act 2011 outlined two possible paths for the legislation depending on the results of the popular vote.[62] If there was a majority of votes in the referendum for the proposed changes, then the Secretary of State was to introduce an order bringing the changes in legislation into force. If there was a majority of votes against the changes, then the Secretary of State was to bring an order repealing it. The enabling legislation for the Brexit referendum, by contrast (the European Union Referendum Act 2015), made no such provisions for the outcome of the vote.[63] The enabling legislation for the Alternative Vote

[62] '(1)The Minister must make an order bringing into force section 9, Schedule 10 and Part 1 of Schedule 12 ("the alternative vote provisions") if—(a)more votes are cast in the referendum in favour of the answer "Yes" than in favour of the answer "No", and (b)the draft of an Order in Council laid before Parliament under subsection (5A) of section 3 of the Parliamentary Constituencies Act 1986 (substituted by section 10(6) below has been submitted to Her Majesty in Council under section 4 of that Act. (2) If more votes are not cast in the referendum in favour of the answer "Yes" than in favour of the answer "No", the Minister must make an order repealing the alternative vote provisions.' Parliamentary Constituencies and Voting Act 2011 s 8.

[63] This point was stressed by the UKSC in *Miller* where the majority stipulate: 'Both sides of the argument proceed on the basis that the referendum on membership of the EU was held under the European Union Referendum Act 2015 ("the 2015 Act"), which resulted in a vote to leave the EU, does not provide the answer. The Secretary of State's argument proceeds on the basis that the Crown has taken the decision under Article 50(1), accepting the result of the referendum. The Miller claimants argue only that Parliament can take that decision. Both the Secretary of State and the Miller claimants proceed on the basis that the referendum result was not itself a decision by the UK to withdraw from the EU, in accordance with the UK's constitutional requirements, and that the 2015 Act did not itself authorise notification under Article 50(2). In these circumstances, there is no issue before the court as to the legal effect of the referendum result. Nor is this an appropriate occasion on which to consider the implications for our constitutional law of the developing practice of holding referendums before embarking on major constitutional changes: a matter on which this court has heard no argument.' *R (Miller) v Secretary of State for Exiting the European Union* [2017] UKSC 5 [171].

referendum is important because it shows that in the past referendums have been used as limits on the actions of representatives in the United Kingdom.

The prevailing view of referendums in the United Kingdom is not as limits on the actions of representatives but rather temporary replacements for representatives. This is not a welcome development. It does not reflect the traditions of liberal democracy. Leyland captures this worry well when he says: 'The role of the Westminster Parliament and the wider democratic process is in danger of being defined by the growing use of referendums as substitutes for traditional politics under the banner of "popular sovereignty." '[64] There is much to commend the 'referendums as substitutes' view. There is value in seeing referendums as processes that encourage deliberation among voters. Nevertheless, the better approach—especially in the United Kingdom—is treating referendums as limits on the actions of representatives. Consider now why this is the case, before turning to how some of the shortcomings of the Brexit referendum are the treatment of referendums as expressions of popular sovereignty.

V. The case for the 'referendums as limits' approach

In this section, I will make a case that the 'referendums as limits' approach is the better account of their use both in theory and in practice. In making the case in practice, I will focus in particular on the case of the United Kingdom and the 2016 Brexit referendum.

A. The case in practice for the 'referendums as limits' approach

Referendums work better when used post-legislatively as limits on the action of representatives. This approach provides greater clarity for voters about what they are voting on, legislators on what voters' preferences are, and the executive on how to execute proposals for reforms. UCL's 2018 Independent Commission on Referendums offers a five-part rationale for post-legislative referendums. Post-legislative referendums offer: (i) a closer connection between votes and the outcomes of those votes; (ii) clarity for elected representatives; (iii) higher feasibility of proposals put to a vote; (iv) the pre-legislative process may raise public awareness; and (v) civil servants can prepare for

[64] Leyland (n 11) 145.

outcomes.[65] Referendums are blunt instruments for aggregating political will, they are very well placed to tell us what voters do not want, but not well-placed to articulate specific reasons or reforms.[66]

Even those like Tierney who take the 'referendums as substitutions view' do not argue that referendums can be entirely decoupled from their representative context. The small 'c' conservative account of referendums offers an account of referendums that is more closely integrated into the system of representative democracy as a whole, which is necessary because votes do not exist in a vacuum. Representatives are required to determine what it is that voters will vote about, even if the question is not asking voters to approve a Bill or proposal for reform. This is particularly the case in the United Kingdom given the requirement of enabling legislation. This agenda-seeing stage of determining what question is put to a referendum and under what conditions is hugely significant to the referendum process itself.[67] The potential for elite manipulation at this stage is significant.[68] Representatives are also required in order to interpret and execute the outcomes of representatives. The substantive and structural challenges of the Brexit referendum were compounded by an accountability vacuum. When referendums are not used post-legislatively, when debates take place about arguments in the abstract, then there is a difficulty in tying commitments to specific representatives. There is also less incentive to play by campaign finance rules when the umbrella organizations (unlike political parties) fade away once the process has finished.

Votes in referendums can never be separated from votes for the representatives engaged in the referendum process itself. Even in non-authoritarian countries, referendums are used to bolster personal legitimacy.[69] This is all to say: representatives are a necessary prerequisite for referendums. They cannot be supplanted, even temporarily, to consider political questions. It both normatively and practically better to confront the necessity of representatives head-on and to use referendums as a way of guiding and limiting representatives rather than seeking to supplant them temporarily.

[65] 'Independent Commission on Referendums' (n 33) 85.

[66] 'Votes in referendums are very well placed to tell us what voters do not want. Given the variety of views that voters have when they vote, referendums are not well placed to articulate what voters do want out of a proposal for constitutional reform. When referendums begin processes for reform they are too blunt an instrument to aggregate political will about what those reforms should include.' ibid. 83.

[67] Tierney (n 18) 51.

[68] Shipman argues that there is a plausible case that by the time the condition of the referendum had been decided, remain had already lost. Tim Shipman, *All Out War: The Full Story of How Brexit Sank Britain's Political Class* (Harper Collins 2016).

[69] 'Referendums five political actors the political legitimacy to pursue change and potentially alter status quo institutions.' M Walker, *The Strategic Use of Referendums: Power, Legitimacy, and Democracy* (Springer 2003) 3.

B. The normative case for the referendums as limits approach

The two approaches to referendums outlined here reflect different approaches to democracy. Those approaches to democracy in turn reflect different views of why democracy is justified. On the civic republican approach, the value of democracy is principally procedural in nature. This is Tierney's aim in drawing on the civic republican tradition. He argues 'the primary claim of the deliberative democrat is that the more deliberative a decision-making process, the more legitimate the decision it reaches.'[70] This is at the core of the theoretical disagreement between the two approaches. On Tierney's view, the better the process the better the outcome. But the liberal approach to democracy, going back to Mill, justifies democracy in a different way.[71] On the liberal view, democracy is also justified on instrumental reasons. As Dworkin says, each of these democratic traditions offers different answers to the question 'what is good about democracy?'[72] 'Are good ... democratic outcomes good because they are democratically chosen, or are they democratically chosen because they are good?'[73] Proceduralists take the former view arguing that democratic decisions are good principally because of the way democratic decisions are made. Instrumentalists take the latter view arguing that democracies are good because they produce good outcomes, or better outcomes than alternative systems. The aim of identifying these two traditions is not to oversimplify them. Proceduralists think that democratic processes have instrumental value. Proceduralists such as deliberative democrats think that the process of engaging citizens in the terms of their governance is almost certain to lead to better decisions. Tierney himself argues that referendums are justified, in part, because they re-engage people in democracies.[74] I am not arguing that referendums have only instrumental rationales, but rather that they must have at least some instrumental rationale. Further, I will argue that this instrumental rationale must be provided—in part—by representatives.

The procedural approach rests principally on a majoritarian rationale. Referendums are valuable processes because they give everyone an equal say. The difficulty is that a proceduralist, majoritarian argument alone is not enough to justify either democracy or the use of referendums. As Dworkin

[70] Tierney (n 18) 285.

[71] JS Mill, *Considerations on Representative Government* (OUP 1991) Chapter Three.

[72] Ronald Dworkin, *Is Democracy Possible Here?: Principles for a New Political Debate* (Princeton University Press 2008) 66.

[73] ibid.

[74] Tierney (n 18) 41.

rightly argues, it must be the case that democracy is more than a majoritarian process. Dworkin says:

> The majoritarian conception of democracy is defective because it cannot explain, on its own, what is good about democracy. Mere weight of numbers, on its own, contributes nothing of value to a political decision. We need a deeper and more elaborate account that tells us what conditions must be met and protected in a political community before majority rule is appropriate for that community.[75]

Those who take a proceduralist approach like Tierney argue that the very demanding standards for deliberative they set mitigate against the dangers of majority decision-making. I disagree. While the principles and approach to democracy advocated by deliberative democrats are *prima facie* good and *ceteris paribus*, decisions made under conditions of reciprocity and accountability are better than those that are not, they do not necessarily lead to good or better outcomes than alternative processes. Referendums, and all democratic processes, are instruments that can be used to a variety of ends. This is all to say: the proceduralist account of referendums and democracy such as civic republicanism are compelling, but they do not offer a sufficient basis to justify democracy or to evaluate the success of particular democratic processes such as referendums. These substantive values, limits, and procedural–independent standards which make democracy more than majoritarianism are provided by representatives and institutions. Representatives are necessary to execute, interpret, enforce, and apply the preferences of the larger group voting in a referendum. When processes are working well, it is representatives that ensure that referendums are consonant with human rights. Consider a thought experiment. Even if it were preceded by the most deliberative process, a referendum which held that people with blue eyes no longer have the right to vote is not democratically defensible. Some further explanation of what makes a decision democratic is required. This further rationale is supplied by the standards that make a process good in the first place, and when a system is working in a defensible way, referendums are a necessary part of setting that framework.

The normative case for the referendums as limits is that this account better reflects what is good about referendums and what is good about democracy. The civil republican rationale focuses on the procedural value of referendums. Doubtless referendums have procedural value, but procedural rationales are

[75] ibid. 70.

neither necessary nor sufficient to justify referendums. Referendums and democracy are also instrumentally valuable, and they are instrumentally valuable because they lead to good democratic outcomes providing direction to representatives. Democracy in general must be both procedurally and instrumentally valuable, and this is true of referendums too.

The argument here is complex so it is worth restating its parts. I have argued: (i) democracy cannot be understood as only a procedural ideal because substantive limitations, protections on equality (for instance) must be in place in order to protect the very possibility of procedural ideals at all: (ii) these substantive limitations and ideals mean that democracy must involve more than rule by the majority; (iii) unlike arguments for democracy in general, referendums are often justified on a principally procedural, majoritarian basis; (iv) the principles for democracy in general should apply to referendums in particular. Why think that the justification for a particular type of democratic process such as a referendum would be different than for the system in general? (v) the instrumental value of referendums is supplied by representatives in two ways. First, representatives make democracy possible in terms of executing, implementing, and adjudicating decisions. Second, it is representatives and institutions that set the requisite procedure-independent standards that make democracy possible in the first place.

VI. Brexit and two accounts of democracy in the United Kingdom

The debate about what 'Brexit' means reflects a deeper disagreement about the significance of the referendum in 2016. The outcome of the Brexit referendum meant some change in the relationship between the United Kingdom and the European Union, but the content of that relationship was inchoate. Did it mean leaving the single market and the customs union? Was it the beginning of a process of constitutional reform or the end? These are the debates that drive the debate about Brexit more than three years after the referendum. What were people voting for? What views can be imputed to voters by supporting a proposition? MPs and voters disagree among themselves about whether the referendum was a decisive expression of the coherent will of 17.4 million people or the direction to representatives to begin a process of reform. The debate about the meaning of Brexit is in part a debate about what the referendum itself meant, and whether it answered this question. The Brexit referendum was the result of longstanding structural instability in the treatment of referendums in the United Kingdom. It was called by Prime Minister David Cameron in response to an election that he never expected to win and was perhaps included in the Conservative manifesto in order to be traded away as a concession to a coalition with the Liberal Democrats. While David Cameron's use of referendums was tactical, short-sighted, and poorly planned, this poor design of the Brexit referendum in 2016 reflects the broader failings with the use of referendums in the United Kingdom; particularly with respect to European integration. The Government declined to hold referendums on either the Maastricht or the Lisbon treaties, and in doing so John Major and then Tony Blair helped sow the seeds of Brexit.

The Government's position on the Maastricht referendums,[76] that referendums are not required in the United Kingdom's constitutional arrangements, could have remained the prevailing view.[77] New Labour reintroduced referendums after an 18-year hiatus, however, and used them to consider a range of questions.[78] Further, Tony Blair promised a referendum on the Constitution Treaty and then did not hold one on the Lisbon Treaty, despite this promise. These decisions not to hold referendums to ratify treaties of European integration continue to resonate today. Not using the referendum as limits on the actions of representatives at the time to approve the treaties meant they never received the broad public support that referendums can demonstrate. This created an unresolved political problem both in the United Kingdom in general and especially for the Conservative Party in particular.[79] Further, because referendums were not used as a device of approval, it potentially led to confusion on

[76] 'The government states its position, in terms that deserve to find a place in textbooks on the constitution, in the mass circulation of a booklet it published last December to mark the British presidency. It offers this answer to the question "Why can't we have a referendum like the Danes, the Irish and the French?" The British system is a parliamentary democracy: the Government are accountable to Parliament and Parliament is accountable to the electorate. The House of Commons approved the negotiating position pre-Maastricht and the results afterwards. It has also given a second reading, after the election, to the Bill which would enable the Government to ratify the Treaty. Parliament will have a thorough and detailed discussion of the Bill in Committee stage. The government believe that is the right way to proceed in a parliamentary democracy.' David Baker, Andrew Gamble and Steve Ludlam, 'The Parliamentary Siege of Maastricht 1993: Conservative Divisions and British Ratification' *Parliamentary Affairs*, 1 January 1994 37, 48.

[77] Although referendums have always been closely tied to European integration, so as long as there were moves towards European integration, referendums would have likely been a political consideration, at least for a minority of voters. The Referendum Party received 2.7% of the vote in the 1997 general election. For more on the Referendum Party see Ian McAllister and Donley T Studlar, 'Conservative Euroscepticism and the Referendum Party in the 1997 British General Election' (2000) 6 Party Politics 359.

[78] New Labour mentioned referendums 11 times in their 1997 manifesto and held four referendums within their first year of taking office.

[79] Although of course, a referendum alone would never have solved the underlying problems, Tim Oliver, 'To Be or Not to Be in Europe: Is That the Question? Britain's European Question and an in/out Referendum' (2015) 91 International Affairs 77.

what exactly the meaning of the 2016 referendum on the United Kingdom's membership of the EU was. The significant degree of European Integration since the 1975 referendum, without further ratifying referendums on new treaties, created the possibility of a legal and political crisis. There might have been specific stages in the process of European Integration, for instance the Maastricht or Lisbon treaties, that a majority of voters found objectionable?[80] Had referendums been used consistently as a process of ratification then there would have been a case, as section 6 the European Union Act 2011 suggested, of holding referendums only on further integration.[81] Ratifying referendums have a clearer structure. They isolate one aspect of the European Integration, rather than trying to unpick a range of potential relationships in a binary way. The challenges of the Brexit referendum and its aftermath demonstrate how difficult it is to disambiguate a range of relationships with the European Union from a binary choice. The ineffective all-or-nothing structure of the Brexit referendum is, at least in part, a result of the decisions not to hold a ratifying referendum on the Maastricht and Lisbon Treaties. Had referendums been used to approve these treaties, it would have begun to establish a consistent role for referendums as approving stages of European integration; a role that as a democratic process they are far better placed to play.

There is a movement sometimes to treat the 2016 Brexit referendum as a 'second' referendum and the referendum in 1975 as the first. This statement is made pejoratively to suggest that there are endless referendums unless one is taken to be a dispositive once in a generation event. I think this is mistaken. The content of the question being put to the voters in the 1975 referendum was entirely different; the relationship with the European Union (it was then the EEC) is entirely different. That is not the same question, not the same relationship, as was being voted on in 1975. Ever since the 2016 referendum, there have been calls for further referendums to clarify the meaning of Brexit. This additional vote would be a part of the same process providing further direction to representatives. While this additional vote is defensible, it is by no means a perfect solution. As the Independent Commission on Referendums rightly argues, when two votes are required, it is important that this is identified at the outset so that the rules are clear in advance.[82] This disagreement about the meaning

[80] Which seems at least plausible given that they affirmed EEC membership in 1975, at some point in the integration process a majority of voters became disenchanted. Or it might have been that different generations had different views of European Integration.

[81] European Union Act 2011 s 6, but this has now been repealed by the European Union (Withdrawal) Act 2018

[82] 'Independent Commission on Referendums' (n 33) 89.

and merits of another referendum on Brexit further confirms the argument made above: it not clear what role this referendum in general, or referendums in particular, were playing the process of constitutional change. This disagreement about the meaning of Brexit and the merits of another referendum persist. At the time of writing in the autumn of 2019, I see no prospect of this disagreement being resolved.

VII. Conclusion: Referendums in the United Kingdom post-Brexit

The future of referendums is more certain than the future of Brexit. The trend is for referendums to beget referendums. The use of referendums on particular topics creates precedents, as the EEC referendum did in 1975, and voters' expectations of their role in the process of constitutional change shifts. The trend, especially since the 1970s, has been towards increasing use of referendums in general.[83] This is not itself necessarily a bad thing. Referendums can be effective democratic processes. What would be disastrous, however, is if referendums continue to be used without a clear underlying rationale. This chapter has argued that referendums are not themselves problematic, they are a democratic process like any other, but not all uses of referendums are the same and they are not all created equal. There are competing visions of referendums currently at play in the United Kingdom's constitutional arrangements. The case for small 'c' referendums is imperfect and cannot address all of the failings with the use of referendums in the United Kingdom. Nevertheless, it is a better approach than treating referendums as temporary substitutions for representatives. This because referendums can never in practice be separated from the representative context of which they are apart. It is also because referendums can only be justified in theory if, like democracy in general, they have instrumental as well as procedural value. It is the necessary role of representatives that gives referendums their instrumental value and rationale.

[83] Tierney (n 18) 1.

8

Deciding on the Future[1]

First Nations Ratification Processes, Crown Policies, and the Making of Modern Treaties

Janna Promislow

I. Introduction

Indigenous peoples in Canada regularly make decisions about their constitutional futures. First Nations,[2] for example, make collective decisions under legislation to move away from *Indian Act*[3] regimes on matters of membership and elections, or to adopt a land code under the *First Nations Land Management Act*.[4]

[1] This title is a variation of a slogan used by the Maa-nulth Treaty Society in promoting the Maa-nulth Final Agreement to its constituencies: Maa-nulth Treaty Society, "*Choosing your Future*" (September 2007), online: <http://www.maanulth.ca/downloads/Roadmap-Brochure_FINAL.pdf> accessed 28 January 2022.

[2] This chapter is focusing on First Nations contexts. First Nations is a term that is often used as preferred terminology for the legal entity known as Indian Bands, the language under the *Indian Act*. First Nations is also used to refer to people and peoples who do not fit under the *Indian Act*. This term is used in both senses in this chapter, with a preference for referring to the statutory actor as *Indian Act* bands to make the differences clear where relevant. The concerns with *Indian Act* definitions of both status-Indians and recognized bands is a central concern in this chapter and will be discussed directly. The chapter does not, however, attempt to address the specificities of community votes that are unique to Métis, Inuit, and non-status First Nations contexts.

[3] RSC 1985, c I-5 [*Indian Act*]. The *Indian Act* is much decried colonial legislation, but has, paradoxically, provided a form of recognition of Indigenous communities and their rights. The treaty process discussed in this chapter is one route for First Nations to move out from under the *Indian Act*. Federal government efforts at wholesale reform of this legislation have failed. Current reform efforts are proceeding in a piecemeal fashion. For discussion, see Royal Commission on Aboriginal Peoples. "Chapter 9: The Indian Act" in *Report of the Royal Commission on Aboriginal Peoples: Looking Forward, Looking Back*. Volume 1 (Ottawa: the Royal Commission on Aboriginal Peoples, 1996) 235–308; *The* Indian *Act: Breaking Its Stubborn Grip*, a special issue of Policy Options Politiques (Fall 2017), online: <https://policyoptions.irpp.org/magazines/september-2017/the-indian-act-breaking-its-stubborn-grip-2/> accessed 28 August 2020; and, Hayden King, "Wholesale Rapid Removal of the Indian Act Without Alternatives Will be Met with Resistance" (Yellowhead Institute, 16 June 2018), online: <https://yellowheadinstitute.org/2018/06/16/wholesale-rapid-removal-of-the-indian-act-without-alternatives-will-be-met-with-resistance/> accessed 28 August 2020.

[4] SC 1999, c C-24 [*First Nations Land Management Act*]. For discussion of this regime, see Shalene Jobin and Emily Riddle, *The Rise of the First Nations Land Management Regime in Canada: A Critical Analysis* (Yellowhead Institute, 2019), online: <https://yellowheadinstitute.org/wp-content/uploads/2019/09/fnlma-report.pdf> accessed 28 August 2020 and Malcom Lavoie & Moria Lavoie, "Land

Janna Promislow, *Deciding on the Future* In: *The Limits and Legitimacy of Referendums*. Edited by: Richard Albert and Richard Stacey, Oxford University Press. © Janna Promislow 2022. DOI: 10.1093/oso/9780198867647.003.0009

The negotiation and enforcement of section 35 rights similarly involve collective decision-making of a constitutional order. Decisions to launch a rights case, to negotiate a treaty, or to support proponents who consult them on projects that potentially threaten the lands, waters and resources that sustain Indigenous nations, all engage definitional and fundamental questions for those communities. Each such decision involves an exercise of political will and, potentially, a measure of self-determination, moving a community's authority over important jurisdictions out from under federal supervision or advancing their economic, cultural and political futures through section 35 rights processes. And yet, each such decision is made under the long shadow of *Indian Act* rules and associated policies that have for so long interfered with and colonized Indigenous societies.

There are many factors and dynamics that can make collective decision-making in Indigenous contexts difficult and complex. Communities are small and both Canadian and Indigenous law inform ethics and accountabilities in political decision-making. Generations of colonial policy, some of it very recent, has arbitrarily excluded people, women more than men, from *Indian Act* status and therefore from large portions of internal First Nations decision-making. Community members are also often dispersed, a lingering dynamic unleashed by past and present colonial policies and socio-economic conditions on reserve.[5] Communicating complex scientific, governmental, and policy issues across resident and non-resident populations with potentially large variations in formal education levels and internet access is onerous. And, as recent pipeline controversies have brought to the fore, the polity and institutions through which decisions are made (or should be made under Indigenous law), may not have legislative or other state recognition. Yet, *Indian Act* governments remain the primary and sometimes only decision-maker involved in such decisions.

The discussion that follows considers the dynamics of collective decision-making about self-determination when the polity, and the institutions through which the decisions are made, have colonial genealogies. My argument focuses

Regime Choice in Close-Knit Communitites: The Case of the First Nations Land Management Act" (2017) 54 OHLJ 559–607, online: <https://digitalcommons.osgoode.yorku.ca/ohlj/vol54/iss2/15> accessed 28 August 2020.

[5] These dynamics were addressed in *Corbiere v Canada (Minister of Indian and Northern Affairs)*, [1999] 2 SCR 203, in which the right to vote in band elections by off-reserve band members was protected under s. 15(1) of the *Charter*. See generally John Borrows, "Physical Philosophy, Mobility and the Future of Indigenous Rights" in Ben Richardson, Shin Imai & Kent McNeil, eds, *Indigenous Peoples and the Law: Comparative and Critical Perspectives* (Oxford: Hart Publishing, 2009) 403.

on whether ratifying a treaty can enhance self-determination for Indigenous peoples.[6] This chapter presents a critique of the state policy environment and how it shapes or restricts the choices of Indigenous collectives around decisions of significance for their path of self-determination, focusing on comprehensive land claim (CLC) agreements, also known as modern treaties. As a vehicle to remove the strictures of the *Indian Act*, deciding to ratify a modern treaty not only reformulates of the Indigenous party's authority, lands, section 35 rights, and legal status in Canada, but also its own internal constitution.[7] Although current policy flux includes encouraging directions that respond to longstanding critiques of federal policy, ratification processes have not received much attention in policy discussions. Training established critiques on ratification votes, and pursuing arguments and discussions that resonate beyond the comprehensive claims context, I argue that state policies, policy omissions, and non-adherence to policies obstruct self-determination for the Indigenous parties involved.

Rather than being concerned with whether an *Indian Act* band can legitimately negotiate or lead the ratification process, my evaluation is concerned with the conditions of the involvement of *Indian Act* band governments, and what conditions may support an exercise of constituent power to form a viable new or renewed collective. I accept that, to some extent, Indigenous decision-making relating to self-determination involves colonial institutions.[8] For some, this starting point might suggest that there is no possibility of achieving legitimate expressions of political will through or involving such institutions.[9] My starting point is more pragmatic: legitimate or not, ratification votes (or

[6] For discussion of self-determination, see S. James Anaya, *Indigenous Peoples in International Law*, 2d ed. (Oxford University Press, 2004), Part II. See also Jacob Levy, "Self-Determination, Non-Domination, and Federalism" (2008) 23 *Hypatia*, 60–78.

[7] There also much at stake for the state's constitution as well. Modern treaties are understood in the jurisprudence as a significant moment, if not *the* moment, of reconciliation of the pre-existing sovereignty of Indigenous peoples with assumed Crown sovereignty: *Haida Nation v British Columbia*, 2004 SCC 44 [*Haida Nation*] at para 20.

[8] A related topic, not pursued in this chapter due to limitations of size and method, is whether an anonymous voting process, such as a ratification or community vote, is itself an obstacle to legitimacy amongst Indigenous cultures with a long tradition of consensus decision-making. This dispute has surfaced in relation to tensions internal to the Gitxsan people over who represents them in treaty negotiations: *Spookw v Gtixsan Treaty Society*, 2014 BCSC 1100 (*Spookw v GTS*, 2014), upheld on appeal: 2017 BCCA 16, and *Re Section 85 of the Society Act, Gitxsan Treaty Society*, 2013 BCSC 974. The issues at stake include the Gitxsan Treaty Society's efforts to align their corporate structure with Gitxsan governance traditions and institutions, based on hereditary leaders and houses, and Gtixsan people who want to see a broader "democratized" (understood as one person, one vote) membership with the involvement of Gitxsan *Indian Act* bands (*Spookw v GTS, supra* at para 81).

[9] See, for e.g., Taiaike Alfred: "The structure and logic of *Indian Act* precludes the validity of any agreement signed by an institution that is itself a creation of the Canadian government." (*Deconstructing the British Columbia Treaty Process*, First Nations Governance Centre, 2000, at 21) [Alfred, 2000].

community votes) are used extensively in First Nations contexts and often involve or are led by *Indian Act* band governments.[10] It is therefore worth considering the policies that shape these referendum processes. Further, I accept that acts of collective will always start from somewhere and that somewhere is often not ideal. As Hans Lindhal explains, the pursuit of the legitimacy or normative justification of a constituting act is misdirected because "constituent power never operates in a void, it is never *ex nihilo*: it is subject to practical constraints both normative and factual."[11]

After a brief introduction to the CLC and British Columbia Treaty Commission (BCTC) processes, I take a "bookends" approach, looking at who is expected and permitted to initiate treaty negotiations and then how this entity is expected and permitted to conduct the ratification vote under these policies. At the front end of the issue, I consider crown and BCTC policies regarding the Indigenous parties that may negotiate treaties, including policies on shared or overlapping territories. To understand my argument that internal issues of representation can be obscured within a larger set of issues about identifying Indigenous polities and rights-holders, this section canvasses some key concerns about *Indian Act* band governments and the colonial detritus that layers present day political processes in First Nations. At the backend of the treaty negotiation process, I focus on the conduct of ratification campaigns and votes, highlighting two key concerns: 1) fairness in ratification campaigns, focusing on funding issues and "information and engagement" strategies; and 2) the structure of the ratification vote, focusing on decision thresholds and regional or sub-group representation.

Together, these foci highlight parameters within treaty processes that potentially marginalize dissent and minorities sub-groups within the polity. Similar to what Stephen Tierney describes as a dynamic of "unwarranted homogenisation" through referendums in federal states,[12] I argue that greater attention to, and patience with, decentralized and regionalized Indigenous polities is required from negotiating state governments. Not doing so is a failure to take Indigenous politics and polities seriously, which risks continuing the colonial trajectory and continuing divide and conquer dynamics through decisions to ratify a final agreement. Policy directions that avoid these risks are not simple

[10] The Crown's fiduciary obligations to *Indian Act* bands and in relation to reserve land may require the involvement of the band in treaty and other decisions that disrupt those obligations. See discussion and citations accompanying *infra* notes 143 and 144.

[11] Hans Lindahl, "Constituent Power and the Constitution" in David Dyzenhaus and Malcolm Thorburn, eds, *Philosophical Foundations of Constitutional Law* (OUP, 2016) 141–159 at 152.

[12] Stephen Tierney, "Referendums in Federal States: Territorial Pluralism and the Challenge of Direct Democracy" (*in this volume)*.

and may not be politically palatable; nevertheless, I conclude with brief comments reflecting on the Crown's obligations and options for better directions for Crown policy to support Indigenous self-determination through treaty and ratification processes.[13]

The topics I address here are difficult and divisive issues for communities. Before engaging, I owe it to those affected by the politics discussed to identify myself as a non-Indigenous academic who is not directly implicated in political questions internal to Indigenous nations. I am affected only indirectly, as a Canadian citizen and observer aspiring to contribute to discussions and knowledge that might assist in moving towards renewed and improved state relationships with Indigenous peoples and better public policy and law. While my argument in this chapter is critical of modern treaty processes, it is emphatically not a critique of those who have entered into agreements with the provincial and federal crowns. First Nations who have entered into the long negotiation process of a CLC agreement are invariably seeking a better situation for their communities. Waiting for a "better" political or legal moment may not be viable nor is political process on these issues predictable. Instead, my critique is aimed at shedding light on the complexity of community decision processes in First Nations contexts and addressing crown polices and obligations that would better support processes of self-determination.

II. Treaty processes

The CLC and related treaty processes date from 1973, prompted by the recognition of Aboriginal title in *Calder* and the political agitations around the Trudeau (Sr.) government's White Paper.[14] CLC Agreements have, to date, been the primary policy vehicle for the state to respond to assertions of Aboriginal title by Indigenous peoples who have not signed a treaty that expressly cedes their land. Through these agreements, governments aim to achieve "certainty" by settling outstanding title claims, which have the potential for proof under section 35 of the *Constitution Act, 1982* (or the common law before 1982).

[13] For a related discussion of the need to make changes within Canadian law to accommodate the expression of Indigenous law, see Alan Hanna, "Spaces for Sharing: Searching for Indigenous Law on the Canadian Legal Landscape" (2018) 51 UBC L Rev 105.

[14] Terry Fenge, "Negotiation and Implementation of Modern Treaties between Aboriginal Peoples and the Crown in Right of Canada" in Terry Fenge & Jim Aldridge, *Keeping Promises. The Royal Proclamation of 1763, Aboriginal Rights, and Treaties in Canada* (Montreal & Kingston: McGill-Queen's University Press, 2015) 105 at 108 [Fenge]; See generally, Christa Scholtz, *Negotiating Claims* (New York & London: Routledge, 2006).

These agreements are also the primary negotiations vehicle through which First Nations can enlarge their land base and replace governance structures and related federal ministerial supervisions that remain in place under the *Indian Act*.[15] However, despite the aim of settling right claims, the process has not been "rights-based." As Eyford explained, "Canada is prepared to make a general recognition that a treaty group has Aboriginal rights, including title, in the preamble to a treaty but is not prepared to provide ... specific recognition."[16] A policy-based approach has meant that federal negotiations mandates may be broader or narrower than what a judicial declaration of rights may provide (and covers more topics than may be addressed in rights case), and presumes that parties will prefer to negotiate rather than risk their day in court over the definition of the rights that catalyzed the CLC process.

The CLC has evolved since 1973. Where the policy originally required that Indigenous parties "extinguish" their Aboriginal rights and title in exchange for the benefits, rights, and lands set out in the treaty for the sake of certainty, the language shifted in 1986 to modification of the non-land rights[17] and today includes options of "suspension", "non-assertion", or "non-exercise" of those rights.[18] Another important shift was the eventual ability of Indigenous parties to negotiate self-government at the same time as land, achieved in 1995.[19] A further key evolution was the creation of the British Columbia Treaty Commission (BCTC) in 1992 pursuant to an agreement of a tri-partite task force[20] made up of the federal and provincial crowns with the First Nations Summit (a political body representative of BC First Nations interested

[15] There are also legislative avenues for moving out of parts of the *Indian Act*, such as the *FNLMA*; see discussion cited in *supra* notes 3 and 4. See also Naiomi Metallic, "Indian Act By-Laws: A Viable Means for First Nations to (Re)Assert Control over Local Matters Now and Not Later" (2016) 67 UNBLJ 211.

[16] Douglas R Eyford, "A New direction: Advancing Aboriginal and Treaty Rights A report " Report of the Ministerial Special Representative on Renewing the Comprehensive Land Claims Policy (20 February 2015) [Eyford Report] at 45, online: <https://www.rcaanc-cirnac.gc.ca/eng/1426169199009/1529420750631> accessed 1 April 2019.

[17] Fenge, *supra* note 14 at 116–117.

[18] Standing Committee on Indigenous and Northern Affairs, *Indigenous Land Rights: Towards Respect and Implementation*, 42nd Parliament, 1st Session, February 2018 [Standing Committee Report, 2018] at 42.

[19] From 1986 to 1995, the policy was that Canada "would negotiate agreements in respect of self-government, but would not, 'as a matter of policy' include self-government in a comprehensive land claims agreement in the absence of a further constitutional amendment." (Jim Aldridge, "The 1998 Nisga'a Treaty" in Terry Fenge and Jim Aldridge, *Keeping Promises. The Royal Proclamation of 1763, Aboriginal Rights, and Treaties in Canada* (Montreal & Kingston: McGill-Queen's University Press, 2015) 138 at 147. The change to allow both land and government at the same time came with Canada's adoption of the Inherent Right of Self-Government Policy, following the failure of the Charlottetown Accord: Aldridge, ibid. at 147–148; Fenge, *supra* note 14 at 123–124.

[20] Chief Joe Matias et al, *The Report of the British Columbia Claims Task Force* (28 June 1991) [BC Task Force, 1991]. The Commission was created by both federal and provincial legislation: *Treaty Commission Act*, RSBC 1996, c 461; *British Columbia Treaty Commission Act*, SC 1995, c 45.

in pursuing treaty negotiations[21]). Pertaining to negotiations in BC only, the BCTC is mandated to facilitate and provide a public education and information on the treaty process.[22] Although still anchored in the federal CLC, the adaptations of the process for a "made-in-BC" approach specifically responds to the particular geo-political landscape in which there are very few historical treaties in place and in which more than 100% of the lands within its boundaries are claimed as traditional territories by Indigenous nations, leading to what is commonly identified as the problem of overlapping claims and/or shared territories.[23]

There have been numerous critiques of the CLC and calls for reform. The slow progress of the agreements is frequently cited as a problem. Since the policy was first introduced over 45 years ago, only 26 final agreements have been reached across Canada, mostly in the northern territories where political and demographic dynamics are significantly different than in the southern provinces.[24] According to the federal government, the average negotiating time is 15 years with 8% of agreements taking more than 26 years to conclude.[25] A further and longstanding critique targets the insistence on obtaining "certainty" by requiring Indigenous parties to relinquish, modify, or exchange

[21] For information on the First Nations Summit, see online: <http://fns.bc.ca/> accessed 28 August 2020.

[22] There is also a "made-in-Nova Scotia" process for negotiations in Atlantic Canada, where historical Mi'kmaq treaties exist but did not include land cession provisions. See Kwilmu'kw Maw-Klusuaqun/Mi'kmaw Rights Initiative, online: <http://mikmaqrights.com/negotiations/made-in-nova-scotia-process/> accessed 28 August 2020, and the Mi'kmaq-Nova Scotia-Canada Framework Agreement, 23 February 2007, online: <https://www.rcaanc-cirnac.gc.ca/eng/1100100031915/1529422708421> accessed 28 August 2020.

[23] BC Treaty Commission, *Mission Statement. Monitoring Adherence to the BC Claims Task Force Report*, online: <http://www.bctreaty.ca/sites/default/files/Mission_Statement.pdf> accessed 28 August 2020; Dene Moore, "It's Up to First Nations to Resolve Overlapping Claims: B.C. Treaty Commission Report" *The Globe and Mail*, 7 October 2014.

[24] Crown-Indigenous Relations and Northern Affairs Canada, "Treaties and Agreements" (last modified 30 July 2020), online: <https://www.rcaanc-cirnac.gc.ca/eng/1100100028574/1529354437231> accessed 28 August 2020>. This number includes Yale First Nation Final Agreement, which has not been implemented: Rob Shaw, "Yale First Nation Puts Hold on Treaty Implementation" (11 February 2016), online:<http://vancouversun.com/news/local-news/yale-first-nation-puts-hold-on-treaty-implementation accessed 10 April 2019. See also Mark Hume, "Yale First Nation Rejects B.C. Treaty, Citing 'Critical Flaws'" (11 February 2016), online: <https://beta.theglobeandmail.com/news/british-columbia/yale-first-nation-rejects-bc-treaty-citing-critical-flaws/article28739680/?ref=http://www.theglobeandmail.com&> accessed 10 April 2019. Elsewhere, the federal government reports 29 CLCs "and/or self-government agreements" have been "ratified and brought into effect": Crown-Indigenous Relations and Northern Affairs Canada, "General Briefing Note on Canada's Self-government and Comprehensive Land Claims Policies and the Status of Negotiations" (16 Aug 2016), online: <https://www.rcaanc-cirnac.gc.ca/eng/1373385502190/1542727338550> accessed 6 March 2019 [General Briefing Note].

[25] These statistics are as of 2014 and include both comprehensive claims and self-government negotiations: Indigenous and Northern Affairs Canada, *Fact Sheet—A Results-Based Approach to Comprehensive Land Claim and Self-government Negotiations* (31 July 2014), online: <https://www.aadnc-aandc.gc.ca/eng/1406824128903/1406824211834> accessed 6 March 2019.

future rights claims in favour of the rights specifically set out in the agreement, known as "extinguishment."[26] At a more general level, the CLC policy has been repeatedly and convincingly critiqued, particularly by Indigenous scholars, as an example of how the hegemony of the colonial state is extended through "the asymmetrical exchange of mediated forms of state recognition and accommodation."[27] Given this critique and experience, Johnny Mack, a member of the Toquaht tribe, struggled to understand how the Maa-nulth First Nations came to participate in the process and celebrate the treaty they reached under this policy.[28] He concluded that it is hard for people to turn down the treaty when it actually may be an opportunity to improve their lives, accepting that it may be an avenue for "pragmatic progress" that does not disrupt colonial power imbalances or advance self-determination.[29] Mack's valuable insights underscore that the CLC is not about a wholesale moment of change, from colonial oppression to self-determination. Optimistically, and with reform of the policy and negotiations process, achieving a CLC agreement is not *the* moment of self-determination, but, potentially, a step towards it.[30]

[26] See, for e.g., Russell Diabo, "Idling Some More: AFN & 100's of Chiefs Capitulate to Harper's Termination Plan" (Jan.-Sept. 2013) 11 First Nations Strategic Bulletin 1, online: <http://d3n8a8pro7vhmx.cloudfront.net/idlenomore/pages/710/attachments/original/1381176797/FNSB_Jan-Sept_13.pdf?1381> accessed 31 August 2017 [Diabo]; Arthur Manuel & Grand Chief Ronald M Derrickson, *Unsettling Canada: A National Wake-Up Call*, (Toronto: Between the Lines, 2015) at 201 [Manuel]; Shiri Pasternak, *Grounded Authority. The Algonquins of Barriere Lake Against the State* (Minneapolis: University of Minnesota Press, 2017) at 252 [Pasternak]. Recently, the Standing Committee on Indigenous and Northern Affairs commented, "It is ... unlikely that making the extinguishment of rights a condition for settling claims is consistent with a nation-to-nation relationship of equals," and recommended that this aspect of the CLC be put to an end: Standing Committee Report, 2018, *supra* note 18 at 42–43, 55.

[27] Glen Coulthard, *Red Skins, White Masks: Rejecting the Colonial Politics of Recognition* (Minnesota: University of Minnesota Press, 2014) at 15. See also Taiaiake Alfred, *Peace, Power, Righteousness: An Indigenous Manifesto* (Oxford University Press, 1999); Paul Nadasdy, *Hunters and Bureaucrats. Power, Knowledge and Aboriginal-State Relations in the Southwest Yukon, rev ed.* (Vancouver: UBC Press, 2005) [Nadasdy, 2005]; Colin Samson, "Canada's Strategy of Dispossession: Aboriginal Land and Rights Cessions in Comprehensive Land Claims" (2016) 31 CJLS 87 [Samson]; Andrew Woolford, "Transition and Transposition: Genocide, Land and the British Columbia Treaty Process" (2011) 4 New Proposals: J of Marxism and Interdisciplinary Inquiry 67; James Tully, "Consent, Hegemony, and Dissent in Treaty Negotiations" in Jeremy Webber & Colin M Macleod, eds, *Between Consenting Peoples. Political Community and the Meaning of Consent* (Vancouver: UBC Press, 2010) 233; and Stephanie Irlbacher-Fox, *Finding Dahshaa: Self-Government, Social Suffering, and Aboriginal Policy in Canada* (Vancouver: UBC Press, 2009).

[28] Johnny Camille Mack, *Thickening Totems and Thinning Imperialism* (LLM Thesis, University of Victoria, 2007, *unpublished*) [Mack].

[29] *Ibid.* at 31, 32.

[30] For differing evaluations of the Nisga'a Agreement's contributions to self-determination, see Tracie Scott, *Postcolonial Sovereignty? The Nisga'a Final Agreement* (UBC Press, Purich Publishing Ltd., 2012); Carole Blackburn, "Producing Legitimacy: Reconciliation and the Negotiation of Aboriginal Rights in Canada," (2007) 13 Journal of the Royal Anthropological Institute 62; and Ross Hoffman & Andrew Robinson, "Nisga'a Self-Government: A New Journey Has Begun" (2010) 30 Cdn J of Native Studies 387–406 [Hoffman & Robinson]. Relatedly, implementation of completed agreements is significant to the potential contributions of modern treaties to self-determination; see Martin Papillion, "The Two

In light of the critiques and calls for reforms, and with the blossoming of discussions and processes on rights recognition and implementation under the Trudeau government,[31] it is appropriate to question whether the CLC has a future[32], and relatedly, why this policy framework is the focus of this chapter. Regardless of policy flux, negotiations are ongoing across the country and commitments to modern treaties have been renewed by the House of Commons Standing Committee on Indigenous and Northern Affairs in 2018[33] and by the tri-partite principals (the federal and provincial crowns, and the First Nations Summit) to the BC treaty process in December 2018.[34] Whatever the future of the CLC specifically, negotiated resolutions of rights and shared or competing jurisdictions have been, and will remain, fundamental to Indigenous-state relations in Canada. Ratification processes will remain a critical, and, to date, underexamined step in finalizing the products of negotiation. Whether this growth of interest in reform and alternatives to the CLC better achieves the potential of contributing to self-determination depends not only on the substantive aspects of the treaty and rights recognition policies, but also on how the processes impact the formation/re-formation of the Indigenous polities involved and their internal decision processes. Realizing the potential for moving towards self-determination depends heavily on whether power imbalances and colonial advantage are mitigated in the process of negotiation and

Faces of Treaty Federalism" in J Bickerton & A.G. Gagnon (eds), *Canadian Politics*, 7th ed (University of Toronto Press, 2020) 217, and Standing Committee Report, 2018, *supra* note 18.

[31] Crown-Indigenous Relations and Northern Affairs Canada, "Overview of a Recognition and Implementation of Rights Framework", 10 September 2019 [CIRNAC, Rights Recognition], online: <https://www.rcaanc-cirnac.gc.ca/eng/1536350959665/1539959903708;> accessed on 2 December 2019 and Crown-Indigenous Relations and Northern Affairs Canada, "About Recognition of Indigenous Rights and Self-Determination Discussion Tables", 20 December 2019 online <https://www.rcaanc-cirnac.gc.ca/eng/1511969222951/1529103469169> accessed on 30 June 2020. Currently, there is an "interim policy" in place for comprehensive land claims negotiations, developed by Canada at the same time as it appointed Douglas Eyford to conduct an engagement process and report, delivered in 2015 (Eyford Report, *supra* note 16). Information about the CLC itself are found in "Renewing the Comprehensive Land Claims Policy: Towards a Framework for Addressing Section 35 Aboriginal Rights" (last modified 18 June 2018), online: <https://www.rcaanc-cirnac.gc.ca/eng/1408631807053/1544123449934> accessed 1 April 2019 [Renewing the CLC] and General Briefing Note, *supra* note 24.

[32] See, e.g., the Assembly of First Nations' evidence before the Standing Committee, that "the department has shifted toward an "exploratory process" or "rights and recognition tables."" (Standing Committee Report, 2018, *supra* note 18 at 39) and Bruce McIvor, "Have we just witnessed the end of the Modern Treaty process?" First Peoples Law (28 June 2018), online: <https://www.firstpeopleslaw.com/index/articles/361.php> accessed 1 April 2019.

[33] Standing Committee Report, 2018, *supra* note 18, recommending reforms while reiterating the importance of CLC agreements.

[34] Principals' Accord on Transforming Treaty Negotiations in British Columbia, 1 December 2018 [Principals' Accord]. This Accord builds on reform proposals put forward in 2016: Multilateral Engagement Process to Improve and Expedite Treaty Negotiations in British Columbia: Proposals for the Principal's Consideration (17 March 2016, endorsed by the Principals 24 May 2016).

ratification. Thus, in the next section, I turn to examine specific features of the BCTC and CLC frameworks, focusing on how these treaty processes alleviate, continue or even worsen the seemingly inexorable power imbalances and dynamics of domination.

III. Indigenous polities and ratification processes

A. How are Indigenous polities identified and represented?: The "overlapping and shared territories" issue as overbroad and a misnomer

The hurdle known as "overlapping and shared territories" in treaty negotiations relates to who may initiate negotiations on behalf of Indigenous peoples and how the government parties respond when presented with more than one Indigenous party claiming rights in relation to the same territory. In this section, I tackle these issues by first setting out some necessary context on the identification of Indigenous polities in Canadian law and policy, with particular attention to the rights-holding collective in the Aboriginal rights jurisprudence and *Indian Act* band governments. I then introduce the policies regarding who can initiate modern treaty negotiations and how overlapping and shared territories are addressed, provide illustrations of the shortcomings of these policies, and discuss the implications.

1. Indigenous polities in constitutional law

The section 35 Aboriginal rights jurisprudence has only recently begun to address the twin issues of identifying the collectivity that holds section 35 rights and the institutions that represent the collective body of rights-holders.[35] The collectively held nature of these rights[36] presumes a collective to hold

[35] This has received more attention in relation to Métis rights, with the Supreme Court setting out preliminary criteria for assessing whether there is a historical rights-bearing community in *R v Powley*, 2003 SCC 43, [2003] 2 SCR 207 at paras 21–23. For discussion see Kent McNeil, "Aboriginal Title and Indigenous Governance: Identifying the Holders of Rights and Authority" (2020) 57:1 OHLJ 127 [McNeil, "Rights Holders"]; Karen Drake, "A Right without a Rights-Holder is Hollow: Introduction to the OHLJ Special Issue on Identifying Rights-Bearing Aboriginal Peoples" (2020) 57:1 OHLJ, *forthcoming*; Naiomi Metallic, "Searching for 'Superchief' and Other Fictional Indians: A Narrative and Case Comment on *R v Bernard*, 2017 NBCA 48" (2020) 57:1 OHLJ, *forthcoming*; Brent Olthuis, "The Constitution's Peoples: Approaching Community in the context of Section 35 of the Constitution Act, 1982" (2009) 54 McGill L.J. 1; Kerry Sloan, "Always coming Home: Metis Legal Understandings of Community and Territory" (2016) 33 Windsor YB of Access to Justice 125; and Adam Gaudry & Chris Anderson, "*Daniels v Canada*: Racialized Legacies, Settler Self-Indigenization and the Denial of Indigenous Peoplehood" (2016) 36 Topia 19.

[36] *Behn v Moulton Contracting Ltd*, 2013 SCC 26 at paras 30, 35, [2013] 2 SCR 227.

these rights, and institutions and actors that can act to represent the rights and rights-holders in courts and negotiations.[37] Historical jurisprudence addressed these assumptions by inquiring into the competence of a party to sign historical treaties, which is a legal and political act on behalf of a collective (if not a nation).[38] The jurisprudence evolved away from these questions, but has recently returned with renewed attention to the difference between identifying the rights-holding collective and assessing the litigating party's claim to representative it.[39] *Indian Act* bands have long been the litigant in Aboriginal rights and related cases, without challenge to their representative capacity by any party. However, a strong line of cases has emerged demonstrating awareness of the limitations of *Indian Act* bands as *the sole* representative of the collective rights-holders.[40]

[37] It is beyond the scope of this chapter to consider how the collectives that hold constitutional rights relates to the idea of Indigenous nations. In this chapter I assume that the rights-holding collective (and the party or parties that speak for that collective) should be part of negotiations that address/modify/continue those rights. I do not, however, go so far to assume that the rights-holding collective is the nation. The geographic or territorial scope of the rights-holding collective is an issue that has begun to be addressed in cases (particularly in the Métis rights context) and is discussed in *R v Bernard*, Metallic, and Drake, all *supra* note 35. See also Gordon Christie, "Potential Aboriginal Rights-holders: Canada and Cultural Communities versus Indigenous Peoples and Socio-political Bodies" (2020) 57:1 OHLJ 1.

[38] It was a question that was as relevant in relation to signatories on behalf of the crown as to Indigenous leaders. See *R v Sioui*, [1990] 1 SCR 1025, 7 DLR (4th) 427, in which the treaty pre-dated the British sovereignty under the Royal Proclamation of 1763. In *R v Simon*, [1985] 2 SCR 387, 24 DLR(4th) 390, the Supreme Court adopted a *sui generis* approach to Crown-Indigenous treaties, distinguishing these treaties from those made by sovereign states under international law and thereby avoiding the requirements of international law regarding the capacity and status of the treaty signatories. Regarding such issues in the history of Indigenous-settler relations, see Janna Promislow, "One Chief, Two Chiefs, Red Chiefs, Blue Chiefs: Newcomer Perspectives on Indigenous Leadership in Rupert's Land and the North-West Territories" in Hamar Foster, Benjamin L Berger & AR Buck, eds, *The Grand Experiment: Law and Legal Culture in British Settler Societies* (Vancouver: UBC Press for the Osgoode Society for Canadian Legal History, 2008) 55.

[39] See, for e.g., *Hwlitsum First Nation v Canada (Attorney General)*, 2018 BCCA 276 at para 25. There is also significant, longstanding civil procedure case law on the status of the Indian Act band chiefs to act in a representative capacity to bring actions on behalf of the band, given the unusual legal status of bands; see Jack Woodward, *Native Law*, Chapter 1, G., 3, "Nature of an Indian Band as a Legal Entity" and Chapter 20.1 "Practice Matters—Proceedings Involving Bands" (Thomson Reuters, 2017—looseleaf, access through Proview).

[40] "It is settled law that the definition of 'Indians' and 'bands' in the *Indian Act* is not an exhaustive definition of the aboriginals who may assert rights that are protected by s. 35 of the *Constitution Act*." *Campbell v British Columbia (Minister of Forests)* 2011 BCSC 448 at para 96 [*Campbell* (2011)], appeal dismissed as moot given that logging in issue was already complete: 2012 BCCA 274. The rights claimant in this case, the Sinixt (or Arrow Lakes) First Nation, was declared "extinct" by the Canadian government in 1956 for the purposes of *Indian Act* band status. Some members of this nation remained in Slocan Valley area of BC while others became members of neighboring Okanagan nations or the Colville Confederated Tribes in the US. In *Campbell* (2011), the court rejected the efforts of the Sinixt Nation Society to get an injunction to stop logging pending judicial review due to the Society's failure to satisfy the judge of their representative capacity in relation to the Sinixt rights-holding collective (at para 61). The Sinixt have nevertheless successfully established an Aboriginal right to hunt for food, social, and ceremonial purposes: *R v Desautel*, 2021 SCC 17 [*Desautel*].

This acknowledgement has evolved through a growing sophistication in the cases around the collective entity that holds section 35 rights.[41] Courts have recognized that Indigenous peoples must define their own rights-holding collectives; as the BC Court of Appeal said in *Tsilhqot'in Nation*: "the definition of the proper rights holder is a matter to be determined primarily from the viewpoint of the Aboriginal collective itself."[42] This principle is, on its own, unassailable. However, the consultation cases demonstrate the limited utility of this principle without further consideration of who represents that collective.[43] In consultation contexts, competing and multiple Indigenous consultation parties—such as multiple representatives of both the same rights-holding collective and of different, sometimes competing, rights-holding collectives in relation to a particular territory– are not uncommon. Understanding such multiple representations requires familiarity with the colonial history of the particular geographies and peoples in issue as well as with the fluidity of nationhood and decentralized governance in many Indigenous traditions. These traditions belie assumptions that Indigenous territories are organized according to the same geo-political principles as the sub-units such as provinces within the state.[44] Such assumptions can lead to complicating Indigenous politics by misguided demarcations of matters as internal and external to the Indigenous groups. These complications amplify when, outside of the *Indian Act* structure, unrecognized bands, traditional or hereditary governments, and

[41] Although there has been confusion at courts as well. See, for e.g., *R v Bernard*, 2017 NBCA 48 and commentary by Metallic, *supra* note 35.

[42] *Tsilhqot'in Nation*, BCCA at para 149. On the other hand, the Supreme Court decision in *Tsilhqot'in Nation v British Columbia*, 2014 SCC 44, [2014] 2 SCR 256 [*Tsilhqot'in Nation*, SCC] glossed over issues and arguments at lower levels, such as the Province's view that the Xeni Gwet'in band was the holder of rights and title in the claim because of evidence that decisions were, historically, typically made a the "encampment or band level" and, similarly, evidence that historically the Tsilhqot'in people did not have a "national" level chief or political organization. (*Tsilhqot'in Nation*, BCCA, at paras 459, 468). It also glossed over issues of the governance rights attaching to title. For related discussion, see Gordon Christie, "Who Makes Decisions Over Aboriginal Title Lands?" (2015) 48 UBC L Rev 743 and McNeil, "Rights Holders," *supra* note 35.

[43] For more on the consultation context, and the limitations of *Indian Act* bands as consultation partners and Impact Benefit Agreements as signals of consent, see Dayna Nadine Scott, "Extraction Contracting: The Struggle for Control of Indigenous Lands" (2020) 119 The South Atlantic Quarterly 269.

[44] For analysis and critique of how modern treaty policies assume familiar geo-political borders, see Brian Thom, "The Paradox of Boundaries in Coast Salish Territories" (2009) 16 Cultural Geographies 179–203; Brian Thom, "Reframing Indigenous Territories: Private Property, Human Rights and Overlapping Claims" (2014) 38 Am. Ind. Culture and Research J 3 [Thom, 2014]; Christopher Turner & Gail Fondahl, " 'Overlapping claims' to territory confronting treaty-making in British Columbia: Causes and Implications" (2015) 59 The Canadian Geographer 474–488 [Turner & Fondahl]; and Paul Nadasdy, "Boundaries among Kin: Sovereignty, the Modern Treaty Process, and the Rise of Ethno-Territorial Nationalism among Yukon First Nations" (2012) 54 Comparative Studies in Society and History 499–532. For a discussion of the historical fluidity of Anishinaabe people, see Heidi Stark, "Marked by Fire: Defining Anishinaabe Nationhood" (2012) 36 American Indian Quarterly 119.

alternative or newer governance bodies, such as tribal councils and urban organizations, seek recognition in consultation processes.

Against this backdrop, the jurisprudence provides tentative directions on these issues by requiring claimant organizations or individuals to prove both their connection to a historical rights-bearing community and meet the requirements of civil procedure in the representative structure of their community.[45] Moreover, in consultation contexts the general thrust of the emerging law is that all entities representing people with a credible claim to collective rights and an appropriate mandate from the people it claims to represent should be part of a consultation process. This is true even if—possibly especially if—the entities represent the same or constituent parts of the same rights-holding collective but articulate different positions on the project or decision in issue.[46]

2. Indian Act band governments: roles and limitations

While the identification of Aboriginal rights-holders and their representatives may be attracting renewed attention in the rights jurisprudence, critiques of *Indian Act* bands are well established.[47] Critiques include *Indian Act*

[45] This should not be taken to suggest that courts should adjudicate the rights-holder or proper representative(s) of the rights-holder. For cautions on this point, see Christie, "Potential Aboriginal Rights-holders: Canada and Cultural Communities versus Indigenous Peoples and Socio-political Bodies" (*supra* note 37); and Paul Chartrand, "Rethinking the Doctrine of Aboriginal Rights: the Métis Cases" OHLJ 173. For related cases, see *Desautel, supra* note 40; *John Voortman & Associates Limited v The Haudenosaunee Confederacy Chiefs Council*, [2009] 3 CNLR 117 at para 73; *Fond du Lac Denesuline First Nation v Canada (Attorney General)*, 2010 FC 948, [2010] 4 CNLR 1 at para 163 (affirmed, without addressing this issue, 2012 FCA 7, 430 N.R. 190); *Native Council of Nova Scotia v Canada (Attorney General)*, 2007 FC 45, [2007] 2 CNLR 233 at paras 42–44 (affirmed 2008 FCA 113, [2008] 3 CNLR 286, without addressing this issue); *Enge v Canada (Minister of Indian Affairs and Northern Development)*, 2017 FC 932 [*Enge*] at paras 78–124); *Yahaan v Canada*, 2017 FC 725, aff'd on appeal, 2018 FCA 41), and *R v Bernard, supra* note 41.

[46] For e.g., *Nlaka'pamux Nation Tribal Council v Griffin*, 2009 BCSC 1275, [2009] 4 CNLR 213; Enge, *supra* note 45; *Kaska Dena Council v Yukon (Government of)*, 2019 YKSC 13; and *Ogichidaakew v Ontario (Energy)*, 2014 ONSC 5492 discussing the "Kelly v Canada order" to join individual Indian Act bands to judicial review proceedings initiated by an aggregate treaty body, Grand Council Treaty 3, without resolutions from the individual bands. See also Kerry Wilkins, "Aboriginal Law: The Duty to Consult: To Whom Is the Duty Owed", Canadian Encyclopedic Digest (Ontario), 4th ed. (Toronto: Carswell, 2008), vol. 1, title 2 at §10. More recently, judicial reviews of decisions at various stages of negotiations and implementation demonstrate the potential of modern treaties to negatively impact the constitutional rights or rights claims of neighbouring collectives who are not party to the treaty; See esp Enge, *supra* note 45 and Gamlazyeltxw, discussed further at *infra*, note 98.

[47] See, for e.g., Frances Abele, *Like an ill-fitting boot: Government, governance and management systems in the contemporary Indian Act.* National Centre for First Nations Governance. Ottawa, Ontario, Canada, 2007; online: <http://fngovernance.org/ncfng_research/frances_able.pdf> accessed 20 September 2017. See also John Borrows, *Seven Generations, Seven Teachings: Ending the Indian Act.* National Centre for First Nations Governance. Ottawa, Ontario, Canada, 2008 [Borrows, "Seven Generations"]; online: <http://fngovernance.org/resources_docs/7_Generations_7_Teachings.pdf> accessed 20 September 2017; and Shin Imai, "The Structure of the Indian Act: Accountability in Governance" National Centre for First Nations Governance, Ottawa, Ontario, Canada, 2007, online: <http://fngovernance.org/ncfng_research/shin_imai.pdf> accessed 1 April 2019.

mandated governance institutions, membership rules, and their imposition on and relationship to Indigenous political institutions more generally. These critiques raise questions regarding the representative capacity of *Indian Act* band councils to negotiations aimed at greater self-determination.[48]

Critiques have noted the poor governance associated with notoriously short governance terms (two years) under the *Indian Act* and anonymous voting mechanisms that do not respect Indigenous traditions around the selection of leaders or ideas of leadership that may be role-specific (e.g., war or peacetime, resource allocations, trade relationships) and based on authority earned through an ethic and practice of generosity and intensive accountability, rather than a delegation of authority made by an elected government.[49] As further discussed below, *Indian Act* reforms under which bands may adopt their own leadership and electoral systems may address some of these concerns.[50] However, the issues are far from resolved.[51] The legislative history of excluding women and others from *Indian Act* band membership is also well known.[52] Several iterations of *Indian Act* registration rules have discriminated against generations of women and their children and grandchildren. Following further litigation and a third round of legislative amendments,[53] the federal

[48] Alfred, *supra* note 9.

[49] Ibid. Regarding Indigenous governance and leadership, see Kiera Ladner, "Governing Within an Ecological Context: Creating an AlterNative Understanding of Blackfoot Governance" (2003) 70 Studies in Political Economy. A Social Review 125–152 and Val Napoleon, "Gitxsan Democracy: On its Own Terms" (Draft paper, on file with author, May 2020), forthcoming in a collection edited by James Tully (Cambridge University Press). See also "One Chief, Two Chiefs", *supra* note 38.

[50] There are at present, two routes for an *Indian Act* band to establish a different regime for selecting its leadership: a customary approach and a newer regime under the *First Nations Elections Act*, SC, 2014, c 5 and in force since 2015. As of 2016, there were 200 bands under the "default" *Indian Act* regime: Indigenous and Northern Affairs Canada, "Leadership selection in First Nations, online: <https://www.aadnc-aandc.gc.ca/eng/1323195944486/1323196005595> accessed 1 April 2019.

[51] The adoption of customary systems of governance for reserves is not a panacea for shedding the colonial strictures of the *Indian Act*. For an unfavourable account of particular cases, see Robert Jago, "Canada's Hollow Concern for First Nations Democracy" *The Walrus Online* (19 July 2019): <https://thewalrus.ca/canadas-hollow-concern-for-first-nations-democracy> accessed 30 July 2020.

[52] For overviews of this history, see Bonita Lawrence, "Gender, Race, and the Regulation of Native Identity in Canada and the United States: An Overview" (Spring 2003) 18 Hypatia; Val Napoleon, "Extinction By Number: Colonialism Made Easy" (2001) 16 Can J L & Soc 113; Sarah E. Hamill, "McIvor v Canada and the 2010 Amendments to the *Indian Act*: A Half-Hearted Remedy to Historical Injustice: (2011) 19 Constitutional Forum constitutionnel 75, online: <https://journals.library.ualberta.ca/constitutional_forum/index.php/constitutional_forum/article/viewFile/17264/13867>; Kirsty Gover, "When Tribalism Meets Liberalism: Human Rights and Indigenous Boundary Problems in Canada" (2014) UTLJ 206–242; and Sebastien Grammond, "Discrimination in the Rules of Indian Status and the McIvor Case" (2009) 35:1 Queen's L.J. 421.

[53] *Descheneaux c Canada (Procureur général)* 2015 QCCS 3555, prompting An Act to amend the Indian Act in response to the Superior Court of Quebec decision in *Descheneaux c Canada (Procureur general)*, SC 2017, c 25. For an overview, see: Norah Kielland & Marlisa Tiedemann, "Legislative Summary of Bill S-3: An Act to amend the Indian Act (elimination of sex based inequities in registration)" Library of Parliament Research Publications, Publication No. 42-1-S3-E (2017), online: <https://lop.parl.ca/sites/PublicWebsite/default/en_CA/ResearchPublications/LegislativeSummaries/421S3E>accessed 21 August 2020.

government is still grappling with the incompleteness of reforms to date.[54] First Nations also struggle with this legacy of exclusion and how to rebuild their own sense of community boundaries, particularly in resource strained environments where federal funding and the land base on the reserve do not keep pace with population growth in the community.[55] This history of discrimination means that many individuals who likely belong to the rights-holding collective (and the political community more generally) have been arbitrarily excluded from *Indian Act* band membership,[56] the unit that often represents First Nations rights-holding collectives. As previously excluded individuals gain status through statutory reforms, they are not automatically members of an *Indian Act* band nor are they necessarily welcomed into the political life of a community. Knowledge of these exclusions thus presents a significant caution against relying on the decisions of an *Indian Act* government as fully representing the political will of a First Nations community on rights or other matters.

Furthermore, when "traditional" or "hereditary" governance structures make themselves heard beyond their nation, they may do so to contradict the decisions of related *Indian Act* bands. These are governance institutions that pre-existed the *Indian Act*, and have often continued to exist along-side *Indian Act* councils, both competing and cooperating (or integrating) with legislatively imposed/recognized councils.[57] In the context of consultations and

[54] Crown-Indigenous Relations and Northern Affairs Canada "Remaining inequities related to registration and membership"(28 Nov 2018), online, <https://www.rcaanc-cirnac.gc.ca/eng/1540403281222/1568898803889> accessed 21 August 2020. Most recently, a challenge to exclusion from status as a result of a grandparent's "enfranchisement" has succeeded: *Hele c Canada (Attorney General)*, 2020 QCCS 2406.

[55] For e.g., bands may make their own membership codes, such that membership rules may be different than federal-registration (status) rules. For discussion, see Val Napoleon, "Aboriginal Discourse: Gender, Identity, and Community" in in Benjamin J. Richardson, Shin Imai & Kent McNeil, eds., *Indigenous Peoples and the Law. Comparative and Critical Perspectives* (Oxford & Portland, Oregon: Hart Publishing, 2009) 233–255.

[56] Often referred to as "non-status Indians"; see *Daniels v Canada (Indian Affairs and Northern Development*, 2016 SCC 12, [2016] 1 SCR 99.

[57] For e.g., the Six Nations, which identifies itself as the proper governance authority of the lands allocated to it by treaty, following its alliance with the Crown in its wars with the emerging United States of America. See Darlene Johnston, "The Quest of the Six Nations Confederacy for Self-Determination" (1986) 44 UTFL Rev 1 [Johnston]. For discussion of past clashes with the imposed *Indian Act* band government, see Peter Maxwell Jacobsen, "Who Rules the Valley of the Six Nations? A discussion of Isaac v. Davey" (1976) McGill LJ 131 online: <http://lawjournal.mcgill.ca/userfiles/other/5226663-08.pdf> accessed 20 September 2017; and *Logan v Styres* (1959) 20 DLR (2d) 416 (Ont HC). For an example of the integration of *Indian Act* bands and traditional governance institutions into a national governance structure, see the Council of the Haida Nation, online: <http://www.haidanation.ca/index.php/chn/> accessed on 1 April 2019, and discussion in Gid7ahl-Gudsllaay (Terri-Lynn) Williams-Davidson "Weaving Together Our Future: The Interaction of Haida Laws to Achieve Respectful Co-Existence" unpublished materials prepared for the Continuing Legal Education Society of British Columbia, November 2012 at 6.2.4, online: <http://www.whiteravenlaw.ca/wp/wp-content/uploads/Weaving-Together-Our-Future.pdf> accessed 1 April 2019>.

treaties, leaders with hereditary titles governing through systems of clan and house appear to face off with elected chiefs wielding authority from the *Indian Act*, but the actors involved sometimes have roles in both the legislative and hereditary systems.[58] A recent example from Wet'suwet'en territory involved members of the Gitdimt'en clan and supporters, who barricaded access to the worksite for the Coastal GasLink pipeline in 2019 while five Wet'suwet'en *Indian Act* band councils had signed agreements with Coastal GasLink supporting the project.[59] After solidarity protests across the country in early 2020 and involvement of the RCMP at the construction site, the federal government pursued and signed a memorandum of agreement with the hereditary chiefs of the Wet'suwet'en recognizing them as the Aboriginal rights and title holders and committing to a schedule of negotiations.[60] Media reports during this conflict demonstrated the confusion of governments and observers over the phenomenon of "emerging" traditional or hereditary systems of government, while others noted the ongoing presence and renewed of vitality of authorities deriving from Indigenous law.[61] As attention to the house system with its hereditary government and ownership of Aboriginal title grew, media reports also began to note dissent within that system[62] and concerns raised by *Indian Act* band councils about their role in the process.[63] As this

[58] E.g., the *GTS v Spookw* litigation, *supra* note 8.

[59] Citizen News Service, "All First Nations Agreements Now in Place for Coastal GasLink Pipeline" *Prince George Citizen*, (19 Sept 2018). This article cites a Coastal GasLink news release as indicating that support for the agreements comes from both "traditional and hereditary" leaders.

[60] Memorandum of Understanding Between Canada, British Columbia and Wet'suwet'en, 29 Feb 2020 (signed 14 May 2020), online: <https://www.rcaanc-cirnac.gc.ca/eng/1589478905863/1589478945624> accessed 21 August 2020. This agreement did not resolve the particular dispute about the Coastal GasLink pipeline. See Justine Hunter, "'Milestone' Proposed Deal Between Wet'suwet'en Nation, Ottawa, BC Would Recognize Hereditary System," *The Globe and Mail*, 2 March 2020, online: <https://www.theglobeandmail.com/canada/british-columbia/article-wetsuweten-nation-proposed-deal-land-title-coastal-gaslink-pipeline/> accessed 21 August 2020; Leyland Cecco, "Canada: Wet'suwet'en Sign Historic Deal to Negotiate Land Rights" *The Guardian*, 15 May 2020, online:<https://www.theguardian.com/world/2020/may/15/canada-wetsuweten-historic-deal-land-rights-pipeline> accessed 21 August 2020.

[61] For quotes of both responses, see comments of BC Premier John Horgan and retired anthropologist Antonia Mills, reported in David P Ball, "Wet'suwet'en Hereditary System 'Never Ceased, It Just Went Underground'" *The Star Vancouver*, 10 January 2019. [Ball, *The Star Vancouver*].

[62] Brent Jang, "Hereditary House Chief Declares Support for Coastal GasLink Plan" *The Globe and Mail*, 9 March 2020, online: <https://www.theglobeandmail.com/canada/article-hereditary-house-chief-declares-support-for-coastal-gaslink-plan/> accessed 26 May 2020; Brent Jang & Kirsty Kirkup, "Wet'suwet'en Matriarch Calls for Hereditary Governance to Reflect Views of Elected Councils", *The Globe and Mail* (10 March 2020), online: <https://www.theglobeandmail.com/canada/article-wetsuweten-matriarch-calls-for-hereditary-governance-to-reflect/> accessed 26 May 2020.

[63] Olivia Stefanovich, "Signing of Wet'suwet'en Agreement Could Land Ottawa in Court" *CBC News* (14 May 2020), online: < https://www.cbc.ca/news/politics/wetsuweten-agreement-signing-1.5567760> accessed 26 May 2020; Chantrelle Bellrichard, "Wet'suwet'en, BC, and Canada sign MOU on Negotiations for Legal Recognition of Title," *CBC News* (14 May 2020), online: <https://www.cbc.ca/news/indigenous/wetsuweten-mou-title-negotiations-signing-1.5570128> accessed 26 May 2020.

episode demonstrates, the relationship between the two forms of government is much more complicated than a simple dichotomy of "legitimate" and "illegitimate." As Val Napoleon commented, "There's no sharp line within the Wet'suwet'en people. Some of the people on the band council are also hereditary chiefs. You're talking about the same families, house groups and clans, all people linked by history, family and being part of a historic society that has its own legal order that's been undermined."[64] Under this nuanced framing, the actors are using the tools they have to express their political preferences, which are informed by obligations and jurisdictions that come from at least one of, if not both, state and Indigenous legal systems.

In law, the *Indian Act* band has a long history as something more, or other, than just a statutory creation, including recognition of inherent Indigenous governance authority and beyond statutory delegations.[65] One example is that, subject to Ministerial imposition to the contrary, the *Indian Act* defines band councils as selected through an electoral process that accords with "the custom of the band,"[66] a term that does not necessarily imply a "traditional" method of election but rather "serves to distinguish band councils elected pursuant to the *Indian Act* from those elected according to rules established by the band."[67] Courts have viewed this authority as originating in Indigenous law and Aboriginal rights.[68] Regardless of their status at law, many communities have become accustomed to *Indian Act* bands despite impositions that clash with and distort local governance norms.[69] As Brian Thom explains with respect to Coast Salish peoples, "[t]hough identifications with long-standing networks of extended kin continue to resonate for Coast Salish social and cultural lives, people also strongly identify with their Indian band. The strength

[64] Quoted in *supra* note 61. See also Val Napoleon, "Indigenous Women Talking: The Work of Indigenous Feminism" draft paper, June 2020, on file with author and forthcoming in Emily Synder, Val Napoleon, Rebecca Johnson, eds, *Indigenous Feminist Studies* (working title) (University of Toronto Press). See a brief video interview with John Borrows regarding the governance work of rebuilding out of the *Indian Act* structures: "Exploring the implications of agreement between Wet'suwet'en and government, *The Globe and Mail*, 7 May 2020, online: <https://www.theglobeandmail.com/canada/video-exploring-the-implications-of-agreement-between-wetsuweten-and/>

[65] See generally, *Campbell v British Columbia (AG)*, 2000 BCSC 1123, [2000] 4 CNLR 1. See also Woodward, *Native Law*, supra note 39, chapter 1.

[66] *Indian Act*, s 2, "*council of the band.*" Ministerial authority to impose the *Indian Act* regime is found in s. 74. Bands may also "revert" to "custom" elections, subject to meeting federal policy requirements. For discussion see: Report of the Standing Senate Committee on Aboriginal Peoples, *First Nations Elections: The Choice is Inherently Theirs* (May 2010) [Senate Committee Elections Report, 2010] at 31–34. More recently, bands may also choose to conduct their elections in accordance with the *First Nations Elections Act*, *supra* note 50.

[67] Senate Committee Elections Report, *supra* note 66 at 8.

[68] *Gamblin v Norway House Cree Nation Band Council*, 2012 FC 1536 at para 34. See also *Pastion v Dene Tha' First Nation*, 2018 FC 648.

[69] John Borrows, "Seven Generations", *supra* note 47.

of this village-based identity is underscored by *Indian Act* driven membership codes, through which eligibility to receive benefits and services . . . is derived."[70] A contextual approach is thus important to understanding the nature of a particular *Indian Act* band, and how it might relate to the inherent governance authority and institutions of the local and regional Indigenous polities. In relation to territory, however, the limits of the representative authority of the *Indian Act* band may be clearer. The geo-political territory of the *Indian Act* band, on which legislatively delegated (and potentially inherent) jurisdiction are exercised, is the reserve. Reserve lands often do not define the main or only territories over which Indigenous peoples hold and exercise constitutional rights in pursuit of both livelihood and culture, and over which they assert title and/or assert governance authority.[71] The leading Aboriginal title cases in Canada, brought forward by nations with significantly different Indigenous cultures, both involved assertions of ownership by collectives different from the *Indian Act* bands in the same territory.[72] Nevertheless, rights and title cases continue to also be brought forward by *Indian Act* band chiefs, in their representative capacity.

Acquired significance does not override the colonial critique of *Indian Act* bands or a history of federal dominance and neglect. Nevertheless, the strands of history and law suggest that without further inquiry, a blanket dismissal of *Indian Act* bands as at least one representative of Indigenous political communities and their legal traditions may be as inappropriate as a blanket acceptance of their representative status as complete.[73] Instead, the *Indian Act* band can be understood as, at best, a proximate body to express the political will of the collectivity that holds constitutional rights and at worst, a body that represents the will of only a sliver of the rights-holding collective and competes with other

[70] Thom, 2010 *infra* note 86 at 34. For other examples of contextual understandings of the *Indian Act* band, see, for e.g., Pasternak, *supra* note 26 at chapter 7; and Johnston, *supra* note 57.

[71] Christie, *supra* notes 37 and 42;Thom, 2010, *supra* note 70 at 34.

[72] In *Delgamuukw v British Columbia*, [1997] 3 SCR 1010, the Gitxsan and Wet'suwet'en claimants were the traditional or hereditary chiefs of the houses, which are the owners of land under their respective legal traditions. In *Tsilqhot'in Nation*, *supra*, an inland nation without a house structure, the claim started under one First Nation (*Xeni Gwet'in*) was put forward at the national level, involving six *Indian Act* band councils. Discussions of an appropriate form of governance among Tsilhqot'in bands and their shared Tŝilhqot'in National Government are ongoing, as part of the now tri-lateral negotiation process with British Columbia and Canada: *Gwet'sen Nilt'I Pathway Agreement*, (25 June 2019), online: <http://www.tsilhqotin.ca/Portals/0/PDFs/Press%20Releases/2019_Gwets%27enNilt%27iPathwayAgreement.pdf> accessed 26 May 2020. Currently, Haida title is being pursued by the Council of the Haida Nation, a government institution that combines traditional and *Indian Act* governance structures and has been in place since 1974: <http://www.haidanation.ca/?page_id=20> accessed 1 April 2019.

[73] From my survey of the Statements of Interest submitted by First Nations in the BCTC, it appears that there are roughly 3 times as many negotiations tables led by individual communities/*Indian Act* bands than by tribal councils and/or hereditary leaders. Many of those nations describe their authority as customary or as both customary and legislative.

representatives, obscuring both the existence of the polity and identification of its will. Given this spectrum of representativeness, one might expect negotiations and ratification policies to involve an active assessment—perhaps by an independent third party with Indigenous membership and expertise—of the potential Indigenous parties in a given territory and context,[74] and support for intra-and inter-Indigenous discussions and dispute resolution before negotiations progress with state parties. While some supports are available alongside growing recognition of the need for supports for inter- and intra-Indigenous processes,[75] the CLC and BCTC negotiations and ratification policies, outlined below, fail to treat the identification of negotiating polities with the complexity required.

3. Modern treaty policies and experiences

On the surface, the relevant treaty negotiations policies are "hands-off," leaving important choices of representation to Indigenous peoples themselves and emphasizing the accessibility of the process. At first glance, this ethic of non-interference appears to support self-determination. On a closer examination, however, these policies do not account for the dynamics unleashed within and between Indigenous groups by the recognition accompanying state parties' choices to enter into negotiations with self-identified Indigenous parties. That recognition—and the state support that comes with it—sets the reformulation

[74] Related proposals include the Royal Commission on Aboriginal People's recommendations for the creation of Treaty Commissions as "permanent, independent and neutral forums where negotiations as part of treaty processes can take place" including mediation and binding or non-binding arbitration on matters, and conducting expert fact-finding (Royal Commission on Aboriginal Peoples, *Report of the Royal Commission on Aboriginal Peoples* (Ottawa: Minister of Supply and Services, 1996) [RCAP Report], vol 2, ch 3, at 85, 87) and the Aboriginal Lands and Treaties Tribunal, to provide adjudicative support for treaty processes (*ibid.*, vol 2, ch 3, at 87). Val Napoleon has suggested Indigenous law as an important resource in resolving such disputes, specifically in the Treaty 8 context regarding overlaps with Lheidli T'enneh First Nation, "Thinking About Indigenous Legal Orders," Research Paper for the National Centre for First Nations Governance (June 2007) at 9-10. David Rosenberg and Tim Dickson have called for a joint First Nation and government body to be created to map lands in BC that are subject to Aboriginal title: "Mapping Aboriginal Title in British Columbia" (2016) 7 Advocate 505 at 514. See also Shin Imai, "Sound Science, Careful Policy Analysis, and Ongoing Relationships: Integrating Litigation and Negotiation in Aboriginal Lands and Resources Disputes" (2003) 41 Osgoode Hall L J 587.

[75] The federal government's articulation of "potential" approaches in its rights recognition framework shows signs of moving in these directions, stating, for e.g., that "The Governor in Council could act on the recommendation of the Minister to add recognized Nations or other Collectives and their governments to a schedule of the act. In making his or her recommendation to the Governor in Council, the Minister could be required to take into account independent advice, provided either by an ad hoc advisory committee or an institution" and also noting the possibility of dispute resolution services in relation to 'shared or overlapping' territories; CIRNAC, Rights Recognition, *supra* note 31. See also, "Shared Territories and Overlaps", presentation from the BC Cabinet and First Nation Leaders' Gathering, 5 Nov 2019, online: <https://firstnationsleadersgathering.gov.bc.ca/assets/Breakout_2_Shared_Territories_and_Overlaps.pdf> accessed 21 August 2020.

of the Indigenous polity on a course that is very difficult to undo, even if modern treaties are living, evolving agreements. In the end result, the "hands-off" polices are not hands-off in effect.

The policies of both the CLC and the BCTC leave it open to Indigenous parties to choose or create entities to conduct negotiations or to rely on *Indian Act* bands. Treaty negotiations thus proceed with *Indian Act* bands, or treaty societies and organizations, which may be an aggregation of *Indian Act* bands or may be led by and/or include input from elders and hereditary leaders. Federally, aggregation for the purposes of treaty and self-government negotiations is encouraged: "Canada considers aggregation as an effective and affordable way for resource management and governance administration."[76] The BCTC, however, moved away from encouraging aggregation, viewing the federal policy, and particularly an early federal emphasis on "province-wide organizations", as a failure.[77] In BC, First Nations' options for creating their negotiating body is limited only by the need to satisfy the BCTC of their representative capacity and the crown that the body represents *a* rights holder (as opposed to "*the*" rights holder).[78] Optimistically, the BCTC has focused on the treaty process as an expression of self-determination: "Integral to the self-determination of First Nations is the ability to define citizenship, articulate who is eligible to vote, and collectively shape a common future. Building this new future begins with a committed membership and continues through the enrolment process. It crystallizes through the will of the First Nations citizenship, as expressed through the ratification vote."[79] Under these access-oriented policies, negotiations towards agreements in BC have often proceeded with individual communities; four of the six collectives that have reached the point of holding a ratification vote on a Final Agreement under the BCTC began negotiations as individual *Indian Act* bands.[80]

[76] Renewing the CLC, *supra* note 31. For discussion regarding the origins of this policy, see Christa Scholtz, "Land Claim Negotiations and Indigenous Claimant Legibility in Canada and New Zealand" (2010) 62 Political Science 37 at 38.

[77] BC Task Force, 1991, *supra* note 20 at 19.

[78] BC Task Force, 1991, *ibid.*; For details on what the BCTC requires from a First Nation to begin negotiations, see "Stage 1: Criteria", online:<http://www.bctreaty.ca/policies/stage-1-criteria> accessed 1 April 2019.

[79] BC Treaty Commission, Guide to First Nations Ratification. Building Our Future (February 2017) [BCTC, Ratification Guide] at 4.

[80] The four were the Sliammon First Nation, now the Tla'amin Nation (in implementation), Tsawwassen First Nation (in implementation), Lheidli T'enneh (ratification failed, 2006 and 2018), and Yale First Nation, (ratified, but not implemented). The other two are Nisga'a, which proceeded outside of the BCTC process, and Maa-nulth. Maa-nulth is itself comprised of five individual communities with self-government being implemented at that level, and those five communities split off from a larger group of 12 that had originally joined together for negotiations; see Mack, *supra* note 28. The ratio of negotiations being pursued by an single community/*Indian Act* band compared to an aggregated collective across all stages of negotiations is 3:1 (based on information available in 2019 from the BCTC,

That negotiations are often led by individual communities contributes to the phenomenon known as overlapping or shared territories. The CLC defines shared territory and overlap issues as "situations in which more than one Aboriginal group has potential or established Aboriginal and treaty rights in the same geographical area."[81] In these situations, the CLC and BCTC processes rely on Indigenous peoples to resolve potentially competing rights and territorial claims amongst themselves, although the BC and federal governments recognize that all parties have an interest in these claims and overlaps being resolved.[82] The BCTC advises that First Nations must identify potential overlaps when they first seek to initiate negotiations and indicates that "[o]verlap disputes" should be resolved before the conclusion of an Agreement in Principle (AIP). More attention to these issues in the last decade has resulted in increased support from the BCTC for dispute resolution between Indigenous groups[83], and recognition that the crown "has a constructive role to play in the resolution of these issues."[84] Nevertheless, negotiations have often continued past the AIP phase without such resolutions[85] and the tools and policies to guide the crowns' role are as yet undeveloped.

Concerns arising from single community or *Indian Act* band led negotiations do not preclude a small or local community pursuing self-government on a scale that is manageable and corresponds with local aspirations. Indeed, colonial experiences with divide and conquer dynamics may make aggregation

"Negotiations Update", online:<http://www.bctreaty.ca/negotiation-update> accessed 1 April 2019). This means that most treaties currently under negotiation in BC are proceeding with individual communities, some of which report well under 500 members at the beginning of their negotiations (ibid.).

[81] Renewing the CLC, *supra* note 31.

[82] Ibid. and British Columbia, First Nations Summit, and Canada, *Recognition and Reconciliation of Rights Policy for Treaty Negotiations in British Columbia*, 4 September 2019 [BC Rights Recognition Policy] at para 56, online: <https://www2.gov.bc.ca/assets/gov/british-columbians-our-governments/indigenous-people/aboriginal-peoples-documents/recognition_and_reconciliation_of_rights_policy_for_treaty_negotiations_in_bc_aug_28_002.pdf> accessed 1 October 2019.

[83] The BCTC indicates that "Where all parties to the overlap agree, the Commission may facilitate or assist the parties to obtain dispute resolution services as required." BCTC, "Stage 4, Resolving overlaps" [BCTC, Resolving overlaps], online:<http://www.bctreaty.ca/policies/monitoring-commission-0> accessed 1 April 2019.

[84] BC Rights Recognition Policy, *supra* note 82.

[85] In such cases, the BCTC now provides an assessment report to First Nation parties and the crowns assessing "the nature of the dispute, and whether best efforts have been made by all parties to resolve it through a process, such as the First Nations Summit's Recognition Protocol, agreed to in earlier stages": BCTC, Resolving overlaps, *supra* note 83. See generally, Christopher Devlin & Tim Theilman, "Overlapping Claims: In Search of 'a Solid Constitutional Base'" *CBA Aboriginal Law Section Annual CLE* (June 2009) [Devlin & Theilman], online: http://www.dgwlaw.ca/wp-content/uploads/2014/12/Overlapping_Claims.pdf accessed 21 August 2020. Regarding the CLC, Eyford stated: "The 1981 and 1986 Policies established that no land in areas of shared territory would be granted as part of the comprehensive land claim unless boundary disputes had been resolved" and noted that the 1993 Policy was silent (Eyford Report, *supra* note 16 at 66).

unthinkable in the present moment.[86] However, treaty processes are not simply about the governance choices of Indigenous nations. Treaties are also inextricably about the constitutional rights of Indigenous peoples. These rights are grounded in economic and cultural practices that are often exercised across large territories, and Indigenous territories and polities are not limited to reserves and village-based governance systems.[87] An overly localized approach to treaties thus increases the probability that the rights-holding collective or collectives are not properly represented in negotiations that address those rights.[88] In effect, the "overlapping and shared territories" phenomenon is as much the product of a misfit between who is negotiating and what is at stake in the negotiations as it is about the identification of constitutional rights and title that may be shared within a given geography.

Some of the potential problems of the non-interference and access policies under the BCTC are demonstrated by a treaty process in Secwepemcúl'ewc (the territory of the Secwepemc people, located in the interior of BC). The Northern Secwepemc te Qelmucw (NStQ) signed an AIP in July 2018 following a referendum process to confirm the mandate in 2016. NStQ is an aggregate body of four *Indian Act* bands, which reported overlaps and/or shared territories reported with several other nations from differing language groups but also with the "other Secwepemc nations."[89] The other Secwepemc nations share a language group and history. One recent account of that history and law suggests the historical and ethnographic evidence, including oral histories, "strongly emphasized the collective nature, at the Secwépemc nation level, of land tenure."[90] More southerly Secwepemc communities, represented by the Shuswap Nation Tribal Council (SNTC), view the treaty process as inadequate and oppose the NStQ decision to negotiate. They view the land at stake as the

[86] See Brian Thom, "The Anathema of Aggregation: Toward 21st Century Self-Government in the Coast Salish World" (2010) 52 Anthropologica 33 [Thom, 2010]. However, negotiations with single community political units entrenched by the *Indian Act* has also been criticized as a poor foundation for self-determination; see, for e.g., RCAP Report, *supra* note 74, Vol. 2, chapter 2 at 158, 169-170, and Diabo, *supra* note 26.

[87] The identification of Aboriginal rights and title is fact-driven, such that the size of an Indigenous harvesting area or Aboriginal title will depend on the particular claim. However, as established in *Tsilhqot'in Nation*, SCC, *supra* note 42, the concept of Aboriginal title is not restricted to village sites and the exclusivity of Aboriginal title does not preclude the possibility of joint ownership; see Kent McNeil, "Exclusive Occupation and Joint Aboriginal Title" (2015) 48 UBC L Rev 821.

[88] The evolving rights jurisprudence has also led to recommendations that the negotiations process must involve more attention to assessing and describing the rights at stake: Eyford Report, *supra* note at 16 at 46. See also Devlin & Theilman, *supra* note 85.

[89] BC Treaty Commission Annual Report 2018 at 38 [BCTC AR 2018].

[90] Marianne Ignace and Ronald E Ignace, *Secwépemc People, Land, and Laws. Yerí7 re Stsqeys-kucw* (McGill-Queen's University Press, 2017) at 288. Ronald Ignace is a well-known politician from Skeetchestn, a southern Secpwepemc *Indian Act* band.

land of the Secwepemc nation as a whole and that important decisions about that land rest with the entire nation. Amongst the actions taken against the NStQ process was an open letter sent to Secwemepc community members by the Tribal Chief of the SNTC to encourage a "no" vote[91] and picketing at the voting station in one of the NStQ communities by some members of different Secwepemc communities (for which they had no mandate from SNTC) to encourage voting against the NStQ AIP. One of the protestors—a member of an NStQ band—smashed the ballot box and delayed the voting process in Williams Lake.[92]

At the time of the voting disruption, Chief Anne Louie of the Williams Lake band (the affected voting community) described the SNTC letter as "illegal interruption because they aren't voting members of . . . the communities involved with this treaty. They seem to think they represent all Secwepemc but they don't."[93] Whether she knew that the voting disruption involved an NSTQ band member or not, Chief Anne Louie recognized the larger dispute as one of representation. Past BCTC Chief Commissioner, Sophie Pierre, has also commented that external nation-to-nation or inter-tribal issues are separate from internal issues and require different approaches.[94] The policy, however, treats all disputes as ones of competing claims to territory and rights. If the framing of the problem does not encompass questions of who is the holder of the land and rights at stake and who may speak for that rights-holding collective(s), the BCTC's view of the treaty process as "nation rebuilding"[95] is on a rocky path. Moreover, as will be further addressed in the next section, this line drawing marginalizes dissenting voices.

The logic of the current approach —proceeding to finalize treaties in the presence of known "overlaps" —was well expressed by Robert Nault, the Federal Minister of Indian Affairs and Northern Development when the Nisga'a Agreement was completed. Both before and after ratification and implementation, challenges to the Nisga'a Agreement came from internal and external sources, including the Nisga'a's Gitxsan and Gitanyow neighbours.[96]

[91] Wayne Christian, Tribal Chief, *Shuswap Nation Tribal Council, open letter to Secwepemc community members,* 25 January 2016, available online: <https://es-la.facebook.com/shuswapnation/posts/january-25-2016secwepemc-community-membersre-nstq-treaty-agreement-in-principle-/10153893783864747/> accessed 19 March 2019.

[92] Monica Lamb-Yorski, "NStQ Treaty Referendum Vote Halted Thursday at Sugar Cane" *The Williams Lake Tribune* (11 February 2016), online: <https://www.wltribune.com/news/nstq-treaty-referendum-vote-halted-thursday-at-sugar-cane/> accessed 19 March 2019.

[93] Ibid.

[94] "Interview with Sophie Pierre", *BC Treaty Commission Annual Report 2014*, at 13–15.

[95] BCTC AR 2018, *supra* note 89 at 14–16.

[96] Challenges also came from non-Indigenous British Columbians, including the efforts of then opposition leader Gordon Campbell; see Tony Penikett, *Reconciliation: First Nations Treaty Making in British Columbia* (Vancouver: Douglas & McIntyre, 2006). For discussions of the challenges from

In his address to the Senate Committee during hearings on the constitutionality of the legislation to ratify the agreement, Minister Nault acknowledged that it is always preferable for Aboriginal groups to reach agreement on overlapping territories amongst themselves, but emphasized that the federal government was prepared to move forward with the Nisga'a treaty in the absence of agreement following unsuccessful negotiations between the Nisga'a and the Gitanyow. He set out three criteria for moving forward with a treaty in these circumstances:

The group that is ready to settle has negotiated with its neighbours in good faith; measures taken to resolve the impasse have proven to be unsuccessful; and the treaty contains an explicit statement that it will not affect any Aboriginal or treaty rights of any other Aboriginal group.

The federal policy on overlaps recognizes that in the face of unresolved impasses on overlap issues the only solution may be to negotiate a treaty with each group in turn, while respecting the rights of other affected Aboriginal groups.

The Gitanyow have remained in negotiations.[97] Nault's explanation appears to still be current, providing the most explicit statement of the crown's negotiations policy on these issues available. Under Nault's account, government unavoidably chooses one treaty partner over another group. The government chooses the more flexible negotiating partner willing to negotiate now rather than wait for further evolution in the treaty process or rights jurisprudence to better meet their needs and aspirations. In doing so, the policy of not interfering with the resolution of inter-Indigenous (and intra-Indigenous) disputes goes out the window. Further, as Nault explains, one key premise for favoring groups in the treaty process over ones who have remained outside of it (or are just not as advanced in their negotiations) is non-derogation of the non-treaty group's rights. However, Nault's confidence in non-derogation to protect Indigenous collectives with rights claims associated with territories subject to a different group's treaty, implemented through the eponymous non-derogation clauses in the treaty, is out of date. Recent duty to consult jurisprudence has signaled that treaty rights can negatively impact the accommodation of

internal parties and neighbouring nations, see Carole Blackburn. *Negotiating Rights, Reconciling History: The Nisga'a Treaty and the Terms of Inclusion in the Canadian State* (PhD Dissertation. Ann Arbor, MI: UMI Dissertation Services, 2003); and Neil J Sterritt, *Tribal Boundaries in the Nass Watershed* (Vancouver: UBC Press, 1998); and Neil J Sterritt, "The Nisga'a Treaty: Competing Claims Ignored!" (1998/99, Winter) 120 BC Studies.

[97] In 2021, the Gitanyow Hereditary Chiefs signed a Governance Accord with BC and Canada, which the BC Treaty Commission describes as providing "a new path forward in the BC treaty negotiations process guided by the Rights Recognition Policy" *Annual Report 2021* at 11, online: <https://www.bctreaty.ca/sites/default/files/BCTC_Annual_Report_2021.pdf> accessed 31 January 2022.

unproven rights claims in government decision-making.[98] If the intent is to pursue a policy of non-interference with Indigenous self-determination, it may also be critical to stop moving forward with agreements that alter section 35 rights before the communities at stake can agree (or agree to disagree) on issues of representation as well as overlap.

B. Ratification processes: funding and fairness

The marginalization of dissenting and minority voices within Indigenous polities begins with the lack of status of sub-groups who may not be represented by the negotiating body. In this section, I turn to examine the aggravation of this marginalization through funding supports to the Indigenous negotiating body and further funding and support for the information and engagement campaigns that precede the ratification of a final agreement. In respect of both, it is apparent that past and ongoing forms of investment in the treaty process, by both government and Indigenous parties, can thwart the rebuilding of Indigenous nations through treaties.

1. Funding Indigenous parties: loans

Indigenous parties' participation in negotiations were funded by loans until 2018. As the first charge against the capital that would be transferred under a ratified agreement, negotiations loan debts were enforceable against a First Nation should they choose to leave the negotiation process before concluding a treaty. Over the extended timelines of treaty negotiations, the loan program—and more specifically the debt load it created if parties left the treaty process—generated perverse incentives for parties to keep negotiating instead of encouraging quick settlements.[99] Unsustainable negotiations debt burdens threatened the financial viability of communities outside of treaty settlements, particularly given that many negotiations have been pursued with a single band-level community.[100] In a 2011 review of the BC process, James Lornie

[98] *Gamlazyeltxw v British Columbia (Minister of Forests, Lands & Natural Resource Operations)*, 2020 BCCA 215 [*Gamlazyeltxw*] The case involves a dispute over the Crown's obligations in relation to claimed Gitanyow harvesting rights in the Nass Wildlife Area, which is part of the Nisga'a treaty territory but also subject to Gitanyow litigation of rights and title (and presumably treaty negotiations). The BC Court of Appeal stated that "the existence of treaty rights may limit any accommodation a rights claimant may seek, as the Crown cannot be required breach a treaty in order to preserve a right whose scope has not yet been determined" (at para 13).

[99] Eyford Report, *supra* note 16.

[100] For e.g., Xaxli'p First Nation spent over 14 years in the BCTC process before deciding to withdraw after reaching the agreement in principle stage of the process. The band did not start repaying the loan in the next five years. Indian and Northern Affairs Canada contacted Xaxli'p to address the

concluded that debt burdens meant there was "no viable exit strategy" from the treaty process, creating disincentives to completing the agreements.[101] The recent loan forgiveness program and shift of the funding model to contributions rather than loans has been well-received by many,[102] and is clearly responsive to numerous critiques and recommendations on this issue. However, the incentives involved in funding Indigenous parties to negotiate and the potential to influence the directions taken by these parties, do not end with the loan program. It is nevertheless a time for optimism that future directions will do a better job balancing power in the funding arrangements to support negotiations.

Lheidli T'enneh First Nation's long journey through the treaty process illustrates the counter-productive incentives of both the now defunct loan funding regime and the continued lack of regulation of ratification campaigns, discussed further below. A small *Indian Act* band, near Prince George, BC, Lheidli T'enneh was one of the first bands to enter into the BC treaty process in 1993 and reached a final agreement that was put to a ratification vote in first in 2007 and then again in 2018.[103] Both times, the community voted the final agreement down with more than 50% of voters rejecting the treaty each time.[104] For reasons that remain opaque, but may relate to concerns about repaying

accumulating interest and the threat to the band's solvency, which could potentially place the band under direct financial management by the department. Instead of repaying the loan, the band sought the help of the Indigenous Network on Economies and Trade and pursued a shadow submission to the UN Committee on the Elimination of Racial Discrimination (CERD). Their loan debt was eventually placed in "abeyance" by Canada (Pasternak, *supra* note 26 at 256–257).

[101] James M Lornie, Final Report with Recommendations Regarding the Possibility of Accelerating Negotiations with Common Table First Nations that are in the BC Treaty Process, and Any Steps Required (30 November 2011) [Lornie Report] at 29.

[102] See, for e.g., the BCTC news release, "Debt burden on reconciliation eliminated in Budget 2019" 19 March 2019.

[103] The final agreement was not substantially altered before the vote in 2018, although there were adjustments to update the financial package dollar values to 2017 and other minor clarifications in drafting: *Lheidli T'enneh Final Agreement. Question and Answer Booklet* (Prince George, April 2018) [2018 Q&A Booklet] at 8.

[104] Regarding the 2007 vote, see Jeremy Hainsworth, "Northern BC First Nation Rejects Land Claim Settlement in 53 per cent Vote" *Canadian Press NewsWire*, 31 Mar 2007; Gordon Hoekstra, "BC Treaty Commission Mulls Probe of Why Lheidli T'enneh Dumped Deal" *Canadian Press NewsWire*, 7 Apr 2007 [Hoekstra]. There may be some discrepancies in this reporting, as Lheidli T'enneh reports that there were 111 yes votes out of a total of 273 possible votes (eligible voters), suggesting the rejection rate was actually 59% of eligible voters: [2018 Q&A Booklet, *supra* note 103.] Regarding the vote in 2018, see Press Release, Lheidli T'enneh Ratification Results, 23 June 2018, online: <https://web.archive.org/web/20180813120243/http://yourvoiceourfuture.ca/lheidli-tenneh-ratifcation-results-press-release> accessed 10 March 2019, reporting 185 votes against the treaty to 137 votes for. This press release does not make it clear if 185 against included eligible voters who did not vote. If not, the margin of defeat may be greater.

negotiation debts, the 2007 rejection of the agreement was not "no enough" to end of the process.

At the time of the 2007 rejection, both the First Nation's and BCTC leadership wanted to know why the process failed and efforts were made to investigate the reasons for the "no" vote. Director of Lheidli T'enneh treaty policy at the time, Rick Krehbiel, commented that he believed that a "lack of understanding triggered the rejection."[105] Similarly, *The Globe and Mail* reported that the Chief was convinced that members "may have been unclear on what they were voting for when they rejected the deal,"[106] while consultant and negotiator Tim Raybould commented that "[t]reaties have become way too complicated."[107] By contrast, a Lheidli T'enneh opponent to the treaty, then band councillor Rena Zatorski, was reportedly unconvinced that "there was widespread misunderstanding of [the Treaty]" and expressed concerns that by pursuing a second vote, treaty "proponents [were] looking for an opportunity to mount a stronger campaign [the second] time around."[108] A survey exploring the negative vote was commissioned by the BCTC. A majority of the survey respondents who voted for the treaty explained their support for the treaty as owing to wanting to move away from the *Indian Act* and/or because they saw the treaty as a fair deal, while a majority of the respondents who voted against the treaty explained their position as based on concerns that the nation was not prepared to take on all of the responsibilities of self-government and/or because they thought the final agreement was a bad deal.[109] Lack of information also figured into the survey responses, but not as highly as opinions about the agreement itself and its potential for implementation.

These official reflections on the 2007 experience, however, do not mention that following the "no" vote, the band was required to repay the approximately $7 million it had borrowed to participate in the negotiations. As Shiri Pasternak reports, BCTC advised that holding another vote on the final agreement would stay the repayment of this loan, which would otherwise paid off in five years through payments of $116,666/month.[110] Leading up to the 2018

[105] Hoekstra, *supra* note 104.
[106] Justine Hunter, "Band May Give Rejected Treaty Another Chance" *The Glove and Mail*, S1 (15 August 2007) [Hunter, G&M].
[107] Tim Raybould, "Just Who Needs Treaties?" Letter to the editor, *The Globe and Mail*, A20 (4 Apr 2007).
[108] Hunter, G&M, *supra* note 106.
[109] Mustel Group Market Research, "LheidliT'enneh First Nation Member Survey" (June 2007), online: http://www.bctreaty.ca/sites/default/files/Lheidli_Tenneh_membership_survey.pdf accessed 15 September 2017. [LT Survey]. See also John Curry, Han Donker, and Richard Krehbiel, "Land Claim and Treaty Negotiations in British Columbia, Canada: Implications for First Nations Land and Self-Governance" (2014) 58 The Canadian Geographer 291 [Curry, Donker & Krehbiel].
[110] Pasternak, *supra* note 26 at 255.

vote, website engagement materials were initially clear that, although no further negotiations debts were being accrued, another "no" vote would require the repayment of the negotiations loan while a yes vote would lead to repaying the loan out of an expected capital transfer of $16.1 million.[111] This message later changed. In materials prepared just three months before the vote in 2018, the Lheidli T'enneh Treaty Department noted an expectation that their earlier loan would be forgiven, based on a federal government announcement that it "will engage with affected Indigenous groups on how best to address past and present negotiations loans, including forgiveness of loans."[112] Nevertheless, the logic of persuasion evident in the treaty department's engagement materials leading up to the 2018 re-vote portrayed the treaty as an investment of time and energy that should not be lost. As Legal Advisor George Nicholson wrote in an engagement newsletter ahead of the second ratification vote: "Lheidli T'enneh may reject the Final Agreement, and I fully respect the community's right to choose. However, members should clearly understand that by rejecting the Final Agreement, it is a big step backwards, and other options are very likely to take a lot of time and also be a lot of work."[113] Financial investments through the loan program likely played an unspoken force in this narrative, accompanied by a sense of investment in the process that is not fully alleviated by the removal of debt burden.

2. Ratification: funding and fairness in information and engagement campaigns

The information and engagement strategies prior to ratification votes also demonstrate how investments of both time and money in the treaty process can favour the yes vote, or at least the party advocating for ratification. In the context of ratification campaigns, dissenting and minority views are marginalized by the lack of standards of fairness in electoral politics.

Lheidli T'enneh's experience illustrates how people and leadership, who are presumably neutral and responsive to their community's mandates, become invested in seeing these agreements through to a yes vote. This is not surprising, nor is it necessarily problematic. Indeed, the analysis of the 2007

[111] Bill Stipdonk, "Lheidli T'enneh First Nation. Fiscal Presentation" (June 2016), online: <http://www.yourvoiceourfuture.ca/sites/default/files/documents/fiscal-presentation.pdf> accessed 10 March 2019.

[112] 2018 Q &A document, *supra* note 103 at 68.

[113] "The Long Hard Road to Recognition of Aboriginal Rights" *Your Voice. Your Choice. Our Future. Lheidli T'enneh Final Agreement Decision* (October 2016) at 4, online: <http://www.yourvoiceourfuture.ca/sites/default/files/documents/october_2016_lheidli_tenneh_treaty_newsletter_0.pdf> accessed 10 March 2019.

Lheidli T'enneh vote pointed to the lack of a treaty champion to advocate for the agreement.[114] In other ratification processes, this concern of a treaty champion may have informed problematic forms of support offered by the crowns and/or Indigenous governments to treaty advocates ahead of ratifications votes. For example, Johnny Mack documented that the Maa-nulth treaty team generated an "atmosphere of celebration," fuelled by government chartered flights to the Nass Valley to visit the Nisga'a Lisims (government), or treaty team sponsored beach barbeques for discussions of treaties and cultural events, funded presumably by the $250,000 granted to the Maa-nulth nations in the last two months before the vote.[115] The *Toronto Star* reported allegations by a Tsawwassen band member that "monetary incentives were being dangled [including] $15,000 for each band member aged 60 and older upon approval of the treaty."[116] While the federal government denied that it was improperly interfering with the ratification process in the Tsawwassen treaty, the *Star* reported that the "BC government is not hiding the fact that it will do what it must to convince the aboriginal band's 350 members" to adopt the treaty.[117] A Vancouver area MP, John Cummins, accused the relevant cabinet members of "bribing natives into accepting a controversial provincial treaty ... [commenting that] "[i]f we in this country had a referendum and another nation was interfering in our referendum, we'd be rightfully outraged."[118] When contacted by journalist Brian Lewis, then Minister of Aboriginal Affairs in BC, Mike De Jong's response to these allegations was reported as "guilty as charged, for the most part"[119] an astonishingly flippant response, premised on the perceived need to ensure treaty process success, particularly after the Lheidli T'enneh vote in 2007.

[114] LT Survey and Curry, Donker & Krehbiel, *supra* note 109. In 2007, the community process was led by a Community Treaty Council, formed through family representation and modelled on a traditional governance structure, noted in the analysis as having been non-functioning for many years.

[115] Mack, *supra* note 28 at 123–124. Mack does not indicate the source of the funding. The Tsawwassen were also bused to Nisga'a territory so that they might learn from this success of this treaty signatory (Pasternak, *supra* note 26 at 260). Lheildli T'enneh treaty office website advertised similar events leading up to the 2018 vote.

[116] Richard Brennan, "Ottawa, B.C., Dangling Cash to Get Treaty Signed, MP says" *Toronto Star*, (16 July 2007), at A15. [Brennan]. See also Brian Lewis, "Funds Flow to Ensure Yes Vote on Treaty Deal", *The Province* (12 July 2007) [Lewis]. In submissions to the UN Committee on the Elimination of Racial Discrimination in 2009, the alleged inducement package distributed after the yes vote included $1000 for members under age 60 and was not funded out of the treaty settlement: Pasternak, *supra* note 26 at 257.

[117] Ibid. Brennan, *supra* note 116.

[118] Ibid.

[119] Lewis, *supra* note 116. These details and responses were also enumerated in submissions to CERD, as reported by Pasternak, *supra* note 26 at 257.

In the BC Treaty Commission 2015 Annual Report, there is a quiet statement of crown policy on ratification processes, perhaps responding to these earlier voting "irregularities":

"Canada and BC are of the view that they cannot actively and overtly support the First Nations communications efforts during the ratification process. As a consequence, the First Nation must undertake the process and the vote essentially on their own. The Treaty Commission has increased its involvement in ratification process to fill this gap and to provide support for this critical work. [The Treaty Commission's activities to support ratification processes include] [i]increased funding or additional allocations of Negotiation Support Funding for communications initiatives and community engagement."[120]

This statement suggests that crown learned something from the problems in the earlier approaches, but BCTC still only allocates funding to what is effectively the "yes" side of the treaty debate.

The efforts of Indigenous treaty negotiators to be neutral in their information and engagement work was evident at the end of the second Lheidli T'enneh ratification campaign. In their Questions & Answers document, for example, there was a clear effort to situate the Treaty Department as neutral towards the outcome and address perceptions of the treaty process likely stemming from the earlier campaign and the experiences noted above:

> Q: Why does it seem like everyone who speaks to us, even our chief, is pushing the final agreement on us?
>
> A: Each member must decide for themselves whether or not they agree with the Final Agreement.... The negotiators believe that this Final Agreement meets the mandate given to them by the community and there are strengths that need to be understood. The community engagement process is about explaining the strengths and weaknesses of the Final Agreement so that each person who is affected can make an informed individual decision when they vote in June.[121]

The document further explicitly confirmed that there would not be a payout or signing bonus in the event of ratification.[122] Despite of the obvious care and attention to neutrality, the message from the 2018 Lheidli T'enneh negotiation team still expressed a view of final agreement that was arguably

[120] BC Treaty Commission, *Annual Report 2015*, at 17.
[121] 2018 Q&A Booklet, *supra* note 103 at 10.
[122] Ibid. at 68.

not neutral. For example, in explaining how laws enacted under the Lheidli T'enneh Constitution would be different than bylaws enacted under the *Indian Act*, the document states that under the latter, the Chief and Council "are not given authority to pass bylaws [on reserve land] independently of the federal government" while "the Final Agreement would enable the Lheidli T'enneh Government to enact laws that are equivalent in force to federal and provincial laws."[123] These statements may be true in some contexts, but they do not reflect that Lheidli T'enneh is under the *First Nations Land Management Act*, under which 40 provisions of the *Indian Act* pertaining to land use are replaced with a land management code enacted by the band that also removes Ministerial oversight.[124] These statements also do not reflect case law, which, to date, has only recognized the authority of Indigenous governments under modern treaties as delegated (or subordinate), and not on par with the constitutionally co-ordinate authorities of federal and provincial governments.[125] Regardless of the significance of such points for Lheidli T'enneh voters, the problem is not that the Lheidli T'enneh treaty negotiators were "pro-treaty" in their explanations of the agreement being put forward for ratification. Perhaps inevitably, the engagement process leading up to a ratification vote is a campaign. The problem is that it is not treated as such.

Even with lessons learned from past ratification processes, BCTC's framing still does not address or protect ratification as an exercise of popular will by an Indigenous polity. Instead, the First Nation treaty negotiation team—often a branch of the band government, as it was in Lheidli T'enneh, that has become heavily invested in achieving ratification of the agreement they negotiated– is a vehicle for the delivery of the Treaty Commission's mandate, a recipient of aid and support to achieve its aims. Indeed, the BCTC guide on ratification suggests that engagement committees, who are tasked with education about the

[123] Ibid. at 55.

[124] Crown-Indigenous Relations and Northern Affairs Canada, "First Nations Land Management," (last modified 28 February 2019), which indicates that Lheidli T'enneh has been under this regime since November 2000, online: <https://www.aadnc-aandc.gc.ca/eng/1327090675492/1327090738973> and https://www.aadnc-aandc.gc.ca/eng/1327165048269/1327165134401 accessed 1 April 2019. See also *supra* note 4 for more on the Act and Metallic, *supra* note 15 regarding the recent removal of the ministerial power of disallowance in relation to other band bylaws.

[125] *Sga'nism Sim'augit (Chief Mountain) v Canada (AG)*, 2013 BCCA 49, 359 DLR (4th) 231, lv to appeal to SCC refused, 3530 (22 Aug 2013). The BCCA did not preclude other sources of authority for the laws of such a government but held that the finding of delegated authority was sufficient for the determination of the issues in the case, which challenged the constitutionality of the Nisga'a Agreement. There is a potential irony in interpreting the authority of governments established through land claim agreements in a more circumscribed manner than that of *Indian Act* band councils (see early discussion of the legislative and inherent sources of their authority). For critical commentary on *Chief Mountain*, see Joshua Nichols, "Reconciliation without Recollection? Chief Mountain and the Sources of Sovereignty" (2015) 48 UBC L Rev 515.

treaty in advance of ratification, may choose to run an "assertive yes campaign" as the appropriate engagement strategy.[126] While support for Indigenous nations in their communications strategies is important, the policy stance fails to recognize the importance of dissent in these contexts and of supporting a rigorous political process in Indigenous communities. Ratification chapters in claims agreements detail the creation of bi- or tri-partite ratification committees, the appointment of a Chief Election Officer, and ensure strict protocols for the conduct of the actual vote.[127] In many agreements, the committee is tasked with ensuring that voters are provided with a reasonable opportunity to review the agreements and internal constitutions to be ratified.[128] Such provisions in final agreements are a bare framework that requires further development at a policy level, although the provisions themselves might also be more substantial. In BC, this policy is to fund engagement campaigns that can explicitly be "assertive yes campaigns." Effectively, the votes are regulated but the campaigns are not.[129]

For perspective on how far this varies from what might be considered a model of a fair voting process, consider BC's failed referendum on electoral reform in 2018. Under legislation passed specifically to address this referendum, the Chief Electoral Officer selected groups as the official proponent and opponents of the electoral reform proposals. Each group was awarded $500,000 for public information campaigns. The campaign period was strictly regulated, individual contributions to the campaigns were limited, and a ceiling on expenses was set along with requirements for public disclosure.[130] Elections BC, a well-established neutral party, had the responsibility for neutral public

[126] BCTC *Ratification Guide*, *supra* note 79 at 24.

[127] See, e.g., Chapter 28 of the *Maa-nulth First Nations Final Agreement* [*Maa-nulth Agreement*], online:<https://www.aadnc-aandc.gc.ca/DAM/DAM-INTER-BC/STAGING/texte-text/mna_fa_mnafa_1335899212893_eng.pdf> accessed 21 August 2020.

[128] See, for e.g., Article 7.b. of the *Tla'amin Final Agreement*: <https://www.rcaanc-cirnac.gc.ca/eng/1397152724601/1542999321074#chp23> accessed 21 August 2020. The *Tsawwassen First Nation Final Agreement* included a funding commitment by Canada and BC to Tsawwassen First Nation to carry out the obligations (Article 24.8): <https://www.aadnc-aandc.gc.ca/DAM/DAM-INTER-BC/STAGING/texte-text/tfnfa_1100100022707_eng.pdf> accessed 21 August 2020. The *Nisga'a Final Agreement* also required a debate and resolution to put the Agreement to a referendum from an assembly of the Nisga'a Nation in chapter 22: <http://www.nnkn.ca/files/u28/nis-eng.pdf> accessed 21 August 2020.

[129] Issues relating to the conduct of the ratification campaign were raised by opponents to the Tla'amin Agreement in proceedings to set aside an injunction to prevent their protest and blockade at ratification voting centres: *Sliammon Treaty Society v Point*, 2012 BCSC 1038. In court, the protestors argued for funding of a referendum process that would include balanced representation of positions both 'for' and 'against' the treaty, amongst other things. These arguments were dismissed without much examination by the presiding judge, demonstrating at least that injunction proceedings are not the best forum for addressing these issues: ibid. at paras 7–12, 18.

[130] Elections BC, 2018 Referendum on Electoral Reform, "Opponent and Proponent Groups," online: <https://elections.bc.ca/referendum/about-the-referendum/opponents-proponents-and-advertising-sponsors/opponent-and-proponent-groups/> accessed 19 March 2019.

education. The point of this comparison is not that all of these forms of regulation should necessarily transfer to Indigenous contexts, but that, in the treaty context, matters of constitutional import are not taken half as seriously. There are no sources of funding for those opposed to the treaty in the campaign leading up to ratification votes. Similarly, there appear to be no rules on funding and fundraising leading up to community votes on the final agreements. The idea of a balanced campaign does not even figure into the policy picture.

C. The structure of ratification votes

Ratification thresholds highlight another way in which minority views—and in particular, regional and sub-groups—within the Indigenous polity have not been given an adequate platform within the ratification process. The minimum threshold required by the Crown negotiating partners in ratification referendums is 50%+1 of all *eligible* voters, such that a failure to vote counts as a vote against the treaty. The BCTC describes this threshold as "higher than any other voting process in the country."[131] First Nations are free to and have set thresholds much higher than 50%+1.[132] One might argue, though, that the *Clarity Act*, SC 2000, c 26 has a higher or at least more thoughtful threshold requirement, under which section 2 requires a "clear expression of a will by a clear majority of the population of a province that the province cease to be part of Canada." The House of Commons is to assess the clarity of the majority against: "**(a)** the size of the majority of valid votes cast in favour of the secessionist option; **(b)** the percentage of eligible voters voting in the referendum; and **(c)** any other matters or circumstances it considers to be relevant." While such an approach may not be desirable or appropriate in the treaty context, the *Clarity Act* formulation shows that there are many more ways to define the majority required to set a polity off on an important new governance trajectory.

Higher thresholds are not necessarily the key or only concern in crafting a voting process that will adequately represent the affected political community.

[131] Ibid. at 12. By contrast, the standard required in BC referenda is "more than 50% of validly cast ballots": *Referendum Act*, BCSC 1996, c 400, s. 4. See also s. 9 of the *Electoral Reform Referendum 2018 Act*, SBC 2017, c 22.

[132] For example, Lheidli T'enneh set a threshold of 70% of eligible voters in 2007 but opted for a 50%+ 1 threshold in 2018. The final agreement was rejected by over 50% of voters both times. See Jeremy Hainsworth, "Northern BC First Nation Rejects Land Claim Settlement in 53 per cent Vote" *Canadian Press NewsWire*, 31 Mar 2007 and Press Release, Lheidli T'enneh Ratification Results, 23 June 2018, online: <https://web.archive.org/web/20180813120243/http://yourvoiceourfuture.ca/lheidli-tenneh-ratifcation-results-press-release> accessed 10 March 2019.

Equally important are questions about how sub-groups within the voting population are represented in the vote. For example, in another context, the BC *Recall and Initiative Act*, RSBC 1996, c 398 defines a successful initiative vote as follows:

> **15** (1) Subject to Part 5, the chief electoral officer must declare an initiative vote to be successful if
> (a) more than 50% of the total number of registered voters in British Columbia vote in favour of the initiative, and
> (b) more than 50% of the total number of registered voters for each of at least 2/3 of the electoral districts in British Columbia vote in favour of the initiative.

Section 15(1)(b) ensures attention to regional approval such that the urban vote of greater Vancouver cannot determine the result for the entire geo-political territory of BC. Given the tensions catalyzed by the treaty process within and between Indigenous communities and their representative bodies, consideration of sub-groups within the eligible voting population is important to the BCTC's hopeful aim of ratification expressing "the will of the First Nations citizenship."[133] It is equally, if not more important to ensuring that the rights-holders impacted by the terms of the agreement are adequately represented in the decision.[134]

The BCTC and CLC policies do not prevent differentiations between voting majorities and the requirement of multiple majorities for ratification. For example, when peoples in the Sahtu ratified their agreement in 1999, 75% approval of 2/3 of eligible voters from both Métis and Dene voting lists were required in light of different legal and treaty statuses prior to the agreement, which includes both peoples.[135] The Maa-nulth Agreement required both an overall majority (50%+1) and a majority of each individual community.[136] But

[133] BCTC *Ratification, supra* note 79.

[134] "Ratification of a treaty is not an individual vote as found in other elections. It is a communal vote on constitutionally protected collective rights to lands, self-government, and resources. No other vote involves collective rights to land and resources, so the voting threshold is meant to establish clear evidence of collective will. As a result, the ratification threshold for a First Nation for treaty is higher than any other voting process in the country" (ibid. at 12). Higher thresholds, however, do not answer the questions of who is the rights-holding collective or collectives, and who represents those collectives.

[135] Ratification Process, s. 6, *Sahtu Dene and Metis Comprehensive Land Claim Agreement*, (Minister of Indian Affairs and Northern Development, 1993), online: <https://www.rcaanc-cirnac.gc.ca/eng/1100100031147/1543258621708?wbdisable=true#appd>accessed 1 April 2019.

[136] *Maa-nulth Agreement supra* note 127 at Article 28.2.1(d) and (e). The Agreement also contemplated the course of action should ratification not succeed in all of the individual communities, such that this regional failure would not automatically lead to the failure of the treaty: Article 28.2.10. Such

generally, the lack of attention to regional and less populous groupings within the voting entity has been problematic in BC, as was demonstrated in the ratification process for the Nisga'a, concerning in particular the Kincolith band.[137] In Senate hearings on legislation to implement and ratify the Nisga'a Agreement through Parliament, Mercy Thomas, matriarch from the Nee'is'lis'e'yans wilp and Wolf Clan of the Git Gingolx and Nisga'a, also a member of the Kincolith band, explained that her wilp (house) was geographically isolated and that the negotiation process and resulting agreement would leave them politically isolated as well. Responding to a question as to whether she will have political rights to vote under the Nisga'a Agreement, she explained:

> We will be able to vote. The irony, however, is that there are three other villages in the Upper Nass that will always outvote us. It does not matter what we do. We have been classified as the dissidents.... [I]t is a case of the numbers. The three Upper Nass villages will always outvote Kincolith no matter how we look at it.[138]

Her other evidence indicated that one of the points of dissent was the amount and locations of the land being surrendered through the treaty—a common concern at the time—and particularly, that the land of her wilp was relinquished.[139] Through the treaty, the Nisga'a moved from a wilp-based ownership of and authority over land (common to neighbouring Gitxsan and Wet'suwet'en societies), to a " 'common bowl' approach by which authority over territories is theoretically pooled in the [Nisga'a Nation]. There is no mention of houses in the Nisga'a treaty."[140] As Ms. Thomas' evidence suggests, the pre-existing owners and authorities on behalf of a given territory were not represented as such in the process of ratifying the agreement.

Although such transformation to governance and ownership structures to more state-like entities and arrangements is a much-critiqued aspect of the

concerns, however, do not 'fix' the problems caused by proceeding with this Agreement after the larger Nuu-chah-nuulth nation rejected the treaty at the AIP stage.

[137] There were several concerns about the Regarding the Nisga'a ratification process, and legal interventions by some of the internal actors. For discussion, see Blackburn, 2003, *supra* note 96; and Christopher Roth, "Without Treaty, Without Conquest: Indigenous Sovereignty in Post-Delgamuukw British Columbia" (2002) 17 Wicazo Sa Review 143–165

[138] *Proceedings of the Standing Senate Committee on Aboriginal Peoples*, Issue 7—Evidence. Senate of Canada (Ottawa, 23 March 2000), online: <https://sencanada.ca/en/Content/SEN/Committee/362/abor/07ev-e?Language=E&Parl=36&Ses=2&comm_id=1>accessed on 19 March 2019.

[139] See also discussion in Hoffman & Robinson, *supra* note 30.

[140] Roth, *supra* note 137 at 149.

CLC and government policy more generally,[141] such transformations may be a legitimate and appropriate choice for Indigenous nations to make. Critics generally argue that the CLC is too substantively restrictive to make this a matter of uncoerced choice. The critique I present here adds that the manner of making this choice is itself problematic. Under the BCTC and CLC processes, multiple majority ratification votes are possible and the work sits with Indigenous parties to resolve questions of who can and should represent an Indigenous polity in treaty negotiations and in ratification. However, such work occurs within the pressures stemming from engagement with the BCTC or CLC processes, including the lopsided support for pro-treaty voices discussed above. "Self-determination as non-domination" may require providing positive (external) support for units within a larger self-determining body who may be weaker or more poorly resourced and vulnerable to domination from within.[142] In this context, and although the suggestion may bristle against laudable policy directions towards non-interference with Indigenous self-determination, the onus remains on crown parties to do more and possibly even require more of Indigenous negotiating parties in these situations.

More attention to the structure of the voting majorities may even be a legal obligation on the part of the federal crown. Federal fiduciary duties inform the threshold "floor" of the existing 50%+1 of eligible voters that is adopted by Indigenous parties in most claims contexts.[143] If Nee'is'lis'e'yans wilp, for example, proved Aboriginal title to their claimed territory (or part of the territory), and if this land was ceded by the larger Nisga'a nation and not protected as Indigenous land through the treaty settlement, the Crown might be in breach of its fiduciary obligations by having permitted the land to be ceded without specific permission of the Indigenous title holder.[144] At the very least, there is a duty to consult regarding the impacts of treaties and advanced treaty negotiations on rights-holders in the same geographical area who are not or

[141] See, e.g., Nadasday, 2005 *supra* note 27.

[142] Iris Marion Young, *Global Challenges: War, Self-Determination, and responsibility for Justice* (Cambridge: Polity Press, 2006) at 66, discussed and challenged by Jacob Levy in *supra* note 6.

[143] BC *Ratification Guide, supra* note 79:"The federal government requires this threshold because the federal Crown holds reserve and financial assets on behalf of *Indian Act* bands. The fifty per cent plus one threshold ensures that members agree that assets held by the Crown can be transferred to the new self-governing First Nation." The federal government also has fiduciary obligations to Aboriginal title holders: *Tsilhqot'in Nation*, SCC, *supra* note 42.

[144] A similar concern can be raised regarding the non-involvement of the *Indian Act* band when its assets (reserve lands) are being surrendered by entities that are not the band. An example of this is raised, and dismissed, in *Spookw v Gtixsan Treaty Society, supra* note 8. This issue was addressed in the *Maa-nulth Agreement, supra* note 127 which required a distinct vote of the *Indian Act* band to agree to the transfer of the band assets and dissolve the band (Article 28.3), a process that recognized that the people enrolled and eligible to vote on a treaty can differ significantly from the people who are on the list of an *Indian Act* band.

choose not to be represented by the Indigenous party to the negotiations.[145] While there are cases upholding the propriety of the Crown and BCTC not "interfering" in internal disputes within Indigenous nations and treaty parties,[146] at least the consultation obligations under the honour of the Crown has evolved in a manner that potentially clashes with the hands-off policies of the BCTC and CLC processes.

Regardless of the precise nature of the Crown's legal obligations in ratification votes, we might just expect more of our governments in such lengthy and important negotiations. As Christopher Roth notes with respect to identifying the treaty signatories, "North American history is full of examples in which any signature or 'X' is deemed sufficient to divest whole civilizations of their territories, but in the twenty-first century we might expect more nuanced criteria."[147] The nuance is still wanting in the decision processes to ratify a final agreement. The future trajectory of the treaty and treaty relationships depend on it.

IV. Conclusion

The treaty process has many flaws. It has been soundly critiqued by many observers, participants, and governments, with several points of critique shared across radically different political viewpoints. Where most critiques focus on the substantive limitations of the Comprehensive Claims Policy, some critiques also point to issues of process. As detailed above, This chapter demonstrates the fundamental inattention to basic issues defining fair and democratic decision-making in treaty processes, which aggravate the dynamics unleashed by the burying of the twin issues of who is (or are) the rights-holding collective(s) and who represents that (or those) collective(s) under the rubrique of shared and overlapping territories.

The current policy direction on these issues is one of non-interference with Indigenous collectives and their choices around representation and ratification in the negotiation process. This chapter has argued that while "non-interference" may be an appropriate objective, it cannot be achieved with blind spots on issues of representation, and without policies or support for vigorous and fair campaigns and consideration of sub-groups leading up to ratification. These blind spots marginalize dissent and minority perspectives, and potentially also

145 See *Enge*, *supra* note 45.
146 See, for e.g., *Spookw v Gitxsan Treaty Society*, *supra* note 8.
147 Roth, *supra* note 137 at 153.

allow constitutional rights to be modified without adequate representation of the rights-holders in the decisions. Not only may the honour of the Crown require more from the Crown in these situations, there is no protected bubble of "non-interference" in the colonial landscape in which these negotiations occur. The Crown cannot disregard inter- and intra- Indigenous struggles, many of which are aggravated by the past and present parameters of treaty processes. Treaties are relationships. Crown parties need to be relational in their understanding of the impact of their policies.

The current policy moment is full of fresh energy and frequent policy announcements. Serious issues like negotiations debt burdens, loan forgiveness, and repayment have been addressed. However, current policy directions, and indeed the existing policies on most of the issues covered in this chapter, remain opaque. In 2018, the Standing Committee on Indigenous and Northern Affairs recommended that more information about the new Rights Recognition tables be made publicly available,[148] a recommendation that has more general application. These tables along with other statements of policy both federally and from the BC treaty process Principals suggest that, at the very least, a rights-based process—or more likely, processes—are in the works.[149] The potential for the continuation, as opposed to modification or transformation, of rights through treaties, as well as more express attention to the rights at stake by the negotiating crowns begin to address the concerns I have raised regarding representation, obligations to rights-holders, and the potential and reasonable differences within Indigenous nations regarding their futures. These directions suggest optimism is appropriate. Funding processes that support and allow Indigenous peoples to discuss and consider territorial definition and governance options amongst themselves without negotiations pressures, including dispute resolution, would be reason for even more optimism.

If I might be pessimistic for a moment, I would point out most of these reformist directions have already been around for several years, and that despite more nuanced understandings of the "overlaps" issue, BC's premier recently described hereditary governments as an "emerging" issue.[150] My pessimism is further fuelled by the inattention to ratification processes in policy renewal debates. Apart from the 2017 guide prepared by the BCTC,[151] which does not evidence awareness of the need to also support a "no" campaign, ratification processes are not a topic of current concern. It is not difficult to imagine

[148] Standing Committee Report, 2018, *supra* note 18 at 55.
[149] Principal's Accord, *supra* note 34.
[150] Ball, *The Star Vancouver*, supra note 61.
[151] BCTC *Ratification Guide*, *supra* note 79.

directions for policy development that would help. Minimally, transparency and controls on contribution funding for campaigns in advance of final agreement votes require attention. My call for greater Crown and BCTC action and attention to these issues is not, however, a call for unilateral action that does not respect Indigenous self-determination. As with other areas of policy development involving Indigenous peoples, directions for such policies must emerge through conversations with Indigenous communities and political organizations.

Beyond the treaty policies, a more fundamental shift is required. That shift is embedded in the driving mission behind the CLC, the BC treaty process, and other negotiations processes. The treaty process has long been mired by hopeful but misdirected government plans to achieve "reconciliation", settle the land question, and allow economic development to continue with new and better distributions of the benefits to Indigenous communities. The process has not been understood as one that will continue, or as a nation-to-nation process full of sticky political moments and with the potential to change not just the Indigenous polities but also the character and nature of the Canadian state. The lack of attention to ratification issues and to issues of rights-holders and representation separately from competing territorial claims, is just one symptom that suggests that Indigenous parties remain only marginally understood as political communities with their own political and legal traditions. As political communities, important decisions like entering a treaty to address or settle Aboriginal rights claims and reformulate internal governance are properly and hotly contested. Treaty and rights recognition processes that recognize and support Indigenous nations as polities emerging from a complex and damaging past will represent a tectonic shift in the policy landscape.

9

Plebiscites and Peace

Comparative Lessons from the 2016 Colombian Plebiscite for Peace

Carlos Bernal

I. The Dilemmas on Plebiscites and Peace

A. The Colombian Plebiscite for Peace

On 2 October 2016, in the so-called "Plebiscite for Peace", 50.21 percent of the voters rejected the peace agreement that the Colombian Government had negotiated with the Revolutionary Armed Forces of Colombia [hereafter: FARC].[1] Only 37.43 percent of the eligible voters participated in the plebiscite. The Colombian Constitutional Court had previously ruled that, if the voters rejected the peace agreement, the Government was not empowered to implement it.[2] Instead, the Government ought to negotiate a new agreement, and seek popular ratification again.

Despite that, the Government and the FARC adopted a different strategy. They introduced a few changes to the rejected draft and quickly construed a second agreement. The then President, Juan Manuel Santos, requested that the Congress—in which he controlled a slim majority by virtue of party affiliation and political coalitions—ratify the second peace agreement. The Congress granted the request, and the Constitutional Court upheld the validity of the parliamentary ratification.[3] Consequently, as prescribed by a constitutional amendment, the Congress and the Government gained authority to implement the peace agreement with the enactment of constitutional amendments,

[1] The Revolutionary Armed Forces of Colombia—People's Army (in Spanish: Fuerzas Armadas Revolucionarias de Colombia—Ejército del Pueblo, FARC–EP or, simply, FARC) was a guerrilla movement. This movement was involved in the Colombian armed conflict from 1964. Their members endorsed a Marxist–Leninist ideology. Their operations included terrorism, kidnaping, illegal mining, extortion, and production and distribution of illicit drugs.

[2] Colombian Constitutional Court, Decision C-379/2016.

[3] Colombian Constitutional Court, Decision C-699/2016.

Carlos Bernal, *Plebiscites and Peace* In: *The Limits and Legitimacy of Referendums.* Edited by: Richard Albert and Richard Stacey, Oxford University Press. © Carlos Bernal 2022. DOI: 10.1093/oso/9780198867647.003.0010

laws, and presidential decrees by means of expedite normative production procedures (known as the *fast track*).[4] The same constitutional amendment empowered the Constitutional Court to review the constitutionality of all implementation provisions.[5]

B. The legitimacy dilemma

Two questions arise from an analysis of this scenario. First, can plebiscites—or referendums—confer legitimacy to the implementation of peace agreements? In the Colombian context an answer to this question leads to a dilemma. I will call it: the legitimacy dilemma.

(i) On the one hand, a negative answer is justifiable for three reasons: (a) complexity; (b) manipulation; and (c) the intrinsic legitimacy of peace agreement.

   (a) First, in the Plebiscite for Peace the Government requested the people to vote in favour of—or against—the implementation of a 297 page long, highly technical peace agreement, which addresses complex issues concerning transitional criminal justice, amnesty, recognition of truth, symbolic reparations, land redistribution, the transformation of the FARC into a political party, a plan for removing mines from the war territories, a project for replacing farming of illicit plants with other products, among other matters. What kind of legitimacy can the people confer to an agreement of this level of complexity with a single vote? If none, due to epistemic and deliberative constraints, that legitimacy could only be very limited.

   (b) Second, critics of the outcome of the Plebiscite for Peace argued that opponents to the peace agreement had manipulated the will of the people with a fear campaign. Along the streets of Colombian cities and towns, citizens observed billboards portraying Timochenko, the leader of the FARC, as a Colombian President. At the same time, supporters of the agreement threatened the voters with a reinvigoration of the conflict if the peace agreement were rejected.

[4] See, Legislative Act 1/2016. Under the Colombian Constitution, a Legislative Act is an Act by means of which the Congress amends the Constitution.

[5] Legislative Act 1/2016 granted that empowerment to the Constitutional Court.

Under those conditions, votes of manipulated citizens, ill-informed on the foreseeable outcomes, cannot confer legitimacy to the implementation of the peace agreement.

(c) Finally, regardless of the outcome of the plebiscite, implementing the peace agreement was legitimate by itself because peace is, at the same time, a precondition and a goal of democratic constitutionalism, and the peace agreement was arguably a suitable means to achieve peace. Hence, the outcome of the plebiscite did not matter at all. An approval by the citizens could not add legitimacy to an intrinsically legitimate peace agreement. Also, a rejection by the citizens could not deprive the peace agreement from its legitimacy.

(ii) On the other hand, if, as explained below, actual popular consent engenders legitimacy, then, plebiscites—and referendums—can indeed become sources of legitimacy for the implementation of peace agreements. Following the majority rule, this can only be the case if most of the people vote in favour and give their consent to those agreements. According to the Colombian Constitutional Court this application of the majority rule was also a constitutional tenet.[6] Hence, in the aftermath of the Plebiscite for Peace, the Constitution did not permit political authorities to disregard the popular vote. The Government was under the constitutional and political obligation to respect the will of the people. Seeking the negotiation of a completely new agreement, and a subsequent popular ratification by means of another plebiscite, was the only permissible strategy. Hence, ratifying and implementing a slightly modified second agreement was unconstitutional.

C. The constitutional review dilemma

A second question is whether empowering a Constitutional Court to review the constitutionality of the implementation of a peace agreement can confer legitimacy to that process. Answering this question also elicits a dilemma. I will refer to it as the constitutional review dilemma.

(i) On the one hand, a peace agreement—as a set of transitional justice institutions—is a mechanism that can assist a society in the endeavour of overcoming conflict, when the existing constitutional framework has

[6] Colombian Constitutional Court, Decision C-379/2016.

proved unsuitable. Under those circumstances, a peace agreement could only be an appropriate means to achieve the goals of transitional justice, if it includes provisions that somehow conflict with the Constitution, e.g. amnesty laws, exceptions to the obligation to compensate victims, the creation of special parliamentary seats for ex-combatants, etc. Hence, the question about including a mechanism of constitutional review within a process of implementation of a peace agreement should receive a negative answer. What would be the point of entrusting a Constitutional Court with the task of reviewing the constitutionality of provisions enshrining transitional justice institutions, if the very nature of those institutions is at odds with the Constitution?

(ii) On the other hand, if the purpose of a peace agreement is the institutionalization of democratic constitutionalism, then a mechanism of constitutional review of the implementation norms can be a suitable source of legitimacy. Thus, the answer to the above stated question should be positive. A Constitutional Court can ensure that the transitional justice institutions are not a façade for window-dressing arrangements that can contradict the very essence and purpose of a constitutional democracy.

D. Aim and claims

Based on an analysis of the Colombian case study of the Plebiscite for Peace, its implementation, and the judicial review by the Constitutional Court, this chapter aims to evaluate the legitimacy and the constitutional review dilemmas, and to suggest appropriate solutions.

The outcome of the analysis are two claims: (i) Plebiscites—and referendums—can confer legitimacy to a peace agreement if and only if they are the final step of a fair and inclusive deliberative process. If it is foreseeable that those conditions cannot be met, institutional designers should avoid scheduling participatory strategies of this kind within transitional justice processes. Instead, or additionally, (ii) they should include mechanisms of constitutional review of norms implementing peace agreements. Constitutional Courts can ensure that peace agreements are an advancement towards the entrenchment of democratic constitutionalism. Naturally, this can only be the case if Constitutional Courts are impartial and independent.

The second claim leads to a nuanced notion of transitional constitutionalism, in which the legitimacy of peace agreements depends on their coherence with the core elements of democratic constitutionalism. In the Colombian case, the process of constitutional review conferred to the peace agreement some legitimacy that it could not gain from the Plebiscite for Peace. However, due to the political influence of former President Santos over the majority of the Constitutional Court, some decisions by the Court were unable to provide that legitimacy.

E. Outline

The outline of this chapter is the following. In Section II, I present a short description of Colombia's internal conflict and I explain how the peace agreement process was structured under the 1991 Colombian Constitution. In Section III, I account for the circumstances in which the Plebiscite for Peace took place. In Section IV, I critically analyse the aftermath of the popular rejection of the Peace Agreement, particularly, concerning the congressional ratification of the second version of the agreement, and its constitutional review. In Section V, I explain what I will understand under legitimacy for the purpose of the analysis of the legitimacy and constitutional review dilemmas that I carry out in Section VI and Section VII.

II. Colombia's internal conflict and the peace agreement

A. On Colombia's internal conflict

Since its independence from Spain in 1810, the political history of Colombia has been dominated by an endless fratricidal war. From the beginning of the nineteenth century until the middle of the twentieth century, war between the members of the two traditional parties, the conservatives and liberals, caused bloodshed on a scale comparable only to that of the Mexican revolution. This critical situation was mitigated in the 1970s, when the parties signed an agreement for alternate power sharing with a formula called the National Front. According to this formula, each Government was succeeded by a Government from the opposing party. Despite its benefits, that formula excluded the claims of the working class, indigenous peoples, and small farmers from the policies based on the consensus reached by conservative and liberal elites.

The closure of the political system during the National Front was conducive to the emergence and consolidation of various guerrilla groups. At the beginning, the guerrillas fought under a kind of leftist political credo, bearing elements of Marxism and Maoism. Backed by military assistance from the United States, the Government tried to exterminate the guerrillas, which, for their part, received financial, military, and ideological support from the then existing USSR and Cuba. However, neither side could defeat the other. The guerrillas always exercised *de facto* military control over extended parts of the national territory and survived through different mutations. The most remarkable, following the fall of the Berlin Wall and the demise of the USSR, was the loss of ideological direction. Then, they transformed themselves into a lucrative business of organized crime, kidnapping, and drug production and trafficking.

Constant attacks by the guerrilla on landowners, and the inability of the State to enforce State law in rural areas, gave rise to paramilitary groups. Supported by the landowners, and by the drug cartels, those groups intensively fought the guerrillas. Those groups also deployed a strategy of elimination of civilians accused of funding the guerrillas, and funded their activities through similar, nefarious means. These developments resulted in outrageous massacres and systematic violation of human rights.

B. The enactment of the 1991 Constitution

The 1991 Constitution emerged as a sign of hope against the backdrop of a beleaguered State with armed guerrillas engaged in outright conflict. The 1991 Constitution is the outcome of the first democratic constitution making process in the history of Colombia. Representatives of the most heterogeneous groups and classes participated in the discussion, drafting, and enactment of the text. Its main motto was pluralism. The Constitution was designed to open up the political system and to guarantee the participation of everyone, even members of guerrilla groups that, such as the M-19, demobilized before the election of a Constitutional Assembly in December 1990. In addition, a wide-ranging declaration of socio-economic rights with binding force compelled the State to work actively towards achieving a better level of social justice and distribution of wealth to benefit vulnerable groups.

Three popular votes granted legitimacy to the initiative of drafting and enacting the 1991 Constitution. In the official elections of March 1990, a movement of young students proposed to voters to include an additional ballot—the so called "seventh ballot"—requesting the election of an extra-constitutional National Constituent Assembly. More than one million citizens deposited their seventh vote. Due to this fact, President Virgilio Barco decided to call a referendum to officially vote for the formation of the National Constituent Assembly during the following presidential elections in May 1990. Five million voters approved the formation of that Assembly in an official referendum. Then, in December 1990 the people elected their representatives for that Assembly, which in July 1991 enacted the Constitution.

C. Transitional justice under the 1991 Constitution

Even under the 1991 Constitution the State lacked adequate political and military power to control the guerrillas and paramilitary groups. For this reason, two processes of transitional justice were set in motion. The first began in 2005 with the enactment of a normative framework of institutionalized mechanisms for rendering the members of paramilitary groups judicially accountable, and enabling their victims to achieve clarification of the truth, compensation, and land restitution.[7] More than 35,000 members of paramilitary groups have so far demobilized. However, this process has been strongly criticized for resulting in impunity, and insufficient reparations to victims.[8]

The second transitional justice process was inaugurated in 2012 with the enactment of a constitutional amendment that made provision for peace negotiations with the FARC.[9] The amendment granted five transitional and exceptional powers to Congress: (i) to give privileges to the members of guerrilla groups willing to sign a peace agreement; (ii) to create judicial and extrajudicial procedures for prosecuting crimes, clarifying the truth, and ensuring compensation to victims; (iii) to create a truth commission; (iv) to determine selection criteria for prioritizing the prosecution of those "most responsible" for systematically perpetrating crimes against humanity, genocide, and war, and refraining from prosecuting other offenses and agents, suspend sentences, and commute criminal penalties for "extrajudicial sanctions" or "special arrangements"; and (v) to determine what crimes can be deemed as "political offences" such that their perpetrators will remain eligible for political participation.

The adjectives "transitory" and "exceptional" create the impression of a transitional constitutional framework for peace. Moreover, the transitory articles

[7] This framework included the Act 975/2005, the Decision C-370/06 of the Constitutional Court, and other legislative (Acts 1424/2010, 1448/2011, and 1592/2012), and administrative norms (such as the Decree 1290/2008).

[8] See, Nicole Summers, "Colombia's Victims' Law: Transitional Justice in a Time of Violent Conflict?" (2012) 25 *Harv. Hum. Rts. J.* 219–235.

[9] Legislative Act 1/2012.

purport neither to derogate nor interrupt the validity of essential principles of the constitution, but to subsist within its framework. Nevertheless, some of these grants of power appear to be at odds with essential constitutional principles, such as the principle of equality and the rule of law. The principle of equality, for example, entrenched in Article 13 of the Constitution, is in tension with granting special political and criminal justice benefits to former FARC guerrilla members. Furthermore, the rule of law, entrenched in Article 1 of the Constitution, requires (among other things) a strict enforcement of criminal laws, the prosecution of all crimes, and the allocation of full compensation to victims. This is in tension with some criminal law and liability benefits granted under the peace agreement.

D. Constitutional difficulties of transitional justice

These tensions engendered constitutional difficulties. The Constitutional Court dealt with those difficulties when it reviewed the constitutional amendments that framed the peace negotiations,[10] and the norms implementing the peace agreement.

The Constitutional Court approached those issues with a balancing perspective.[11] According to the Court, the potential of some provisions of the constitutional amendment that framed the peace negotiations for satisfying the constitutional right to peace outweighed the degree in which they interfered with essential constitutional principles.[12] For instance, the Constitutional Court held that the government obligation to guarantee human rights and to enforce criminal laws against human rights violations was outweighed by the goal of "achieving a stable and lasting peace".[13] The Court reasoned that

[10] Article 241 of the 1991 Constitution empowers the Constitutional Court to review the constitutionality of constitutional amendment on procedural grounds. Nevertheless, the Constitutional Court has created and applied an established "constitutional replacement doctrine", according to which constitutional amendments inconsistent with the essential principles of the Constitution are invalid. On this doctrine, see Carlos Bernal, "Unconstitutional Constitutional Amendments in the Case Study of Colombia: An Analysis of the Justification and Meaning of the Constitutional Replacement Doctrine" (2013) 11(2) *Int'l J Const L* 339–357.

[11] See, the decisions C-579/2013 and C-577/2014.

[12] Article 22 of the Constitution guarantees a right to peace.

[13] In Decision C-579/2013, the matter under review was the provision in Act 1/2012 empowering the Congress to determine selection criteria for use by the Attorney General to give priority to the prosecution of those "most responsible" for "systematically perpetrated" crimes against humanity, genocide, and war. According to the same criteria, the Attorney General may refrain from prosecuting "all the cases", and may also suspend sentences, and commute criminal penalties into "extrajudicial sanctions" or "special arrangements". The plaintiff sought a declaration that the expressions "most responsible", "systematically perpetrated", and "all the cases" implied a constitutional replacement. The plaintiff claimed that these expressions implicitly replaced an essential constitutional element, namely,

prosecuting only the "most responsible" agents is a suitable approach to assure the non-recurrence of crimes, dissolve criminal macro-organizations, and reveal patterns of human rights violations. At the same time, this policy of criminal prosecution represents only a mild interference with the government obligation to protect human rights, because it does not amount to an absence of investigation of war crimes, genocide, and human rights violations. It only empowers the office of the Attorney General to focus its attention on "those agents who played an essential role in the perpetration" of those violations. Furthermore, the Court held that the powers vested in the legislature expressed a proportionate relation between the duty to guarantee human rights and enforce criminal laws and the goal of achieving a stable and lasting peace, provided their exercise meets certain conditions related to the guarantee of the rights of the victims.

In the same vein,[14] the Constitutional Court upheld the constitutionality of a provision included in a constitutional amendment, which empowers the Congress to deem certain offences as "political crimes".[15] The effect of that provision is that those who have committed "political crimes," but who have demobilized and reintegrated into civil society during the peace process, remain eligible to participate in politics. The Article sets a constraint to the exercise of this legislative power, namely, that crimes against humanity and genocide cannot be deemed "political crimes". The plaintiff maintained that, by excluding including war crimes, drug trafficking offenses, and acts of terrorism in the list of offenses that cannot be deemed "political crimes", this Article replaces an essential element of the constitution. That element is the requirement of minimum moral standards for candidates who intend to represent the people as political office holders.

The Constitutional Court did not agree with the plaintiff. The Court held that not including the above-mentioned offenses in the list of crimes that cannot be deemed political crimes enhances the possibilities of future political participation for participants in the historical conflict. This is a suitable means to achieve three of goals of transitional justice, namely, reconciliation, a

the State duty to guarantee human rights protection for victims and society generally by means of the strict enforcement of criminal laws against all human rights violations and all infringements of international humanitarian law. According to the plaintiff, Act 1/2012 would unconstitutionally empower the Congress to replace this essential element of the Constitution by restricting the State duty to enforce criminal laws against only some human rights violations and only some infringements of international humanitarian law, namely, the violations and infringements "systematically perpetrated" by the "most responsible agents".

14 Constitutional Court, Decision C-577/2014.
15 Article 3 of Legislative Act 1/2012.

stable and lasting peace, and building a new and inclusive legitimacy for political institutions.

III. The Plebiscite for Peace and the Decision C-376/2016

Under the powers granted by the Legislative Act 1/2012, between 2012 and 2016 the Government carried out negotiations with the FARC. As a strategy to endow the outcome of the negotiation with legitimacy, in 2015 President Santos presented to the Congress a bill calling for a plebiscite concerning "the endorsement of the final agreement for the termination of the conflict and construction of a stable and lasting peace". The 1991 Constitution did not require undertaking such plebiscite. The agreement could have been implemented by means of constitutional amendments, laws, and decrees. However, in a context of backlash against the peace negotiation, the Government—and its supporters in the Congress—decided to consult the people by means of a plebiscite.[16] According to the Act of the plebiscite for peace,[17] only a low participation threshold (13%), and a simple majority was required for the ratification of the plebiscite. In addition, the outcome of the plebiscite was binding for all matters concerning the constitutional and legal implementation of the peace agreement.

In accordance with Article 241 of the Constitution, the Constitutional Court undertook a constitutional review of the bill, and in the Decision 376/2016 endorsed the constitutionality of the Act of the plebiscite for peace. The Court clarified that the decision by the people was political in nature and did not imply the incorporation of the peace agreement into the legal system. According to the Constitution, the President can convene a plebiscite when he aims to consult the people on a political decision within the scope of the Government's powers. Hence, the approval by the people endows the decision with legitimacy and represents a political mandate, which is binding on the President but not on other State institutions, such as the Congress. After popular ratification, the peace agreement ought still to be implemented by means of ordinary mechanisms for legal production. Finally, the Court stated that the consequence of the popular rejection of the peace agreement was the impossibility to implement

[16] Article 104 of the Constitution institutes plebiscites as mechanisms of popular participation, in the following way: "The President of the Republic, with the approval of the ministers and the prior approval of the Senate of the Republic, may consult the people on matters of great national importance. The people's decision will be binding. Such consultation may not coincide with another election."

[17] Statutory Law 1806/2016.

it. In that scenario the President ought to negotiate another agreement and request the people to ratify it in another plebiscite.

The Plebiscite for Peace took place on 2 October 2016. The 13% participation threshold was reached. However, 50.21% of the voters rejected the agreement after a campaign in which both supporters of the approval, and supporters of the rejection were the target of criticism. On the one hand, critics challenged the very idea of requesting the people to approve a highly technical document on transitional justice. Even experts had difficulty in understanding most of the contents of the peace agreement. Furthermore, the people were asked to approve or to reject in block the whole 297 long page agreement. The voters could neither introduce modifications to the document nor approve certain sections while rejecting others. Additionally, supporters and detractors of the peace agreement appealed to intimidation during the campaign. Rejecting the peace agreement could mean the end of the ceasefire and the restart of the conflict. Approving it could lead to the transformation of Colombia in another Bolivarian Republic—like Venezuela—with the immediate loss of liberal constitutionalism.

There is no doubt that supporters and opponents of the peace agreement also defended legitimate arguments. On the one hand, the agreement incorporated a sophisticated design of a Special Jurisdiction for Peace, which arguably complies with international standards on criminal liability in times of transitional justice,[18] while, at the same time, incentivizing the guerrilla members to agree to its conditions. On the other hand, the agreement did not foresee any specific commitment of the guerrillas to compensate their victims from their

[18] Such as: securing accountability of the most responsible agents, recognition of the victims, and that "prosecution initiatives aim to ensure that those responsible for committing crimes, including serious violations of international humanitarian law and gross violations of international human rights law, are tried in accordance with international standards of fair trial and, where appropriate, punished". See, Secretary General of the United Nations, *Guidance Note of the Secretary-General. United Nations Approach to Transitional Justice* (2010), available online at: https://www.un.org/ruleoflaw/files/TJ_Guidance_Note_March_2010FINAL.pdf (accessed 08.05.2020). See also, United Nations Secretary-General, *The Rule of Law and Transitional Justice in Conflict and Post-Conflict Societies* (2004), available online at: http://www.unrol.org/files/2004%20report.pdf (accessed 19.03.2020); UN Commission on Human Rights, *Updated Set of Principles for the Protection and Promotion of Human Rights through Action to Combat Impunity*, E/CN.4/2005/102/Add.1, 8 February 2005, available online at: http://daccess-dds-ny.un.org/doc/UNDOC/GEN/G05/109/00/PDF/G0510900.pdf?OpenElement (accessed 19.03.2020); and UN General Assembly, *Basic Principles and Guidelines on the Right to a Remedy and Reparation for Victims of Gross Violations of International Human Rights Law and Serious Violations of International Humanitarian Law*, A/RES/60/147, 21 March 2006, available online at: http://www.ohchr.org/EN/ProfessionalInterest/Pages/RemedyAndReparation.aspx (accessed 19.03.2020). See also, Peter Dixon and Chris Tenove, "International Criminal Justice as a Transnational Field: Rules, Authority and Victims" (2013) 7 *International Journal of Transitional Justice* 393–412; Ruti Teitel, "Transitional Justice and Judicial Activism— A Right to Accountability?" (2015) 48 *Cornell International Law Journal* 386 f.; and Carsten Stahn, "The Geometry of Transitional Justice: Choices of Institutional Design" (2005) 18(3) *Leiden Journal of International Law* 425–466.

own resources. In addition, the negotiating parties bizarrely defined the peace agreement as a special agreement, in terms of Article 3 common to the Geneva Conventions.[19] By means of this characterization, the negotiating parties aimed to include the peace agreement into the so-called constitutional block,[20] and to accord to it supra-constitutional rank into the Colombian legal system.

IV. The Colón Theatre Agreement, the ratification by the Congress, and the Decision C-699/2016

In the aftermath of the Plebiscite, and after brief deliberations with the opposition, the Government conveyed to the FARC some proposals to renegotiate the rejected peace agreement. With the fear of losing momentum, the Government included only few points in a second version of the agreement. The changes in the text amount to a very small percentage. Certainly, a more specific commitment of the FARC with regard to the compensation to victims was agreed. However, the core of the deal remained unchanged.

A few months earlier the Government had managed to obtain the congressional approval of another amendment to the Constitution, namely, Legislative Act 1/2016. This amendment created three special mechanisms for the implementation of the peace agreement, that is, its transformation into legally binding norms: first, a shorter procedure to amend the Constitution; second, a legislative procedure for peace that enabled the Congress to pass laws at a faster pace; third, an empowerment to the President for issuing decrees with legal force implementing sections of the agreement and policies connected to it. The legislative decrees have the legal capacity to amend and derogate previous laws and regulate matters reserved by the Constitution to the Congress. The three mechanisms were known as *fast track* procedures. Their configuration aimed to achieve a faster implementation of the peace agreement and to avoid risks associated with delays and lack of effectiveness of transitional justice mechanisms.

According to Article 5 of Legislative Act 1/2016 the implementation of the peace agreement by means of fast track mechanisms was only legally possible

[19] The relevant text of this provision is the following: "The Parties to the conflict should further endeavour to bring into force, by means of special agreements, all or part of the other provisions of the present Convention."

[20] Under Article 93 of the Constitution, the case law coined the term "constitutional block" for referring to the block of norms belonging to the international human rights treaties ratified by Colombia. Norms belonging to the constitutional block prevail over the domestic law.

after "ratification by the people". Naturally, the semantic reference of this latter expression was the approval of the agreement in the Plebiscite for Peace or, according to the Decision C-376/2016, an approval of another, different, agreement in a second plebiscite. Despite the rejection of the agreement by a slim majority of the voters, the Government did not call for a second plebiscite but asked the Congress to ratify the renegotiated agreement, in the name of the people, by means of a political motion. Evidently, the amended agreement—known as the Colón Theatre Agreement—was not a new peace agreement but a second slightly changed draft of the original one. The Government feared that voters would reject this version too. Furthermore, the Government was not prepared to expose its main policy to the objections by the opposition party, led by former President Uribe, that found increasingly popular support. Finally, the trust of the guerrilla leaders in the process was quickly deteriorating, and the phantom of a return to the war darkened the political scene.

Within this background, the Constitutional Court reviewed the constitutionality of Legislative Act 1/2016.[21] Using the constitutional replacement doctrine, the Court raised two legal issues. First, whether the amendment replaced the Constitution by introducing faster and more flexible constitutional amendment and legislative mechanisms. Second, whether the extraordinary faculties granted by the Congress to the President breached the principle of separation of powers in such a degree that implies a constitutional replacement. The Court gave a negative answer to both questions and accepted that the ratification of the Colón Theatre Agreement by the Congress amounted to a popular ratification for empowering the Congress and the President to employ the fast track mechanisms. Indeed, the Court attributed to the Congress the authority to decide what "popular ratification" meant under Article 5 of the Legislative Act 1/2016. In this way, the Court enabled the Congress not only to ratify the Colón Theatre Agreement but to begin its implementation via fast track.

V. A conception of legitimacy

Within this framework the relevant question of this chapter is how to solve the legitimacy and the constitutional review dilemmas. Answering those questions presupposes clarifying the conception of legitimacy that I will employ in the present analysis.

[21] See, the Decision C-699/2016.

The concept of legitimacy is a matter of debate in legal theory and political philosophy.[22] There are at least three senses of "legitimacy": a legal, a sociological, and a normative one.[23] In a legal sense, legitimacy is a feature of norms. It refers to their validity, that is, the existence—and consequential binding force—resulting from the fact that they have been enacted by the competent authorities and appropriate procedures, according to the legal system.[24] Concerning plebiscites or referendums, legal legitimacy points to the question whether they have been convened and carried out according to the procedures foreseen by the Constitution and the laws.

From a sociological perspective, Weber defined legitimacy as the "belief by virtue of which persons exercising authority are lent prestige".[25] As applied to plebiscites—and referendums—, sociological legitimacy relates to the questions whether the authorities convening the plebiscite and the people participating are considered as politically trustworthy in their endeavour, and whether the outcome of the plebiscite is accepted (as a matter of fact) as deserving of respect or obedience.

In the normative sense, when predicated about plebiscites, "legitimacy" denotes the virtue of generating acceptability or justifiability of the resulting outcomes as worthy to be transformed into law. If those outcomes are linked to constitutional norms, then normative legitimacy points to their acceptability as higher law, intended to endure for long periods,[26] and to represent what Ackermann calls: "the constitutional judgment of [. . .] the People".[27]

Concerning plebiscites—and referendums—, it is possible to assess the normative legitimacy of three abstract objects: the process, the outcome, and the subject of a plebiscite. For instance, in the Colombian case it is possible to assess the normative legitimacy of the process of the plebiscite for peace, of its outcome—that is, the rejection of the peace agreement by a slim majority—, and of its subject—namely, the peace agreement as such. A plebiscite that is procedurally legitimate can communicate legitimacy to its outcome. Moreover, if the outcome is the approval of the political proposal, then the process and the

[22] For a critical analysis of the debate, see Fabienne Peter, "Political Legitimacy", *Stanford Encyclopedia of Philosophy* (2016), available online at: <https://plato.stanford.edu/entries/legitimacy/> (accessed 29.03.2020).

[23] David Beetham, *The Legitimation of Power* (Humanities Press International 1991) 4–5. Similarly, Richard Fallon identifies three senses of legitimacy as well. he calls them legal, moral, and sociological. See, "Legitimacy and the Constitution" (2005) 118(6) *Harvard Law Review* 1794 f.

[24] Hans Kelsen, "Der Begriff der Rechtsordnung" (1958) (3–4) *Logique et Analyse* 94.

[25] Max Weber, *The Theory of Social and Economic Organization* (Talcott Parsons (ed.), Free Press 1964) 382.

[26] See, Zachary Elkins, Tom Ginsburg, and James Melton, *The Endurance of National Constitutions* (Cambridge University Press 2009).

[27] See, *We the People: Foundations* (Harvard University Press 1991) 9.

outcome can also communicate legitimacy to the approved subject. However, legitimacy of the process is neither a necessary condition for the legitimacy of the outcome nor of the subject of the plebiscite. Hence, the legitimacy of a peace agreement, about which there has been a plebiscite, can derive—even exclusively—from its content. In any case, from the procedural legitimacy of a plebiscite in which the people has expressed their views concerning a political matter arguably follows an obligation—at least prima facie—to abide by the outcome.[28]

What does make the process and the outcome of a plebiscite normatively legitimate? Actual and hypothetical consent are two plausible legitimacy conferring properties. Concerning actual consent, general claims about its legitimacy conferring value are applicable here. Locke, for instance, claimed that "no one can be put out of this estate and subjected to the political power of another without his own consent".[29] Rawls refers to actual consent as "originating consent,"[30] and holds that it should be explicit for conferring legitimacy. In the same vein, according to Simmons, legitimacy "depends on one's actual consent".[31] Furthermore, Barnett claims that legitimacy depends on "actual unanimous consent to the jurisdiction of the lawmaker".[32] According to Rousseau, citizens' explicit expression of their common will is a necessary condition for legitimacy.[33] Analogously, a plebiscite process is legitimate if it channels the expression of the actual consent of the people about a political matter. Also, the outcome of a plebiscite is legitimate if it represents an expression of the actual consent by the people.

Due to the risks concerning the manipulation of actual consent by the people, other normative theorists endorse hypothetical consent as the legitimacy conferring property. For instance, according to Kant, the legitimacy-conferring feature is not actual consent but whether individuals could have consented to the norms they ought to obey.[34] This depends, at least in part, on the fairness of the processes in which the relevant norms are created. Similarly,

[28] On the connection between the legitimacy of an authority and the duty to obey its commands, see John Rawls, *A Theory of Justice* (Harvard University Press 1999) 343. In the case of a referendum or a plebiscite the authority is the people itself.

[29] John Locke, *Second Treatise on Civil Government* (C.B. MacPherson (ed.), Hackett 1990 [1690]) 52.

[30] John Rawls, *Lectures on the History of Political Philosophy* (Harvard University Press 2007) 124.

[31] A. John Simmons, Justification and Legitimacy: Essays on Rights and Obligations (Cambridge University Press 2001) 137.

[32] Randy E. Barnett, "Constitutional Legitimacy" (2003) 103 *Colum. L. Rev.* 111.

[33] Jean-Jacques Rousseau, *On the Social Contract 1762* (Hackett 1988) II:4 and I:3. Within this context, the reference of concept of will is equivalent to the concept of consent.

[34] Immanuel Kant, "On the Common Saying: 'This May be True in Theory, but it does not Apply in Practice'" in Hans Reiss (ed.), *Kant: Political Writings* (H. B. Nisbet (translator), Cambridge University Press 1991) at 75–76.

Waldron talks about a qualified form of "hypothetical consent,"[35] and conceptualizes legitimacy of political decisions in terms of whether the relevant decisions are made according to the right procedures.[36] Moreover, according to Barnett, legitimacy requires law-making "procedures which assure that they are not unjust".[37] Analogously, the outcome of a plebiscite is legitimate if the procedure leading to it was fair. In this context, a process is fair if it is open, and inclusive of all relevant stakeholders,[38] if they are informed concerning the matter about which they will express their consent, if they have not been manipulated or threatened, if they can participate in the plebiscite in equal conditions and in a meaningful way, and if the process leading to the vote allowed for a rational deliberation concerning the advantages and disadvantages of the possible outcomes.[39]

The best standard for assessing normative legitimacy is a combination of both properties. Also achieving normative legitimacy is a matter of degree. Thus, the following rule is valid: the fairer the process of a plebiscite is and the more its outcome is an expression of the actual consent by the people, the more legitimate is the result of a plebiscite. The opposite also applies.

Finally, it is also possible to assess the normative legitimacy of the subject in a plebiscite concerning the approval or the rejection of a peace agreement. The appropriate standard is twofold. On the one hand, the legitimacy of a peace agreement depends on its suitability to achieve the aims of transitional justice. This refers to the institutionalization of "processes and mechanisms associated with a society's attempts to come to terms with a legacy of large-scale past abuses, in order to ensure accountability, serve justice and achieve reconciliation".[40] A peace agreement is a device by means of which a political community seeks to overcome a past of severe and systematic violations of human rights, and to "repair and rebuild" State institutions within the confines of the rule of law.[41] Its aims are justice, truth, reparation, guarantees of non-repetition,

[35] Jeremy Waldron, "Theoretical Foundations of Liberalism" (1987) 37(147) *The Philosophical Quarterly* 127–150.

[36] Jeremy Waldron, "Rights and Majorities: Rousseau Revisited" in John W. Chapman and Alan Wertheimer (eds.), *Majorities and Minorities* (New York University Press 1990).

[37] Randy E. Barnett, "Constitutional Legitimacy" (2003) 103 *Colum. L. Rev.* 111.

[38] On the relevance of open public deliberation, see, Thomas Christiano, *The Rule of the Many* (Westview Press 1996) 35.

[39] On the connection between rationality and inclusiveness, on the one hand, and legitimacy, on the other: see, Fabienne Peter, *Democratic Legitimacy* (Routledge 2008).

[40] United Nations Secretary-General, "The rule of law and transitional justice in conflict and post-conflict societies" (2004), available online at: http://www.unrol.org/files/2004%20report.pdf (accessed 03.07.2020).

[41] J. E. Méndez, "Constitutionalism and Transitional Justice" in M. Rosenfeld and A. Sajó (eds.), *The Oxford Handbook of Comparative Constitutional Law* (2012) 1271.

and the construction of a new constitutional framework punctuated from the old.[42] On the other hand, the legitimacy of a peace agreement depends on its suitability to entrench, enhance, or improve the basic elements of democratic constitutionalism: the rule of law, the principle of the separation of powers, some sort of protection of individual rights or—at least—interests that are guaranteed under the Constitution or the legislation, and an entrenchment of the democratic idea.[43]

In sum, I will approach the analysis of the legitimacy and constitutional review dilemmas using the following legal and normative conception of legitimacy: (i) the outcome of a plebiscite is legally legitimate if it is convened and carried out according to valid legal norms; (ii) the fairer the process of a plebiscite is, and the more its outcome is an expression of the actual consent by the people, the more normatively legitimate is the outcome of a plebiscite; (iii) the more a peace agreement is suitable to achieve the aims of transitional justice and to entrench, enhance, or improve the basic elements of democratic constitutionalism, the more normatively legitimate it is.

VI. The legitimacy dilemma and the Colombian Plebiscite for Peace

The question eliciting the legitimacy dilemma is whether plebiscites can confer legitimacy to the implementation of peace agreements.

If analysed in the Colombian scenario of the Plebiscite for Peace, this question should receive a negative answer, concerning the normative perspective of legitimacy.

From the legal point of view, that Plebiscite was convened according to the Constitution, and to the Jurisprudence of the Constitutional Court. However, it was not constitutionally required to convene the plebiscite. The Government was permitted to implement the Peace Agreement without popular ratification.

From the normative point of view, the Plebiscite could have never granted legitimacy to the Peace Agreement. From the outset, it was not foreseeable that the Plebiscite had the capacity to frame a fair and inclusive deliberative process. This was the case for to several reasons. First, the Plebiscite took place in

[42] R. G. Teitel, *Transitional Justice* (2000), 191 f.

[43] This concept underpins Articles 2 and 16 of the French Declaration of the Rights of Man and of the Citizen. Article 2 states that the aim of all political associations [that are created by means of a constitution] is the preservation of the rights of human beings. Article 16 states that a "society in which the observance of the law is not assured, nor the separation of powers defined, has no constitution at all".

an ambiance of polarization. The Government had not included representatives of the opposition, the military, and the victims in the negotiation of the peace agreement with the FARC. Thus, those groups radically opposed the ratification of the agreement. Second, the voters were ill-informed about the content of the peace agreement. The Government should have displayed a pedagogic campaign explaining to the citizens at least the core elements of the agreement. Third, the organizers should have spelt out the question of the Plebiscite in a way that allowed the citizens to express their views concerning each component of the peace agreement—criminal justice, amnesty, political transition, reparations, demining, land reform, etc. The only question was: "Do you support the final agreement for ending the conflict and building a stable and lasting peace?". Fourth, the Government should have forbidden any kind of intimidation of the citizens during the campaign leading to the popular vote.

In addition, the only admissible interpretation of the real outcome of the plebiscite was the rejection of the Peace Agreement by the citizens. Hence, given that the Plebiscite for Peace was convened and carried out following the constitutional, legal, and jurisprudential rules, the following conclusions derive: the outcome of the plebiscite was legally legitimate; hence, the citizens did not give their actual consent to the peace agreement. Accordingly, the second draft of that agreement lacked any legal and normative legitimacy. As a consequence, the Congress and the Constitutional Court infringed the constitutional and legal rules about plebiscites by, respectively, ratifying and validating the ratification of the second draft of the rejected agreement. This infringement reinforced political polarization. The opposition parties that supported the rejection of the Plebiscite for Peace still consider the implementation of the Peace Agreement as a democratic fraud.

A comparative lesson arises from this analysis. Institutional designers of transitional justice processes should not convene plebiscites or referendums requesting the people to approve or reject peace agreement if it is foreseeable that: (i) the plebiscite reinforces conflict or polarization; (ii) citizens lack the appropriate knowledge to understand the decisions they are making (and it is not possible to display a pedagogical campaign); (ii) citizens cannot make a separate decision about every aspect of the peace agreement; (iv) the vote will probably be manipulated; and (v) the peace negotiation process has not been fair, open, and inclusive, in a way that allowed genuine deliberation concerning all relevant matters.

VII. The constitutional review dilemma and the Colombian Plebiscite for Peace

The question eliciting the constitutional review dilemma is whether empowering a Constitutional Court to review the constitutionality of the implementation of a peace agreement can confer legitimacy to that process. A positive answer should solve this dilemma. Indeed, a process of constitutional review of the implementation norms of a peace agreement performed by an impartial and independent constitutional court can confer normative legitimacy to the whole process.

Within this context, the role of a Constitutional Court is twofold. First, from a procedural perspective, the Court ought to review the normative framework of the peace negotiations and the peace agreement as such. The Court ought to ensure that all those norms are legally legitimate, in the sense that they have been enacted by competent authorities and by means of the appropriate constitutional and legal procedures. This role is analogous to the function that constitutional courts have played in some constitution-making processes.[44] The paradigmatic example of this is Section 71(3) of the 1993 South African Interim Constitution, granting power to the Constitutional Court to certify that the new Constitution complied with the "constitutional principles" stated in the interim constitution. Reflecting on that example, Arato correctly suggests that constitutional courts are institutions suitable for guaranteeing at least procedural fairness in a constitution making process.[45] *Mutatis mutandi*, constitutional courts are appropriate institutions for ensuring procedural fairness of transitional justice processes.

Second, the Constitutional Court ought to guard the essential principles of the permanent Constitution from degradation along the transitional justice process. Also, the Court ought to guarantee that the implementation of a peace agreement achieves an equilibrium concerning collisions between constitutional and transitional justice principles, and between different transitional justice principles. The doctrines of constitutional replacement (above-mentioned), and principle of proportionality are appropriate methodologies for that aim. The Court should apply them in the context of international human rights and transnational frameworks for transitional justice. The Report of the Secretary-General of the of the United Nations entitled *The rule of law and*

[44] A. Arato, "Redeeming the Still Redeemable: Post Sovereign Constitution Making" (2009) 22 *Int J Polit Cult Soc* 427–443, at 433.
[45] Ibid.

transitional justice in conflict and post-conflict societies of 23 August 2004,[46] leading international human rights cases (such as *Barrios Altos* and *Almonacid*, in which the Inter-American Court of Human Rights protected the victim's right to reparation despite the existence of domestic amnesty laws)[47] and instruments (such as the Reports 28 and 29 of 1992 of the Inter-American Commission on Human Rights, concerning the amnesty laws in Argentina and Uruguay),[48] and leading precedents from foreign jurisdictions,[49] are sources that a constitutional court should use for undertaking that balancing tasks.

In 2017 the Colombian Constitutional Court carried out both endeavours. In the remarkable Judgment C-322/2017, the Court declared unconstitutional two of central features of the fast track legislative and constitutional amendment procedures, as they were foreseen by the Constitutional Amendment 2016. Those features were: (i) the prohibition to members of the Congress to introduce modifications to the bills of law or constitutional amendments implementing the peace agreement, without explicit approval by the

[46] United Nations Secretary-General, "The Rule of Law and Transitional Justice in Conflict and Post-Conflict Societies" (2004), available online at: http://www.unrol.org/files/2004%20report.pdf (accessed 30.07.2020). Other international documents on topics related to transitional justice include: UN Commission on Human Rights, "Updated Set of Principles for the Protection and Promotion of Human Rights through Action to Combat Impunity", E/CN.4/2005/102/Add.1, 8 February 2005 and the accompanying reports by Diane Orentlicher, "Independent Study on Best Practices, Including Recommendations, to Assist States in Strengthening Their Domestic Capacity to Combat All Aspects of Impunity", E/CN.4/2004/88, 27 February 2004 and "Report of the Independent Expert to Update the Set of Principles to Combat Impunity", E/CN.4/2005/102, 18 February 2005, available online at: http://daccess-dds-ny.un.org/doc/UNDOC/GEN/G05/109/00/PDF/G0510900.pdf?OpenElement (accessed 26.08.2020); and UN General Assembly, "Basic Principles and Guidelines on the Right to a Remedy and Reparation for Victims of Gross Violations of International Human Rights Law and Serious Violations of International Humanitarian Law", A/RES/60/147, 21 March 2006, available online at: http://www.ohchr.org/EN/ProfessionalInterest/Pages/RemedyAndReparation.aspx (accessed 26.08.2020).

[47] Inter-American Court of Human Rights, *Barrios Altos v. Peru*, Judgment of 14 March 2001, Ser. C, No. 75; *Almonacid Arellano et al. v. Chile*, Judgment of 26 September 2006, Ser. C, No. 154.

[48] Inter-American Commission of Human Rights, Annual Report 1992–93, Report 28/92, Cases 10.147, 10.181, 10.240, 10.262, 10.309, and 10.311, Argentina, 2 October 1992, and Report 29/92, Cases 10.029, 10.036, 10.145, 10.305, 10.372, 10.373, 10.374, and 10.375, Uruguay, 2 October 1992.

[49] In *Azanian Peoples Organization (AZAPO) and Others v. President of the Republic of South Africa and Others* (CCT17/96) [1996] ZACC 16; 1996 (8) BCLR 1015; 1996 (4) SA 672 (25 July 1996) the South African Constitutional Court considered the international and transnational legal framework on transitional justice for reviewing the constitutionality of section 20(7) of the Promotion of National Unity and Reconciliation Act 34 of 1995. This section empowered the Committee on Amnesty established by the Act to grant amnesty to a perpetrator of an unlawful act associated with a political objective and committed prior to 6 December 1993. The section also determined the effects of the amnesty. The Court upheld the constitutionality of the section on the basis that it implied a limitation to the right to access to court justifiable by s 22, 33(1) and (2), and the epilogue of the interim Constitution. Despite the fact that the Court ought to consider the constitutionality of that section only against the interim Constitution, speaking for the majority, in his opinion Mahomed DP cited the use of amnesty for criminal acts in the transitional justice processes in Chile, Argentina and El Salvador (par. 22 to 24). He also acknowledged that the interim Constitution directed the Court "to "have regard" to public international law if it is applicable to the protection of the" fundamental rights entrenched in chapter three of that Constitution (par. 27). However, Mahomed DP considered that none of the international instruments quoted by the applicants assisted their case.

Government; and (ii) the obligation to members of the Congress to vote bills in block, that is, for or against the whole bill, and not article by article. In a very controversial 5–4 decision, the majority held that those provisions implied denaturing the structure of deliberative democracy and other essential principles in the congressional implementation of the Peace Agreement. With those provisions, the Government aimed to nullify the political rights of the opposition parties to modify the Peace Agreement. Those parties (including the Democratic Centre, led by the then Senator, former President Alvaro Uribe) had supported the "no" vote in the Plebiscite for peace (and, in this sense, had achieved victory in that plebiscite). Nevertheless, they were a minority in the Congress. According to the reasoning of the Court, entrenching deliberative democracy, political pluralism, and the attenuation of hyper-presidentialism are essential principles of the 1991 Constitution. The above-mentioned provisions of Legislative Act 2016 denatured those principles in the domain of legislative implementation of the Peace Agreement. They stripped opposition parties, which represented the voters who rejected the Agreement in the Plebiscite, of their political rights and powers to seek, in the implementation of the Peace Agreement, that balance between the benefits for former combatants, on the one hand, and the reparation of the victims, truth telling, justice, and commitment to non-repetition, on the other.

Former President Santos and the leaders of the FARC severely criticized this decision. The Constitutional Court had a transitional composition when the decision was made, on 16 May 2017. Four justices favourable to the agenda of President Santos remained in the Court, along with two politically independent justices (Ortiz and Guerrero). The independent justices were joined by two acting justices (who, at that time, were in charge of two chambers of the Court; they were waiting for new justices to be elected), and myself. I received most of the criticism. I had been nominated by President Santos. However, I did not promise fidelity to him but to the Constitution, and to the values of impartiality and judicial independence.

After this decision, President Santos and his majorities in the Congress secured that the remaining justices, who were to be elected in 2017, were committed to guarantee fidelity to him and to the implementation of the peace agreement as drafted by the Government and the guerrillas. The outcome of this strategy was the configuration of an undefeatable majority at the Constitutional Court that, with only few exceptions concerning certain isolated provisions, upheld the validity of all constitutional amendments, laws, and legislative decrees that implemented the Peace Agreement.

Many of those constitutional amendments, laws, and legislative decrees are clearly compatible with the Constitution. Some of them aim to strengthen the institutions for improving land redistribution between small farmers in conflict zones,[50] for bettering the schools,[51] housing,[52] economic planning and development,[53] agricultural innovation,[54] and environmental protection systems in those territories.[55] Other norms purport to secure an environment for the exercise of political rights[56] (in particular, of opposition parties[57] and former combatants),[58] create peace keeping institutions,[59] improve safety conditions for the demobilized combatants[60] (including foreign citizens),[61] ensure an appropriate demobilization of minors[62] and guarantees of their rights,[63] suspend arrest orders for demobilized FARC combatants,[64] facilitate their reintegration to a normal social[65] and economic life,[66] create security conditions for human rights leaders,[67] institute plan for replacing plantation of illicit drugs with other products,[68] among other topics.

However, some of those constitutional amendments, laws, and legislative decrees are constitutionally flawed. With some of the legislative decrees, President Santos overstepped the boundaries of the powers to implement the Peace Agreement and the competences of the Congress.[69] Moreover, the Government and the Congress did not make provision for actual and effective

[50] See, Legislative Decree 2204/2016, reviewed in the Judgment C-160/2017.

[51] See, Legislative Decree 882/2017, reviewed in the Judgment C-607/2017; and Legislative Decree 892/2017, reviewed in the Judgment C-535/2017.

[52] See, Legislative Decree 890/2017, reviewed in the Judgment C-570/2017.

[53] See, Legislative Decree 893/2017, reviewed in the Judgment C-730/2017.

[54] See, Constitutional Amendment 01/2017, reviewed in the Judgment C-674/2017.

[55] See, Legislative Decree 870/2017, reviewed in the Judgment C-644/2017.

[56] See, Legislative Decree 895/2017, reviewed in the Judgment C-555/2017.

[57] See, Statutory Bill 03/2017 Senate and 006/17 Chamber of Representatives, reviewed in the Judgment C-018/2018.

[58] See, Act 1830/2017, reviewed in the Judgment C-408/2017, and Constitutional Amendment 03/2017, reviewed in the Judgment C-027/2018.

[59] See, Legislative Decree 885/2017, reviewed in the Judgment C-555/2017.

[60] See, Legislative Decree 154/2017, reviewed in the Judgment C-224/2017; Legislative Decree 298/2017, reviewed in the Judgment C-331/2017; and Act 1865 of 2017, reviewed in the Judgment C-026/2018.

[61] See, Legislative Decree 671/2017, reviewed in the Judgment C-433/2017.

[62] See, Legislative Decree 831/2017, reviewed in the Judgment C-460/2017.

[63] See, Legislative Decree 891/2017, reviewed in the Judgment C-541/2017.

[64] See, Legislative Decree 800/2017, reviewed in the Judgment C-518/2017.

[65] See, Legislative Decree 897/2017, reviewed in the Judgment C-554/2017.

[66] See, Legislative Decree 899/2017, reviewed in the Judgment C-569/2017.

[67] See, Legislative Decree 898/2017, reviewed in the Judgment C-013/2018.

[68] See, Legislative Decree 249/2017, reviewed in the Judgment C-289/2017; and Legislative Decree 896/2017, reviewed in the Judgment C-493/2017.

[69] For instance, by undertaking a whole land reform for the country (see, Legislative Decree 884/2017, reviewed in the Judgment C-073/2018 (see my dissenting opinion)), and a modification of the legal framework for electric energy in country zones (see, Legislative Decree 902/2017, reviewed in the Judgment C-565/2017 (see my dissenting opinion)).

reparations from the perpetrators of human rights violations for their victims;[70] they also left ambiguities concerning the Special Jurisdiction for Peace allowing drug dealers to receive the same criminal benefits as the members of the FARC.[71] Those authorities also extinguished any kind of criminal prosecution against perpetrators of war crimes and crimes against humanity, extremely weakened the extradition process for members of the FARC (even in cases in which they kept perpetrating crimes), and allowed for sexual predators of children to receive criminal justice benefits.[72]

Due to the control that President Santos maintained over a majority of justices of the Constitutional Court, the Court did not strike down provisions establishing those unconstitutional regulations. Because of the lack of impartiality and independence, the constitutional review undertaken by the Court could not confer normative legitimacy to those provisions that are at odds with key tenets of a conception of transitional justice compatible with democratic constitutionalism.

From this analysis arises a comparative lesson. Transitional justice designers should foresee a constitutional review of rules implementing peace agreements as a way to endow them with normative legitimacy. However, such a review should only be carried out by an impartial and independent Constitutional or Supreme Court. Naturally, such Court should never disregard the outcome of a plebiscite or referendum. Judicial supremacy should never trump popular sovereignty.

[70] For instance, by undertaking a whole land reform for the country (see, Legislative Decree 884/2017, reviewed in the Judgment C-073/2018 (see my dissenting opinion)), and a modification of the legal framework for electric energy in country zones (see, Legislative Decree 902/2017, reviewed in the Judgment C-565/2017 (see my dissenting opinion)).

[71] See, Legislative Act 1/2017 and the Statutory Law of the Special Jurisdiction for Peace.

[72] Ibid.

10

Are the People the Masters? Constitutional Referendums in Ireland

David Kenny and Aileen Kavanagh

Contemporary constitutional practice is marked by an increased reliance on referendums and other forms of "citizen-led constitutional change".[1] In order to ensure that ordinary people can have some democratic ownership of their constitution, many countries across the world are experimenting with novel forms of participatory and plebiscitary constitutional change, leading to claims that we are now living in the "Age of the Referendum".[2] In part, this move towards direct popular engagement in constitutional change is a corrective to the growing disaffection for democratic politics in consolidated democracies.[3] It is also an obvious response to the perennial tension between democracy and constitutionalism. But the rise of the referendum is also fraught with concerns that it will usher in a crude populism which will obliterate constitutional constraints and lead—ironically—to executive dominance, authoritarianism and deep forms of democratic decay.[4] Therefore, whilst referendums hold out the promise of constitutional self-government, we need to be mindful of the pitfalls and problems which attend them.

In exploring the potential of a democratic constitutionalist vision which gives people the power to decide on the terms of their constitution, Ireland offers a promising testing ground. The Irish Constitution—Bunreacht na hEireann (literally "The Basic Law of Ireland")—came into force in 1937 following a state-wide plebiscite. Viewed as a potent expression of Irish independence

[1] Xenophon Contiades and Alkmene Fotiadou, "Participatory Constitutional Change" in Zenophon Contiades and Alkmene Fotiadou (eds), *Participatory Constitutional Change: The People as Amenders of the Constitution* (Routledge, 2018) 1, at 2.

[2] Stephen Tierney, "Europe is Entering the 'Age of the Referendum', But there is Nothing to Fear for European Democracy if Referendums are Properly Regulated", Scottish Constitutional Futures Forum, available at <https://www.scottishconstitutionalfutures.org/Default.aspx?tabid=1767&articleType=ArticleView&articleId=4188> accessed 3 February 2022; Stephen Tierney, *Constitutional Referendums: The Theory and Practice of Republican Deliberation* (OUP, 2012).

[3] Colin Hay, *Why We Hate Politics* (Polity Press, 2007).

[4] Larry Diamond, "Facing Up to the Democratic Recession" (2015) 26 Journal of Democracy 141.

David Kenny and Aileen Kavanagh, *Are the People the Masters? Constitutional Referendums in Ireland* In: *The Limits and Legitimacy of Referendums*. Edited by: Richard Albert and Richard Stacey, Oxford University Press. DOI: 10.1093/oso/9780198867647.003.0011

from British rule, the drafters of the Irish Constitution were keen to ensure that the Irish people would have ownership of their own Constitution for generations to come. Therefore, they provided that if the Constitution needed to be amended, it could only be done by referendum of the people of Ireland.[5] As one of the Constitution's chief political architects—Eamon de Valera—observed: "If there is one thing ... that is clear and shining through the Constitution, it is the fact that the people are the masters."[6] As we will argue, although it may be exaggerated to say that they are the "masters" of the Constitution, they are certainly key constitutional players with real power to influence, shape and direct constitutional change. Referendums are now a regular and prevalent feature of the Irish constitutional landscape and have been the medium through which large-scale social, economic and political changes in Ireland have been achieved, including on issues such as divorce, abortion and same-sex marriage.

On the surface, one might think that Ireland's referendum process would fall victim to many of the common concerns about referendums. In initiation and formulation, the process is open to elite capture because the government gets to propose and formulate the referendum proposal which is put to the people. The process is purely majoritarian; 50% plus one of the voters on referendum day can approve any change. Any change can be proposed, however radical. Minority rights have been put to referendum vote. Ireland's rules and regulation of campaign advertising and debate are loose and scant and seem unlikely to combat disinformation. Yet, when examined closely, Ireland stands as a *counterpoint* to many of the criticisms and fears which surround referendums. Elite dominance, though formally prevalent, is offset by a substantial role for civil society in initiation and campaigning. Bare majority vote is supplemented by widespread participation and deliberation, which appears to be nuanced and robust, whilst minority rights have been vindicated when voted on. The process has not been subject to political exploitation for sweeping or abusive constitutional change.[7] Though the record is far from perfect, referendums work reasonably well in Ireland, commanding high levels of popular participation and engagement, which go well beyond the mere act of ratifying or rejecting a referendum proposal at the ballot box and extend to widespread, relatively well-informed and committed popular deliberation. During a constitutional

[5] Articles 46 and 47, Constitution of Ireland (Bunreacht na hEireann).

[6] Eamon de Valera, Dáil Debates (Debates of the Lower House of the Irish Parliament), Vol. 67 No. 1, 11 May 1937.

[7] See David Kenny, "The Risks of Referendums: 'Referendum culture' in Ireland as a solution?" in Maria Cahill, Colm Ó Cinnéide, Seán Ó Conaill, Conor O'Mahony (eds), *Constitutional Change and Popular Sovereignty in Ireland* (Routledge, 2021).

referendum in Ireland, a national conversation takes place about what people want their Constitution to mean. As such, Ireland is a crucial case-study in exploring the promise—and perils—of constitutional referendums.

In Section I, we give an overview of the Irish constitutional referendums process and its use since 1937. In Sections II and III, we examine two recent and high-profile referendums—on same-sex marriage and abortion—providing a textured narrative of the involutions of those referendums from initiation to the campaigns. These referendums were some of the most important and challenging ever to take place in Ireland and were widely perceived to be a great success. In Section IV, we probe more closely the role of the people in the referendum process and the way in which popular, grassroots movements for change interact with the political elites. We conclude that the Irish process has virtues in its successful combination of popular empowerment with political and elite constraint, illustrating this by reference to elements of our two case-studies. Those case-studies demonstrate significant citizen participation and civil society involvement, robust deliberation and rigorous fact-checking, combined with an engaged electorate. In terms of potentially exporting or transplanting the Irish experience, we enter a note of caution given that the reasons for success are partly embedded in the political and popular culture in Ireland in ways which are difficult to replicate in other countries. In the concluding section, we show how the Irish referendum process is embedded within a "referendum culture"[8] which has developed over time. Transposing Ireland's process to other systems without the attendant cultural, legal and political supports is, therefore, risky. But whilst Ireland may not give us a playbook for referendum success, it provides deep insight into how constitutional referendums can flourish as a form of democratic constitutionalism where "the people" have meaningful input, agency and effect.

I. Ireland's referendum process

A. Broad power of amendment

Article 46.1 of the Irish Constitution states that "Any provision of this Constitution may be amended, whether by way of variation, addition, or repeal, in the manner provided by this Article." The proposal to amend the Constitution must first be introduced in Dáil Éireann (the Lower House of the

[8] Ibid.

Irish Parliament) as a Bill, "and shall upon having been passed or deemed to have been passed by both Houses of the Oireachtas [Parliament], be submitted by Referendum to the decision of the people in accordance with the law for the time being in force relating to the Referendum."[9] Article 47 provides, amongst other things, that this referendum is decided by simple majority of those voting on any given day.[10] All citizens entitled to vote for in Dáil elections can vote in a referendum. If the majority of votes cast at the referendum are in favour of the change, the President signs the Bill into law and the Constitution is then amended.[11]

Since Ireland has a Westminster system of government, the government is almost always in control of the lower house. Therefore, the power to initiate referendums rests primarily with the 15-member cabinet. The Attorney General, the government's chief legal advisor, plays a significant role in shaping the language of the proposal and advising on the possible legal consequences of the changes. In terms of the scope or the subject-matter for a referendum, the text of the Constitution contains no explicit limits. The courts have held that there is no implicit limitation—formal or substantive—on the amendment power: the people can amend the Constitution in whatever form they might like, and no part of the Constitution is insulated from change.[12] In holding this, the courts have stressed the primacy of popular sovereignty in the Irish Constitution: "The will of the people as expressed in a referendum providing for the amendment of the Constitution is sacrosanct and if freely given, cannot be interfered with. The decision is theirs and theirs alone."[13]

B. Use of the amendment power

Since 1937, there have been 37 constitutional referendums which have resulted in 30 amendments to the Irish Constitution. About two-thirds of those amendments have taken place in the last 30 years. These amendments can be divided into the following three broad categories: 1) *social and moral issues*;

[9] Article 46 provides two rules of form; the Bill must be expressly described as "'An Act to amend the Constitution"; and such a Bill cannot contain any other provision alongside the amendment.

[10] Article 47.1.

[11] Article 47. For further information on the process and practice of referendums in Ireland, available at <https://www.citizensinformation.ie/en/government_in_ireland/elections_and_referenda/referenda/constitutional_referendum_in_ireland.html> accessed 3 February 2022.

[12] See *Re Article 26 and the Information (Termination of Pregnancies) Bill 1995* [1995] 1 IR 1; Gerard Hogan, Gerry Whyte, David Kenny and Rachael Walsh, *Kelly: the Irish Constitution* (Bloomsbury Professional, 2018) at [8.1.17].

[13] *Hanafin v Minister for Environment* [1996] 2 IR 321 at 425.

2) *constitutional structure* and 3) *international affairs*. Within these categories, 14 amendments related to rights or "hot button social issues",[14] including abortion, divorce and same-sex marriage. Eight relate to the powers of government, including reform of the courts, voting entitlements and local government. Nine have related to the ratification of international agreements, predominantly the EU treaties.

Eleven other proposals put to the people by referendum were rejected. Six of these were political reform proposals ranging from minor (lowering the eligibility age for the Presidency) to major changes (abolishing the upper house, empowering parliamentary enquiries and twice attempting to change the electoral system). Three failed proposals—on divorce and on ratification of the Nice and Lisbon Treaties—were later carried in repeat referendums. The other two failed proposals both related to attempting to overturn or limit the effect of Supreme Court ruling allowing abortion in cases where the life of the mother was at risk from suicide.[15] Therefore, it cannot be said that the Irish people are overly acquiescent to the elites who propose constitutional changes. Certainly, when a matter is put to referendum in Ireland, the outcome of that vote is rarely assumed or taken for granted. After all, the people have rejected 25% of the proposals put to them. Some of these matters were supported broadly by all major political parties; some of these matters related to fundamental and consequential matters of political reform.[16] Doyle postulates that this indicates "a wariness of simply accepting whatever the political classes recommend"[17] which may in turn create caution on behalf of the political elites proposing constitutional changes, since it expends political capital and there is a real chance that they will fail.[18]

Interestingly, 13 constitutional amendments have involved a direct response to Court decisions interpreting the Constitution, including on children's rights, citizenship, abortion and bail for those facing criminal charges.[19] Of course, conducting a popular debate on the nuances of judicial decisions in referendum campaigns can be challenging, as can attempts to overturn court

[14] See Oran Doyle, *The Irish Constitution: A Contextual Analysis* (Hart, 2018) 201.

[15] Elements of *Attorney General v X* [1992] 1 IR 1 would have been overturned by the 12th and 25th Amendment Bills 1992 and 2002.

[16] An amendment to empower parliamentary enquiries failed in 2011; an attempt to abolish the upper house of parliament failed in 2013; and the people twice refused, in 1959 and 1968, to alter Ireland's electoral system on Proportional Representation by Single Transferable Vote.

[17] Doyle (n 14) 199.

[18] Ibid.

[19] Gerry Whyte, "The Role of the Supreme Court in Our Democracy" (2006) 28 DULJ 1; Conor O'Mahony "Constitutional Amendment and Judicial Restraint: How Restrained Should an Irish Court Be?" in Eoin Carolan (ed), *The Constitution of Ireland: Perspectives and Prospects* (Bloomsbury Professional, 2012); See.

rulings that turn on nuanced points of constitutional law.[20] Nonetheless, the Irish example shows that even when courts are empowered to strike down legislation,[21] it does not follow that judges thereby get "the last word" on constitutional issues.[22] In Ireland, the constitutional amendment formula provides a democratic response mechanism, ensuring that it is the people (and the political branches)—not the courts—who ultimately get the final decision on what the Constitution requires.[23]

C. Judicial intervention in the referendum process

The courts have played an important role in shaping the Irish referendum process in two significant respects: 1) insisting that the ratification of certain EU treaties required a constitutional change referendum, and 2) in constitutionally regulating referendum campaigns.

In *Crotty v An Taoiseach*,[24] the Supreme Court held that the ratification of the Single European Act by legislation was not permissible, notwithstanding a constitutional provision stating that any action necessitated for EU membership could be taken by the State. The Court held that if the Treaty involved ceding new powers of government not previously given away—as the SEA did in respect of foreign policy—then this required constitutional authorisation. The SEA was thus put to referendum, as has every core EU Treaty change since then. However, the rule is not absolute: constitutional change is required only if new powers of government are ceded to an international body. In *Pringle v Government of Ireland*,[25] the Court held that ratification of the European Stability Mechanism Treaty—establishing a mechanism and fund to administer bailouts to Eurozone members—did not require a referendum as no powers of government were given to that body to be used without the Irish government's consent.

Moreover, the courts have crafted rules which control and constrain the conduct of government and the broadcast media in respect of campaigns.[26]

[20] Oran Doyle and David Kenny, "Constitutional Change and Interest Group Politics: Ireland's Children's Rights Amendment" in Richard Albert, Xenophon Contiades and Alkmene Fotiadou (eds), *The Foundations and Tradition of Constitutional Amendment* (Hart, 2017) 199.

[21] Bunreacht na hEireann, Article 34.4.

[22] Aileen Kavanagh, "A Hard Look at the Last Word" (2015) 35 Oxford Journal of Legal Studies 825.

[23] Eoin Carolan, "Leaving Behind the Commonwealth Model of Rights Review: Ireland as an Example of Collaborative Constitutionalism" in John Bell and Marie-Luce Paris (eds), *Rights-Based Constitutional Review: Constitutional Courts in a Changing Landscape* (Edward Elgar, 2016), 109–111.

[24] *Crotty v An Taoiseach* [1987] IR 713.

[25] *Pringle v Government of Ireland* [2012] IESC 47.

[26] See Hogan et al. (n 12) [8.1.39] et seq.

In *McKenna v An Taoiseach (No. 2)*,[27] the Supreme Court held that the government's use of public funds to promote a Yes vote in the 1995 divorce referendum was an unconstitutional interference with the campaign. Hamilton CJ held this was "an interference with the democratic process and the constitutional process for the amendment of the Constitution and infringes the concept of equality which is fundamental to the democratic nature of the State."[28] The Court affirmed this principle during the 2012 Children's Rights Referendum campaign, finding that a government (supposedly neutral) information campaign breached the *McKenna* standard in subtly advocating in favour of the proposal.[29] Relatedly, the courts have restricted on the conduct of public broadcasters in referendum campaigns. In *Coughlan v Broadcasting Complaints Commission*,[30] the Supreme Court held that the public broadcaster, RTÉ, should not have allowed political parties—all of which supported a Yes vote—to air political broadcasts on the 1995 divorce referendum without any equivalent broadcast from NGOs opposed to the referendum. This rule, as applied by broadcasters, has become very strict. Stopwatches are often used in assigning time; "balance" in debate in insisted upon even outside the formal campaign period.[31]

The Supreme Court, however, has been loath to overturn referendum results *even if* there has been unconstitutional campaigning. This seems to be linked to the courts' firm belief in the sanctity of the popular will. The courts refused the "awesome undertaking" of overturning a result, even when there has been an unconstitutional information campaign and a remarkably close result.[32] The Supreme Court standard for overturning a result is whether "it is reasonably possible that the irregularity or interference identified affected the result".[33]

[27] *McKenna v An Taoiseach (No. 2)* [1995] 2 IR 10.

[28] *McKenna v An Taoiseach (No 2)* [1995] 2 IR 10 at 42.

[29] The government's individual members can personally campaign for the proposal and use general government resources (eg transportation) in the course of a referendum campaign, once they do not dedicate specific funds to advocating for a particular result.

[30] *Coughlan v Broadcasting Complaints Commission* [2000] 3 IR 1. See Hogan et al. (n 12) [8.1.44]

[31] See "Second Report—Articles 46 And 47, Amendment Of The Constitution And The Referendum" April 2009 at 79.

[32] See *Hanafin v Minister for Environment* [1996] 2 IR 321 on the divorce campaign of 1995, where there were two unconstitutional campaign interventions, and only 50.3% of people voted in favour, and the result was still upheld.

[33] *Jordan v Minister for Children and Youth Affairs* [2015] IESC 33 at [85]. A key factor is whether "a reasonable person would be in doubt about, and no longer trust, the provisional outcome of the election or referendum".

D. Campaign regulation

Aside from the broad rules enunciated by the higher courts, there is a surprisingly light regulatory framework on referendum campaigns.[34] There is some control over donations to referendum campaigns, but no overall spending limits.[35] An ad-hoc Referendum Commission, typically chaired by a judge, is set up for each vote to inform voters that the referendum is taking place, but it does not engage in substantial regulation of campaigns or campaign information.[36] Broadcast advertising of political matters is generally not allowed[37] but there is no check on print or digital advertising, and social media is entirely unregulated. Fear that this complete lack of regulation would lead to problems led social media advertisers to impose their own restrictions in the 2018 abortion referendum: Facebook refused to allow foreign advertising, and Google decided not to accept any advertising related to the campaign on its platforms.[38] The Citizens' Assembly recently considered the referendum process and made recommendations as to how it might be structured more effectively.[39]

II. The same sex marriage referendum 2015

In a 24-country study between 1999 and 2002, Ireland was reported to have been to be one of the most homophobic countries in the western world.[40] If putting minority rights to a referendum vote is a dubious idea, putting this same-sex marriage to a vote in Ireland might be seen to be particularly risky. Yet, in 2015, Ireland became the first country in the world to legalise same sex marriage by referendum. The referendum passed with a large margin of victory and was considered a triumph for the LGBTQ cause.

[34] See generally Conor O'Mahony, "Legal Regulation of Referendum Campaigns", paper delivered to the Citizen's Assembly, 13 January 2018.

[35] There is a limit of €100 for anonymous donation; of €200 per individual and corporation unless they are specially registered; and foreign donations are banned. There are related donation disclosure requirements.

[36] The Commission at one point gave pro/con arguments on the proposal; this practice was stopped when it proved problematic. See Hogan et al. (n 12) [8.1.60].

[37] Ibid [8.1.44].

[38] See Adam Satariano, "Ireland's Abortion Referendum Becomes a Test for Facebook and Google" *New York Times*, 25 May 2018.

[39] See Hogan et al. (n 12) [8.1.58].

[40] Diarmaid Ferriter, *Occasions of Sin: Sex and Society in Modern Ireland* (Profile Books, 2009) 509, citing the *Evening Herald*, 24 April 2007.

A. Constitutional issue

Same-sex marriage was a constitutional issue by virtue of the unusual text of Article 41 of the Irish Constitution. Article 41.3.1 states: "The State pledges itself to guard with special care the institution of Marriage, on which the Family is founded, and to protect it against attack." Though marriage was not defined in the constitution, in "guarding" the institution of marriage, and "protecting it", the text seemed to suggest a conservative and preservationist, rather than expansive, view of marriage. While Civil Unions were introduced in 2010, it was thought that introducing same-sex marriage would require constitutional change.[41] Advocacy organisations thus focused on lobbying the government for constitutional change to allow for same-sex marriage.[42]

B. Lobbying for change and the constitutional convention

A general election, held in 2011, saw a breakthrough for the organisations—such as the Gay and Lesbian Equality Network (GLEN) and the Irish Council for Civil Liberties (ICCL)—that had been lobbying for this change. The Labour Party—which formed part of the government after the election—committed to legalising same-sex marriage as part of their election manifesto. In negotiating with Fine Gael on a programme for coalition government a compromise was reached: to convene a Constitutional Convention to consider a variety of topics for possible constitutional reforms, including same-sex marriage. The Convention was envisaged as a mixed-member deliberative forum which would include a randomly-selected but representative group of ordinary citizens, together with sitting politicians who were members of parliament.[43] The decision to set up this deliberative forum was seen by many as a stalling tactic, and as political cover for the majority government party—Fine Gael—with its core support amongst middle class rural voters.[44] The Convention bought

[41] In a 2006 High Court case which considered a claim that marriage was open to same-sex partners, the court held that the definition of marriage in the Constitution had "always been understood as being opposite sex marriage". *Zappone and Gilligan v Revenue Commissioners* [2008] 2 IR 417, 505. See contra Conor O'Mahony, "Principled Expediency: How the Irish Courts can Compromise on Same-Sex Marriage" (2012) 34 DULJ 199.

[42] See <http://www.marriagequality.ie/about/history/> accessed 3 February 2022.

[43] See Jane Suiter, David Farrell, Clodagh Harris and Eoin O'Malley, "The First Irish Constitutional Convention: A Case of 'high legitimacy'"? (2019) 23(1) Participations 123; David Farrell, Jane Suiter, Clodagh Harris and Kevin Cunningham, "The Effects of Mixed Membership in a Deliberative Forum: The Irish Constitutional Convention of 2012-2014" (2020) 68 Political Studies 54–73.

[44] Gráinne de Burca, "Reinvigorating Democracy in the European Union: Lessons from Ireland's Citizens Assembly?" in Aleksandra Gliszczyńska-Grabias and Ulad Belavusau (eds), *Liber Amicorum*

several years to see how public opinion on the issue would settle. Tellingly, the Government made no commitment to hold a referendum on any of the proposals made by the Convention;[45] its recommendations were advisory only.[46]

The Constitutional Convention held a series of monthly meetings throughout 2013. With a membership of 66 ordinary citizens and 33 politicians, there were fears that the political elites would set the agenda, control the process and dominate the discussion. But that danger did not materialise.[47] Despite initial scepticism, the Convention was considered a success in terms of deliberative engagement and citizen participation. More than 1,000 people/groups made submissions on the issue of same-sex marriage. The Convention reported on the matter in April 2013, recommending overwhelmingly that the Constitution be changed to allow same-sex marriage, with 79% of members in favour. There was also overwhelming support for enacting legislative arrangements for guardianship and parentage alongside same-sex marriage. The government acquiesced to the Convention's recommendation, agreeing to hold a referendum on same-sex marriage in the first half of 2015. Later, the Fine Gael Taoiseach (Prime Minister) publicly declared his support for the proposal and his intention to campaign for it, having previously been unwilling to take a position. On 21 March 2015, the government's proposed wording for the change was announced, and was shortly after approved by the legislature without change. It proposed to insert the following provision into Article 41: "Marriage may be contracted in accordance with law by two persons without distinction as to their sex."[48]

C. The referendum campaign

By the time the referendum campaign began in earnest ahead of the May 2015 vote, the four major political parties—Fine Gael, Fianna Fail, Labour and

Wojciech Sadurski (OUP, 2020); Oran Doyle and Rachael Walsh, "Deliberative Mini-Publics as a Response to Populist Democratic Backsliding" in Maria Cahill, Colm O'Cinneide, Sean O Conaill and Conor O'Mahony (eds), *Constitutional Change and Popular Sovereignty: Populism, Politics and the Law in Ireland* (Routledge, 2021).

[45] See Gráinne Healy, Brian Sheehan and Noel Whelan, *Ireland Says Yes: the Inside Story of How the Vote for Marriage Equality was won* (Merrion Press, 2016), 17 et seq.

[46] David Farrell, Clodagh Harris and Jane Suiter, "Bringing People in the Heart of Constitutional Design: The Irish Constitutional Convention of 2012-14" in Xenophon Contiades and Alkmene Fotiadou (eds), *Participatory Constitutional Change: The People as Amenders of the Constitution* (Routledge, 2017), 121.

[47] Ibid 126–127.

[48] Article 41.4.

Sinn Féin—all supported the proposal in a rare instance of cross-party political agreement. An umbrella campaigning group—Yes Equality—was formed from several advocacy groups to pursue a unified campaign for the proposal.[49] Though the political parties campaigned, the Yes campaign was chiefly led by this civil society group. Engaging young voters was a key priority, and many young people registered to vote.[50] A massive canvassing effort was undertaken by the Yes side, visiting hundreds of thousands of homes throughout the country.[51] Campaigners told personal stories about how the referendum would affect their own lives. A core message of Yes Equality, the biggest campaign group, was "I'm voting yes, ask me why",[52] encouraging voters to engage Yes supporters. The Yes campaign made concerted efforts to keep tone civil and modest and not seem "pushy" or entitled, seeking to appealing to the median voter whose mind was not yet made up. Experiences in the United States showed that tone and perception of the different sides could be crucial in winning over undecided voters.[53]

In the campaign, several major arguments had to be dealt with and rebutted by the Yes campaign, and fact-checked by journalists. Examining these issues give us some insight into the way in which Irish referendum campaigns are carried out.

1. Surrogacy and children

Commentators expressed concern about the elision of the issues of same-sex marriage and adoption and family rights, which had been raised by opponents at the Constitutional Convention. Marriage equality advocates knew that the issue of children was potentially significant for middle-aged voters.[54] Since opposite-sex married family has particularly strong rights under the Constitution, including rights in respect of children, opponents argued the expansion of marriage would extend these rights.[55] To prevent these issues from swamping the central issue of marriage equality, the government wished to enact legislative reform of this area in advance of the vote.[56] While there

[49] See Healy et al. (n 45) 14. On the campaign generally, see Oran Doyle, "Minority Rights and Democratic Consensus: The Irish Same-Sex Marriage Referendum" (2020) 15(1) National Taiwan University Law Review 21.

[50] Ibid 25.

[51] Ibid 80–86.

[52] Ibid 39–55.

[53] Ibid 150.

[54] Ibid 42.

[55] These rights are defended in Articles 41, 42 and 42A of the Constitution.

[56] Christine Bohan, "Alan Shatter: Same-sex marriage referendum is not a vote about parenting" theJournal. ie, 17 December 2013, available at <http://www.thejournal.ie/same-sex-marriage-debate-dail-1228224-Dec2013/> accessed 3 February 2022.

was reform in respect of adoption and custody of children, the government was unable to agree surrogacy regulation, meaning that surrogacy was left almost entirely unregulated. It became a major issue in the campaign.[57] The posters erected by opponents almost all addressed this theme in some form. One pictured a smiling baby being kissed by its parents with the slogan "Children Deserve a Mother and a Father".[58] Another showed a sad-looking girl with the word "Surrogacy" and the slogan "She Needs Her Mother For Life, Not Just For Nine Months".[59]

The response of the Yes side to the argument about parenting was to deny any claim that same-sex families were sub-optimal or inferior. They noted that same-sex parenting and adoption arrangements were now regularised by the recent legislation introduced by the Government—an argument which proved sufficiently strong to disarm the issue. Surrogacy was more difficult, being unregulated and an unfamiliar issue for many people. In the end, fears seemed to be quelled by the Government's assurance that the issue would be regulated for all couples, but was also bolstered by assurances given by the Chair of the Referendum Commission (an independent body set up to communicate factual information about referendums and provide impartial information)[60] as well as from a variety of legal experts, saying that there was no entitlement for any couple to access surrogacy, and that it could and would be regulated for all couples even if the referendum passed.[61] This illustrates that the referendum campaign engaged in depth and in detail with complex issues and key concerns, counteracting and minimising disinformation, whilst weaving in comment and input from expert commentators.

2. The adequacy of civil partnership

Another argument against the proposal was that marriage was simply an unnecessary step: that same-sex couples were given many of the entitlements and privileges of marriage in the form of civil partnership. One of the posters on the No side read: "We Already Have Civil Partnership; Don't Redefine Marriage". Polling suggested that if Civil Partnerships could be shown to be similar enough to marriage, it could potentially convince voters that marriage was not

[57] Healy et al. (n 45) 19.
[58] Ibid 118.
[59] Ibid 119.
[60] On the Referendum Commissions, available at <https://www.citizensinformation.ie/en/government_in_ireland/elections_and_referenda/referenda/referendum_commission.html> accessed 3 February 2022.
[61] Prime Time, 14 May 2015. See Healy et al. (n 45) 138.

required for equality.[62] Yes campaigners chose not to focus on legal differences, but on the special status of marriage, the value of constitutional recognition for same-sex relationships, and "the sense of exclusion which civil partnership communicates".[63] Focusing on these rhetorical points proved effective. A late addition to the No campaign's argument tried to redress this by suggesting giving constitutional status to civil partnership.[64] Ultimately, however, the argument that separation would frustrate equality seemed to prove persuasive.

3. Religious ceremonies and practices

Issues about the ability of religious bodies to deny same-sex couples access to religious marriage, and issues about conscientious objection, were also raised in the campaign. This issue was headed off at the pass when the government clarified that religious officiators would not be compelled to perform ceremonies.[65] Nevertheless, question of civil and religious marriage were elided somewhat during the campaign, including by Irish Bishops, who weighed in on the No side.[66] These concerns were ultimately implausible given the strong protections for religious freedom in the Irish Constitution, rendering it very unlikely that religious organisations could ever be compelled to marry anyone,[67] and the issue did not gain traction.

4. Avoiding an anti-establishment vote

A tangential concern was that the referendum, being supported by government and all major political parties, could be subject of a protest vote by those dissatisfied with the austerity measures that Ireland was enduring after the economic crash of 2008 and subsequent EU-IMF bailout. The government parties performed poorly in local and European elections a year before, and the country was in the grip of a wave of protests about recently introduced water charges. Several referendums proposed by the government in the preceding years—including abolition of the upper house of parliament and increasing the power of investigative parliamentary committees—had failed. It was possible that dissatisfaction with the government could be taken out in a vote such as this. This risk was abated because several of the political parties who opposed austerity

[62] Healy et al. (n 45) 120. 46% of respondents in a Red C poll on 1 May 2015 agreed with the statement "Same-sex couples have full legal protection and can enter State-recognised civil partnerships. There is no need to go further and completely change the definition of marriage."

[63] Ibid 120.

[64] Ibid 151.

[65] Patsy McGarry, "Diarmuid Martin Not Calling For 'Conscience Clause' In Vote" *The Irish Times*, 23 March 2015.

[66] Healy et al. (n 45) 121–122.

[67] See Article 44 of the Constitution of Ireland; Hogan et al. (n 12) [7.9.01] et seq.

most strongly in favour of the measure and urged voters not to vote against the measure on the basis of dissatisfaction with government. The Socialist Party poster, for example, asked its supporters to save their protest until the General Election the next year: "2015 Vote for Equality. 2016 Vote Against Austerity".[68]

D. Result

The final result was emphatic. With a high turnout of 60%, 62% of votes were cast for Yes, a total of 1,201,606. There were majority Yes votes in all but one electoral area. The nature of the Irish experience is significant. As well as being the first country to legalise same-sex marriage with a popular vote, the large majority in favour and the fact that the campaign was led by civil society "put the lie to the suggestion that marriage equality was a policy concocted and enforced by elites".[69]

III. The abortion referendum 2018

In 2018, Ireland voted by a large majority to remove the right to life of the unborn from the Irish Constitution, essentially lifting the constitutional ban on any liberalisation of Ireland's very strict abortion regime. Again, although putting this question to a popular vote was both controversial and risked failure and a perpetuation of Ireland's very strict regime, in the end this referendum campaign was considered to be something of a triumph of deliberative democracy.

A. Constitutional issue

Abortion in Ireland was made a constitutional issue not by the courts, but by the people in a referendum. In the 1980s, in response to (probably unjustified) fears of judicial intervention in the style of *Roe v Wade*,[70] a lobby group known

[68] Healy et al. (n 45) 70–71.
[69] Healy et al. (n 45) 174.
[70] See David Kenny "Abortion, the Irish Constitution, and Constitutional Change" (2018) 5(3) Revista de Investigações Constitucionais/Brazilian Journal of Constitutional Research 257, 259–260. Though the Irish courts were interventionist in the 1970s, they had on several occasions commented that the Irish Constitution, far from protecting a right to privacy that might legalise abortion, perhaps contained implied rights to life of the unborn.

as the Pro-Life Amendment Campaign (PLAC) campaigned extensively to have a clause inserted into the Constitution to prevent this.[71] They were successful in having this proposal put to the people, who voted by a large majority[72] to insert Article 40.3.3, which became commonly known as "the Eighth Amendment". This provided:

> The State acknowledges the right to life of the unborn and, with due regard to the equal right to life of the mother, guarantees in its laws to respect, and, as far as practicable, by its laws to defend and vindicate that right.

The effect of this clause was to constitutionally prohibit abortion, as any attempt to significantly liberalise the regime would not be in keeping with the right to life of the unborn. However, as the Attorney General had warned in advance of the vote, this was not a clear constitutional provision,[73] and it had several unexpected effects. It was held to prohibit the publication of information about abortion services elsewhere.[74] In 1992, a major controversy arose as to how to balance the right to life of the unborn with the equal right to life of the mother if the threat to life was risk of suicide, and relatedly, whether a person could be prevented from leaving the jurisdiction if their intention was to obtain an abortion. This question arose in a case called *Attorney General v X* (commonly known as the *X* case),[75] which concerned a 14-year-old girl who had been raped, and wished to go with her parents to England to have an abortion.[76] The Supreme Court held that the life of the mother must take precedence when it is at risk (including from suicide) so that a termination in that case would be constitutional. In such circumstances, the right to travel must be respected. However, the Court ruling did not of itself change the legislation on abortion, and successive governments were unwilling to legislate in line with the ruling.

There were also still many unanswered questions and gaps in the law. Indeed, there were no fewer than four further referendums on abortion: one designed to overturn the information decision; another to bolster the travel ruling; and

[71] See Brian Girvin, "Social Change and Moral Politics: The Irish Constitutional Referendum 1983" (1986) 34 Political Studies 61.

[72] More than two-thirds of people voted in favour, by 841,233 votes to 416,136 on a 50.3% turnout.

[73] See 339 Dáil Debates col. 1357 (9 February 1983).

[74] *Attorney General (SPUC) v Open Door Counselling* [1988] IR 593.

[75] *Attorney General v X* [1992] 1 IR 1.

[76] For an overview and examination of this case, see R Mac Cormaic, *The Supreme Court* (Penguin Ireland, 2016), 285–296; Aileen Kavanagh, "The Irish Constitution at 75 Years: Natural Law, Christian Values and the Ideal of Justice" (2012) XLVIII Irish Jurist 71, 86–96.

twice unsuccessfully to augment or overturn the suicide ruling.[77] The result of this was that many thousands of women travelled to the UK to access abortion services, which perhaps allowed the issue to lie partially dormant.[78] However, despite this, no legislation was passed to allow for abortion in cases where the mother's life was at risk (from suicide or otherwise) and this left medical practitioners in a state of uncertainty.[79]

Several events in the early 2010s brought this issue to a head,[80] and the government legislated for abortion in the case of risk of suicide, in line with the Supreme Court judgment.[81] In the context of debating this Bill, various parliamentarians suggested a slightly more expansive liberalisation, but were told these would be unconstitutional,[82] drawing attention to the strictures of the constitutional ban. In the aftermath of this, pro-choice groups—including the Abortion Rights Campaign (ARC), the National Women's Council of Ireland (NWCI) and the Irish Family Planning Association (IFPA)—began a campaign to remove the constitutional bar, or, as the slogan went, to "Repeal the Eighth". However, in view of the imminent referendum on same-sex marriage, campaigners, though keeping the issue in the public eye, took something of a back seat until that vote was passed.[83] From mid-2015, the campaign began in earnest.

B. Lobbying for change, the Citizen's Assembly, and the Eighth Amendment Committee[84]

As pressure mounted from these civil society groups, the Fine Gael minority government elected in 2016 again decided to put the question to a citizen's

[77] See the Twelfth, Thirteenth and Fourteenth Amendment to the Constitution Bills 1992, and the Twenty Fifth Amendment to the Constitution Bill 2002.

[78] Between 1980 and 2016, in the region of 170,000 people travelled for this reason; Irish Family Planning Association, available at <https://www.ifpa.ie/ifpa-welcomes-cabinets-approval-of-eighth-amendment-referendum-wording/> accessed 3 February 2022.

[79] See Peter Boylan, *In the Shadow of the Eighth: My Forty Years Working for Women's Health in Ireland* (Penguin, 2019) 71–100.

[80] Major events were the death of a woman called Savita Halappanavar in an Irish hospital, and critical European Court of Human Rights Ruling in *A, B & C v Ireland* [2010] ECHR 2032, (2011) 53 EHRR 13. See ibid 71–86; 101–102.

[81] The Protection of Life During Pregnancy Act 2013.

[82] Michael O'Regan, "Government Defeats Daly's Abortion Bill with Big Majority" *The Irish Times*, 10 February 2015.

[83] See Gráinne Griffin, Orla O'Connor, Ailbhe Smyth and Alison O'Connor, *It's a Yes!* (Orpen Press, 2019), 41–42.

[84] In the interests of full disclosure, it should be noted that one of the authors presented to both the Citizen's Assembly and the Eighth Amendment Committee on matters related to the abortion question.

deliberative body. A Citizen's Assembly, composed of 99 randomly[85] selected citizens and chaired by a senior judge, would consider the abortion issue, hear from experts and interest groups and deliberate before making non-binding recommendations.[86] As with the Constitutional Convention, this was initially seen by critics as a stalling tactic, buying time and potentially providing the government with political cover.[87]

The Assembly considered the abortion issue over six months, with testimony from legal, medical and ethical experts; people telling personal stories about their experience of Ireland's abortion regime; and campaigning groups presenting their arguments. The citizens were allowed to ask questions and were given ample time to discuss matters amongst themselves. In April 2017, the Assembly made its final recommendations, and to the "shock of almost all present", they were very expansive.[88] The Assembly recommended: removal of the constitutional prohibition on abortion, to be replaced by a simple clause affirming the power of the legislature to regulate the area; and a fairly permissive legislative regime that would allow for abortion without restriction as to reason up to 12 weeks, and for stated reasons thereafter.[89] Since many had expected a modest proposal—perhaps inserting certain listed grounds for abortion into the Constitution—this was surprisingly liberal. Naturally, this result was warmly welcomed by pro-choice groups, but condemned by pro-life groups.[90]

The government inserted yet another intermediate layer into the process: a special parliamentary committee, composed of members from across the political spectrum and from both sides of the abortion question, as well as those in middle. It was not clear that the government would accept the recommendations of the Assembly[91] and this was seen as another possible delay tactic or a way to "water down"[92] the Assembly recommendations. However, over the course of the Committee's many weeks of hearing testimony, even some of the

[85] Citizens were selected with an eye to representative demographic composition; David Farrell and Jane Suiter, *Reimagining Democracy Lessons in Deliberative Democracy from the Irish Front Line* (Cornell University Press, 2019).

[86] For a detailed overview of the role of this Citizen's Assembly, see Oran Doyle and Rachael Walsh, "Constitutional Amendment and Public Will Formation: Deliberative Mini-Publics as a Tool for Consensus Democracy" (2022) 20 ICON (forthcoming).

[87] Griffin et al. (n 83) 57–58.

[88] Ibid 70.

[89] See First Report and Recommendations of the Citizens' Assembly, 29 June 2017, available at <https://2016-2018.citizensassembly.ie/en/The-Eighth-Amendment-of-the-Constitution/Final-Report-on-the-Eighth-Amendment-of-the-Constitution/Final-Report-incl-Appendix-A-D.pdf> accessed 3 February 2022.

[90] Simon Carswell, "Citizens' Assembly: Reaction From Both Sides Of Abortion Debate" *The Irish Times*, 23 April 2017.

[91] Griffin et al. (n 83) 81.

[92] Griffin et al. (n 83) 86.

sceptical members of the Committee came around to the view that anything short of the Assembly recommendations were unworkable.[93] In the end, in its December 2017 report, the Committee recommended liberalising the law along similar lines to the Assembly's recommendations, but differed as to the form of the constitutional change: it suggested removing the constitutional bar entirely, with no replacement.

Neither of these processes imposed any legal obligation on the government, which retained political discretion in terms of what if any amendment to propose. However, the political pressure to generally follow the recommendations of the Assembly and Committee was significant. In the end, the Government decided to put the issue to referendum with the suggested replacement of the clause on the right to life of the unborn with an enabling provision: "Provision may be made by law for regulation of termination of a pregnancy."[94] The Attorney General, taking the same view as the advice given to the Assembly, believed that this would reduce uncertainty in the proposal: without a clause empowering the legislature (and by implication making courts less likely to intervene) it might be possible for the courts to use unenumerated rights of the unborn or the pregnant person to make the law more liberal or more conservative.[95] This language was designed to remove this as an issue in the campaign, making it apparent that the legislature was to have the final word. Furthermore, the government committed to supporting legislation allowing abortion for 12 weeks without restriction as to reason, and for stated reasons thereafter. There was dissent on this issue from some government ministers,[96] and a free vote (not subject to parliamentary whip) was promised in the legislature, but this had the effect of making the terms of referendum debate clear: if the referendum were passed, this legislation would likely follow.

C. The referendum campaign

Seventy pro-choice groups banded together to form a civil society organisation called "Together for Yes".[97] Though the government and several other political parties supported the change and contributed to the campaign, it was led by

[93] Griffin et al. (n 83) 84. Billy Kelleher, "Why I Was Persuaded Abortion Up To 12 Weeks Should Be Allowed" *The Irish Times*, 21 March 2018.
[94] 36th Amendment to the Constitution Act 2018.
[95] See Kenny (n 70) 267–268.
[96] In particular from Tánaiste (Deputy Prime Minister) Simon Coveney. See Boylan (n 79) 201–202.
[97] Griffin et al. (n 83) 95.

civil society. This group faced difficult questions about how to advance their case; many campaigners felt "tone policed" by instructions to not seem shrill, angry or extreme in their views. However, the leaders of this group did attempt to avoid perceptions of anger or extremity for fear of alienating voters. They avoided the word "choice" in the name of the group. They emulated strategies used by the Yes campaign in the same-sex marriage referendum, including maintaining a "calm, rational tone".[98]

A crucial part of their strategy was to use personal stories of those affected by Ireland's restrictive regime, both in media and in direct contact with voters.[99] The Yes campaign launched a large grassroots canvassing effort, with an estimated at 19,000 volunteers knocking on as many as 500,000 doors to talk directly to voters.[100] In doing this, they had careful messaging, focusing on terms like "personal decision" and "never easy" and avoiding terms like "choice" and "on demand". They attempted to frame the issue as "care" and "doctor's care",[101] and medical experts such as Dr Peter Boylan, chair of Institute of Obstetricians and Gynaecologists, were prominent in the Yes campaign.[102] The campaign focused on explaining the rationale for access to abortion for 12 weeks without restriction as to reason, which was a sticking point for many voters,[103] and refuting the idea of abortion used as contraception.[104] Opponents of the proposal were led by two civil society groups, Love Both and Save the 8th. Their core messages were that politicians could not be trusted with this issue;[105] that the 12 weeks period would not be the actual limit in practice, with posters wrongly suggesting liberalisation up to six months was the aim of the change;[106] and that the liberalisation would allow the abortion on the grounds of non-fatal foetal disability.[107] The latter two claims were untrue and following rigorous fact-checking by the Referendum Commission and news outlets, did not gain traction. The claim that politicians could not be trusted did not seem to resonate.

[98] Ibid 92–93, 111; 119–120.
[99] Ibid 170–172.
[100] Ibid 130, 148.
[101] Ibid 119, 140.
[102] See Boylan (n 79).
[103] Griffin et al. (n 83) 138–139. Exit polls showed this supposition was correct, and many Yes voters still harboured reservations about this.
[104] Ibid 139.
[105] Ibid 116, 153.
[106] Ibid 142.
[107] Aoife Barry, "FactCheck: Are 90% of Babies with Down Syndrome in Britain Aborted?" theJournal.ie, 3 February 2018, available at <https://www.thejournal.ie/factcheck-babies-abortion-3823611-Feb2018/> accessed 3 February 2022.

During the campaign there was great concern about unregulated social media advertising, and that it might allow foreign interference or radically change campaign dynamics. In response to this, the tech advertising platforms simply opted out: Facebook ceased to allow any advertising outside of Ireland; Google went further and stopped any advertising on the issue on its platforms.[108]

D. Result

In the end, the result of the referendum was emphatic; the Yes side won the referendum by 66.4% to 33.6%, with a voter turnout of c. 64%.[109] It was a "stunning victory"[110] which few had predicted in the run up to the referendum, where the narrative was that there was a strong a perhaps silent No vote and that the result would be very close.

IV. The people as constitutional actors

If we are living in the "Age of the Referendum",[111] then Ireland provides an illuminating exemplar of how constitutional change can be achieved by popular referendum in a process that achieves robust social and political legitimacy, whilst generating widespread citizen engagement and deliberation. Moreover, by supplementing its long experience of constitutional referendums with deliberative mini-publics and Citizens' Assemblies, Ireland is now at the forefront of constitutional design innovations which translate deliberative democratic ideals into concrete constitutional practice. It might be an exaggeration to say, as Eamon De Valera did, that the people are "the masters" of the Irish constitution. They are, however, key constitutional actors in the ongoing, iterative process of democratic constitutionalism in action. Indeed, Ireland is a counterpoint to common fears and dominant critiques of referendums—critiques which stem from their susceptibility to elite domination, popular disinformation and lack of constitutional constraint. Though the formal terms of the referendum process set out in the text of the Irish Constitution leave the process wide open to such dangers, they have not materialised in practice. The lived experience of referendums in Ireland over the last 30 years has resulted in a practice which is characterised by relatively high-quality debate and deliberation;

[108] See Satariano (n 38).
[109] The vote was 1,429,981 in favour to 723,632 against, on a turnout of c. 64%.
[110] Griffin et al. (n 83) 197.
[111] Tierney (n 2).

robust levels of participation and popular engagement; and strong perceptions of social and political legitimacy. The referendums have engendered a popular sense of ownership—and even part-authorship—of the Irish constitution. The Constitution of Ireland is an historic document which marked Ireland's full independence from Britain over 80 years ago. But thanks in part to the participatory and plebiscitary power of amendment by referendum, it is also a living Constitution that grows and develops in tandem with deep changes in Irish society.

In order to fully appreciate the role of the people as key constitutional actors in the Irish constitutional order, a number of important points must be borne in mind. First, although the power to initiate a referendum lies formally with the political elites, in practice citizens and interest-groups make a significant contribution to the initiation and even formulation of the referendum proposal. This ground-up dimension of amendment dynamics is vividly on display in our two case-studies of the referendums concerning same-sex marriage and abortion, which reveal a complex interplay between grassroots reform movements, popular demands and elite engagement. In both cases, we see the pivotal role of civil society in stimulating and initiating change, as well as the citizen participation in shaping the outlines of that change. Far from merely ratifying a proposal sown up by the political elites, individual people, interest groups and larger civil society have a significant agenda-setting role.

In fact, the political elites were actually trying to avoid grappling with the thorny and politically divisive issues surrounding same-sex marriage and abortion. But they were ultimately forced to confront them by effective civil society lobbying. Under intense political pressure, these elite actors were left with little choice but to address these issues in some way.[112] Even when the political parties eventually agreed to put these issues to referendum, these pressure groups led the referendum campaigns in practice. In the two cases discussed above, the political elite—arguably as an exercise in political cover—involved ordinary citizens in the process of initiation and in shaping the proposal in question by setting up the Constitutional Convention. In each case, but especially in the case of abortion, these processes proved influential in shaping the constitutional proposal, as well as the broader debate on the issue. The Citizen's Assembly clearly influenced the outline of the constitutional and legislative solutions that were ultimately adopted, and its deliberations and conclusions persuaded several high-profile political actors to change their mind. It would have been hard for the government to ignore its recommendations.[113]

[112] Farrell et al. (n 46) 121.
[113] Ibid.

These processes proved so successful that they have continued: the Citizen's Assembly went on to consider other issues,[114] and a new Assembly on gender equality, to include consideration of constitutional reform, met in early 2020.[115] This is still a new phenomenon, and only time will tell if this form of deliberative mini-public will become the norm. However, there are indications that there may be a developing political convention that significant/contested reform proposals should begin with a citizen-led deliberative process. This is will only be known over time as this quasi-convention is tested by experience.[116] At least in relation to same-sex marriage and abortion, Irish citizens were deeply involved at every stage of the process: from agenda-setting to initiation, from proposal to deliberation, from grassroots campaign to momentous constitutional change on deeply controversial moral and social issues.

All told, the fear about elite "control" or even domination of the process has not been the constitutional reality in Ireland. We should beware of equating formal power with political effect in this context. The reality is that the people are involved in the process much earlier than a formal account would suggest. Instead of elite control and domination, the initiation process is more accurately viewed as a complex collaboration between political elites and popular input, where ordinary people stimulate, shape and inform the nature of the referendum proposal, as well as the detailed texture of the referendum campaign. For their part, the political elites—who, after all, are elected representatives of the people—are responsive to popular demands for constitutional change.

Second, suspicion of establishment proposals show that the people have real power that they can assert against political elites. People are not overly prone to voting on second-order preferences such as mere dislike of government, at least in recent referendums;[117] during the same-sex marriage referendum, an anti-establishment vote was feared but did not manifest. However, an anti-elite sentiment may have defeated two political reform proposals in the 2010s, on stronger parliamentary enquiries and abolition of the Senate, both of which failed and which featured prominent arguments about the political elite

[114] David Farrell, Jane Suiter and Clodagh Harris, "'Systematizing"' Constitutional Deliberation: the 2016-18 Citizens' Assembly in Ireland" (2019) 34 Irish Political Studies 113–123

[115] See Laura Fletcher, "Citizens' Assembly Favours Changes 'Women in the Home' Clause" RTÉ News, 16 February 2020, available at <https://www.rte.ie/news/ireland/2020/0216/1115644-citizens-assembly/>.

[116] Geoffrey Marshall, "What are Constitutional Conventions?" (1985) 38(1) Parliamentary Affairs 33.

[117] See generally Marsh Michael, John Garry and Richard Sinnott "'Second Order' Versus 'Issue-Voting' Effects in EU Referendums: Evidence from the Irish Nice Referendums" (2005) 6(2) European Union Politics 201; Catherine Lynch, *Explaining the Outcome of Rejected Referendums*, Oireachtas Library & Research Service Note, 23 February 2018, 5.

seeking extra power.[118] More generally, major political reform proposals have struggled to pass.[119] Thus, the people have a genuine checking power over proposals of the political elite.

Third, whilst one fear about referendums is the risk of elite domination, there is also fears about unconstrained populism: the priority of emotional soundbites instead over in-depth deliberation, vague unwieldly questions which are not amenable to popular deliberation, compounded misinformation and propaganda which stymies informed and balanced debate. For the most part, the Irish experience has managed to steer clear of these problems or at least avoid their worst excesses. How? For one thing, the requirement that the referendum proposal must be agreed by a majority in both Houses of the Oireachtas places constraints on the type and formulation of the proposal. Subjecting the question to parliamentary debate and scrutiny means that politicians, legal experts, political pundits, interest-groups, civil society and the media are on notice of the proposal and stand ready to spot potential loopholes and vague wordings which may be a hostage to fortune. Experience with referendums over 30 years has shown that vaguely worded proposals cause confusion and frustration, not least in working out what a "yes" or "no" vote actually means in the end result. The fact that referendums are required to amend the Constitution is another constraint which focuses minds—including legal minds—on the requirement to product a concrete textual proposal which will have its intended legal effects. This requirements focuses referendum debates on the details of the proposals and their specific legal and practical consequences.[120] Therefore, whilst constitutional referendums in Ireland are an instance of direct democracy—in the sense that people vote directly on constitutional questions—the will of the people is channelled, constrained and mediated through multiple mechanisms which give elected representatives, the courts, the media and other constitutional actors a significant role in contributing to a reticulated referendum process.

The role of elected representatives in contributing to this process and ensuring that the referendum worked well is clearly evidence in the abortion referendum, where the government and legislature ensured that a number of thorny ancillary issues related to abortion were addressed in the legislative process, thus providing clarity so that the people could focus on the central question. Had they not made these critical interventions, the debate about

[118] See Kenny (n 7).

[119] Doyle (n 14) 199–200.

[120] See Doyle and Kenny (n 20) 209–210.

abortion might have otherwise been swamped by uncertainty, confusion and scare-mongering about dire hypothetical scenarios. This shows that the Irish referendum process is shored up by a variety of legal rules, political practices and social conventions, which bear out Sujit Choudhry's and Mark Tushnet's hypothesis that "preparing citizens for working the gears of a constitutional democracy might necessitate careful adherence to institutionalised procedures for deliberation and decision and formal legality".[121]

Examples of such formal legal constraints in the Irish context include the constitutional requirement of equal funding to both sides of the referendum campaign and balanced coverage in the broadcast media.[122] The independent Referendum Commission bolsters a climate of responsible debate, which is suitably responsive to the facts. Moreover, since the campaigns on either side of a referendum proposal want to attract the median voter, this curbs constrains and moderates the tone of the debate, since all those involved in the referendum campaign are fully aware that lack of civility or open vituperation for the other side will alienate the Irish electorate and undermine the reputation of that side of the campaign.

Experience of referendums over many years on a wide array of issues has now given rise to what could be described as "a referendum culture"[123] in Ireland. As a set of beliefs, norms and practices which has grown up over time, the Irish referendum culture emphasises:

a) the importance of having a clear question at the outset;
b) even-handed coverage of the debate where all sides get an fair chance to put their point across;
c) rigorous fact-checking of the information which feeds into the debate;
d) due respect—but not reverence—for expert opinion and its inclusion into the debate;
e) lack of undue deference towards political elites;[124] and
f) a general appreciation amongst the populace as a whole that a constitutional referendum is significantly different from an ordinary party-political election.

[121] Sujit Choudhry and Mark Tushnet, "Participatory Constitution-Making: Introduction" (2020) 18 ICON 173, 175.

[122] See above, at (n 30).

[123] Kenny (n 7).

[124] Thus, one of the innovative features of the Irish Constitutional Convention was that it included political representatives, generating fear that "ordinary" people would defer to the political elites. However, this did not occur, see Jane Suiter, David Farrell and Clodagh Harris, "The Irish Constitutional Convention: A Case of 'High Legitimacy'" in Reuchamps and Suiter (eds), *Constitutional Deliberative Democracy in Europe* (ECPR Press, 2016), 34ff

This last point is partly a product of experience over decades; but it is also due to the fact that referendums can see cross-party alliances or divides which differ from the ordinary alignment of party politics.

To be clear, we are not claiming that Ireland has created a referendum nirvana, blissfully free from any hint of underhand political tactics, cheap rhetoric or misinformation. Such problems inevitably surface to some degree in all referendum campaigns, and in some more than others. Nor should we overstate the quality of Irish referendum campaigns in controlling misinformation; there have been issues with misinformation in referendums in the past.[125] Insofar as misinformation is effectively controlled, this is in spite of, not because of, formal rules governing information and campaign, which are few and far between. Nonetheless, viewed in global perspective or in comparison with the Brexit referendum in the United Kingdom, the Irish experience performs relatively well across the dimensions of participatory engagement, deliberative quality and social legitimacy.

Indeed, a remarkable feature of the Irish referendum process is the broad and deep acceptance of result of the results of the process even in cases where the issue under discussion is extremely divisive, and appreciation for the virtues of the process. In the exit poll for the 2018 abortion referendum, 72% of those in favour of the proposal, and 62% of those against, said that they would accept the outcome of the referendum even if it went against them.[126] 74% of all voters said it was fair to resolve the issue by referendum; only 8% said it was unfair.[127] 72% of voters stated that "important issues should always be decided by referendum"; again, only 8% disagreed.[128] That voters would feel so positive about this divisive referendum, and the referendum process in general, is a testament to highly functional process, and to a sense that the people feel respected and empowered within it. This is testament to the widespread belief that the referendum process was fair and even-handed and gave all sides a reasonable chance to make their views known. This phenomenon of widespread popular acceptance of a referendum outcome was most marked when the referendum proposal to legalise divorce in 1995 was won by the slenderest majority of 50.3% of Irish voters after a highly contentious campaign, and with

[125] Again, the first Nice and Lisbon Treaty votes seemed replete with misinformation. However, upon close analysis, the reasons for the votes failing seems to be related to lack of public engagement/understanding and lack of any clear explanation of the proposal by the government, leading to a depressed turnout; see Cathryn Costello, "Ireland's Nice Referenda" (2005) 1 EuConst 357.

[126] See Ian McShane, *RTE and Behaviour and Attitudes Exit Poll on Thirty-sixth Amendment to the Constitution*, 25 May 2018, 45.

[127] Ibid 31–32.

[128] Ibid 37–38.

court challenges over the fairness of the campaign. Even then, the issue was widely and promptly treated as settled.[129]

V. A cautionary conclusion

In exploring the nature, scope, constraints and culture surrounding constitutional referendums in Ireland, we have highlighted the complex, iterative relationship between grounds-up popular movements and top-down elites, where the people are key constitutional actors who play pivotal roles in initiation, agenda-setting, campaigning, deliberation and, finally, voting on what the Irish Constitution means in the 21st century. Combining and supplementing the referendum process with the Constitutional Convention and the Citizens' Assembly, Ireland has also engaged in innovative experiments in "constitutional deliberative reform"[130] which builds on the referendum culture which has grown up in Ireland over the last 30 years.

Of course, it might be tempting to dismiss the Irish success with participatory and deliberative methods of constitutional change as irrelevant to global debate on referendums, since Ireland is a "small and relatively homogenous society".[131] With a population of 4.5 million inhabitants, 82.7% of whom have been born in Ireland,[132] there are certainly grounds for believing that "size matters" when it comes to generating meaningful citizen-engagement and deliberative communities. Perhaps it is difficult to scale up these experiences to larger, more pluralistic states where there is greater political, social, racial and religious diversity and polarisation. This is one reason for caution before attempting to transplant the Irish experience to larger countries. However, it would be too quick to assume that the referendums which have taken place in Ireland over the last decades were subjects on which there was an easy societal consensus. In fact, they concerned some of the most deeply contentious and potentially divisive issues of our time, which could easily have polarised along the dimensions of age, class, religious background or the urban/rural divide. The fact that issues such as same-sex

[129] For a retrospective on that referendum, see Fiona Gartland, "'Hello Divorce: Goodbye Daddy' 20 years after Irish said yes" *Irish Times*, 24 November 2015.

[130] Jane Suiter and Min Reuchamps, "A Constitutional Turn for Deliberative Democracy in Europe?" in Reuchamps and Suiter (eds), *Constitutional Democracy in Europe* (ECPR Press, 2016), 5.

[131] Ibid; Doyle and Walsh (n 86).

[132] Central Statistics Office, "Census 2016: Summary Results Part 1", chapter 5, available at <https://www.cso.ie/en/media/csoie/newsevents/documents/census2016summaryresultspart1/Census2016SummaryPart1.pdf> accessed 3 February 2022.

marriage or even abortion were debated in a spirit of relative civility and resolved as part of a process which was deemed fair and legitimate on all sides, cannot be taken for granted. After all, these were the kinds of deeply-held moral issues which had divided the Irish population and the political elites down the middle for decades.

Nonetheless, it is also true that the two referendums we canvas here were extraordinary and unusual events which were particularly salient amongst Irish people. Other referendums—especially on issues of constitutional structure and the European treaties—have not garnered the same degree of public interest, engagement or debate.[133] There are examples in Ireland's recent constitutional past that suggest that the Irish electorate might fare less well with such polycentric questions with complex legal ramifications, but the evidence on this is itself complicated.[134] If the Irish experience is a positive one, this is a product of experience which has created a "referendum culture"[135] over time. Ireland has had many constitutional change referendums in recent decades—experiences, good and bad, of framing and deliberating such change. Many of the positive elements of Irish practice seem to depend on informal, conventional or cultural mechanisms that help to shape formation, debate, campaigning and voting behaviour. These informal cultural mechanisms are hard to instigate or replicate in other cultural environments. Ireland seems more likely to provide for rules of thumb—heuristics as to how to proceed—than any kind of precise roadmap to guarantee success in holding a referendum.

Moreover, being made up of informal practices, there is no guarantee that Ireland's successful culture is resilient or will persist. The dominance of civil society in many of the recent high-profile referendum campaigns, and the use of citizen participation in formulating referendum proposals, are relatively new phenomena. Circumstances could change: social media advertising might disrupt campaigns and rigorous fact-checking, fundamentally altering campaigns; citizen's participation—which is at the gift of the

[133] For example, the establishment of the Court of Appeal in 2013, the failed vote to lower the eligibility age for the presidency, and the successful vote to remove the crime of blasphemy from the Constitution in 2018 all received very little attention.

[134] The first votes on the Lisbon and Nice Treaties, for example, may be examples of this, but the example is complicated; see European Commission, *Lisbon Treaty Referendum Survey: Analytical Report* (European Commission, 2009); Richard Sinnott, *Attitudes and Behaviour of the Irish Electorate in the Referendum on the Treaty Of Nice* (European Commission, 2002); Jane O'Mahony "Ireland's EU Referendum Experience" (2009) 24(4) Irish Political Studies 432; Lynch (n 117) 20–23.

[135] For a more detailed account, see Kenny (n 7).

government—could stop. Nonetheless, as referendums are held under real-life conditions where people disagree deeply and fervently about the crux moral issues of our time, Ireland provides grounds for a modicum of hope that constitutional deliberation can occur in a spirit of "robust civility",[136] following a process which even the losers can accept as fair.

[136] Timothy Garton Ash, *Free Speech: Ten Principles for a Connected World* (Atlantic Books, 2016), 208ff.

Index

For the benefit of digital users, indexed terms that span two pages (e.g., 52–53) may, on occasion, appear on only one of those pages.

Tables are indicated by *t* following the page number